Reviews of *Swords in Their Hands*

A superbly detailed and documented history of an obscure chapter of American history, Swords in Their Hands: George Washington and the Newburgh Conspiracy is a simply fascinating study and strongly recommended reading for anyone with an interest in the emergence of the United States as a political entity in general, and the contributions of George Washington to American governance in particular. A seminal work of impressive scope, Swords in Their Hands: George Washington and the Newburgh Conspiracy is very highly recommended for community and academic library American History collections.

The Midwest Book Review

Swords in Their Hands: George Washington and the Newburgh Conspiracy is a meticulously researched study of a little-known but important event in American history.

The tension between states' rights and those of a centralized federal government is as old as America itself. The details of how Congress and Washington struggled to fund the war and to prod the new republic into honoring promises made to its army form the bulk of *Swords in Their Hands*. Richards has done a fine job of marshaling and presenting the myriad facts of the case.

This nonfiction book will be essential reading for professional and amateur historians, and for academics like me.... The story pulls you along and tells a little-known tale of historic significance for our country.

Hendersonville (NC) *Times-News*

Americans continue to view George Washington as the nation's greatest hero, the courageous man who led the American forces to a surprising victory over the British. But few Americans realize that in March 1783 General Washington had to stare down an uprising by disgruntled army officers known as the Newburgh Conspiracy.

In this comprehensive study of the conspiracy, Dave Richards tells the dramatic story of Washington's role in quashing a military rebellion against the Congress. Well-researched, clearly written, and carefully argued, Swords in Their Hands tells a gripping story that makes an important contribution to the history of the Revolutionary War.

Dr. David Shi
President, Furman University (2004-10)

Pisgah Press

Pisgah Press was established in 2011 to publish and promote works of quality offering original ideas and insight into the human condition, the realm of knowledge, and the world around us.

Copyright © 2013 David T. Richards

Printed in the United States of America

Published by Pisgah Press, LLC
PO Box 1427, Candler, NC 28715
www.pisgahpress.com

Cover design: MyOwnEditor

All rights reserved. No part of this publication may be reproduced, stored in a retrieval system, or transmitted, in any form or by any means, electronic, mechanical, photocopying, recording, or otherwise, without the prior written permission of Pisgah Press, except in the case of quotations in critical articles or reviews.

Library of Congress Cataloging-in-Publication Data
Richards, David T.
Swords In Their Hands: George Washington
and the Newburgh Conspiracy/Richards
Library of Congress Control Number: 2013954113

Includes bibliographical references and index

ISBN 13: 978-0985387587
ISBN 10: 0985387580
History/United States History

First Edition
First Printing
April 2014
Second Printing
September 2014

Printed in the United States of America

Swords in Their Hands:

George Washington and the Newburgh Conspiracy

Dave Richards

Preface

I DO NOT recall ever reading or hearing about the Newburgh Conspiracy when I studied history in school. The impression I got from the textbooks my teachers assigned and their lectures was that nothing of importance happened in the Revolutionary War from the time America achieved a great victory at Yorktown in October 1781 until Congress ratified articles of peace in April 1783. It was only after more than two decades had passed since my graduation from high school, at a time when I was teaching English overseas, that I learned otherwise. I had by that time become something of a history buff and a person in search of a subject to write a book about—some important event or figure ignored by our historians. However, for quite some time I was unable to find anybody or anything really significant that had escaped their pens. Finally, one day when I was reading an outstanding book about the writing of the Constitution, *Decision in Philadelphia: The Constitutional Convention of 1787*, I found my subject—the Newburgh Conspiracy. The authors, James Lincoln Collier and Christopher Collier, had briefly mentioned it when emphasizing how respected George Washington was and how important his presence at the Constitutional Convention was.

Over the years many books about the Revolutionary War and biographies of the key figures associated with the Newburgh Conspiracy—George Washington, Henry Knox, Horatio Gates, Alexander McDougall, John Armstrong, Robert Morris, Gouverneur Morris, and Alexander Hamilton—have been published. Virtually all devote no more than a few pages or a chapter to the plot. Some do not even mention it. Only William Fowler's *American Crisis: George Washington and the Dangerous Two Years After Yorktown, 1781-1783* is an exception; excluding back matter, it has more than ninety pages of material relating closely or loosely to the Newburgh Conspiracy. The bulk of it, though, deals with other subjects.

The purpose of this book is to give the Newburgh Conspiracy the attention it deserves. It may be the closest thing to a coup that America has ever experienced; if it had succeeded, our country might have broken up and become a collection of Balkanized states. The chain of events that led up to this event and its actual happening are connected with the writing of the Constitution, and its story has particular relevance today because it deals with the whole issue of the size of our national government and the balance of power between it and the states. Also, it serves as a warning to those who feel our large national debt poses no danger to us.

Swords in Their Hands is the first book-length account of the Newburgh Conspiracy. It is the culmination of more than eight years of research and writing. It includes, among other things, material from published and unpublished eyewitness accounts, memoirs, correspondence, manuscripts, general orders, diary and journal entries, notes, and other papers written by key military officers and political figures.

Dave Richards
August 2013

Contents

Preface v
A Note on the Text viii

Introduction 1

PART I: The Neglected Army

1. We Are without Money 7
2. Taking Up the Business at This Desperate Crisis 17
3. The Brink of Ruin 30
4. We Will Be Forgot and Neglected 43
5. The Salvation of the Cause 48
6. The Public Creditors Should Unite and Use Their Influence 57
7. There Never Was so Great a Spirit of Discontent 68
8. No Officer Was More Distinguished 82
9. We Have Borne All That Men Can Bear 93
10. The Most Intelligent Members Were Deeply Affected 105
11. Brutus 109

PART II: The Plot And The Flame

12. The Army Have Swords in Their Hands 129
13. Mr. Hamilton Had Let Out the Secret 145
14. Guide the Torrent 161
15. The Political Pot in America Boils 177
16. The Old Leven 193
17. Faith Has Its Limits 207
18. The Most Anxious Moment of His Life 218

PART III: The Hero And Advocate

19. Almost Blind in the Service of My Country 233
20. A Conduct Truly Admirable 245
21. An Advocate for Their Rights 251
22. A Dangerous Instrument to Play With 255

PART IV: The Sad End

23. Like a Rope of Sand 263
24. Compelled to Leave the Army 270
25. A Foundation to Enslave This Free People 277

Afterword 285
Acknowledgments 294
Illustrations 296
Chapter Notes 298
Bibliography 345
Index 359

A Note on the Text

In most instances when quoting participants in the events described in this book, I have not modernized the capitalization, spelling, punctuation, or sentence structure. I have retained in this text the actual style of writing used during the Revolutionary War. Often that means leaving spelling and grammar mistakes, poor punctuation and sentence structure, and unnecessary capital letters intact. When I have made corrections or changes, or added one or more words for the sake of clarity, I have used brackets to alert readers. When entirely modernized quotes appear in the text without brackets, they usually have been drawn from other authors' works. In all cases, whether the quote is from a primary source, such as collections of Revolutionary War-era papers or letters, or from another author's work, I have cited the source in the section titled Chapter Notes.

Swords in Their Hands:

George Washington and the Newburgh Conspiracy

Washington's headquarters, Newburgh, N.Y.

Introduction

NEWBURGH'S HISTORY CAN be said to have begun in mid-September 1609, when the little *Half Moon* carrying explorer Henry Hudson and his crew of nineteen Dutchmen and Englishmen entered the highlands that would eventually bear his name. As they sailed past the Klinkersberg (later named Butter Hill) in their sloop, the sun broke through the dark clouds over the Mahakeneghtuc—the Mohegan name for the Hudson River—and they beheld the magnificence of their surroundings. Mountains, deep valleys, and untouched forests dressed in fall colors reflected off the river's surface. Everywhere Hudson turned "the lethargy of uncivilized nature reigned in undisturbed solitude. The wild game sprang from their familiar retreats startled by the echoes which ... rolled through the ancient forests, as the roar of the Dutch trumpets blew ... inspiring airs ...." It was "as beautiful a land as one can tread upon." It was "a very pleasant place to build a town on."[1]

Although the area was pleasant, settlement of it did not begin until the arrival of Palatines in New York during the spring of 1709. The Palatinate, a German district by the Rhine River, had served for some time as a refuge for Protestants fleeing from persecution. It was one area that had been touched by King Henry IV's Edict of Nantes, which in 1598 had ended Catholic France's wars of religion and given Protestants the freedom to worship as they pleased in some parts of his realm.

That freedom, though, came to an end in 1685, when Louis XIV revoked the edict. When he learned that Austria and Holland were about to initiate hostilities against France, he decided to take preemptive action against the German heretics in the Palatinate and sent the Dauphin into the district with one hundred thousand men. The invasion led to the surrender of a small number of cities, but French Minister of War Louvois's appetite for vengeance was not sated; he wanted the Palatinate razed to the ground. Its inhabitants were given three days to gather what they could and leave. "Men, women and children, clinging to their last, were driven to the fields, in the heart of winter, and left to perish of cold and hunger, while their dwellings were reduced to ashes, their property seized, and their possessions pillaged. More than forty cities and an infinite number of villages were burnt; the palaces of the Electors razed to the ground, and their tombs opened in search of hidden treasures."[2] Its churches, vineyards, and gardens were destroyed.[3]

Fifty thousand Palatines had to move to Protestant cities throughout Europe, where many found themselves dependent on others' charity. In 1708 some fifty of them relocated to England. There they received a warm welcome, which they related in letters sent back to friends and neighbors, and soon more than ten thousand other needy Palatines made their way to the island.[4]

Not long after coming to England, the minister for the first group of Palatines to relocate began eyeing a move to America.[5] A petition was sent to the Lords Commissioners of Trade and Plantations, who then submitted a report to the Royal Council. There were forty-one Palatines "very necessitous and in the utmost want, not having anything … (but what they get by Charity, to subsist themselves)," seeking to leave. "They have been reduced," the report continued, "to this miserable condition by the ravages committed by the French in the Lower Palatinate, where they lost all they had."[6]

In May the Royal Council granted them their wish, ordering that "they be sent to settle upon Hudson's River … where they may be useful to this kingdom, particularly in the production of Naval Stores [turpentine, tar, pitch, and rosin], and as a frontier against the French and their Indians."[7] The group that eventually set sail for America included the minister, farmers, vineyardists, and cloth makers.[8]

After the Palatines arrived in New York, they moved north to the area the Algonquin Indians called Quassaick—"stony land."[9] There they began establishing a hillside town, though a patent for the land originally granted had not yet been and would not be issued until 1719.[10] In all, nine families settled in the area. They received a total of 2,190 acres.[11]

The Parish of Newburgh replaced Quassaick as the official name of the settlement in March 1752. Much had happened between the time the original settlers began building homes and the renaming of the area. Most of them had left Quassaick for the more fertile valley lands, and newcomers had arrived, spurring years of accelerated commercial development that began around 1728. And the predominance of the Lutherans, which was what the Palatines were, had come to an end; later arrivals, an early historian of the town believed, were probably loyal to the Church of England.[12]

The town became very important in trade. Produce and goods brought in were shipped south to New York City, and many profited from the traffic running through the area, including a tall, black-haired merchant and mill owner named Jonathan Hasbrouck.[13]

Although Newburgh was called a "nest of Tories,"[14] an old history of the town asserts that after

Lexington the inhabitants "embraced with quick and unflinching zeal the cause of their country."[15] And in the first year of the Revolution 174 people did sign a pledge, vowing that they would "NEVER … BECOME SLAVES" and that they would support the actions taken by the Continental Congress and the New York Provincial Convention to protect their independence. They would oppose Parliament until the Americans and British reconciled their differences.[16] However, 54 people refused to sign the pledge. They were "the most daring, presumptuous villains," people often guilty of "threatening lives, properties and individuals, damning Congress and Committees," and expressing an intent to "join the enemies" if afforded the chance to do so.[17]

The results were discouraging, but on the day those names were sent to the New York Provincial Congress, July 14, 1775, fifteen of the fifty-four people listed as not having signed that pledge and six others previously not accounted for came forward to sign a second one. The twenty-one claimed they were doing so of their own free will, but in fact they had been pressured to do so.[18]

A small number of people were later detained for behavior deemed unlawful or for displaying suspect loyalty, and some renounced the pledge they had signed. Their change of heart resulted from the patriots' decision to pursue independence instead of reconciliation and their willingness to harshly punish anybody whose loyalty was the least bit in question.[19]

Newburgh was not a scene of great battles during the Revolutionary War. Situated on a hill behind the Hudson River's west bank, protected by tightly packed trees in a number of places, the town's small population could not have been touched by the British ships' guns. Additionally, Newburgh and other villages in the area had militias, which might have led the British to rule out landing any troops there; they could easily be summoned by signal cannon or fires on Butter Hill and flags if the British approached.[20]

After Forts Montgomery and Clinton were taken by the British in October 1777, Newburgh's destruction was anticipated, and families living near the river's west bank packed their belongings and moved out of harm's way. The town did endure cannon fire from some British transports that sailed by—a response to musket fire—but no landing was attempted.[21] That was the closest thing to a heated battle that Newburgh experienced.

Although Newburgh was not the site of historic battles, it did play a role in the war. The people of Newburgh established a militia to watch for any landing of British troops on the west bank of the Hudson. From 1777 until the end of the war they maintained a supply depot for such items as lead, uniforms, shoes, and blankets.[22] Their shipbuilding industry produced vessels that transported military supplies and forces.[23] And the people "came forward with every mode of conveyance in their possession eager to transport provisions" when they got news of the men's hardships at Valley Forge.

Newburgh was a rendezvous point for the army, and the officers and soldiers relied on the area to provide billets and food.[24] Also, men from the town served for short periods of time in nearby places such as New Windsor, Esopus, Fort Constitution, Peekskill, Fort Montgomery, and Ramapo; the mountain passes in the last location were guarded in part to protect the Sterling Iron Works.[25]

The aforesaid shows that Newburgh played a role in the war, but the town would not have earned a place in any major histories of the Revolution if not for events that took place a little less than a year after George Washington arrived there in the spring of 1782 and set up his final headquarters. What happened was something called the Newburgh Conspiracy.

Part I

The Neglected Army

General George Washington

Chapter One

"We Are without Money"

GEORGE WASHINGTON PURPOSEFULLY walked towards the lectern and then looked out over the audience in the central hall of the Temple of Virtue. Most of the officers in his army were present; by this time only a small number—those in the South—were not stationed in the Hudson Highlands. They had not expected the general to come to their meeting, and the Commander-in-chief's surprise appearance added solemnity to the scene.[1] The crucial moment had arrived. Copies of an anonymously written address to the officers had been widely circulated, and its words and tone were alarming. Its author, the fiery Major John Armstrong, the young son of a general whom Washington considered to be a friend, was essentially suggesting that the officers present Congress with an ultimatum: Pay the army what it was owed and provide the funding necessary to ensure that the officers received the postwar pensions they had been promised, or else. If peace arrived and the army's grievances still were not redressed, it would refuse to disband, thus stoking the fears of delegates and private citizens, who had always seen standing armies as potential instruments of tyranny. If, on the other hand, the war continued and the army was still being neglected, it would turn its back on the country and sneer at the trembling delegates in Philadelphia when the British marched on them.[2]

Washington understood that Major General Horatio Gates, Colonel Walter Stewart, Armstrong, and the other eight or nine angry officers behind the call for the meeting and the writing of the incendiary address[3]—the two most important actions in what was later called the Newburgh Conspiracy—were threatening the principle that an army had to remain subordinate to elected civil officials. He knew the officers must not be allowed to hang a sword of Damocles over chosen representatives of the people; what they were doing was not much different from plotting a coup.

An army disloyal to the nation's delegates was a danger to individual liberty; it had the potential to destroy America's developing republic.

The general's speech had to cool the officers' passions. The officers had to be made to wait for Congress to do them justice. If Washington failed, their actions threatened to plunge the country into an abyss of "Civil horror,"[4] for the bonds between the various states were not strong: If the national government fell, they all were likely to go their own ways and hostilities between them might ensue.

The officers had to wait for justice because even by this date, March 15, 1783, Congress was still weak and financially incapable of meeting their demands for back pay and funding for pensions; the writers of the Articles of Confederation had not intended to create a strong national government. Congress could govern the country, print bills of credit, raise a wartime army, and buy supplies, but the funds to pay for those things had to come from the states, and they were not providing them and were not anxious to grant the body the taxation authority it needed to raise funds directly; Congress was too far away from most of the citizenry to be effectively scrutinized, which meant it might become omnipotent and oppressive. Many people felt the war had resulted from Parliament's being given too much power, especially the power to impose taxes, so they were unwilling to give Philadelphia more authority. Consequently, the delegates really were able to do no more than go to the states with their hands out for contributions. They had "the Privilege of asking every Thing," and the states had "the Prerogative of granting nothing."[5]

Congress had relieved the individual states of the burden of meeting the Continental Army's huge expenses and assumed that responsibility itself, but without tax revenue it was severely handicapped, and the soldiers and the creditors providing the government with the money to keep them clothed, fed, and supplied suffered greatly. The fighting men often went without pay, and the lenders grew anxious waiting for interest payments and for their loans to be paid back. So up to its ears in debt was Congress that almost every day the government found itself forced to deal with creditors pestering it for the money they were owed.[6]

THE MATTER OF financing the war was problematic for the government from the start; when the struggle began in April 1775 too little specie—gold and silver coins—was in circulation to support an army for even one year.[7] What America had of value was land and commodities, not money.

Congress did get subsidies and loans from France, Spain, and Holland during the war, but most of that money came from 1781 to 1783. What it got from Europe in the early years did not begin to cover costs. The greatest aid it received from overseas then was not money but vital supplies from France.

One way the government obtained money was by selling interest-bearing certificates to Americans through Continental loan offices. Congress established this system in early October 1776. The first certificates were issued in denominations of $300 to $1,000, yielded four percent, and were redeemable in three years. The delegates' goal was to raise an initial $5,000,000, but by February 1777 they realized that the certificates had to be made more attractive to investors. So they raised the interest rate to six percent and offered certificates in lower denominations—from $200 up. Also, they extended the maturity dates and now sought to obtain $15,000,000.

Those changes, and others made later, did not yield great results. In 1781 the government stopped selling the certificates, and in 1782 it stopped paying interest on them. For one thing, people lacked faith in the government's ability to redeem the certificates; for another, only rich colonists could afford them.[8]

Although the intention was for loan office certificates to be purchased as investments, they became "a kind of mercantile currency."[9] They were used by federal agents to pay for expensive goods and services when they had no money on hand, and since the certificates lost value less rapidly than Continental bills of credit—the national currency—merchants readily accepted them. They understood that if they waited for payment in bills of credit, by the time they actually got them in their hands their value would be significantly less than it was at the time of the purchase agreement. The practice of using certificates to pay for goods and services was especially common after March 1, 1778.

National lotteries were also used to raise money. Under a plan adopted by Congress in November 1776, there were four different drawings. Tickets cost ten, twenty, thirty, or forty dollars, depending upon the drawing. For each drawing, one hundred thousand tickets were made available for purchase and thousands of prizes were offered. The value of the prizes increased in relation to the type of lottery. The top prize in the first-class lottery, for example, was a $10,000 certificate, while in the fourth-class lottery it was a $50,000 certificate.

Drawings took place from the beginning of May 1778 to mid-April 1782. The first-class ticket drawing, which had to be put off several times because of the British occupation of Philadelphia and disappointing ticket sales, began the process; the fourth-class ticket drawing, which had to be temporarily suspended when the event's managers went on strike because they were not being paid, lasted more than a year and ended the process. For all four drawings, sales were disappointing, ranging from about twenty to forty thousand tickets sold.

On the first three drawings the government lost an estimated total of $772,000. On the fourth-class ticket drawing it made a profit of $1,200,000, which would have more than offset the disappointing results for the first three drawings if not for one thing—depreciation of the national currency.[10]

More than anything else, though, the government simply printed bills of credit to pay for the war and other operations. Every year it estimated its expenses, printed the money—the bills of credit—it needed to meet them, watched as its estimates turned out to be much too low, and printed more currency. In spite of the public's eventual reluctance to put its faith in the bills, Philadelphia never stopped printing the currency.[11] The result was depreciation.

Depreciation greatly affected George Washington's army. By mid-December 1778, as the currency declined at a rate of five percent per day, the Commander-in-chief was reporting to Governor Benjamin Harrison of Virginia that many of that state's officers were "from absolute necessity … quitting the Service" and that the small number remaining were "sinking by sure degrees into beggary and want."[12] When 1779 arrived the situation did not improve, and in early February the general noted that farmers were showing almost no interest in providing his army with food because the bills had "so little value."[13]

Of course, depreciation meant inflation. During a three-week stretch in May Philadelphians saw prices double.[14] In June Christopher Marshall had to pay eighty dollars for two silk handkerchiefs.[15] In August colonels from five Massachusetts regiments met and decided to petition Major General William Heath, the highest-ranking officer from their state; their pay was in arrears and they realized that if they received it without adjustments for inflation, they would be impoverished. They had a right to be paid on time and, they thought, it was unjust that they were not receiving anything while civilians were becoming rich and living a life of luxury.[16]

With the Continental currency becoming worthless and prices rising so high so fast, public officials simply could not get money quickly enough to keep pace. The army's commissary and quartermaster departments soon started issuing their own certificates to pay for supplies and services. But the certificates were really no more than IOUs from the government, and money to those departments turned out to be "like a pound of Butter to a Kennel of Hounds," adding greatly to the country's already substantial debt. Procurers, though, could not be blamed for issuing certificates so freely because there was no incentive for them to be tough in bargaining for supplies; a purchasing agent's earnings came from commissions based on the amount of money he *expended* on supplies: the more he spent, the more he earned. If he drove a hard bargain for supplies and saved the government money, he deprived himself of earnings. Of course, often the army just impressed supplies. But in those cases the officer in charge could assuage his guilt over plundering a fellow citizen—and ensure himself a commission—by issuing a certificate for a generous sum to the person.

If officials from those departments had been closely supervised, spending might have been held in check. But that was not the case. They were spread out over the country and lines of authority were not tightly drawn. Another problem was that regulations meant to rein in the commissary department were difficult to understand and not closely adhered to by officials. Also, many officers claimed they had not received copies of the regulations.

Although the certificates proliferated and were written for generous sums, they were not a boon to all those who held them. Some were found to be missing information or to have been issued by officers without authorization. Also, they declined in value as the country's currency depreciated and their holders went from one office to another seeking payment. And some certificates did not draw any interest.[17]

In September 1779, Congress made a real attempt to do something about the high rates of depreciation and inflation. Realizing that those two problems resulted from having too many bills in circulation, it set a ceiling on the amount of money that would be allowed to circulate; once it reached $200,000,000, no more bills would be printed.[18]

Then, on March 18, 1780, after that ceiling had been reached, the delegates decided to devalue the old depreciated bills of credit at a rate of forty dollars in paper to one in specie and replace them with new ones issued by the states and guaranteed by the national government. The states were expected to collect the old bills by taxing their inhabitants, send them on a monthly basis for about thirteen months to Philadelphia to be destroyed, and then issue much smaller numbers of the new guaranteed ones for circulation. Congress asked that the total value of the newly released currency "not ... exceed ... one-twentieth part of the nominal sum of the bills brought in to be destroyed." If all $200,000,000 in old currency were brought in, no more than $10,000,000 in new bills would be issued. Not all that new money was to be kept by the states; forty percent of it would be remitted to Philadelphia as requisitioned funds. With much old devalued currency removed from circulation, the delegates believed, inflation was likely to become less severe.[19]

James Madison was not so optimistic. When he wrote Thomas Jefferson on March 27, 1780, only one week after he had begun serving in Congress, he indicated that the country's situation had never been so perilous. The army was being "threatened with an immediate alternative of disbanding or living on free quarter." The Treasury had no money and the government was no longer able to make purchases on credit, so purchasing agents were using their own private credit as much as possible. The delegates were "complaining of the extortion of the people; the people of the improvidence of Congress, and the army of both." The state of the government's finances called for "the most mature & systematic measures," but they would not be forthcoming because there were too few "adequate Statesmen" in Philadelphia to make them possible. Even if Congress passed the right bills, it lacked the authority to compel compliance. And when the states looked at plans that the delegates recommended, they were cool to them because they did not trust the national government.

Would the March 18 plan change any of that? Madison did not think so: "An old system of finance discarded as incompetent to our necessities, an untried & precarious one substituted, and a total stagnation in prospect between the end of the former & the operation of the latter .... If the States do not vigorously proceed in collecting the old money and establishing funds for the credit of the new ... we are undone."[20]

Within half a year after Madison wrote Jefferson, the delegates saw that the plan was not working[21] and that the situation would not improve with time. One problem was that the states had been issuing their own currencies and did not stop doing so even after Congress called for them to do so and to pull out of circulation bills they had issued earlier. Another problem was that the states let their inhabitants use such certificates as had been issued by the quartermaster and commissary departments to pay taxes; if they had accepted only the old devalued bills, as had been intended, more of them could have been removed from circulation and replaced with newly issued ones. A third problem was that, just as Madison had anticipated, the states lacked the vigor to collect the old bills; by June 1781, the deadline for turning all of them in, only $31,000,000 had been retired.[22] Also, the states turned out the new currency too slowly[23] and the government did not have the hard currency to back the new bills.

As the states lagged in their collection efforts and continued to issue their own currencies, Congress printed more and more bills of credit to finance its operations. Whenever it did so, inflation reared its ugly head. As citizens saw this happening, they realized that if they hung on to their money, they invited disaster. They had to spend their dollars when they had maximum purchasing power, so they rushed to get rid of their money before additional newly printed bills appeared and begot more depreciation and inflation.

While that "jockeying"[24] took place, worried businessmen did their share to exacerbate the problem by jacking up prices[25] to protect themselves against losses they anticipated incurring from more depreciation. As a result, many Americans found themselves shelling out exorbitant sums of money for things that cost far less before the war: Thomas Jefferson had to pay $355.50 for three bottles of brandy; John Witherspoon, the president of the College of New Jersey (now Princeton), bought a coat that turned out to be the wrong size for $1,000.[26] Army officers, who made substantially less than a common laborer, saw that a day of traveling would cost them almost all their pay for one month and a reliable horse what they might earn for ten years of service.[27]

As the currency continued to depreciate and inflation raged, drawing up business contracts became more difficult.[28] Stipulations in them had to be written in a way to account for depreciation, but courts and arbitrators differed on how it should be calculated.

People with the resources to make loans to the government were discouraged from doing so by rapid depreciation.[29] The offer of interest on a loan office certificate was not tempting; interest accumulated too slowly to keep pace with the decline of the paper dollar. Lenders understood that to redeem their certificates meant to take losses.

The government in fact had good reason not to think about levying taxes while the bills continued to lose their worth. Whatever it collected from the taxpayers today soon lost value because of rampant inflation, and citizens understood that by simply waiting to pay their taxes as the currency depreciated they would effectively reduce the real amount owed.[30]

Congress's inability to put its financial house in order had serious consequences. As the states and Congress failed to address the army's needs because of their financial problems, officers grew dissatisfied. Lieutenant Colonel Ebenezer Huntington, who had foregone his studies at Yale to be a part of the war effort, hated his fellow countrymen and lambasted them for their "Rascally Stupidity" and neglect of the army. He blamed them for the government's inability to reinforce regiments and provide the men with proper food, clothing, and pay. What were Americans thinking? Did they think the French were going to "fight their battles for them" once they arrived? If so, they were mistaken. The French would never tolerate the kind of neglect the American army had put up with. Once proud of being born in America, Huntington was "now ashamed" to say that this country was his place of birth. The government had to act! It had to bring the regiments up to full strength and pay the men with real money—gold or silver. The army was at its breaking point. "The Insults & Neglects which the Army have met with from the Country, Beggers all description, it must Go no farther they can endure it no longer," he warned. He was "in Rags," had "only a Junk of fresh Beef & that without Salt" for his day's rations, and had gone without pay for more than half a year. He did not like that he was enduring all this for "Cowardly Countrymen who flinch at the very time when their Exertions are wanted, & hold their Purse Strings as tho they would Damn the World, rather than part with a Dollar to their Army."[31]

As a result of the neglect the army experienced, many officers concluded that America needed a stronger central government. "The fundamental defect is a want of power in Congress," the slight Lieutenant Colonel Alexander Hamilton declared in a long letter to New York delegate James Duane in September 1780. "The confederation … gives the power of the purse too intirely to the state legislatures. It should provide perpetual revenues in the disposal of Congress—by a land tax, poll tax, or the like. All imposts upon commerce ought to be laid by Congress and appropriated to their use, for without certain revenues, a government can have no power."[32]

Hamilton would not change his views when he later entered Congress. He would become so determined to see that Congress was given the taxation authority it needed in order to obtain permanent funding that he would come to see the army as an instrument he could use to achieve his objective. He would become a key figure in the Newburgh Conspiracy.

Another person who wanted to see the government receive real taxation authority was George Washington. He felt Congress ought to be given more power because he was apprehensive about the government's ability to finance its operations and the war effort in particular. "We are without money, and have been so for a great length of time," he lamented to George Mason in late October. Throughout the war the army had "lived upon expedients," surviving on "false hopes, and temporary devices, instead of System." Now, though, they could "live no longer."

The powerless Congress was like "a force … constantly fluctuating and sliding from under us as a pedestal of Ice would do from a Statue in a Summers day." It never had the funds to cover the costs of war. That placed Washington at a great disadvantage. The British had a sovereign central government. It was able to tax its citizens to raise the funds necessary to adequately provide for its soldiers, while Philadelphia was unable to do the same for Washington's men because of the unwillingness of Americans to support the creation of a strong central government with taxation authority. Washington might go to the state governments for help, but they had their own local problems to deal with, and the general understood that depending on all or even many of their legislatures to provide funds for a national need—the war effort—was impossible.

Better to give the delegates greater taxation authority to finance the war than to go to thirteen different state legislatures to ask for help. "If we mean to continue our struggles ... ample powers must be lodged in Congress, as the head of the Federal Union, adequate to all the purposes of War,"[33] Washington insisted.

Washington lacked confidence in requisitions—formal requests to the states for funds—for good reason. In theory they appeared to be fine. The delegates would set a quota for each state that was based on an estimate of "the value of all [its] land ... and the buildings and improvements thereon"[34] and it would then tax its residents and pass on the revenue obtained to Philadelphia. Congress would then use the revenue it collected to defray expenses.

But in practice they did not work well, and eventually almost all the states would ignore them. No state wanted to pass on its tax revenue unless its neighbors did likewise, and since none really knew how much revenue others had given up, each feared it had or would surrender more than its fair share to Philadelphia.[35] In the end the states used the revenue that was supposed to go towards their quotas for local needs[36] and regarded money sent to the government as voluntary contributions. And even when states collected money for national needs, they often spent it themselves on behalf of Congress instead of sending it to Philadelphia; in some cases, but not always, their expenditures on the body's behalf were counted towards their requisition quotas.[37]

Congress did not have enough clout to force the states to send the money it requested, and many of its own delegates and the legislatures were not about to enhance its power to obtain revenue. They feared that a Congress with enhanced revenue-obtaining powers would impose oppressive taxes on its citizens and, knowing taxes were very unpopular with the public, they were not willing to incur their constituents' disapproval or wrath. "Many who see the right road [taxes] and approve it continue to follow the wrong road, because it leads to popularity. The love of popularity is our endemi[c]al disease,"[38] Robert Morris later opined to Benjamin Franklin.

In addition to the unpopularity of taxes, other factors undermined the requisitioning process: The values of the states' lands and the improvements made on them were inaccurate; they were too high, the states complained, and Philadelphia had to consider any money received from the states to be loans until better ways of assessment were devised. The British occupied parts of America, which made it difficult for the states to collect taxes. Bureaucrats in that day and age were not models of efficiency, and the requisitioning process was not time-economical; when Congress did requisition funds, delays occurred before the state legislatures acted and again as the taxes were collected. The cost of collection was high, in part because America's population was scattered. And states were not always well off enough to send money to Congress even if they were willing to do so.[39]

The fact that almost all the states eventually chose to ignore the requisitions is important. If they had not done so, Congress would have been better funded and Washington's army would have been paid more regularly. Its officers would then have had less reason to grow angry and become involved in anything like the Newburgh Conspiracy.

As 1780 came to an end and 1781 began, the value of paper dollars continued to plunge. The worthless currency had become "fit for little else but to make the tail of a paper kite with."[40] In December the exchange rate in Philadelphia was seventy-five dollars in paper currency to one in specie;[41] in January it went to a hundred to one.[42]

Although the government had reason to expect aid from France—during the fall of 1780, after meeting with George Washington behind closed doors in Hartford, Connecticut, the gray-haired General Rochambeau had sent his son back home to report that the Americans were in dire shape[43]—by January 1781 it could wait no longer. It needed to pay Washington's soldiers, build up supplies, and purchase clothing. It had to send someone who was able to tell the French how the war was going and describe the condition of the American army. So Washington decided to dispatch one of his favorite aides, the tall twenty-six-year-old Lieutenant Colonel John Laurens, to ask for money and supplies. As a result of "an almost uninterrupted series of complicated distress," the army had just about run out of patience and had grown extremely discontented, the general wrote in his instructions to the well-to-do colonel. It had to receive "speedy relief." Unless he got "an immediate, ample, and efficacious succour of money," it would only be able to "make a feeble and expiring effort the next campaign."[44]

Less than one month after Washington wrote those instructions, in early February 1781, Congress took significant steps to improve its financial situation and the efficiency of the government in general. On February 3 it approved a motion by North Carolina's Dr. Thomas Burke that the body be vested with the authority to collect a five-percent duty on imports, but the proposal could become law only if all thirteen states approved it, and some of them were not willing to give the delegates that power. That the motion was made by Burke, who was responsible for the clause in the Articles of Confederation giving the states their "sovereignty, freedom, and independence, and every power, jurisdiction and right ... not ... expressly delegated to ... Congress," illustrated just how weak the members felt. Earlier Burke had even wanted to get rid of Congress after the war because he feared it would become power-hungry and tyrannical. The money received from the five-percent duty, which is usually referred to as the Impost of 1781, would go towards paying off creditors and helping Philadelphia achieve some financial independence from the states.

Shortly thereafter, on February 7, the delegates established the Departments of Finance, of War, and of Marine to go along with the Department of Foreign Affairs, which they had established in January. The old method of administering affairs through committees and boards had been slow and unwieldy. A civil service with departments headed by individuals elected by the delegates was likely to more effectively carry out the government's policies.[45]

The person unanimously elected to head the Department of Finance was Robert Morris, a wealthy forty-seven-year-old merchant who suffered from asthma and inflammation of the eyes.[46] Merchants with administrative experience and the connections needed to immediately begin carrying out the government's commercial business, like Morris, were in great demand in an age when America had no trained professional bureaucracy to rely upon.[47] He would be the only person in American history to hold the title of Superintendent of Finance.[48] What people called this tall merchant with graying hair and an expanded waistline, though, was simply "the Financier," and that epithet is on his tombstone.[49]

Chapter Two

"Taking Up the Business at This Desperate Crisis"

ROBERT MORRIS,[1] POSSIBLY illegitimate, was only thirteen when he arrived in America from England in 1747. He had been summoned by his father, Robert, Sr., who was working in a small port in Maryland for a British shipping firm. Two years after arriving in America, the younger Morris was sent to Philadelphia to live with a friend of his father, a merchant named Robert Greenway. Not long thereafter he began an apprenticeship with a Philadelphia shipping company owned by Charles Willing. While receiving training there, the boy became friends with "old Square Toes," Mr. Willing's oldest son, Thomas. When Charles left America for a while to visit his father in Bristol, England, and to look after his business in the British Isles, "old Square Toes" was entrusted with the company's American operations. Robert, who had been performing rather mundane tasks, such as cleaning the office and labeling cargo, was given more responsibility, though he was still just in his mid-teens.

Soon Morris learned that the price of flour had gone up in overseas markets. Willing's agents in Philadelphia and surrounding areas were quickly ordered to purchase for export all the flour they could get their hands on, and before long angry city merchants were howling; the boy was guilty of cornering the flour market and they and their children were going to starve as a result! They howled in vain, though; upon returning home, Charles heard out the merchants and was pleased that the boy had acted so decisively.

The boy's responsibilities increased with time. For four years he was in charge of the company's finances, and some time after Charles died from yellow fever, he asked his new boss—"old Square Toes"—to put him in charge of the cargo and commercial concerns of a ship bound for Jamaica.

Now a young man, he made that voyage and a number of others, but one in particular was especially noteworthy. In February 1757, during the French and Indian War, he was taken prisoner by the French just as the ship he was on prepared to unload cargo in Cuba. He, the ship's captain, and the crew managed to escape one night, but they were still in a very unenviable position: They had earlier been disarmed and stripped of much of their clothing; they were without food and water; and the interior of Cuba, through which they were now moving, was hilly and wooded. The group eventually exited the forests and reached a shore area near Havana, but there remained the question of how they would find a way off the island; they had neither money nor a way of transporting themselves home.

Morris's resourcefulness saved him. Coming upon a Frenchman who was struggling with a broken watch, the American offered to help. The Frenchman handed the watch to Robert, who borrowed a knife from someone and then went to work on it with that and whatever else could be adapted to serve as a watch repairman's tools. Once he got the watch ticking again, Morris handed it back to the Frenchman. The grateful Frenchman then directed others in need of repair work to him and before long Robert was making enough money to purchase food and other items he needed.

When an American ship finally entered port, Morris and his captain knew their return home was possible. They boarded the vessel and in April 1757 arrived in Philadelphia. Glad to see Robert back, "old Square Toes" offered to make him a partner. Ultimately the new partner would lead Willing & Morris for about two decades and help it amass great wealth. He forged ties with others in the business world, formed partnerships, and expanded shipping operations all around the globe. He traded flour, tobacco, sugar, indigo, and even enslaved Africans. The only rule was that the commodity had to help the company make a profit.

The successful businessman first became politically active in 1765, after passage of the Stamp Act, but his greatest activity did not come until after the war began, by which time he was a married man. From July 1775 to July 1776 he served as Benjamin Franklin's vice-chairman on the Pennsylvania General Assembly's Committee of Safety, a twenty-five-man committee responsible for all of the state's war-related business, and during that time frame he was selected to be one of the state's seven delegates to the Continental Congress. There he served four terms and, as can be expected, spent much time working for committees that dealt with matters relating to the war and commerce.

By December 1776, if not earlier, Morris recognized that America was in serious trouble. Depreciation—"this evil"[2]—was already a problem and Washington appeared to be in danger of losing his army; men were or before long would be leaving for home as their enlistments ended. Consequently, on December 31 the general had regiments scheduled to be discharged the following day form up in snow-covered streets and fields to hear a personal appeal from him to stay a little longer. Any soldier who stepped forward to answer his call deserved a bounty of ten dollars. Eventually, all but those physically unable to continue their service decided to stay on.

Understanding that promissory notes were not going to satisfy the men—that he had to come up with ten dollars in hard cash for each soldier who answered his call or else his success would turn into a failure—the general sent an urgent letter to Morris, informing him that he had offered them a bounty to stay on a little longer and imploring him to use his personal credit to "borrow Money"[3] so he could keep his promise to the men who had agreed to continue serving.

Morris did not disappoint Washington, reporting to him the next day that he had collected $50,000 in hard cash and that if the general needed "further occasional supplies of Money," he could count on him to act.[4]

The general had to appreciate what Morris had done for him, but the tall delegate's good deed did not prevent him from developing a reputation as a schemer, which would certainly hurt him when he later was linked to the Newburgh Conspiracy. Using his influence as chairman of the Secret Committee,

Robert Morris, "The Financier"

which was the government's primary purchaser of foreign goods, he steered contracts in the direction of his company and friends. By doing so, he made himself an easy target and, in 1779, twice found himself accused of wrongdoing. The first time he was charged with using committee funds—public funds—to compensate his company for a loss of private cargo that had resulted when the British seized a ship called the *Farmer*. The second time he was said to have bought up a recently arrived French vessel's cargo, run a "black market"[5] in flour, planned the export of that commodity as private cargo—a clear violation of embargoes in effect at the time—and caused a big price hike on dry goods that hurt the public. In the end, both cases were looked at and Morris was found to be not violating any laws. In the first case the cargo was not private; it was actually being shipped at the behest of the American government. In the second case he was carrying out the wishes of a business partner acting on behalf of the French army and navy.

The following year, in July 1780, Morris opened the Bank of Pennsylvania to receive "a patriotic subscription of continental money ... for the purpose of purchasing provisions for a starving army."[6] His own subscription of ten thousand pounds and others' provided the bank with enough money to furnish the Continental Army with three million rations and three hundred large casks of rum.

MORRIS'S APPOINTMENT AS superintendent was announced on February 20, 1781. By that time he was solidly in the nationalist camp, the group of politicians who wanted to see the national government's powers enhanced. Nationalists wanted Congress to be able to assume the whole public debt and to have the right to tax the people. They saw both as keys to providing stability for the new country. Morris believed that the government's assumption of the whole debt and the taxes it levied to finance it were going to "prove the strongest cement to keep the confederacy together"[7] and Tom Paine considered "a national debt …a national bond."[8] When civilian creditors and military personnel had to come to Congress with their claims, they naturally had an interest in keeping America afloat because if the country sank, they could not get the money they were owed. And the government had an interest in paying them because it did not want to lose its credit. The end result was foreseeable—the emergence of a moneyed class dependent on Congress.

Letting the states take care of the debt was out of the question in the minds of the nationalists. If each state was left responsible for only its share of the national debt, disunion was going to result: every one of the thirteen would go its own way, imposing duties in a manner meant to not burden its own inhabitants and vying to create the most favorable economic conditions within its borders with too little or no regard for the effects of its actions on its neighbors. Rather than uniting to form one nation, the states were certain to become fierce competitors.[9]

Nationalists such as Alexander Hamilton and Robert Morris were strong supporters of the Impost of 1781, the five-percent duty on imports; they wanted the government to have the power to levy taxes directly. However, they realized that the measure had to be approved by all thirteen states before it became law and they saw that much opposition to it existed; some state legislatures and their delegates in Congress saw the impost as a threat to their states' sovereignty. As time would pass, Hamilton's and Morris's frustration would grow. Eventually, they would come to see the army as an instrument that could be used to pressure recalcitrant state legislatures and their supporters in Congress into giving the government what it needed—real taxation authority; they would became provocateurs of the Newburgh Conspiracy.

As long as the government went without real taxation authority, the army remained neglected. In early April Washington, writing partly in cipher to Laurens in Paris, made clear that the army was facing major food shortages; *teamsters were not delivering provisions because they did not want to be paid in worthless certificates.* The situation had become desperate. *With each passing day the general was seeing more evidence that the war could not be continued unless the colonel succeeded in securing a loan from the French.* Without one Washington had no hopes of keeping his "remnant of an Army" together for even the upcoming campaign, let alone any future ones. "[I]f France delays, a timely, and powerful aid in the critical posture of our affairs it will avail us nothing should she attempt it hereafter," he stressed. The soldiers were "approaching fast to nakedness" for lack of clothing. The army's hospitals lacked medicine, and sick people did not have the type of nutritious food that they required. "[A]ll public works [were] at a stand[still], and the Artificers disbanding." France had to advance America money immediately. "[W]e are at the end of our tether. ... Now or never our deliverance must come," the general proclaimed.[10]

At the time when Washington wrote that letter, the government still did not have anyone heading the Department of Finance. Although Congress had announced Morris's appointment in February, he did not immediately accept the position. Finally, in mid-May, after lengthy negotiations, he agreed to assume the post. As part of the agreement between the two parties, Congress allowed the new superintendent to continue his outside business interests while he held the office.[11] Concern about conflicts of interest was less then than it is now. Mixing government business with one's own was not uncommon and was considered acceptable as long as the government was not cheated.[12]

Both the announcement and Morris's subsequent acceptance of the position were welcomed. Alexander Hamilton opined that nobody else in the whole country exhibited in combination "so many advantages." Independence would be gained "by introducing order into our finances—by restoreing public credit—not by winning battles"[13] and Morris was the man who could accomplish those things. James Wilson of Pennsylvania observed "great and very general Satisfaction." He believed the timing was good; the people now appeared to be open-minded about the need to replace the "so long injudiciously pursued" system of financing government operations. They understood that it was impossible to continue financing the war with a rapidly depreciating currency and expected Morris to greatly reform the government's finances.[14] General Gates predicted "Fame immortal" for him if he succeeded in putting America's finances in order. He deserved to be honored for "taking up the Business at this desperate crisis."[15]

Within three days of agreeing to head the Department of Finance, Morris presented Congress with a plan to establish a national bank and asked the delegates to immediately appeal to the state legislatures for the authority to incorporate it and to ban "all other Banks in these States, at least during the War."[16] In order to use debt to produce a national bond Morris was convinced that he first had to establish a national bank to succeed the Bank of Pennsylvania. A national bank could be "a principal Pillar of American Credit."[17]

The delegates quickly approved his plan. The Bank of North America, as they called it, was expected to help the government manage its finances[18] by holding money for Congress and lending it out in the form of newly issued bank notes so Philadelphia could meet its obligations. These notes were going to become the sole usable currency for the whole country, the currency used in trade and to pay taxes, replacing the various types of worthless paper money printed by the states and the government.

The plan called for starting capital to be raised by selling shares of the bank to interested investors. The first thousand were to be sold at $400 apiece in gold or silver. When the bank turned a profit its directors were going to pay those initial investors dividends and thereby establish its credit[19] "firmly in the minds of the Stock holders."[20] New shares were then going to be offered to the public and purchased by confident investors. Within four years the bank would have $4,000,000 and the government would be able to borrow and use its money to spur economic development. "The small Sums advanced by the Holders of Bank Stock may be multiplied ... so as to increase the Resource[s] which Government can draw from,"[21] Morris explained.

The problem for Morris, though, was that he did not have the luxury to wait four years. For all practical purposes, the Continental currency lost all its value that spring and became the subject of ridicule. "A large body of inhabitants with paper dollars in their hats ... paraded the streets of Philadelphia, carrying colors flying, with a DOG TARRED," the *Royal Gazette* reported in May, "and instead of the usual ... feathers, his back was covered with Congress' paper dollars." Right behind them came "the jailor, who refused accepting the bills in the purchase of a glass of rum, and afterwards ... the traders of the city, who shut their shops, declining to sell any more goods but for gold or silver."[22] Some Rhode Islanders supposedly performed a mock burial of the currency, at which someone delivered the appropriate words for the occasion.[23] Whether those events actually happened or were just stories that someone made up probably cannot be determined, but such accounts may accurately reflect how far the paper currency had fallen in the eyes of Americans.

In mid-July the Financier noted the currency's collapse in a letter to the Governor of Cuba and asked for a $400,000 loan.[24] But what he really wanted more than the loan was for all the states to approve the impost. Some states had not approved it and others had attached certain conditions to their approval. In a circular written later that month Morris pointed out to six of them that every time the government went to the creditors it had to pledge the faith of the United States and that the various legislatures had to come up with the funds the government needed to honor those pledges. If the states did that, the government could restore its credit. But if they did not do that, its enemies were going to be able to strongly argue that the government was "Unworthy of Confidence, that our Union [wa]s a Rope of Sand, that the People [we]re Weary of Congress, and that the Respective States [we]re determined to reject its Authority."

There was no reason for the states to be wary of Congress, Morris thought. It was "composed of Representatives freely Chosen and ... of Consequence under the Control of those by whom they were Appointed," the states. Therefore the states ought to give the delegates "all necessary Powers," real authority to levy taxes to obtain the revenue they needed to fund the debt. That would "dishearten the enemy."[25]

But not all the states were ready to give Congress that authority, and Morris had to find money now for the coming Yorktown campaign.[26] Washington wanted hard cash because he had to pay for boats to convey his soldiers down Chesapeake Bay and move heavy guns the last few hundred miles, and his men had to see some of the money they were owed for their past service. "I must entreat you, if possible, to procure one months pay in specie for the detachment under my command," Washington wrote to Morris on August 27. "Part of those troops have not been paid any thing for a long time … and have upon several occasions shewn marks of great discontent. The service they are going upon is disagreeable to the Northern Regiments, but … a douceur of a little hard money would put them in proper temper. If the whole sum cannot be obtained, a part of it will be better than none, as it may be distributed in proportion to the respective wants and claims of the Men."[27]

By the beginning of September Washington was still waiting in vain for the money he had requested; without it he could not placate the army and leave to join forces with Lafayette. Finally, on the sixth, he wrote Morris again. Morris had to send him money immediately, "a Month's Pay at least … on the Wings of speed."[28]

Since the Treasury was empty and would not be full for some time, Morris went to his many American friends and acquaintances who owed him for past favors. Unable to obtain enough hard cash for the Yorktown campaign from them, he then met with Rochambeau and other French officers at French Minister Luzerne's home in Philadelphia to ask that they lend America $20,000.

Rochambeau, however, had only $40,000 in his war chest. How could he lend America half of what he had when he was not even able to pay his own men? Furthermore, the loan could not be made, even if desirable, because the intendant of the French army had already departed for Head of Elk, Maryland, where the allies would be stopping on their way to Yorktown.

Morris was not deterred. "I'll ride south with you until we find him," he replied. "We must have money for the men, or it's all over with us."[29]

The following morning Morris and the French officers mounted their horses and headed south to catch the intendant. Accompanying them was Gouverneur Morris, who spoke French well enough to act as a translator. When the party approached Chester, Pennsylvania, they were overtaken by a courier from Washington. A fleet under Admiral DeGrasse had arrived with funds and the French were able to lend America the money she needed! It had to be paid back by October—from the cash obtained by Laurens in France. "We share again,"[30] Rochambeau declared.

That loan, in hard currency, plus Morris's willingness to dig into his own resources, rescued the campaign. Though ships to move the men south by water were not secured, the transport of artillery and heavy stores by boat was financed; necessary supplies were furnished; and one month's pay was advanced to all men in good standing to ensure that they didn't balk at marching to Yorktown.

The arrival of Deputy Paymaster General Philip Audibert at the Head of Elk produced a sea change in the morale of the men encamped there. The sight of men knocking in tops of wooden kegs and silver half-crowns spilling to the ground "raised the spirits to the required level."[31] One New York major thought he was witnessing something historic: "This day will be famous in the annals of History for being the first in which the Troops of the United States received one month's Pay in specie."[32]

Morris also arranged for thousands of silver coins sitting in Boston—some of the cash brought back from France by Laurens—to be sent to Philadelphia. Like the army, Congress needed the money now. So to save time, nobody attempted to count the money; it was simply weighed and put in small strongboxes for transport. Once twenty of them had been filled, they were put in extremely large chests, each weighing a ton. The chests, which like the strongboxes had been made from sturdy oak, were then nailed shut and secured to the axles of oxcarts with heavy iron straps welded by blacksmiths to prevent their being opened while en route to the capital. To haul just a single chest to Philadelphia one horse and four oxen had to be employed.

According to Tom Paine, sixteen teams were needed to haul all the money. Morris biographer Charles Rappleye, though, puts the number at fourteen. Whatever the case, the eventual journey was made under heavy guard and over unfriendly country roads and took two months or more. The armed teamsters used a circuitous route, and the money passed through Worcester and Newburgh before reaching Philadelphia not long after the American victory at Yorktown. There it was used by the government to help establish the Bank of North America, to pay debts incurred during the Yorktown campaign, and to meet other obligations needing immediate attention.[33]

After the victory at Yorktown, Morris desperately wanted to create a system that would give the government permanent funding. The impost and the bank were essential but by themselves not enough. Other specific duties besides the impost were necessary if the government wanted to ensure that creditors need not worry about their loans being repaid. "It is high Time to relieve ourselves from the Infamy we have already sustained, and to rescue and restore the national Credit. This can only be done by solid Revenue,"[34] he announced to the states on October 19, 1781.

Assisting Robert Morris in his work would be the rakish Gouverneur Morris, a large-framed man of French Huguenot descent with a receding hairline and a peg leg. Like Robert Morris, he would become a key figure in the Newburgh Conspiracy.

GOUVERNEUR MORRIS[35] CAME into the world on January 31, 1752. He was one of five offspring, Lewis and Sarah Morris's only son. As a young child he grew up on a huge estate called Morrisania, located by the Harlem River and run by his father—a judge—with the help of forty-six slaves.

Gouverneur received some schooling in New Rochelle and then was sent to the Academy of Philadelphia to get "the best education ... to be had in Europe or America."[36] He arrived there in 1761 and after three years was ready for King's College, though he was only twelve years old. Morris apparently did not display any great zeal in his studies and in his second year even got in trouble with the trustees for circulating a "scandalous report ... virulently attacking the Moral Character"[37] of a mathematics professor. The college conducted a hearing and found the professor not guilty of any inappropriate behavior. Morris and one of the two other students involved in the matter were then brought before an assembly of their peers and scolded by the college president.

In 1768 the teenage boy began an apprenticeship with a prominent Loyalist lawyer named William Smith. Upon completing that training, he received a Master of Arts degree and began practicing law. Though he was not yet twenty years old, he earned a good reputation and achieved financial success. Much of his early legal work dealt with commerce and real estate.

When America and England began to part ways, Morris still hoped for their reconciliation and worked to bring it about. He wanted to avert a war and did not join the angry patriots in 1774–75. Those zealous men who held meetings and rallies to oppose measures taken by Parliament were too unruly, and he did not want them to take control of the government. "I see, and see it with fear and trembling," he wrote in May 1774, "that if the disputes with Britain continue, we shall be under the worst of all possible dominions … the

The peglegged Gouverneur Morris, the Financier's assistant

domination of a riotous mob."[38] An oppressive government far away was dangerous to American liberties, but so were groups of rioters who disturbed the peace and caused anarchy.

Morris entered the New York Provincial Congress in 1775 and in late May was made a member of a committee tasked with considering whether a Continental paper currency should be printed. The morning after the committee was established Morris had a report ready.

In short, his view was that the national government—Congress—had to take the lead in financing the war. He pictured it printing all the bills of credit and issuing each state its share. Each state then had to be responsible for the share apportioned to it. The bills would be used for making purchases and later be redeemed by the states when the creditors holding them came knocking at their doors to be paid back. If a state did not meet its obligations to creditors, Philadelphia assumed the debt.

Having all the states bound to one central authority—Congress—to meet their obligations essentially unified them. And such a plan for financing the war was more efficient; if each state were free to come up with its own plan to pay for its war needs, all sorts of wild ideas eventually proven ruinous to the war effort were sure to be advanced.

The plan Morris put forward was approved first by the New York Provincial Congress and later by the Continental Congress.

Early the following year Gouverneur gave up all hopes for reconciliation. To no avail he had proposed a "plan of accommodation"[39] to let the mother country regulate the colonies' trade but not allow it to force them to provide funds for the British Empire's defense. Now he was siding entirely with the Americans. Thinking that as one of the better members of society he ought to serve his country as an officer, the tall young man sought a commission. Congress did not grant him his wish and later he admitted that he was better suited for "the deliberations of the Cabinet than the glorious Labours of the Field."[40]

While serving in the New York Provincial Congress, Morris became acquainted with Captain Alexander Hamilton, the commander of a New York artillery company, and began a long friendship with George Washington. More importantly, in the spring of 1776, he saw the "Hickey Plot" unfold. Washington was going to be taken prisoner and turned over to the British or killed by being fed poisoned peas or by some other means. Other high-ranking officers also were going to be targeted. The magazines where gunpowder was kept were going to be blown up. The army's guns were going to be rendered useless by American soldiers enticed with cash to join the British. New York City was going to be set fire and the only bridge available to the rebels for escape from Manhattan brought down. Everything was supposed to begin upon arrival of the British fleet.

After authorities learned of the "Hickey Plot," which was named after a member of Washington's guard, incriminating letters were gathered and witnesses gave testimony. One member of the committee created by the New York Provincial Congress to look into the plot was Morris. He served as a key interrogator of New York Mayor David Matthews, who was believed to be receiving money from Governor William Tryon and passing it on to American soldiers for their allegiance to the British and to buy arms for Loyalists.

Another member of the committee was Colonel Alexander McDougall. That he and Morris played the roles of patriots in the story of the "Hickey Plot" now seems ironic. Later, when both were involved in another plot, the Newburgh Conspiracy, they played very different roles.

In the event, a defiant Matthews served some time in Hartford but was later released. Thomas Hickey was not so lucky; on June 28, 1776, he was brought to a Manhattan field and hanged in front of twenty thousand spectators just before midday, the first soldier in the Continental Army to be dispatched in such a manner. Washington impressed upon his young soldiers that the fate of Hickey should serve as a lesson to "particularly avoid lewd women, who by the dying confession of this poor criminal, first led him into practices which ended in his untimely and ignominious death."[41]

In the spring of 1777 the state of New York got its first constitution. Morris had been instrumental in drafting it, but the final product was less than what he had hoped for. One of its shortcomings was that it did not give the governor enough authority. Later Morris would feel the same way about the Articles of Confederation, that they did not give Congress enough authority.

Not long after the constitution was proclaimed, Morris was chosen to be one of his state's five delegates to the Continental Congress. News of the appointment pleased Washington, but Morris was not able to take his seat until about eight months later. By that time Congress had fled to York because of the British occupation of Philadelphia.

Immediately after taking his seat, he was put on the Committee at Camp. The assignment meant a trip to Valley Forge, where he helped Washington come up with a plan for reorganizing his army. There he saw firsthand "the Skeleton of an Army ... in a naked starving Condition out of Health out of Spirits."[42] He learned of desertions and resignations, but did not blame the men and officers. They were "Poor Dogs ... without Cloaths to wear, Victuals to eat, Wood to burn or straw to lie on." He was surprised that any of them stayed.[43] Months had passed since the men last received supplies.

What Morris saw led him and the other committee members to support the recommendations Washington included in a report he prepared for them. He backed the general's recommendation that the officers be given postwar half-pay pensions because he and the other members had heard from the officers themselves during their visit that they wanted them. Though there was strong opposition to giving the officers any type of pension, especially half pay for life, the committee lobbied hard for postwar compensation, and on May 15, 1778, its efforts paid off; Congress approved its proposed compromise, half pay for seven years to officers who served for the duration of the war. He and the other committee members also pressed the body to make the reforms necessary to ensure that the states furnished the men with the supplies that had been requisitioned. And he tried to address the men's pay concerns.

A couple of months before half pay was approved, Morris had written Governor George Clinton that in order to finance the war Congress had to do something about its inability to impose taxes. Simply allowing the debt to grow and waiting for money from the states was not an option. "The Want of Money in the several Departments is a Complaint reverberated to us from all Quarters and arises as much as any Thing from Neglect in those who should have thought a little more of paying while very liberal in contracting Debts," he charged. The problem was "the bad Policy of delaying Taxation" and, Morris fumed, "the People ought to take exemplary Vengeance upon those whoever they may be who are Causes of such Delay."[44]

That spring he began working on a plan to address the government's financial impotence. His idea was to have states claiming western lands cede them to Congress. The ceded lands were then to be used by the body to create a new state for veterans and to provide the government with collateral for foreign loans. In exchange for ceding those lands, the states were going to see their shares of the national debt reduced.

To ensure that revenue was always flowing into the government's coffers, Morris included in his plan duties on imports, a head tax of one dollar on Americans, a poll tax, and fees for postal services. He wanted states to be free to trade with each other without restrictions, but he did not want them to print their own currencies; he envisioned one stable currency for the whole nation and called for the lifting of price controls that were then in effect to demonstrate a faith in it. He also called for the government to publish a record of its debt.

Gouverneur presented his plan in late September. Efforts to come up with a sound financial policy continued thereafter, but his attempt to strengthen the government and provide it with a steady cash flow, however rational, went nowhere. Delegates simply were not ready for his most radical recommendations, including the one for duties on imports. That being the case, the same old systemic problems persisted for the next few years.

Not long after presenting his plan, Gouverneur drafted instructions for Benjamin Franklin, the American minister to France. One of Franklin's tasks was to "lay before the court the deranged state of our finances."[45] To aid him in doing so, Morris provided Franklin with a number of "Observations on the Finances of America." The most important point Franklin had to convey to the French was that America's financial situation could be rescued only "by very considerable loans or subsidies in Europe."[46] Domestic loans and taxes were not capable of supporting the depreciating Continental currency.[47]

Morris left Congress in November 1779, after having been rejected for another term. Though out of office, he still remained concerned about America's finances. In February 1780, while working in Philadelphia as a lawyer, he began writing on that subject for the *Pennsylvania Packet*. Using the printing presses to finance the war was not an answer to America's problems. What the country had to have, "an American"—Morris—wrote in the last of his essays for the newspaper, was a government with greater powers. That meant the authority to levy taxes—many taxes. If it did not get that, the confederation was certain to break apart, victory or no victory in the war.

As that year progressed, no victory in the war appeared likely. In mid-May Charleston fell. Later that month two Connecticut regiments mutinied. In August General Gates suffered a great loss in Camden. And in September Benedict Arnold's treason was discovered.

If those setbacks for the country were not enough to depress Morris, he also had to contend with a personal loss—the loss of his left leg one morning in mid-May. Intending to go out into the country for an extended visit with Maryland delegate George Plater and his wife, Morris had his carriage brought to the front of his house. Without first tethering the two large, gray horses that had drawn it there to a fixed object, he climbed aboard and shouted out one or more commands, though he had not yet taken the reins. The roused horses started to run away. Morris battled with them for several hundred yards but eventually was thrown from the carriage. As he fell to the ground and the carriage turned over, he caught his left ankle between the spokes of a turning wheel and dislocated it and suffered multiple fractures of his leg.

This was not the first time in his life that he had hurt himself badly; as a mischievous fourteen-year-old boy at Morrisania, he had knocked over a kettle of boiling water, badly burning his right arm and side of his body. In that case, though, he did not lose a limb as a result. This time he was not so lucky. When two doctors looked at his injured leg, it appeared so badly damaged that they recommended the lower half be amputated. Morris accepted their advice and had a peg leg of oak made. A friend trying to comfort him thought the episode would leave him a moral person by curbing his desire for a dissolute lifestyle, but Morris viewed the situation differently. "[Y]ou argue the matter so handsomely, and point out so clearly the advantages of being without legs," he replied, "that I am almost tempted to part with the other one."[48]

Gouverneur received his official appointment as assistant to Robert Morris in early July 1781. Within a month the Financier was already noting his "Capable and Usefull" assistant's "Genius and Abilities" in his diary.[49]

THE TASK BEFORE the Financier and his assistant appeared daunting. By this time only specie was being accepted in markets and the phrase "not worth a Continental," which probably had first appeared the year before, was very familiar.[50] The severe decline in the currency that started well before the Financier assumed his position and continued during the last half of 1781 affected everybody: Delegates faced thousand-dollar laundry bills;[51] Tom Paine had to pay $300 for a pair of woolen stockings;[52] and James Madison sometimes did not want his pay because it would be worthless by the time he received it.[53] By the end of 1781 an American needed $1,000 or more in Continental bills to get just one dollar in specie. "If I could buy anything with it, I would not until the last necessity; … it will buy nothing, so that it must be burnt as soon as it honestly can,"[54] the Financier wrote to Benjamin Franklin in late November.

Chapter Three

"The Brink of Ruin"

GEORGE WASHINGTON WAS in Philadelphia when the Financier wrote his letter to Benjamin Franklin. After the victory at Yorktown in October 1781 the general's northern regiments had headed for the Hudson Highlands, while the men from Virginia, Maryland, and Pennsylvania had marched south to join Major General Nathanael Greene in South Carolina. Washington would ultimately join his northern regiments in the Hudson Highlands, but he did not immediately follow them there. First, on November 5, the tall general with a pockmarked face and sunken chest stopped at his brother-in-law's estate in Eltham to see the dying John "Jack" Parke Custis, his twenty-eight-year-old stepson, who had come down with a camp fever at Yorktown. Then, less than a week later, he rode off to Fredericksburg in hopes of seeing his seventy-four-year-old mother, but she was not there. After that he went to Mount Vernon for a short stay, and from there he left for Philadelphia by carriage with Martha. As they made their way north, they encountered enthusiastic crowds and, when they reached Philadelphia, passed homes with windows illuminated to honor the general. Covering many of them were large transparent paintings displaying patriotic sentiments, such as images of Washington wearing a crown of laurels.[1]

Not long before Washington's arrival Congress had called on the states to levy taxes to raise revenue for Philadelphia. The money each state raised and forwarded to Congress would equal its requisition quota for 1782.[2] But in the past the states had not responded to requisitions, and Robert Morris and Gouverneur Morris did not expect the call for special taxes to solve the government's funding problems.[3] So that fall and the following winter, they, Washington, Secretary of War Benjamin Lincoln, Secretary of Congress Charles Thomson, and Secretary of Foreign Affairs Robert Livingston met one or two evenings a week on the second floor of the Department of Marine for the purpose of "Consulting and Concerting Measures to promote the Service and the Public Good."[4]

Since Robert Morris understood that Americans were not necessarily going to like the medicine they prescribed—the Impost of 1781—he began an intense letter-writing campaign to drum up support for it and convince reluctant delegates that it was needed if they hoped to finance the war. "The public Debt is considerable," he noted in a letter to the governors of Massachusetts, Rhode Island and Maryland, "and the public Credit must be lost, if the Interest of it be not provided for." Congress was doing the right thing in asking for funding and he was doing his duty "in soliciting a Compliance with their request." If the opponents of funding succeeded, they would "be responsible for the Consequences" and everybody, including among others the government's creditors, would hold them accountable.

"The Hope of our Enemy, is in the Derangement of our Finances," he emphasized, "and … when revenue is given, that Hope must cease." Anybody who comes out against the impost "not only opposes … the Dictates of Justice, but … labors to continue the War … to shed more Blood, to produce more Devastation, and to extend and prolong the Miseries of Mankind."[5]

Four days after Morris wrote that letter, on January 7, 1782, the Bank of North America opened its doors for business. Hard currency had arrived from France during the fall of 1781; the bank's success appeared likely.

The demand for gold and silver was going to be great, though. Stories about how the bank first tried to attract investors are perhaps apocryphal, but they at least reflect how important it was for the bank to appear to have full vaults. Bank employees were said to have brought boxes conspicuously labeled "Silver" up to the cashiers from the cellar vaults or carried them back down there from the banking room. Boxes were pulled up by belt or chain, lowered onto counters, and raised to allow the silver coins inside to spill out into brilliant piles that grew in size as they were picked up by the bank's reflectors and seen by potential depositors. Men withdrawing silver were approached by secret agents working for the bank and urged to redeposit what they were taking out.

The charade enabled the bank to gain a reputation for being well funded. However, it actually was not on such solid ground. Morris's original plan to raise starting capital by selling shares in the bank to interested investors proved fanciful; few people were able to pay as much as $400 a share to invest in the bank. If all the silver Laurens had brought back from France—more than $460,000—could have been used by the bank as starting capital, Morris would have had enough money; he had reasoned that the bank was going to need $400,000 to begin operating. But before the bank opened for business, close to half of that silver had already been expended.[6]

Still, the Bank did help alleviate some of the army's supply problems and bring a little order to the economy. Money was lent to the government and, Morris believed, the country was saved "from the efforts of her avowed [enemies] and from the intrigues of her concealed enemies, from those who, while they clamor loudly against the administration for doing so little, sedulously labor to deprive it of the means of doing anything."[7]

The delegates' call on the states to levy taxes to meet requisition quotas for 1782 and the opening of the bank aside, the Financier and his assistant still knew they needed to look abroad for funds. When Gouverneur Morris wrote America's diplomatic agent to Spain, John Jay, on January 20, he concluded his letter by urging him to get aid from the Spanish court in Havana. "For Heaven's Sake, convince them of the Necessity of giving us Money," he demanded. "With money we can do every Thing." And if Jay did get money from Havana, he was to conceal his success from Congress; Morris wanted the finance office to be able to "plead Poverty to the States," even if the government was as "rich as Croesus."[8]

The Financier and his assistant could have employed army officers unhappy over their pay arrears to pressure legislators into giving Congress greater power, but when some of them asked Tom Paine in late January to write a petition to Washington about the matter, the finance office showed no inclination to use them as a pressure group. Robert Morris wanted instead "to keep them quiet."

Soon thereafter, in early February, the officers drafted a petition "to their respective States on the Subject of their Pay," which was brought to Morris by Paine. Morris "proposed some alterations tending to make it rather more Continental which he [Paine] approved and promised to adopt."[9]

At that time the author of *Common Sense* was not yet formally working for the finance office, although his services were greatly desired. Back in September 1781 the Financier had called him and "proposed that for the Service of the Country he should write and publish ... Pieces respecting the propriety, Necessity and Utility of Taxation" because the government had to have revenue in order to finance the war.[10] Morris, though, did not offer to pay the writer for his labor and, as a result, his call for help went unanswered for several months.

Finally, on February 10, 1782, "taking into Consideration the important Situation of Affairs ... the Propriety and even necessity of informing the People and rousing them into Action; [and] considering also the Abilities of Mr. Thomas Paine as a Writer," the Financier agreed with Livingston and Washington on an annual salary of $800[11] for some articles intended to urge state legislatures to grant Congress greater taxation authority and "to prepare the minds of the people for such restraints and such taxes and imposts as are absolutely necessary for their own welfare."[12] The money was to be drawn from a secret fund at Morris's disposal. The salary was important because Paine was broke at the time, but the public could not be informed that the writer was being paid by the government;[13] it was far more likely to seriously consider his call for the delegates to be granted greater taxation authority if he appeared to be a disinterested party.

The day after the question of Paine's pay was resolved, Morris wrote Congress. Massachusetts, Rhode Island and Maryland had still not approved the Impost of 1781 and Virginia, which had ratified it, was reportedly not going to apply the law until all the other states had voted for it. That meant the government could not pay the public creditors the interest they were owed. "To expect that under such Circumstances others will confide in the Government would be Folly and to expect that Foreigners will trust a Government which has no Credit with its own Citizens would be madness," Morris warned. He was disgusted with the states and some members of Congress; the former were ignoring the requisitions for 1782 and the latter were slow to censure them out of "Delicacy." He was not going to "be deterred from waking those who slumber on the Brink of Ruin," but he had to have Congress's help: "My Voice, Sir, is feeble and I must therefore pray to be assisted by the Voice of the United States in Congress. Supported by them I may perhaps do something. But without that Support I must be an useless Incumbrance."[14]

Sixteen days later Morris recommended that Congress pass land, poll, and liquor taxes. However, the delegates were not ready for his taxes, no matter how well they recognized that something had to be done to fund the debt. They established a three-man committee made up of members opposed to additional taxes—Arthur Lee of Virginia, Samuel Osgood of Massachusetts, and Abraham Clark of New Jersey—to review and report on his proposal and it recommended that the taxes not be adopted.[15]

About one week after the Financier recommended those taxes, Gouverneur Morris wrote Francisco Rendon, Spain's representative in Philadelphia, to explain why it was so difficult for America to finance the war by taxing its citizens. He began by urging patience, pointing out that no country's citizens liked taxes because the benefits derived from them became apparent only later, while the financial pain caused by them was felt sooner. After giving a detailed history of the government's financial problems—among them currency depreciation, the loss of public credit, and the failure of states to respond to requisitions—Morris again urged patience, reminding Rendon "how extremely difficult … it is to establish a system of taxation adapted to the country and the people of it." In America's case, the problem was that its citizens were unaccustomed to paying taxes and until they became used to "bearing them," the country would need financial assistance from abroad.[16]

On March 5, the same day that Gouverneur Morris wrote Rendon, Paine completed work on a long essay in support of taxation. The plan was for states to levy two types of taxes—one to address their own needs and another to obtain the funds Congress requested. The two were to be clearly differentiated and kept separate.[17] In the past the states had not made such distinctions when levying and collecting taxes and had just ignored requisitions, saying their own wants were so great they could hardly be expected to forward some of their tax revenue to Congress.

Later, not pleased with his initial effort, Paine revised his essay and had it printed in the *Pennsylvania Journal*. The Pennsylvania General Assembly had done the right thing when it levied new taxes to meet its quota, he said. "Huzzas for liberty" and politicians' eloquence mean nothing. They neither "fill the soldier's belly, nor clothe his back." And they will "neither pay the public creditor, nor purchase our supplies."[18] To do those things Congress needs tax revenue.

Not all states did the right thing, though; the New York General Assembly had voted to use some of the funds requisitioned by Congress to pay troops of its line and, pleading poverty, had not sent any money to Robert Morris since his appointment as superintendent. Morris did not understand why New York even considered taking such actions. If all the other states followed her example, some would "pay better than she can," causing dissatisfaction among its soldiers and officers. With that in mind, Morris urged Livingston to persuade the governor "to stop any payments until the Legislature me[t] again" and he had an opportunity to "lay the Consequences before them, so that they may at least act with their Eyes open."[19]

AS MORRIS COMPLAINED about the actions of the legislature in Albany, George Washington settled in at his new headquarters in Newburgh, New York, up in the Hudson Highlands. He had arrived with Martha by barge on either March 31 or April 1, 1782,[20] after an almost four-month-long stay in Philadelphia and a brief stop at Morristown, New Jersey. While in the capital he had been fêted as only a hero can be. He had gone to more parties than he cared to go to, attended plays, been the guest of honor at lunches and receptions, and shaken hands with people who had traveled great distances to meet the victor of Yorktown.

More important, though, he had also tended to military matters. He had met with Robert Morris, Secretary of Foreign Affairs Robert Livingston, and Secretary of War Benjamin Lincoln, and reminded everyone that the war was not yet over. He wanted the states to provide Philadelphia with money for the next campaign, noting that he had heard talk of mutiny and observing that he couldn't guarantee how the army would react if it were shortchanged on pay, food, and clothing. The mood of "Officers, in particular," was not good; they had been promised a generous postwar pension by the government, but the states had yet to provide the funds needed to pay for it.

Despite his efforts, Washington had little to show for the army when he finally arrived in the Hudson Highlands. He had succeeded in getting the delegates to agree to ask the states for more new troops for 1782, but he had nothing for the disgruntled officers.[21]

IF WASHINGTON HAD known what was going on across the ocean while he was in Philadelphia, he would have worried less. The situation there had changed a great deal; Yorktown had dashed all British hopes for victory. When Prime Minister Lord North first learned of the defeat from Lord Germain on the evening of November 25, 1781, he reportedly reacted to the news as though he had "taken a ball in the breast. For he opened his arms exclaiming wildly, as he paced up and down the apartment during a few minutes, 'Oh, God! It is all over! It is all over!'"[22]

King George III, on the other hand, did not panic. Yorktown was a loss and nothing more. They would get more cheerful news before long. "A good end … to this war" was still possible, the fast-talking sovereign with bulging eyes reassured those present, but only if they did not lose hope.[23]

Soon the King had a reason to despair, though. On February 22, 1782, a motion calling on him to end the war came within one vote of passing. Then, less than a week later, Parliament changed course and approved the call to bring it to a close by a vote of 234 to 215.

In early March the House of Commons agreed to brand anyone who tried to prolong the war as an enemy of King and country and gave George III the power to end hostilities with America. The branding decision was the last straw for Lord North. On March 20 he offered his resignation, which the King accepted, and two days later Lord Rockingham took over as prime minister. "At last the fatal day is come,"[24] the King elegized.

That month George III considered abdicating but eventually decided not to do so. In the draft message announcing his plans to leave the throne the lamenting sovereign averred that "the change of Sentiments of one Branch of the Legislature … totally incapacitated Him from either conducting the War with effect, or from obtaining any Peace but on conditions which would prove to be destructive to the Commerce as well as essential Rights of the British Nation." For that reason he believed he was not able to "be of … further Utility to His Native Country."[25]

GEORGE WASHINGTON DID not know about those events. What he did know was that the British had about twelve thousand troops in New York City[26] and they might decide to move up the valley, take control of the Hudson and capture the outposts in the area. So he wanted to be in position to watch them and prevent that from happening.

The Hudson Highlands were the perfect location for him. The area where the Hudson River flows through the highlands was known as Martyrs' Reach,[27] and the waters around West Point were especially treacherous. Intruders had to deal with unpredictable winds and the narrowness of the river, and make a difficult ninety-degree turn. To do so they had to slow down and make changes to their rigging, turning them into easy targets for gun batteries on both shores. And if they survived a barrage from heavy guns, they still had a great iron chain blocking their entrance to the highlands and preventing them from threatening American forces there.

The chain had first been stretched across the river in April 1778. The Americans had frustrated the British in their attempt to sever New England from the mid-Atlantic and southern colonies and close off the Hudson by defeating them at Saratoga in October, but the destruction of Forts Clinton and Montgomery was evidence that something still had to be done to stop enemy ships from using the river; sunken vessels joined by timber, weighted barrels, underwater chevaux-de-frise—wooden obstacles with protruding stakes—fire rafts and ships, and the first iron chain had not been effective barriers,[28] but none of them had been placed in the waters by West Point. A better chain in a better location promised to be the answer.

The new chain was supposed to be strong enough to stop a forty-four-gun British warship backed by an advantageous wind and tide, yet not so heavy that it couldn't be removed when ice started forming in the river. The earlier chain, which had been constructed by the Ringwood Furnace in New Jersey and placed across the river at Fort Montgomery, had proved ineffective; the diameter of its links was too small and the quality of its iron poor. Therefore the new chain had to be made elsewhere.

Peter Townshend's Sterling Iron Works had been in operation since well before the troubles with England began, and the iron it made was well regarded.[29] It was also located only about twenty-five miles from West Point. It was the logical choice for the job.

Townshend was asked to make the chain by Colonel Timothy Pickering one evening in early March 1778, and by the following morning his forges and men were beginning work on it.[30] Thanks to their around-the-clock operations[31] and the purposeful Lieutenant Thomas Machin, who superintended the forge at New Windsor that assembled the links produced at the Sterling Iron Works, the chain was completed in only six weeks.

The finished product was about one-third of a mile long,[32] weighed one-hundred-forty to one-hundred-fifty tons,[33] according to Townshend, and probably had seven-hundred-fifty links. Making those links was no simple process. An iron bar was heated in a hearth, positioned onto an anvil and kept steady with giant tongs as a huge water-powered trip hammer pounded it into a workable shape. It was then heated again to level its ends. After that it was bent with a mandrel until its ends were sufficiently curved to allow their being welded together into a link. Each link was said to be about thirty inches long and likely weighed more than one hundred pounds.

The links were then connected to form sections of the chain, which were carted on ox-driven sledges by New England teamsters from Townshend's ironworks to New Windsor. There they were secured to large rafts made from pine logs protected with tar and oakum. Finally, the forge's work was sent downriver to its proper place[34] and "fixed to wooden Crates filled with stone,"[35] and anchors were dropped to provide even greater stability. The barrier, which would be called "General Washington's Watch Chain" by the Americans and the "Yankee Pumpkin Vine"[36] by the British, was "conjectured to be 8 feet in breadth and the height 10"[37] on both sides of the river.

WASHINGTON'S NEW HEADQUARTERS—Jonathan and Catherine "Tryntje" Hasbrouck's fine Dutch fieldstone farmhouse—was located a few miles north of the chain and West Point. It stood on elevated land and was finely situated in the southeastern part of Newburgh. Its front faced westward; its rear was to the Hudson River. From his new perch Washington was able to look out and see the twelve-mile-long bay, mountains like Dans Kammer up north and the steep Butter Hill (now Storm King Mountain) down south, and a beautiful lake. Further south was New York City. About six miles to the west was the New Windsor Cantonment, where most of his army would later be encamped. From both Newburgh and New Windsor there was a route that the army could take right to New Jersey and Pennsylvania. Not far away were key officers, including Gates and Major General Henry Knox.

Jonathan Hasbrouck, a colonel in his district's militia, had died in much pain from "a stoppage of his water"[38] less than two years before Washington's arrival, but Mrs. Hasbrouck and a small number of officers had continued to occupy the house until that time. She apparently was not too happy about the Commander-in-chief establishing his headquarters in her home, though she would be paid a small amount of rent.[39] When she learned that he was going to be residing there, the tall, thin, black-haired woman "sat some time in sullen silence."[40]

His new headquarters was "neither vast nor commodious."[41] It had a basement where perishable goods could be stored, two floors, and an attic. There was "a post and rail fence around it," according to Newburgh's James Donnelly, "and an orchard on the west and south side."[42]

The most noteworthy room was located in the back of the house on the first floor. During Washington's stay it had seven small blue doors that provided access to most parts of the building, one glass window but no curtain, two small dining tables, a stone hearth and a masonry "fireback" that was part of one wall. This huge fireplace had no sides. As one visitor noted, "The fire is in the room itself."[43] The floor was made of hardwood and the large beams supporting the ceiling may have been made from poplar.

Two other rooms on the first floor served as offices, one for Washington and the other for his aides-de-camp. The aides' bedchambers were the first room to the right of the front entrance and hall. They slept in portable camp beds. The first room to the left was used as a parlor during the day and was where guests stayed when sleeping over. Behind that room was George and Martha's bedchamber. Their bedstead, bought after they arrived, was foldable and small; the Commander-in-chief slept sitting up because that was believed to promote better breathing by opening up the airways. The last room on the first floor, the one appearing to be in the back left corner to anyone standing in the front yard, was Martha's dressing room and a place for storing trunks of cloths. It also was where her personal servant slept.[44]

Much work was done to transform the house and the immediate environs into a suitable place for the general and his entourage before and after their arrival. Good but reasonably-priced furniture, such as the bedstead, was bought. Lightning rods were put up. Barracks and stables were constructed. So too was a pen and slaughter house, possibly across the river. Several guardhouses were erected a good distance from the house. A lab for producing gunpowder was built by the river. The nearby wharf was repaired. And, thanks to Martha, flower beds were prepared, lined with bricks, and then sown with seeds that produced many a colorful blossom. Those were just some of the examples of the work done for the general's stay.[45]

One thing that did not have to be constructed was a large barn; that and an enormous hay barracks already existed before the general's arrival, somewhere to the south of the house.

After Washington settled in, he often watched his Life Guard "parade in the door-yard west of the house. They were a fine body of men—every one six feet or over in height." The noncommissioned officers and privates who made up this corps were "sober, young, active, and well made, of good character and proud of appearing clean. Their uniform consisted of blue coats with white facings, white waistcoats and breeches, black half gaiters and cocked hats with blue and white feathers. They carried a banner upon which was painted ... one of the Guard holding a horse, and in the act of receiving a flag from the Genius of Liberty, standing by the side of the Union shield and the American eagle. On the banner, upon a ribbon, was the motto, *Conquer or Die.*" The size of the corps did not remain constant; apparently as many as two-hundred-fifty guards were attached to Washington at Morristown but by some time in 1783 they would number only sixty-four.[46]

While at the Hasbrouck House, the "Old Man" and "Patsy"[47]—George and Martha—frequently hosted lavish three-course dinners for the general's staff officers and invited guests. The food was prepared by a German cook, and those who attended the dinners were expected to show up in full dress. The silverware used for the occasions was polished. Dinner began at five in the evening, when Washington or the chaplain said grace, and usually continued for two hours. It always included wine, meat, vegetables, pastries, nuts, tea and coffee, and often butter, cider, apples, cranberries and roots.

At nine in the evening supper was served. It would last two hours and consist of a small number of light dishes, fruit, and nuts. Upon its conclusion, toasts would be made and wine consumed.[48]

Washington would live and work in these "confined quarters" until mid-August 1783, leaving Newburgh only for military matters elsewhere in the state and for a brief rest at Mount Vernon during the summer of 1782.[49] In addition to Martha, a number of others stayed with Washington at his headquarters: His mulatto attendant Billy Lee, at least one maid, cooks, scullions, laundresses, and a housekeeper made up the civilian ranks. Lieutenant Colonel Tench Tilghman and another two to five aides and secretaries made up the military family.[50]

Of all the houses that Washington lived in during the war, the farmhouse would earn the distinction of being his longest-serving headquarters. Nonetheless, he still hoped to return to Virginia. The farmhouse was, in his words, a "dreary mansion in which we are locked by frost and Snow."[51]

IN MID-APRIL 1782 Robert Morris was visited by Pennsylvania's Colonel Richard Humpton and "pressed ... to give orders for the Settlement of the Accounts of the Army." The Financier, in response, sent for the paymaster general and consulted with him.[52] He knew the officers should be paid, but he also wanted the public creditors to get what they were owed. When he wrote the President of Congress, John Hanson, on the twenty-fourth in regard to a claim made by Captain Pierre Landais, he made that perfectly clear. "There is no doubt but he ought to receive the Balance due to him, if our Affairs would admit of such payments," he declared, "but there are numerous Creditors of the Public, whose Claims are equally just, and … deserve at least equal attention … and should arrangements … Calculated to administer equal Justice among the Public Creditors be broke through in particular Instances, Congress will very soon find their Table Covered with Memorials and Petitions which having Justice for their Foundation, cannot be rejected after the precedent is set, and which cannot be granted for Want of Means."53

The reason the government lacked the means to pay the army and the creditors was, as always, resistance from the states. Morris thought the government should have "Obligatory and coercive Clauses on the *States*." He had done his best "to stimulate them to Exertions" and had urged them to support his ideas on funding but to no avail. He saw that all the state legislatures had "Characters too full of Local attachments and Views, to permit sufficient attention to the general Interest."54

IN THE HUDSON highlands, on May 3, the need to find the means to pay the army became especially clear. Sometime that morning Colonel Herman Swift learned that some Connecticut men were planning to mutiny; they would "meet that afternoon under pretence of playing ball to concert their operations" and begin executing their plan when they heard the drums beat for reveille at 4 a.m. the following day. Swift, who would be away during the day, requested that his officers gather intelligence while he was absent. When the colonel returned to his men in the evening he learned from the officers the names of "some principal actors" and found out that one-hundred-fifty men had assembled. Later he had some of his officers lead sixty soldiers to the various regiments to round up men whom he "expected to obtain more particular intelligence" from. Eventually, he learned the names of the soldiers the regiments had appointed to lead them and the mutineers' plans: Before going to bed on the third, the Connecticut men would "prepare their packs and … sleep on their arms"; the following morning they would gather on the grounds of their encampment when they heard the drums beat for reveille, wait for someone to take command of them, and then march out of camp and head to Fishkill. There they would "take possession of some fieldpieces, draw their provisions and march to Hartford," where they planned to demand that their state legislature pay them.

The three sergeants whom Swift considered to be the ringleaders were charged with attempting to incite a mutiny and with failing to disclose the hatched plan to their officers. They were then tried by court-martial on the twelfth. One of them was found guilty on both counts and hanged the following day, but the other two were completely acquitted.55

TROUBLE WAS NOT confined to the army in the Hudson Highlands. Sometime during the period when those three sergeants were waiting to be tried—probably on the ninth—Morris received an alarming letter from Nathanael Greene. The general had written the letter only two days after the arrest of a Pennsylvania sergeant for plotting a mutiny that could have resulted in Greene and his staff officers being seized by one-hundred-fifty British cavalrymen and the removal of his army from the war effort. He feared that the Pennsylvania men were succeeding in sowing "the seeds of discontent and mutiny … through the whole army" and told Morris that the sergeant was going to be executed. Any others found guilty of such wrongdoing, he implied, were also going to be punished.

But Greene knew he had to do his utmost to lessen his men's suffering, the fuel for the army's growing "discontent and dissatisfaction." So many of his men were deserting or being discharged that he could not help but lose hope. Now "even … the Officers" were finding "service in this Country … disagreeable"; the poor quality of the army's rations, the "very bad water and the want of money" were causing them to be "continually in a petulant and discontented disposition."

What would help ease the officers' minds was relief for their soldiers. They were "literally naked" and had for the last half year received only promises of pay, not real cash. The gimpy-kneed Greene had done everything in his power to help them but that was not enough. "Unless this Army receive pay before the sickly season approaches it will cease to exist," the general warned. He had been assured that before long much clothing was going to arrive, but only if it came with pay for his men would "the evil … be removed."[56]

Not long after receiving that letter, an especially strident Morris wrote the governors. He had asked for less than what the war really cost, but still far too little revenue was flowing into the government's coffers. The states were guilty of "a dishonorable Neglect," one putting America in peril. He did not elaborate at this point but, given what Greene had written, must have pictured a mutiny of at least two thousand soldiers, something similar to what had happened on January 1, 1781, when the men in the Pennsylvania Line left their quarters, seized arms and cannon, wounded some of their officers, and marched towards Philadelphia. The states were looking out for their own interests at the expense of the nation. "Little local Objects have postponed those Measures which are essential to our Existence so that the most fatal Consequences are now suspended by a Thread," he grumbled. He was writing to inform them of the "Public Danger" and to assure them that he would try to meet the obligations of his office "like an honest Man." However, he could do nothing as long as the states paid no attention to the requisitions from Congress. Only New Jersey had provided funds for 1782. "Now … should the Army disband and should scenes of Distress and Horror be reiterated and accumulated," Morris went on, "I again repeat that I am guiltless for the Fault is in the States. They have been deaf to the Calls of Congress, to the Clamors of the public Creditor, to the just Demands of a suffering Army and even to the Reproaches of the Enemy who scoffingly declare that the American army is fed, paid, and cloathed by France. That Assertion, so dishonorable to America, was true, but the kindness of France has its Bounds and our army unfed, unpaid and uncloathed will have to subsist itself or disband itself."

The governors might not like his choice of words, but Morris felt posterity would show that the blunt language was justified: "This Language may not consist with the Ideas of Dignity which some Men entertain. But Sir Dignity is in Duty and in Virtue not in the sound of swelling Expressions. … I have borne with Delays and Disappointments as long as I could and Nothing but hard Necessity would have wrung from me the Sentiments which I have now expressed. … Unless vigorous Exertions are made to put Money into the Treasury we must be ruined."[57]

The following day the Financier wrote Hanson. His situation was "extremely delicate." He believed they had been "reduced to the Brink of Ruin" by the states and that funds were not forthcoming. Consequently, his appeal to them for cash had been "couched in Terms so pressing as to stimulate if possible their Sluggishness into Exertion." But he understood how dangerous it would be if his strongly worded letter ended up in "improper Hands." He also realized, though, how unwise it would be if, out of fear, he did not send the letter; "if any fatal Consequences should ensue from the continued negligence of the States," they would claim that they were not adequately forewarned. Finding himself facing such a dilemma, Morris asked Congress whether he should forward his letter.[58]

On the evening of May the twentieth Morris met with a five-man committee that had been established to consider his letter to the states. The Financier gave its members—Madison, Jesse Root, John Lowell, John Rutledge, and George Clymer—"a true Picture of their present Situation but after much Conversation they appeared to be disinclined to sending the Circular Letter," so he suggested sending delegations to the states to lobby their governors and legislators. The committee members liked the idea and a short time later Congress gave its approval and sent two delegates to the North and two to the South to urge the states to comply with the requisitions.[59]

Morris also wanted the states to ratify the Impost of 1781. He knew that the impost alone might not generate enough revenue to pay even the interest on the debt but felt the tax measure would "lay the Foundation" for a more elaborate system of funding.[60] He saw it as being crucial to the survival of the government and the country. If all the states ratified it, they would be recognizing that Congress had to tax the American people directly in order to obtain the money it needed to fund its operations. They would be saying that the national government did not have to go through the states every time it needed funds; it could go straight to the people, levy taxes, and then collect the revenue from them. They would be giving up some of their sovereignty for sake of the whole nation. They would be recognizing that they had to work together under one strong head—the national government—and stop acting like thirteen countries with separate and independent legislatures.

But while Morris and other nationalists saw the impost as something Congress had to have in order to fund its operations and to unify the nation, some states and their supporters in Congress viewed it as a threat to their liberties. They did not want to give Congress the power to go into their states and directly tax their people. Eventually the two sides in the debate would become polarized and some officers would lose hope that the government was going to get the funding it needed in order to pay them what they were owed. The officers who did lose hope would grow angry. The angriest among them would become involved in the Newburgh Conspiracy.

Chapter Four

"We Will Be Forgot and Neglected"

ON MAY 22, 1782, one month from the day Nathanael Greene had written that the officers were finding their service disagreeable, George Washington received a remarkable letter from an old Pennsylvania colonel named Lewis Nicola, the commander of the Corps of Invalids in nearby Fishkill. It was a wakeup call for the recently arrived Washington, an ominous sign that officer discontent was not confined to the southern army.

Feeling the pinch caused by inadequate pay and depreciation, the colonel began his seven-page letter by charging some of the state legislatures and heads of government departments with harming the army's "pecuniary rights." In their effort to save money they were acting unjustly. He and his fellow officers were not optimistic about the future and they feared that they were not going to get the pensions Congress had promised them. Once the war came to an end and the army was not needed, little attention would be given to "the men's just demands." After having "born the heat and labor of the day," they were going to "be forgot and neglected by such as reap the benefits without suffering any of the hardships."

The colonel asked how it could be claimed that the army had been compensated for depreciation when the compensation itself came in the form of more "depreciated paper money and certificates … of little benefit to original possessors." And because of the dire straits they were in, they were already selling them "to speculators for a part of their value, never more … than one tenth, but often less."

Based on his talks with officers and conversations "overheard among soldiers," Nicola felt that the army would not allow itself to be disbanded when the war ended unless Congress redressed its grievances and kept the promises it had made. If their grievances were not redressed, if they were asked to "forego claims" that they and their families were relying on, "a new scene of blood and confusion" was to be anticipated.

Nicola did not explain why bloodshed should be expected if the army was asked to forego its claims, but one can surmise that he had in mind something even bigger than the January 1, 1781 mutiny of the Pennsylvania Line, which had resulted in more than two thousand men receiving discharges or long furloughs and one officer being killed. In that case only privates and sergeants in one state line had mutinied; officers had opposed them, both fearing they might join the British and trying to prevent them from marching on Philadelphia. In this case he must have envisioned the roughly seventy-five-hundred to eight thousand privates and sergeants and the several hundred officers from the state lines stationed in the Hudson Highlands participating in the mutiny. The officers would join their soldiers once peace arrived and they saw that Congress planned to disband all the northern regiments without giving them the back pay they were owed and obtaining the funding needed to provide them with the pensions they had promised. The specter of such a large army marching on Congress to get justice at the ends of their bayonets had to appear frightening.

Nicola also probably feared that the national government might then fall. If such a thing happened, the weak bonds between the states would break and they would go in thirteen separate directions, causing much confusion and leaving the United States defenseless.

That scenario, of course, was possible only because the national government—Congress—remained weak; it had no real taxation authority and the states were content to ignore the delegates' requisitions. At this time the nascent American republic really did not resemble a unified nation; the states jealously guarded their sovereignty and showed little interest in making sacrifices for the greater good of the whole country.

The colonel did not count himself as a "violent admirer of a republican form of government." There had been other republics in the not too distant past and their glory had not lasted long, expiring like "a blaze." Holland's case was illustrative. Its government was similar in form to America's and it had to get protection for its commerce from "a neighboring monarch." Wouldn't America have to do the same? Congress was simply not "able to draw forth all the internal resources" of the country and "oppose or attack the enemy with ... real vigour."

Nicola preferred monarchies over republican governments because a monarchy's energy was "more beneficial to the existence of a nation" than a republic's wisdom. Europe's leading monarchies, for example, were still alive and shining brightly, though they had endured "great internal commotions," caused each other uneasiness, and experienced both "periods of vigour & [periods of] weakness." He was not calling for a monarchy unrestrained by laws or a constitution, because he understood that that system of government was seriously flawed. What he wanted was one similar to Great Britain's, which, although imperfect, provided the best form of government.

Returning to the army, the colonel reminded Washington of a promise made by the delegates to grant land to veterans and noted that some but not all the states had given their word to do the same. Believing that those states that had not done so were unable to offer any land, he wanted Congress to assume responsibility for the grants and honor all the promises made "by procuring a sufficient tract in some of the best of those fruitful and extensive countries to the west." Those western lands would then "be formed into a distinct State" and all the veterans settling within its borders would decide on what type of government they wanted there.

Since the war had "shewn to all, but to military men in particular the weakness of republicks," he was certain the veterans choosing to remove to the newly established state would decide to live under "a mixed government," one somewhat monarchical. He realized "some people ... so connected the idea of tyranny and monarchy, as to find it very difficult to seperate them," and thought the title of king for the person to lead the government might need to be rejected in favor of a title that appeared to be less arbitrary, although he felt he could make a case for its use.

As for the belief that the other states would perceive the new one to their west as a threat, that was unfounded. The creation of a new state actually enhanced the others' security by establishing a buffer between them and the various hostile Indian tribes, "a savage and cruel enemy." And those veterans who settled that tract of land were going to be well situated to prevent Canada, which Nicola expected to become an independent monarchy, from menacing the states.

While sharing those thoughts, the colonel also spent some time on the issue of the army's pay arrears. He thought the government should quickly adjust the men's accounts for depreciation and pay them what they were owed; he envisioned the veterans getting both immediate cash payments and quarterly interest-bearing notes. If, however, the government used "certificates of very small comparative value or depreciated paper money" to settle with the soldiers and officers, they were not going to receive what they had really earned. Accordingly, he called for adjustments by the states and Congress. Not only veterans who still had certificates at the end of the war would get compensated but also those who had received their pay in depreciated currency and ones who had sold their certificates to speculators for only a small fraction of what they were worth.[1]

Alarmed by Nicola's vision, Washington wasted no time in responding. He had read "with a mixture of great surprise and astonishment" what the colonel had written, and nothing during the war had caused him more pain than the news "of there being such ideas existing in the Army." He found them abhorrent and extremely reprehensible. He would keep his mouth shut about Nicola's letter for the time being, but only if there was not "some further agitation of the matter." He was "much at a loss" as to what in his own behavior might have encouraged the colonel to write such a letter, one that appeared to be "big with the greatest mischiefs" for the country; the designing Nicola could not have chosen anybody more opposed to his plans than Washington.

Washington wanted "to see ample justice done to the army" as much as or more than anybody else and would do everything he could to achieve that end if an opportunity presented itself, but only "in a constitutional way." He did not want to see any harm come to his country, so he concluded his letter with an earnest appeal to the colonel: "Let me conjure you then, if you have any regard for your Country, concern for yourself or posterity, or respect for me, to banish these thoughts from your Mind, and never communicate, as from yourself, or any one else, a sentiment of the like Nature."[2]

The general kept a copy of his response to the colonel, which an aide and a secretary—Lieutenant Colonels David Humphreys and Jonathan Trumbull, Jr.—attested in writing to being in no way different from the one sent to the colonel.[3] To have had his aides do such a thing was unusual and indicative of his concern.

The letter from Nicola has been called the "Crown Letter," the belief being that the colonel wanted Washington to become King. The general, according to most historians, was shocked that someone would propose that he become King and that is why he reacted so strongly to his letter.

That may be true, but he also must have been alarmed that *officers were now talking about not disbanding until the army's grievances were redressed.* The possibility that blood would be shed if they were not, and Nicola's expressed lack of faith in republican government, had to worry Washington. The general understood how the army's pay problems and the depreciating currency were causing many to lose faith in Congress, but he could not allow officers to threaten Philadelphia with a refusal to disband. Such an action must have seemed extremely disloyal or treasonous to him.

Some sentiments similar to those expressed by Nicola would show up again in an anonymous address written to the officers about ten months later. For that reason the colonel's letter can be viewed as a precursor to the Newburgh Conspiracy.

Nicola answered Washington's response with three letters of his own, the first coming on May 23. The general's rebuke had affected him like nothing else had, and the colonel wanted Washington to believe that his letter had resulted mostly from a "weakness of judgment," not a "corruptness of heart." He did not seek "to disturb the repose of his country" and had thought that his plan would benefit the country, not harm it. But since Washington felt differently, he would regard himself "as having been under a strong delusion" and henceforth do everything he could to "combate … every gleam of discontent."[4]

On the twenty-fourth the colonel, "greatly oppressed in mind & distressed," sent a second letter. Yes, he had "often heard … either directly or by hints" talk that the army would refuse to disband when peace arrived. However, he was in no way involved in the plot; he knew the delegates in Philadelphia had passed resolutions "favourable to the army." The problem was that they had been unable to give effect to them and, therefore, some in the army suspected that the government would not keep its promises to them. If most of the army felt that way when the war ended, it would count on Congress to immediately meet all its obligations. Since he doubted that it could do so, he had offered his plan to Washington as "a compromise."

Nicola then suggested that his own adverse fortunes might have caused him to write the letter that so pained the general. They had left him dispossessed of his "patrimony" and, as a result, his large family, which relied solely on his pay for support, had often gone without food, clothing and the like. His seeing that and fearing for their future might have impaired his reasoning.

"But … the idea of occasioning any commotions in a country I lived in," he continued, "would be daggers in my breast." Rather than live in a country with a government he was not able to support, he would move to another one. If his views on the various types of government were wrong, it was because of "a defect of judgment not a willful shutting of … eyes to the light of reason." Anyway, no matter how mistaken he had been to express himself the way he had, he was certain no damage had been done; he had not disclosed his feelings to anyone else.[5]

The colonel wrote his last reply on the twenty-eighth. He had not expressed himself clearly enough on the twenty-second and that had "so prejudiced" Washington that he was unable to get beyond "detached parts" of the letter and judge it on its entirety. He had not selected Washington "for the purpose of countenancing mutiny or treason." He had wanted to "prevent designs that may some time or other be carried into execution and occasion great mischief."

He did not know if "some of the eastern States" were rejecting the impost because they did not want "officers already reformed" into new regiments as a result of a reduction in forces to receive half pay, as he had heard. But if the officers believed that that was true, that belief might "operate as much as if it were gospel." And officers who thought they were "in danger of being deprived of the fruits of their toils & hazards; of the reward of their services" when peace arrived could unite with "privates … dissatisfied & ready to break out." Realizing how dangerous that would be, Nicola had turned to Washington, who was best able to "influence … the army, to counter act any bad designs."[6]

Nicola then spoke of governments, his scheme for land grants and a new state, and apologized again. Perhaps that apology and his other two letters put Washington's mind somewhat at ease, for the colonel was not punished for his letter of the twenty-second.[7]

Chapter Five

"The Salvation of the Cause"

NICOLA WAS NOT the first officer to feel that his pecuniary rights were being injured. As early as September 1775 a supportive Washington had forwarded to Philadelphia a petition from junior officers for a pay raise. Their low pay was a major cause of the type of friendly relations between officers and soldiers that made it hard to maintain proper discipline and, the general remarked, many of the former were going to leave the army once their terms ended because they were "unable to support the Character & Appearance of Officers."

A committee established by Congress to look into that and other matters went to Cambridge in October and, after holding meetings there with the general and delegates who had been sent by the legislatures of the New England colonies, came out against a raise, but Washington's words carried more weight; in early November the delegates approved an increase of pay for junior officers by a little more than a third: Captains would now make about twenty-seven dollars a month; lieutenants would make eighteen dollars a month; and ensigns would get a little over thirteen dollars a month.[1]

The townfolk of Harvard were alarmed by the size of the pay raise and petitioned their state legislature to lobby Congress to reduce it. They were neither unpatriotic nor unwilling to make sacrifices; they just considered the officers' compensation too great. It had, they believed, "much chilled the spirits of commonalty." They strongly disapproved of how the "distresses of America should prove a harvest to some, and a famine to others." However, as much as they might object to the raise, their legislature apparently did nothing more than pass on the petition to a committee.[2]

Discontent then spread to higher-ranking officers. They knew their British counterparts were making much more than they were and paying less for goods.[3] By late August 1776 Colonel Henry Knox was strongly complaining to John Adams: The officers were "not vastly riveted to the honor of starving their families for the sake of being in the army" and he wanted their pay increased. "I am not speaking for myself," he stressed, "but ... in the behalf of a great number of worthy men who wish to do the country every service in their power at a less price than the ruin of themselves and families."[4]

Congress responded soon thereafter by approving land grants for officers and substantially increasing all but the generals' pay. But if the delegates thought they had ended their discontent once and for all, they were mistaken. Not much time passed before the officers started thinking that they deserved additional postwar compensation besides land grants.[5]

What eight officers had in mind in November 1777, when they sent Washington some proposals for Congress, was a half-pay pension. One had been approved by the government in August 1776, but only for disabled veterans no longer able to work and support themselves.[6] Now many officers were resigning because they were not being sufficiently rewarded for their services. Their commissions had to be made valuable to them. In addition to those "maimed, wounded or incapacitated by loss of constitution," veterans involuntarily retired when forces were reduced upon the arrival of peace should be able to receive the pension until they were recalled.[7]

Washington was skeptical when he saw the officers' plan: "Will not half pay be attended with enormous expence? and would not this, and ... half pay to the Officers of reduced regiment[s] at the end of the War, add such weight to a debt ... of such magnitude, as to send the Colonies under the load of it; & give a great disgust to the people at large?"[8] he asked. He understood that whereas the officers saw themselves as virtuous and deserving of such an expression of gratitude, the average civilian did not hold them in such high regard; he would see the attempt to get such a generous pension as an example of officers trying to benefit personally from the war.

UNLIKE A STATE militia made up of virtuous citizens volunteering to leave civilian life temporarily to serve their country in times of peril, a standing army was viewed by the general public with distrust, as a threat to liberty and the republican form of government. Soldiers were "ever to be dreaded as the ready engines of tyranny and oppression,"[9] patriot leader Dr. Joseph Warren believed. They could "in time ... look upon themselves as a body of men *different* from the rest of the people," Samuel Adams had written in 1768, "and as they and they only have *the sword* in their hands, they may sooner or later begin to look upon themselves as the LORDS and not the SERVANTS of the people: Instead of enforcing the execution of law ... they may *refuse to obey* it ...: Nay, they may even *make laws for themselves*, and enforce them by the *power of the sword*! Such instances are not uncommon in history."[10]

A pension for officers would create such a body different from the rest of the people, argued some members of Congress. This fear was especially prevalent among New Englanders. When the delegates heard that an officer had heaped verbal abuse on the body and its president, they required him to appear in person to apologize to them. The incident prompted Adams to comment that any officer willing to drink to the army before doing so to Congress risked being seen as a supporter of a military dictatorship.[11]

INITIALLY SKEPTICAL, WASHINGTON before long had a change of heart and concluded that the duration officers should get half pay for life. Just before Christmas 1777 he wrote the President of Congress, Henry Laurens, from Valley Forge and told him that "some better provision for binding the Officers by the tye of Interest to the service" was needed. "No day, nor scarcely an hour passes without an Offer of a resigned Commission," he emphasized. If the delegates did not do something for the officers, "the practicability of holding the Army together much longer" was very dubious. But if they did adopt the measure, they would be "making better Officers and better Troops."[12]

The general was not exaggerating how great the problem of officer resignations was. Soon after Washington wrote Laurens, Nathanael Greene saw more than fifty officers in his division at Valley Forge resign in one day.[13]

After receiving Washington's letter, the delegates immediately established two committees. One of them was sent to Valley Forge to gather information. Once that information was sent back to the capital, the other committee, which was made up of Elbridge Gerry, Jonathan Bayard Smith, and John Witherspoon, reviewed it and, in early January 1778, presented Congress with a report recommending half pay for life. The report was discussed and the main reasons for opposition to the plan were reported to Washington. One of those reasons was the country's "Aversion to placemen & pensioners."[14]

Washington knew large numbers of officers wanted half pay and in late January he again urged the delegates to approve it. The hard winter at Valley Forge was driving many officers to resign their commissions or make noise about doing so. Something had to be done to improve their situation or they would continue to leave the military. The days when appeals to sacrifice for the public good were enough to motivate them had passed. "A small knowledge of human nature will convince us, that, with far the greatest part of mankind, interest is the governing principle," he explained. "At the commencement of the dispute, —the first effusions of their zeal, and looking upon the service to be only temporary, they entered into it, without paying any regard to pecuniary or selfish considerations. But finding its duration to be much longer than they at first suspected, and that instead of deriving any advantage from the hardships and dangers to which they were exposed, they … were losers by their patriotism and fell far short even of a competency to supply their wants, they have gradually abated in their ardor; and with many an entire disinclination to the service … has taken place. To this, in an eminent degree, must be ascribed the frequent resignations daily happening and the more frequent importunities for permission to resign. … To this also may we ascribe the apathy, inattention and neglect of duty, which pervade all ranks, and which will necessarily continue and increase, while an officer, instead of gaining any thing, is impoverished by his commission."

The solution to the problem, Washington went on, was not punishment. It was to have "an officer's commission … made valuable to him." If you do that and the officer then fears losing his commission, you will be able to "exact obedience from him." For the officers to feel that their commissions were valuable they had to believe they were being adequately compensated. An officer could not feel comfortable knowing that "after he may have contributed to securing the rights of his country, at the risk of his life, and the ruin of his fortune, no provision was going to be made to prevent him and his family from sinking into indigence and wretchedness." So give the officers postwar half-pay pensions. The promise of them would "reanimate their languishing zeal, and interest them thoroughly in the service."

But if nothing were done, Washington believed, the consequences for the army were sure to be disastrous: "The officers are now discontented with their situation, —if some generous expedient is not embraced to remove their discontent, so extensive a desertion of the service will ensue, and so much discouragement be cast upon those who remain, as must wound it [the army] in a very essential manner."[15]

A little less than two months later, Washington again emphasized the officers' discontent and their inclination to desert in another letter to Laurens. "As it is not improper for Congress to have some idea of the present temper of the Army," the general wrote, "it may not be amiss to remark … that since … August last between two and three hundred Officers have resigned their Commissions and many others were with difficulty disswaded from it." Among those who had resigned were at least six of his Virginia colonels. They were "as good as any in the Service." Their resignations were recent ones and he had heard that more officers were apt to leave.[16]

A couple of days after the general wrote Laurens, on March 26, two members of the congressional committee that had been to Valley Forge proposed that officers who served for the duration of the war and did not hold public office be given half pay after its conclusion. Under the members' plan officers were also free to sell their commissions and if they were killed during service, their widows would receive their pensions. The delegates debated the plan and then, on April 2, decided to set aside the issue until later.[17]

North Carolina's Dr. Thomas Burke did not like the plan, but he knew that officers and soldiers had to be compensated in some way. The argument that it was "unjust to sacrifice the time and property of the men whose lives are every day exposed for us without any prospect of compensation, while so many who are protected by their valor and exertions are amassing princely fortunes" was convincing, and Burke understood that those who insisted "Patriotism and public spirit" should be enough to keep the officers in the army were wrong. His choice was "to trust … some principles of more certain, lasting and powerful influence."[18]

Eight days after Philadelphia set aside half pay, Washington wrote Laurens yet again. He did "most religiously believe the salvation of the cause" was only possible if Congress promised pensions. The pension was a sign of the government's willingness to accord an officer the honor he was due. With half pay, a professional corps of officers would be easier to maintain, but without it, he warned, the corps was going to "moulder to nothing, or be composed of low and illiterate men, void of capacity for this, or any other business."[19]

Washington's problem was that not everybody shared Burke's sympathy for the army. Those opposed to the pension pointed out that the officers had willingly accepted commissions, knowing the hardships. They thought it "unjust in the extreme, to compel thousands of poor industrious Inhabitants" to pay taxes "to pamper the Luxury" of officers; many of them were going to return to great estates and some had "accumulated immense fortunes by purloin & peculation under the Mask of patriotism."

Approval of half pay meant "compliance under menaces"; if the officers did not get pensions, they were going to leave Americans "reduced to the awful alternative of losing the Army & their Liberties." Unsympathetic delegates believed that if they gave in to the officers' demand for the pension, more "arbitrary demands" were sure to follow. And, of course, compliance with their demand "would lay the foundation of a standing army."[20]

When Washington's recommendation reached Philadelphia the reaction must have been apoplectic. So heated did the debate become that an attempt to get members to promise "to support order and preserve decency and politeness" apparently failed, and the untiring Laurens had to warn them "against disorder and intemperate reflections."[21] Delegates from Connecticut characterized the issue as "the most painfull & disagreable question … ever … agitated in Congress."[22] That state and three others—Rhode Island, New Jersey, and South Carolina—adamantly opposed the lifetime pension.[23]

But the delegates had to agree to something or their "fear of all our *best* officers leaving the army"[24] was going to become a reality. Accordingly, on May 15, 1778, they finally settled on a compromise—a postwar half-pay pension for seven years would be given to officers who continued to serve until the war came to an end and did not hold any public office during or after the conflict. The amount an officer could receive was capped at half pay of a colonel. As part of this act, privates and sergeants who fought for the duration were promised a bounty of eighty dollars.[25] It had taken two months to reach an agreement, "by the Grace of God … rid to Death and from the Ashes … produced."[26]

Washington welcomed the news that Congress had approved a pension for the officers. The compromise was less than he had hoped for, but more than he had anticipated. His only regret was that it had not been adopted sooner. He predicted to Laurens that the pension was going to "quiet in a great measure, the uneasinesses which have been so extremely distressing, and prevent resignations which had proceeded and were likely to be at such a height, as to destroy our whole military system."[27]

But by early 1779 he was again recommending that the delegates grant officers half pay for life, knowing they thought there was a big difference between that and the plan approved for them.[28] On May 8 he complained about the lack of harmony among legislators and "the discontents and distresses of the officers" and appeared worried about what the enemy might do to his forces if it chose to really press its advantage during the upcoming campaign. He knew that what he had now was "little more than the skeleton of an army" and he was unaware of any measures that were being taken to improve the situation.[29] "Officers unable any longer to support themselves in the Army are resigning continually, or doing what is even worse, spreading discontent and possibly the seeds of Sedition,"[30] he warned ten days later.

A motion that the pension be for life, rather than for seven years, was made by Gouverneur Morris in late May, but his proposal was overwhelmingly rejected. Then, during the summer, surprised delegates received a petition from officers calling for the more generous postwar benefit; a committee produced a report in favor of it; and Congress passed a resolution urging *the states* to provide the officers with such a plan and any other reward they felt was justified. They also were encouraged to take care of widows. Virginia, Pennsylvania, and Maryland had already promised lifetime half pay to their duration officers and now all the other states were being asked to follow suit.

Some but not all state legislatures heeded Philadelphia's call. Even if all of them had done so, many officers would have been unaffected; the states were not responsible for taking care of those who had been given their commissions by the national government. Consequently, anxious officers could only appeal to Congress, and that's exactly what they did. In autumn the delegates were again petitioned for the more generous pension; if they did not give their word that they were going to grant half pay for life, the officers were going to have to resign. But Congress rejected a motion to enact such a plan and at the beginning of December still one more committee report urging the better plan produced no positive results.[31]

MEANWHILE, THE OFFICERS struggled to support themselves and their families. In April 1779, more than three years before he complained to Washington in his "Crown Letter" about the army's "pecuniary rights" being harmed, Colonel Nicola had to appeal to his state's supreme executive council for a pay raise because currency depreciation and the "exorbitant rise of goods" were eating up his resources to the point that he was unable to clothe himself in a manner befitting an officer. Duty required him to reside in Philadelphia, which meant that he had to cope with "expences … unavoidably greater" than if he had been living in an army camp and his family had been residing in the country.³²

The situation did not improve with time. In September generals held meetings because Congress had, among other things, excluded them from a group authorized to receive a subsistence allowance of $500 a month. When they finally finished writing a petition in mid-November, they noted that they were unable to pay for their clothing, have horses, and entertain others in a way that befitted their high ranks. The generals needed their pay to be raised and adjusted for depreciation, just as it had been for civilians working for the government and lower-ranking officers.³³

As 1779 ended, Colonel Pickering found that he wasn't even making enough money to meet either his food expenses or pay the next year's rent or buy clothes for his children and himself. And he had to have new clothing because his old clothing was "already worn on both sides." The tall, bald, bespectacled son of a Salem deacon had already depleted his personal resources by $10,000 to support himself.³⁴

CHANGES TO THE promised pension plan might not have been made, if not for "the blackest year for American hopes,"³⁵ 1780. In January one hundred Massachusetts men temporarily left West Point because they felt they had completed their enlistments.³⁶ In mid-May the Americans suffered their worst defeat of the war, losing their 5,400-man garrison in Charleston to the British. In late May two hungry Connecticut regiments that had not been paid for five months decided to grab their arms, leave their camp at Morristown, New Jersey, and return home or obtain food by force. Most of them eventually were persuaded to return to their huts,³⁷ but the army's pay problems and shortages did not end, and in June thirty-one poorly clothed and unpaid men from the 1st New York Regiment deserted from Fort Schuyler, announcing that they intended to join the British. However, most of them were killed or caught during their flight; forty Oneida Indians under the command of a Continental Army lieutenant tracked them down and killed thirteen and captured another three.³⁸ In August about eight hundred to nine hundred men lost their lives and another one thousand were captured when General Gates suffered a humiliating defeat at Camden. In September Benedict Arnold's treason was discovered, and the failure of the March 18, 1780 plan—to devalue old depreciated currency at a rate of forty dollars in paper to one in specie and replace it with new bills of credit issued by the states and guaranteed by the national government—became apparent. And throughout the year the states ignored requisitions, and officers resigned everywhere.

Washington knew that his officers had good reason to walk away from their commissions. They were sacrificing more than anyone else for their country's independence yet were not being paid enough to live on. Some of them were "verging fast to the gulph of poverty and distress" and many were "unfit for duty for want of Cloathing."³⁹

They were complaining about all sorts of things, and they had good reason to do so. The states were neglecting them. Only Pennsylvania was doing a good job taking care of its officers, the general felt. That state, he pointed out when he wrote the President of Congress on August 20, had already adopted half pay for life. The delegates in Philadelphia should follow suit because it was "the most politic and effectual [provision]" the body could pass.[40]

Congress did not do what Washington recommended, but it did try to improve the officers' situation. After the petition that the generals had written in the summer of 1780 was delivered to Philadelphia by Major General Alexander McDougall, a five-man committee and other delegates met with him and the body passed a number of resolutions, some of which related to the officers' pension: It repealed the clause in the May 15, 1778 resolution that barred officers from receiving their pensions if they held positions in government. It removed the cap on the amount a general could receive, specifying that his pension would be equal to half of his pay, not half of a colonel's. It approved seven years of half pay for widows and orphans of fallen officers. And it urged that the states either grant half pay for life to duration officers and some type of postwar compensation to duration soldiers in recognition of all they had endured or decide on some other way to reward them.[41]

Those steps were good, but by early fall gloom was pervasive and the army appeared ready to dissolve. On October 3 the delegates had decided to substantially reduce the size of forces in the Continental Army. With this reduction, which was to take effect on January 1, 1781, only officers would be involuntarily retired.[42] It was bound to cause unrest because many officers were likely to be facing a bleak future after leaving the army.

Realizing that the discontent among his officers could infect the whole army, and with an eye on an alarming rate of desertions and resignations, the Commander-in-chief tried to undo the damage. "The temper of the army, produced by its sufferings, requires great caution, in any reforms that are attempted," Washington wrote to the President of Congress on October 11. "The reducing its regiments, and dismissing great part of its officers, is always a matter of delicacy and difficulty. In ours, where the officers are held by the feeblest ties, and are mouldering away by daily resignations, it is peculiarly so. The last reduction occasioned many to quit the service … and left durable seeds of discontent among those who remained. … In the extremity to which we are arrived, policy forbids us to add new irritations. … Too many of the officers wish to get rid of their commissions, but they are not willing to be forced to it."

The officers who remained in the army and those involuntarily retired should get lifetime half pay; the measure was necessary as a safeguard "against the ill effects [of the reduction]." And if that pension could not be given to them, how about whole pay for seven years? Something had to be done or else, Washington believed, so many officers were going to leave the army when their current campaign ended that he would not have enough "even … for common duties when in quarters."[43]

Despite strong objections from the humorless Samuel Adams, Congress by a nine-to-three margin resolved on the twenty-first of October to give the duration officers and those involuntarily retired because of the reorganization of the regiments half pay for their entire postwar lives.[44] The makeup of Congress had changed;[45] new delegates were not as worried about the consequences of giving officers the benefit and making them a privileged class. And they were no doubt influenced by the one-hundred-sixty resignations that had occurred since January.[46]

The pension plan for officers was and would continue to be very unpopular. Many people felt that patriotism alone should be enough to motivate them to fight for independence, and they did not want them to gain any special favor because of their ranks or status in society. Wasn't the promised half pay for life such a favor? Wouldn't the recipients of it become a privileged class of Americans indebted to their benefactors, Congress? Couldn't they then be used as an instrument to enforce unpopular laws by an oppressive government? The pensioners in England had been so utilized.

Also, many people had experienced as severe or even greater hardships than had the officers during the war. Why should the officers get such a pension when other sufferers got nothing for their pains? Hadn't the soldiers done the real fighting? What about militiamen?[47]

And wasn't America's financial health going to be impaired? Weren't the costs of paying for the pension plan going to cause the debt to swell greatly? Wasn't the plan going to make "a great number of People idle Pensioners on the public [dole] who ought to be restored to useful industry?"[48]

During the final fall and winter of the war, when the Newburgh Conspiracy was maturing, the officers would become very concerned about Congress's promise to provide them with a postwar pension. Were the delegates going to renege on their promise to provide them with that compensation once peace arrived and the army was disbanded? If they were, the officers might not be able to escape poverty upon their return home. The army experience, after all, had caused them to "contract habits of Indolence,"[49] and even if they were willing to work, many of them had lost to the war those years that they could have spent learning a trade. "What to do I am at a loss,"[50] wrote one officer upon his departure.

Chapter Six

"The Public Creditors Should Unite and Use Their Influence"

IN NEWBURGH THE "Crown Letter" from Colonel Nicola in late May had undoubtedly left Washington with a feeling that something had to be done. On June 16, 1782, in a letter to Robert Morris, the general implied that the officers were growing impatient[1] and mentioned how he had told them to let their friends back home know that Congress had to have greater taxation authority. That was the only way they were going to be able to solve their problems. The states were ignoring the delegates' requests for money; as of the first of the month, Philadelphia had received only $20,000 of the $8,000,000 it had requested for 1782. That sum was about equal to the average daily cost of the war.[2]

RHODE ISLAND HAD not exactly ignored Philadelphia's request for money; in May its legislators had voted to give Lieutenant Colonel Jeremiah Olney's battalion three months' pay and reduce its requisition quota accordingly. Morris found that unacceptable. "If the States would generally comply with the requisitions of Congress all would be paid and ... all Ground of Complaint would be removed," he wrote to George Olney on June 23, "but partial Payments create more Clamor than if none at all were made." He was not going to allow the reduction approved by that state's legislature to stand.[3]

Three days later, on the twenty-sixth, Morris informed Rhode Island Governor William Greene of this policy against partial payments.[4] Morris's opposition to partial payments extended beyond the army; not only all the soldiers and officers had to be paid, but also all the creditors. The two groups could not be separated. As a matter of fact, if both were united they might be able to exert tremendous pressure on the states to give Philadelphia the funding it needed.

The opportunity to bring about a union between them came when the handsome Colonel Walter Stewart visited Robert Morris on behalf of upset public creditors. It was a role suited for Stewart because he and his father-in-law, a wealthy Philadelphia merchant named Blair McClenachan, were themselves creditors of the government. They were concerned about Morris's decision to suspend interest payments on the loan office certificates they held, which was made because the states had not passed "Continental" taxes—taxes levied solely to obtain funds for Congress. If the situation were not rectified, the colonel warned, "the public Creditors would be much Distressed and their Distresses would make them Clamorous."

Morris defended his action, asserting that interest payments had to be stopped for the sake of the country.

Colonel Stewart was not satisfied. "A meeting of those interested must be Called" because they had to decide on actions that were both in keeping "with the Public Good" and "practicable and necessary for their own Interest."

Unruffled by the angry Stewart, and "very desirous to serve and support ... their Claim to Justice," the Financier recommended that if the creditors did meet, they should establish "a Committee of Sensible cool Men" to look into the matter. If such a committee was set up and did as he suggested, it would see that the real culprits were the states, not Congress.[5]

WALTER STEWART[6] ARRIVED in America from Ireland probably around 1772. When the war began he assembled a company of men for the 3rd Pennsylvania Battalion and in January 1776 he was made a captain, though he was still only nineteen years old. Five months later he became one of General Gates's aides-de-camp and was promoted to major. In November Congress recognized him "as a deserving officer," made him a brevet lieutenant colonel and "presented [him] with a sword of the value of one hundred (100) dollars."[7]

Stewart stayed with Gates until June 1777, when he received a commission as a colonel of a Pennsylvania state regiment. Though made up of inexperienced militiamen, the regiment gave a good account of itself three months later in the Battle of Brandywine. Tasked with covering the main army's line of retreat, Stewart and his men took up positions just skirting a heavily

Colonel Walter Stewart

wooded area about one or one and a half miles to the southeast of Dilworth Village. When pursuit of American forces retreating through that crossroads hamlet brought the British to the area where the Pennsylvanians were deployed, the two sides exchanged heavy fire. Stewart, who was located in the rear, moved about on foot and encouraged his men. For some time the fighting remained intense and neither side appeared likely to give any ground. But eventually Stewart's men ran low on ammunition, darkness descended, the guns became quiet, and the Pennsylvanians retreated to Chester. If not for their stand, the Americans would have suffered many more casualties during the retreat.

The end of that battle did not provide the colonel and his men with a long respite. In early October the Battle of Germantown began. There Stewart and his men forced two enemy companies to take flight and captured their small V-shaped redoubt and three cannon at a crossroads near Luken's Mill. Ultimately, though, Germantown went down as yet another American defeat.

In November Stewart's regiment became the Continental Army's 13th Pennsylvania. The following month George Washington's army established its winter quarters at Valley Forge.

Not long after Washington's army's stay at Valley Forge came to an end, in late June 1778, the colonel moved into New Jersey and saw more action in the Battle of Monmouth. His regiment and two others detached from Brigadier General Anthony Wayne's command and placed under Lafayette were sent out to block a southwestward flanking movement by Major General Henry Clinton from Briar Hill towards the Monmouth Courthouse. The three regiments advanced a short way before halting, Lafayette noticing that American forces in his rear were retreating from the field. The French nobleman engaged the enemy for a while and then slowly fell back, which allowed Major General Charles Lee to withdraw his greatly reduced forces towards the sparsely populated town of Freehold.

The 13th Pennsylvania was ordered to take up a new position in some woods behind an apple orchard located to the east of Freehold. It, two other regiments, and some artillery remained in the same general area east of the road leading to Englishtown for a while, even after General Lee decided to abandon Freehold for a better location to make a stand. As the Americans retreated, enemy dragoons pursued them.

When American regiments reached high ground in front of a meetinghouse, they encountered George Washington. The Commander-in-chief wanted the retreat halted and, after speaking with a colonel who knew the surrounding terrain well, ordered one regiment to move out to an indicated hill and await further orders. Other regiments were then sent to the hill, where they formed up for battle.

As the time for battle drew near, Wayne's men made their way through woods just below the hill. Wayne met Washington and the two generals decided where they should check the British. Wayne positioned two regiments, one of which was Stewart's 13th Pennsylvania, in a wooded area where he felt they could achieve their objective. Soon thereafter the anticipated battle began, and before long Stewart was knocked out of action by a bullet wound to the groin.

Before he had completely recovered from his wound, Stewart and one other colonel were directed by Wayne to go to Philadelphia to reinvigorate support for the war: Legislators, state and national, appeared apathetic about appropriating money for the army's needs, and the general wanted the Pennsylvania General Assembly to be aware that the men's pay was badly in arrears and that they needed clothing to replace their threadbare uniforms before winter arrived.

Stewart did as directed but did not like what he saw in Philadelphia. "How much are we disappointed," Stewart reported back to his friend Wayne, "in respect to the representation in Congress; the pleasing ideas we had formed of it are no more. We unfortunately find a real set of caitiffs have supplied their places. … Nothing but party reigns in different bodies." As for Philadelphians, he continued, "it is all gaiety, and from what I can observe, every lady and gentleman endeavors to outdo the other in splendor and show. The manners of the ladies are likewise much changed. They have really in a great measure lost that native innocence which was their former characteristic and supplied its place with what they call an Easy behavior."

Though the colonel was displeased by what he witnessed, Philadelphia society liked what they saw in the colonel. He became popular with its members and the ladies nicknamed him "the Irish Beauty." Thin-lipped with an aquiline nose and a "fair and florid complexion,"[8] Stewart was said to be the handsomest man in the Continental Army.

Once Stewart had fully recuperated, he took command of the 2nd Pennsylvania, which had been combined with his 13th Pennsylvania only a few days after the Battle of Monmouth. During his time as the commander of the reorganized regiment, the colonel signed a declaration pledging the officers in Philadelphia to hold in contempt and shun any of their brethren who only tepidly supported independence or opposed it and those who approved or encouraged such behavior. Officers who acted thusly damaged the reputation of the army.

In May 1780 Stewart found himself playing the role of peacemaker, speaking to Connecticut soldiers mutinying over pay arrears and reduced rations. The men did not realize how much damage they were doing to their well-earned reputations by mutinying. They had earned "immortal honor … the winter past" for their "perseverance, patience and bravery," but now were throwing it away. It was being done for no purpose; if they took their complaints to their officers, they would not turn a deaf ear to them. Stewart would even go and speak with them himself on behalf of the soldiers.[9]

The young colonel's words eased the soldiers' minds enough to get them to resume their duties, and their hardships were partially alleviated; they received food, though shortages would continue to occur, and some back pay with adjustments for inflation. The mutiny was quelled.

At the beginning of 1781 the colonel once again was trying to help end a mutiny. This time several hundred soldiers from the Pennsylvania Line were involved. They had "not seen a paper dollar in the way of pay for near twelve months," had not received adequate rations, had suffered from a shortage of blankets, and were in great need of new clothing.

Those hardships were bad enough, but worse still was the knowledge that each new recruit was arriving in camp with a bounty of three gold Portuguese half-johannes, which amounted to just over twenty-five dollars, and a promise of a postwar land grant of two hundred acres for just six months of service. Among the new recruits were men who had been released from Philadelphia's jail and allowed to collect the bounties in exchange for enlisting. The experienced Pennsylvania soldiers, on the other hand, had received twenty-dollar bounties and been promised only one hundred acres. They also were being told by their superior officers and Pennsylvania officials that they had signed up for the duration of the war, though they believed they had agreed to serve for only three years.

When the mutiny occurred, Stewart, General Wayne, and Colonel Richard Butler rode out of camp with the mutinying soldiers to ensure that they did not join the British. Two days after their departure from camp the three officers spoke before the soldiers in a field. They made some proposals on how the men could seek redress of their grievances, but failed to sway them to end their mutiny and return to camp. So they wrote the Supreme Executive Council of Pennsylvania and Washington to urge that the former send one or more members to negotiate with a board of sergeants representing the mutinous soldiers and to recommend that the Commander-in-chief remain in place instead of coming to Princeton. The three officers then had meetings with the sergeants and with the President of the Supreme Executive Council, Joseph Reed, and eventually negotiations brought an end to the mutiny.[10]

The following summer Stewart was down south. He supported Lafayette against Cornwallis at Green Spring, Virginia, in July, and then at Yorktown in October. In the latter battle he commanded a reserve regiment "employed in connecting by a ditch and parapet, the two redoubts [nine and ten], and completing and connecting the same with our second parallel."[11]

George Washington Parke Custis described Stewart as "vivacious, intelligent and well educated."[12] Joseph Plumb Martin wrote that "Colonel Stewart was an excellent officer, much beloved and respected by the troops of the line he belonged to."[13]

"THERE IS A well grounded Expectation, that the Clamors of our Creditors will induce the several Legislatures to comply with the Requisitions upon that Subject [the impost],"[14] Robert Morris had written back in the fall of 1781. The same words appeared even more apropos in June 1782.

But the creditors were not going to become clamorous if interest on their loan office certificates continued to be drawn in bills of exchange on France and paid by that country. Consequently, Morris had to stop those payments and force Congress to "look at Home for the Basis of national Credit,"[15] to depend on tax levies as the means to pay its debt. So he sent a letter to the French government that prompted it to announce that it no longer intended to pay America's bills if she did not have sufficient funds in France, and he wrote to Congress to suggest that the body cease drawing bills on France; it should pay the creditors from revenue generated by the Impost of 1781,[16] though the measure had yet to be approved by the states.

Two days after Stewart's visit four other public creditors—Reverend John Ewing, John Shee, Charles Petit, and McClenachan—showed up at the Financier's office; a meeting had been held by the creditors and these four men and Jonathan Dickinson Sergeant had been elected to the committee suggested by Morris. The creditors wanted information on the impending stoppage of interest payments on their loan certificates.[17]

Morris "very readily explained to them the Necessity of stopping the payment … [and] told them they were to be paid in future from the produce of the Impost Law whenever the States would compleat the Grant of that Revenue." Congress had been asking the states to approve the impost since February 1780, and Morris "had solicited the Compliance of the States" from the time he took office. Only Rhode Island had not ratified it, and Morris wished to see "a Speedy Compliance by that State also."

The impost alone, though, was not going to provide the government with enough funds to pay even the interest on the debt. Other taxes were needed to permanently fund the debt. And permanent funding of the debt was something the government had to have. It was "essential to the Interest, happiness, freedom and Glory of the United States, and also … to the interest and Justice due to Individuals." Morris had tried to get permanent funding, "but some Members of Congress did not see things in the same light" as he did, and "many Members of all the [state] Legislatures opposed every kind of Taxation from local and Popular Views." That being the situation, he believed "the public Creditors should unite and use their Influence to turn out Members so influenced" and declared himself "ready to pursue every Reasonable and proper Measure to obtain Justice for the public Creditors."[18]

Three days after that meeting an important deadline arrived; $4,000,000 of the $8,000,000 requisitioned from the states was due. Congress, though, had by that day received less than one percent of what it had requested.[19] It could not even begin to settle with the army or pay creditors what they were owed unless it received much more money. Understanding how important the pay issue was, the government had sent representatives back to state legislatures to make personal appeals, but their pleas had fallen upon deaf ears.

One week later a petition signed by three of the Philadelphia creditors who had visited Morris on June 28—McClenachan, Ewing, and Petit—and Dr. Benjamin Rush was read in Congress. The petitioners claimed to be "among the earliest Promoters of the glorious Revolution … among the foremost to testify their Zeal in supporting the Measures of Congress, as well by contributing their

Substance, as by yielding their personal Services." They had trusted the government and come forward to "cheerfully contribute ... Loans to the United States" but now felt betrayed. They had gone "from a situation of Ease and Comfort to the Depths of extreme Poverty" because it had "deprived [them] of even ... Interest," while unjustly taxing them at least as much as others who had not helped alleviate the government's needs.

The stoppage of interest payments by itself was not the creditors' only problem; depreciation guaranteed that when the government paid back the principal on the loans, the creditors were going to get much less than its original value. Also, if Congress did not act quickly and effectually "to revive that Confidence in the Justice and Integrity of the Public, on which alone any Degree of Public Credit can be founded," these "honest Lenders ... who ... risked their *all* on the Public Faith" were going to have to sell their certificates to predatory speculators for pennies on the dollar.

Since it cost a great deal to finance a war, more than tax revenue was needed. This was especially true for a young nation, the petitioners emphasized. Loans were necessary. However, the government was probably not going to be able to obtain loans unless it got the permanent funding it had to have in order to make regular interest payments and repay the principal.[20]

Congress sent the petition to Morris the same day and asked him to prepare a report. When the Financier summoned the committee of creditors, he informed them that for the time being his office was responsible for the issue they had expressed concern about. He favored "establishing Revenue sufficient to pay the Interest of the whole public Debts" and again urged them to unite and pressure the state legislatures into acting. Once his recommendations for funding the debt were enacted by Congress, they should then get fully behind them but "avoid the language of Threats ... already ... complained of in their proceedings."

The creditors refuted the charge; they were only "in pursuit of Justice" and just treatment of them was in the best interests of the country. "They had pursued their Object with decency" and would continue to do so until they achieved it. Even if they had used such language, they explained, that was only because they "had been excited by Warm and imprudent expressions of Persons who opposed or ridiculed their Pursuit."

If the warning to avoid using threats was not enough to upset the committee, Morris's remark that there would be no interest payments during the current year was. "Mr McClenachan in particular ... would have nothing more to do with the Committee, &c.," if Morris really did stop the interest payments.[21]

As Morris urged the creditors to unite and pressure state legislators into acting, he wrote Virginia's receiver of Continental taxes. "What in the Name of Heaven can be expected by the People of America but absolute Ruin if they are so inattentive to the public Service," Morris complained, bitter over the general public's unwillingness to pay taxes. Money requisitioned by Congress from the states was greatly needed but "not until December will Virginia give any Thing ... towards the Service of the current Year. How, then, are we to carry on those Operations which are so necessary? How is our Country to be defended? How is our Army to be supported? Is this what is meant by the solemn Declarations to support with Life and Fortune the Independence of the United States?"[22]

IN THE SOUTH, Nathanael Greene empathized with Morris. He understood that any superintendent of finance had a difficult job, but Morris's task promised to be especially demanding because the government lacked vigor and "the necessary coersive authority." Well aware of how obstructionist the states were being and not quite despondent only because "the burthen" was on Morris's shoulders rather than on his, Greene assured the Financier that he would do everything in his power to support any financial plan the government approved and that the justness of the army's claims would "facilitate every necessary measure," although they might suffer in the meantime as a result.[23]

NEW YORK RECOGNIZED that Philadelphia had to be given more authority and on July 22 its legislature "unanimously passed a set of resolutions to be transmitted to Congress and the several states proposing a Convention of the states to enlarge the powers of Congress and vest them with funds." It was the first such appeal by any legislative body and it had come only after a visit from one of the delegations that the Financier had urged to be created back in May.

Alexander Hamilton, now employed by the Financier as New York's tax collector, approved of his state's action, but felt the other states were not going to follow suit. A convention was really the only hope to get them "to cooperate in any reasonable or effectual plan." But the problem was that none of the states saw any benefit in acting alone; one would only act in "concert of the others." It was futile to try to reason with any state that took that line, Hamilton told Morris, because "this reasoning ... is founded on all those passions which have the strongest influence on the human mind."[24]

ONE WEEK AFTER New York took its action, Congress received the report it had requested the Financier to prepare in response to the creditors' petition. The proposals within the lengthy work were to be looked at by a thirteen-member grand committee established the week before. In the report, which dealt with public credit and presented a plan for funding the debt, the advantages and disadvantages of domestic and foreign loans were explained, and borrowing as a way to obtain money was judged mostly beneficial. Domestic loans helped bind "the Interests of the moneyed Men" to the government, thereby promising it "Stability." Foreign loans helped generate wealth greatly exceeding the amounts paid in interest.

But to secure foreign loans the government had to do something about its credit. It needed to generate revenue at home to win the public's trust. The sale of western lands was not likely to yield immediate results, so Morris thought the solution was for Congress to have greater taxation authority. That would give the government the permanent revenues necessary to fund the national debt. The Impost of 1781 alone was not enough. Poll taxes, land taxes, and an excise tax on liquor had to be levied. The revenue produced by all of them was to be used to pay the annual interest on the national debt.

Morris anticipated much opposition to the proposed funding program but to his delight, somebody—the "numerous, meritorious and oppressed Body of Men, who are Creditors of the public"—was now aiding him in his battle to get real taxation authority for Philadelphia. They were "beginning to exert themselves for the obtaining of Justice," and that meant Congress would ultimately be able to finance the war effort to a successful conclusion.[25]

The Financier realized that the general public's aversion to paying taxes was really his greatest obstacle. "As to the Complaint made by the People of a Want of Money to pay their Taxes it is nothing new," he wrote to Connecticut's governor, Jonathan Trumbull. "The Complaint is I beleive quite as old as Taxation and will last as long. That Times are hard, that Money is scarce, that Taxes are heavy, and the like are Constant themes of Declamation in all Countries and will be so."

However, that people everywhere had always complained about taxes did not mean they were really too burdensome. "The very Generality of the Complaint shews it to be ill founded," Morris professed. "The Fact is that Men will always find Use for all the Money they can get hold of, and more. A Tax Gatherer therefore will always be an unwelcome Guest because his Demand must necessarily interfere with some pleasurable, or profitable Pursuit. Hundreds who cannot find Money to pay Taxes, can find it to purchase useless Gew Gaws, and expend much more in the Gratification of Vanity, Luxury, Drunkenness, and Debauchery than is necessary to establish the Freedom of their Country."[26]

FROM JUNE 1782 on, dissatisfaction among Massachusetts officers in the Hudson Highlands grew. That month they asked their Commander-in-chief, through General Heath, to allow them to meet and talk about the problems they were enduring. Washington did not object to their meeting for the purpose of "obtaining, in a decent manner, the regular settlement of their Just dues" and, accordingly, gave his consent. The officers then met in July,[27] and General Knox and Colonel Rufus Putnam drafted a petition to their state legislature. They acknowledged that the state had paid the men of the Massachusetts Line what they were owed for their service from January 1, 1777 to December 31, 1780, and had taken steps to compensate them for currency depreciation during that period. But they also reminded the legislators that they had yet to be paid for their service in 1781 and asked that they "send a committee of one or more persons to camp, in order that a settlement may be made … and the respective balances ascertained, upon just and honorable principles."

In addition to back pay, Knox and Putnam informed the legislators, the soldiers were owed "considerable sums due on account of subsistence, detained rations and parts of rations, and deficiencies of clothing … for a number of years past." The committee sent to their camp could pay the men everything they were owed in cash and in interest-yielding certificates. That was not an unreasonable thing to ask for; after all, Connecticut had made "a liberal Settlement of the beforementioned articles" for its troops.

The Massachusetts officers understood that the war was making times difficult for their state, but the legislators had to realize that they and their soldiers had received very little of what they were owed. And nothing, as far as the officers knew, was being done to settle their accounts. "They mentioned this matter with freedom," the two officers continued, "because they have certain information that all expences of civil government, both local and general, are claimed and paid the instant they become due."

The officers had "an unbounded confidence in the integrity of their countrymen," but were "extremely concerned that they should be obliged … to urge facts which have the appearance of complaints." They hoped that the treatment they had received resulted from the financial difficulties "attending a war carried on without funds or revenues," and they did not want the state to forget them once its finances were "in a proper train"; they wanted Massachusetts to reward them with what they justly expected.[28]

Although no mention of it was made in the petition, one thing the officers expected was the promised postwar pension. However, they feared they were never going to receive it. Some in Philadelphia and elsewhere wanted the officers' pension to be declared invalid; they argued that the delegates had been forced to agree to it, that they had approved it only because of the war. Also, a motion to appropriate money for the postwar benefit was not likely to pass Congress; nine states had to vote in favor of it and the delegates were aware that the general public did not like half pay. And if the body approved the appropriation and tried to requisition the funds needed to provide *all the officers* with pensions, the states would likely ignore the requests.

The Massachusetts officers' fears were justified. Connecticut officers involuntarily retired during a reduction in forces at the beginning of 1781 had been promised pensions by Congress back in October 1780, but still were not receiving payments as of July 1782. So that month William Judd and Pelatiah Webster met with Robert Morris and Secretary of War Lincoln and then petitioned Congress on behalf of the officers, urging that the delegates establish a fund to pay for the retired officers' half pay. However, this petition, like one that had been submitted earlier, did not bear any fruit. Although nationalists like Morris and Lincoln wished to see Congress assume responsibility for funding that benefit because that would strengthen their case for giving the government real taxation authority, many delegates did not want to see Philadelphia grow more powerful. They wanted the officers to go to their respective states to receive that benefit. Consequently, the delegates were not able to come to an agreement as to who should bear the expense of half pay—Congress or the states. As temperatures rose during the debate, and before the delegates eventually agreed to set the issue aside until January, Connecticut's Jesse Root warned his fellow members: If the soldiers observing Congress feel they are being "neglected or trifled with they will either quit the service immediately, or refuse to lay down their arms when the war is over."[29]

THE PETITION THAT Knox and Putnam drafted can be considered the first shot in an eight-month war for justice. It represented the beginning of a determined effort by some officers in the Continental Army to get, among other things, the back pay they and their fellow patriots were owed and a guarantee that they would receive the postwar pensions they had been promised.

This war, like the Revolutionary War, would start in Massachusetts. Later it would move to Philadelphia and the Hudson Highlands. It would begin with Massachusetts officers appealing to their state's legislators, continue with nationalists in Philadelphia plotting to terrify their opponents in Congress and the recalcitrant state legislatures they represented into giving the government more power, and reach a climax with hundreds of officers gathering for a meeting in a place called the Temple of Virtue in the Hudson Highlands. The most dangerous part of this war—the plot—would be called the Newburgh Conspiracy.

Chapter Seven

"There Never Was So Great a Spirit of Discontent"

On August 6, 1782, in a letter to Maryland's Matthew Ridley, Gouverneur Morris expressed his private feelings on where the country was and what was needed to preserve the union. The country had seen its population and wealth increase quickly and the people enjoyed much freedom, but it still needed "Vigor, Organization and Promptitude to render this a considerable Empire." Those could "only be acquired by a Continuance of the War which will convince People of the necessity of obedience to common Counsels for general Purposes," he told his merchant friend. War was "a rude, rough Nurse to infant States," one that was possibly going to cause them "to die young," but also one that might allow the states to "grow up vigorous." For the better scenario to play out, the "young Tree"—Congress—had to grow to be "if not large at least solid." Then it would be "tho not showy … surely strong." Now Congress lacked strength. It had not been given enough authority by the writers of the Articles of Confederation. Every day people became more aware of that, and that awareness was going to "remedy the Evil." However, if the war came to an end, so too would the belief that Congress had too little authority. Only when another war came would that "Conviction of our Weakness" return. "And then perhaps it may be too late,"[1] Morris observed.

BY AUGUST 1782 the end of the war did appear to be near. Both sides had begun talking peace back in April, the same month the Dutch had recognized American independence. Sir Guy Carleton, selected to succeed Henry Clinton as the Commander-in-chief of British forces in America for the purpose of overseeing their withdrawal, had written Washington that month and even suggested they conduct negotiations of their own,[2] but the American general was not prepared to take any chances. "We wanted no fresh opiate to increase that stupor into which we had fallen,"[3] he remarked when hearing reports of impending peace. He did not care to risk losing what had been gained from years of fighting, and rumors of peace could be part of a disinformation campaign by the British to cause America's leaders to celebrate and disband the army prematurely. The American victory at Yorktown was "an interesting event and may be productive of much good if properly improved, but if it should be the means of relaxation and sink us into supiness and [false] security it had better not have happened,"[4] he had written in November. "The readiest way to promote lasting and honorable peace is to be fully prepared vigorously to prosecute war"[5] was Washington's axiom.

If the army continued to prepare for war, the officers and soldiers were going to have less free time to recall past grievances. That was important because Washington understood that a neglected army not actively engaged in military operations might grow restless, refuse to obey orders, and even revolt. He knew what the Massachusetts, Connecticut, New York, and Pennsylvania men had done in 1780 and at the beginning of 1781, when they were not involved in actual fighting. He realized that those near mutinies and actual mutinies resulted from the hardships that the soldiers had endured and the bitterness they felt over not being treated justly by their country. He was aware of the shortages of firewood, tents, blankets, cooking utensils, food, forage, medicine, soap, and proper clothing, and he agonized over seeing them go without pay.

The want of pay caused the most uneasiness in the army, especially among men with families. Some of the officers had not been paid in months, if not years. Congress's inability to provide them with money meant they had to dig into their personal resources. Even if they had regularly received their earnings, they were not enough because of inflation. From the beginning of 1778 problems associated with pay—its insufficiency in the face of depreciation and the inflation that accompanied it, arrears, promised bounties not being given to men—fueled much discontent, mutinies, and desertions. Whenever back pay arrived desertions became less frequent.

Hoping to prevent storm clouds from forming, Washington did and would continue to do his best to keep his soldiers' and officers' spirits up and to take their minds off their troubles. He had commissioned exemplary soldiers in the past, but an impending reduction in forces was going to leave his army with fewer officer slots and force him to devise other ways to recognize men for their fine service. So, on August 7, 1782, Washington ordered that each man who had "served more than three years with bravery, fidelity, and good conduct" be rewarded with "honorary badges of distinction," white service stripes that were to be sewn on the lower part of the left sleeve of his uniform.[6]

Another creation of his was the "Badge of Military Merit" or, as it was also called, the "Badge of Merit." This medal was purple and shaped like a heart but, unlike today's Purple Heart, not awarded to soldiers for wounds they suffered in action against the enemy. It was presented to a soldier who had taken "any singularly meritorious action" that could be proved. That meant "not only instances of unusual gallantry, but also of extraordinary fidelity, and essential services in any way."[7] Washington thought the medal was likely to motivate men to do their best by showing them that "the road to glory in a patriot army and a free country is thus open to all."[8] Only three soldiers would receive the medal before the war came to an end.[9]

Rewards were not the only weapon that the Commander-in-chief employed to keep his men from growing restless. He encouraged them to compete in making their living spaces elegant and they responded; one visitor noted, "In front of the tents was a regular, continued portico formed by the boughs of trees in verdure, decorated with much taste and fancy. Each officer's tent was distinguished by superior ornament."[10] He pushed his men to take their newly issued hats and "give them a military and uniform appearance by cutting, cocking or adding such other decorations as they think proper."[11] He urged attendance at Sunday religious services, believing they "tend to improve the morals and … increase the happiness of the soldiery, and must afford the most pure and rational entertainment for every serious and well-disposed mind."[12] He drilled and inspected his men. He assigned them guard duty. And he tasked them with the usual camp details, such as chopping firewood.

Uneasiness among the soldiers had been a constant problem throughout the war. Many mutinies had taken place; some of them involved no more than a squad, others whole regiments.[13] One, the mutiny of the Pennsylvania Line in January 1781, had even resulted in 1,317 men getting discharges and almost as many receiving long furloughs.[14]

The vast majority of officers had remained loyal to Washington and their country when the men rose up. The possibility that officers would join mutinous soldiers and seek justice at the points of their bayonets was not something Washington had had to fear. Their mood was now changing, though, and during Washington's stay in Newburgh he was to see his officers grow more and more uneasy. Hoping to prevent their discontent from boiling over, he granted many extended furloughs to allow them to go home[15] and often urged Congress to take steps to better their situation.

One problem was the officers' awareness that many of their fellow citizens had stayed home during the war and profited greatly from it. Among them were farmers who had gone into the camp by Boston and sold overpriced produce, shoemakers who took money from them for footwear that lasted less than a week, and suppliers who made blankets only one quarter the required size. One officer guessed that their average profit on each contract with the army was fifty percent. He may have been conservative in his estimate; at one point in the war soldiers had not been able to purchase uniforms from some Boston merchants unless the sellers were able to make a profit of at least 1,000 to 1,800 percent. And more than a few of these Americans were doing a healthy business with the enemy.[16]

These war profiteers were "pests of society, and the greatest Enemys … to the happiness of America." They should have been "hunted … down" by the states long ago, Washington had written back in December 1778. The worst of them deserved to be "hung in Gibbets upon a gallows five times as high as the one prepared by Haman."[17]

A contractor that officers especially disliked was Sands and Company.[18] Within three months after beginning to provision West Point and its dependencies the company had begun to draw criticism, and subsequent actions continued to draw the ire of the officers and spark disputes. "By May [1782] the complaints were legion, if not exactly novel."[19] The New York merchant "Mr. Comfort Sands, wrongly named so,"[20] had little concern for the troops' welfare if it meant even a small sacrifice to his flourishing business. He was too tightfisted even when the needs of business called for spending, deceitful when conducting negotiations, excessively scrupulous, and haughty when dealing with officers. The officers were convinced that they were being overcharged, and Washington felt that everything Sands did was done to quench his "thirst of Gain."[21]

The company was required to set up only three issuing stores—too few to match the number of locations where troops were encamped—and they were in places of the contractor's choosing, not the military's. During the winter of 1781–82 a number of regiments found that they had to send teams more than three miles just to get their provisions.

One loser was the hospital near New Windsor. The sick soldiers there could not be issued salt meat. They needed *fresh* meat and they had to draw it in small amounts; otherwise what was not consumed quickly rotted. Smaller amounts meant more trips to the issuing store in Fishkill, which was not easy to reach in winter. As early as January 1782 the hospital found itself without any provisions.

From May 22 to May 24, 1782, General Heath's soldiers also found themselves unable to get any meat. "Why Sir are the Troops without Provisions? why are the deposits which have so often, and so long ago been required by General Heath, and pressed by myself, neglected? Why do you so pertinaciously adhere to all those parts of the Contracts as are promotive of your own Interest and convenience ... and at the same time disregard the most essential claims of the public; thereby hazarding the dissolution of the Army and risking the loss of the most important Post in America?"[22] Washington asked Sands the next day.

In a letter to Robert Morris, who had the authority to decide which private contractors supplied the army, Washington emphasized that he was "experiencing much Trouble from Complaints ... against Mr. Sands's execution of his Contract."[23] The contractor's policy on drawing rations had effectively reduced the officers' meal allowances. If officers were not in camp when rations were handed out to everyone, they could not draw theirs at a later time; they lost those rations. The policy discouraged officers from accepting invitations to visit foreign officers or eat at friends' places and from skipping their daily rations in favor of some poultry purchased at their own expense. It was just another in a long list of actions that angered Washington. Although the use of private contractors saved money, which was important, one could go too far in trying to cut costs. The general did not want to see the government "spin the thread of Oeconomy 'till it breaks" because he understood that "minds soured by distresses are easily rankled."[24]

Other complaints were lodged against Sands and Company and eventually Robert Morris decided to cancel the government's contract with them. He knew Washington had given up on them because they chose to "descend to … *low dirty* tricks" and displayed a "lack of common honesty" just to make a bigger profit.[25]

The officers also were bothered by the actions of Congress. Sensing that the war was coming to an end, the delegates put forth in August a plan that called for the elimination of some regiments to lighten the government's financial burden. Officers and soldiers were going to be discharged and regiments then under strength combined. If small states objected to losing their regiments of the line, they could recruit their own men and pay the enlistment bounties themselves. Why should Congress pay them if it wasn't sure the men were ever going to be needed in battle?

The reduction, which was set to begin on or before January 1, 1783, would result in a large number of officers being let go. That caused apprehension because the officers' back pay was hopelessly in arrears and, unless the government got funding, they anticipated returning home with little, if any, cash in their pockets. They also believed the financially strapped Congress wanted to save money by backsliding on promises it had made to them and feared they might not get the land grants and pensions they were counting on receiving after the war. Many of them had neglected their personal affairs and fallen into debt during the war years. Without some type of financial help from Congress, a return to civilian life for them could mean time in a debtors' prison.[26]

The thought of being sent to a debtors' prison had to weigh on the officers' minds. Although debtors were often not thrown in prisons[27] and some opposition to imprisonment for debt had begun as early as the 1750s,[28] all the states allowed such a punishment.[29] If a debtor was imprisoned, he had to endure a very harsh life. Conditions in debtors' prisons and jail rooms set aside for people in debt were especially poor. In New York City's New Gaol, a three-story stone structure with barred windows, there were four or more people to a small room and debtors with very little status might end up sleeping in a hallway. In that prison and elsewhere debtors often had to share their living space with criminals and, unlike them, they always were required to use their own resources to furnish themselves with food, clothing, and fuel. If they were not able to do that, they had to rely on family members or the charity of others to get those things. Many of the debtors apparently had neither the resources nor the benefactors to enable themselves to get what they needed and, as a result, came close to starving and went cold.[30] In Philadelphia in 1783, for example, one jailer would make a public appeal on behalf of forty of the fifty-seven men and women he was responsible for because they were suffering so greatly from a lack of subsistence.[31] If those problems were not enough to make the imprisoned debtor feel uneasy, he also had to realize that the overcrowding greatly increased the likelihood of him becoming sick and that the presence of criminals made him a potential victim of violence or thievery.[32]

ON AUGUST 28, 1782, Robert Morris wrote Alexander Hamilton. He had "not *even yet* seen the Resolutions … relative to an Extension of the Powers of Congress" that the New York legislature had passed but was pessimistic about their ability to change the situation in Philadelphia for the better. "Power is generally such a darling Object with weak Minds that they must feel extreme Reluctance to bid it farewell," he opined. The states were only going to relinquish it out of "a perfect Sense of absolute Necessity." If they agreed to give Congress more authority, they would do so either as the result of reasoned judgment or out "of Feeling." Consent given as a reasoned decision was "more safe and more certain"; consent given as an emotional response was "always severe and often dangerous." And it had to be given for the sake of the whole country.

But Morris's cynicism led him to doubt that Congress was going to be granted more power. The problem was that in government there were too few patriots "seeking the great good of the Whole on enlightened Principles" and too many of "those vulgar Souls whose narrow Opticks can see but the little Circle of selfish Concerns." What he hoped for was "a firm, wise, manly System of federal Government," but he was not counting on getting one.[33]

Two days later a petition from the Pennsylvania General Assembly was read in Congress. The Assembly was taking up the cause of the suffering Philadelphia creditors, who had sent it two appeals earlier that month. In short, both the legislators and the lenders wanted the suspension of interest payments lifted. The members of the Assembly had always felt Congress was responsible for paying the creditors, assuming it would do so under a general funding plan. Pennsylvania's creditors of the national government were owed more than any other state's, but the state had never asked the delegates in Philadelphia to give preference to its residents when they paid lenders back for supplies and services provided. Now the Assembly wanted to assume responsibility for paying them, unless the delegates came up with a plan to pay the interest on the debt.[34]

AS THE MONTH came to an end, Washington moved "the principal part of the Troops from the Highlands"[35] by flat-bottomed boat down the Hudson to an area around Verplanck's Point, just south of Peekskill. The move was made to enable the troops "to obtain forrage with greater ease & … procure a quantity of Wood for … Garrisons & Posts against the Winter" and be in a better position for a reunion when the French shortly arrived in the Hudson Valley from Virginia.[36] Washington saw another benefit from taking such an action; he was able to see "in what time a large number of Men could embark, debark, and move a given distance by Water."[37]

WHEN SEPTEMBER BEGAN Nathanael Greene wrote Robert Morris and reported that his army remained "in pretty good temper," but his officers and soldiers were finding it difficult to go without their subsistence money and he knew how an army could be "convulsed in an hour and thrown into the greatest disorder." Therefore he wanted Morris to take whatever steps he thought necessary in order to relieve his men, and he promised his support.[38]

Where was Morris going to get money for Greene's army, though? By September no funds had been received from all but Pennsylvania for more than a year, and Congress had only a very small fraction of the $8,000,000 it had requested for 1782.[39] Earlier the states had been asked by Morris to stop ignoring requisitions because promises had been made and there were such things as "sacred Bonds of national Faith and Honour,"[40] but by now he felt that calling on them for money was "like preaching to the Dead."[41]

THAT SAME SEPTEMBER New York creditors upset over congressional inaction met in Albany. The attendees—men such as Philip Schuyler, who chaired the meeting, and Alexander Hamilton, his son-in-law—suggested a convention of New York State creditors to decide on a course of action. They also established a committee to "report petitions to Congress and the Legislature" and to write similarly disaffected lenders elsewhere. Perhaps, they could join ranks and hold a national convention.[42]

The meeting in Albany was, no doubt, a response to the calls of the Philadelphia creditors. In late August they had come out with a broadside titled "To the Citizens of America, who are the Creditors of the United States" and had corresponded with lenders from other states. Through the broadside and letters the lenders learned of the Philadelphians' relations with Morris and the delegates, and they knew the Philadelphia committee expected them to petition Congress both individually and in groups. When the delegates did ask that taxes be enacted, the creditors were supposed to do their utmost to guarantee their states' backing.[43]

New York's creditors were not the only ones to respond to the Philadelphians' call. Lenders in New Jersey met and, a few months later, public creditors from Connecticut petitioned Congress. But the dream of the New Yorkers—a national convention—would not be realized during the war.[44]

MEANWHILE, IN PHILADELPHIA the Grand Committee had finished reviewing the Financier's report on public credit. The members recommended to Congress that it approve the taxes proposed by him and his assistant and disagreed with them only on the sale of western lands, which the committee saw as a good future source of revenue.

But during the debates each of their proposals had its opponents and some of the states lacked adequate representation. Consequently, the committee's recommendations on taxes and its judgment on the sale of western lands were rejected. The best Congress was able to do was ask Morris to stop drawing bills of exchange on France to pay the clamorous creditors the interest they were due; he was to requisition $1,200,000 from the states for that purpose and to make interest payments on other debts. Each state would decide what taxes to levy on its inhabitants and could make the interest payments directly to the creditors, counting them toward its share of the requisition.[45]

Robert Morris knew that far stronger action was needed to solve the government's funding problems and thought annual requisitions were "a futile Measure."[46] However, he did have some reason to be optimistic as autumn approached. He apparently believed Georgia had already passed the impost,[47] although it had not, and during the summer James Varnum predicted that Rhode Island, which had been silent for many months, would soon ratify it.[48]

Varnum, though, was lobbying his state for ratification of the impost, which affected his objectivity. He wanted a strong national government, one with a stable source of revenue. In March 1782 he had produced a number of articles in the *Providence Gazette* in support of the impost.[49]

Those articles had then provoked an immediate rebuttal from David Howell, a strong opponent of taxes. Using the pen name "A Farmer,"[50] the former mathematics and natural philosophy professor produced a number of letters to show where Varnum was wrong. The impost was like the Stamp Act and the Articles of Confederation made clear that the states were sovereign, not subordinate to Congress. The impost hurt a commercial state like Rhode Island, since "any restrictions or duties whatever" were known "to clog and embarrass trade." Even if duties were needed, the state had to be responsible for levying them. Another problem was that under the impost Rhode Island paid a disproportionate share of the country's taxes. After all, it was an importing state and the impost placed the tax burden on the shoulders of importers. And having customs officials appointed by Congress was a bad idea because they would turn over all the money they collected to the national treasury, which could then spend it unobserved by and unaccountable to watchful Rhode Island taxpayers. Rhode Islanders were willing to pay their share of taxes, but only as prescribed by the Articles of Confederation; that is, only their own state officials had the legal right to levy taxes on them.[51]

Howell's position was in line with what his state believed, and in May 1782 he was elected to be one of Rhode Island's four delegates to Congress for the coming term. When a congressional committee wanted to know why his state had not ratified the impost, Howell essentially reiterated the views he had expressed when rebutting Varnum. For one thing, the impost hit Rhode Island especially hard because it had larger mercantile and manufacturing classes than other states, and the merchants were the ones who would pay the higher taxes. They could try to pass on the costs to neighboring states like Connecticut, which because they lacked major ports had to go through Rhode Island to get imported goods, but if those states did not want to pay the higher prices, Rhode Island merchants would go out of business. Rhode Island also thought that if it tried to pass on the costs to neighboring states dependent upon her for imports, they were going to retaliate by charging more for the agricultural goods they sold to the tiny state or by embargoing her. Such a retaliatory action would leave Rhode Island in terrible shape, since it could not produce enough agricultural products to satisfy the needs of its people.

Another thing that bothered him was that the money raised from taxing Rhode Island merchants would not even stay in the state; it would be passed on to Congress by collectors Philadelphia had appointed and sent into the state, which was an infringement on the state's sovereignty. They should be appointed by the state and the money collected should be for its use.

One more factor in Rhode Island's opposition to the impost was the damage it had suffered from the war. Newport now could send out but a few sailing vessels, whereas in 1774 it had been able to send out one-hundred-fifty. The state would need to levy taxes to make up for such losses and to provide for its own defense, especially since the bigger states were still trying to hold on to western lands that Congress wanted them to cede to it.

The last reason for opposing the impost was the belief that future, less honorable congresses might choose not to liquidate the national debt in order to justify prolonging the life of the impost.[52]

IN SEPTEMBER 1782 the French marched north from Baltimore and encamped around Crompond, east of West Point. They remained encamped there until October 22, when they left for Boston to be transported to the West Indies by ship. Before saying good-bye, French officers attended parades and reviews. They got together with their American counterparts and talked about the not-too-distant past. They invited them to dinners at their nearby camp and hosted them in grand style, covering tables with much good food and drink.[53] "It was a real family fête."[54]

Major General Baron von Steuben was determined to match the French hospitality. "I will give one grand dinner to our allies, should I eat my soup with a wooden spoon forever after," the irascible old general vowed. However, he was not able to afford a grand dinner; he had not been paid in more than three years. So he approached Washington to see what he could do about his back pay. Nothing, he was told; that was a problem that only Congress could solve and, Washington admitted, he felt there were "no hopes of any future alteration." But the Commander-in-chief did lend him twenty guineas from his own funds. That sum plus what Steuben got for selling a white horse and a pocket watch that he owned enabled him to host his grand dinner.

The month after the French departed for Boston the general would go to Congress to get what he was due. He left with only one gold coin on his person. Of the $8,500 in hard cash he was owed by the government, he got only $1,700. The rest of the debt was paid by giving him an interest-bearing treasury certificate for $6,800. Eventually, Von Steuben tried to sell it at ten percent of its face value, but to no avail.[55]

Steuben was the exception when it came to hosting dinners. The American officers generally were not able to match their friends' hospitality; they could not offer grand dinners no matter how much they tried. No experience humiliated the American officers more and made their neglect so apparent. How painful for generals to be unable to "invite a French Officer—a visiting friend—or traveling acquaintance to a better Repast than stinking whiskey (& not always that) & a bit of Beef without Vegitable."

Generals, of course, were not the only ones suffering. The Commander-in-chief was seeing "discontents … throughout the Army" when he wrote Lincoln in early October. Soldiers and officers were upset over "the total want of Money," the great debts they had incurred while they were at war, "the distress of their Families … & the prospect of Poverty & Misery before them." It was foolish to believe they would "acquiesce *contentedly* with bare rations" while civilians not enduring anywhere near the number of hardships they endured received their pay on a regular basis.

The officers were also angry that promotions and commissions were being held back and that nothing had been done to ensure they would get the compensation they had been promised. Washington worried about what might happen when the reduction of the army began:

> "I cannot help fearing the Result … when I see such a number of Men goaded by a thousand stings of reflexion on the past, & of anticipation on the future, about to be turned out into the World, soured by penury & what they call the ingratitude of the Public, involved in debts, without one farthing of Money to carry them home, after having spent the flower of their days & many of them their patrimonies in establishing the freedom & Independence of their Country, and having suffered every thing human Nature is capable of enduring on this side of death … without one thing to sooth their feelings, or brighten the gloomy prospects, I cannot avoid apprehending that a train of Evils will follow, of a very serious & distressing Nature. … You may rely upon it, the patience & long suffering of this Army are almost exhausted, and … there never was so great a spirit of Discontent as at this instant."

When men were actively engaged in military operations their discontent, he wrote, could be "kept from breaking out into Acts of Outrage." Once they had gone into winter quarters, though, there was no guarantee that that would continue to be the case.[56]

Others were just as aware of the mood of the army as Washington. The inspector of contracts for the army in the Hudson Highlands, Ezekiel Cornell, saw that all the officers felt "exceedingly distressed for Want of Money" and were complaining.[57] Tench Tilghman also noticed that the officers were "really in a distressed Situation" because they were not being paid and requested that the Financier make "every possible exertion to give two or three Months pay" to them and their soldiers when they went into their winter quarters. "To the Officers it will be the most acceptable thing upon Earth," he predicted. It will "make this Army the most contented of any in the World."

Tilghman then remarked that the army in the Hudson Highlands had "some few grievances" that would not be Morris's responsibility to redress and hoped Secretary of War Lincoln "could find time to make a short visit." The colonel thought he and Morris "could concert measures with him that would do away several disagreeable Matters."[58]

AS CORNELL AND Tilghman wrote Morris, the Financier prepared a letter for the states and enclosed with it a resolution from Congress calling for them to speedily provide the funds that had been requisitioned, because Philadelphia wanted to pay the army.[59] He did not "attempt to display the extraordinary Merit and Sufferings of our Army," which he presumed everybody was aware of, because he was not writing "to ask for our Officers and Soldiers any *Reward* but meerly the Means to do them *Justice*." They were doubly entitled to what the delegates were requesting because they had displayed "exemplary Patience under the Detention of their Dues."[60]

Morris also sent Nathanael Greene and George Washington copies of Congress's plea. He wanted them to keep "any such Officers of Influence and Discretion as may be about to pass from your army to the Legislatures" abreast of the actions taken. By keeping the officers informed, Morris thought, they were able to ensure that "the Views and Efforts of all the public Servants" with like goals "may produce the desired Success."[61]

As he tried to get funds for Congress and urged that the army be paid, the Financier's concern that the war might end too soon for the country's good grew. He hoped "most sincerely and ardently for Peace"—he was tired of the burdens that his position as superintendent placed on his shoulders—but if allowed to speak only as "a Patriot," he would say that the war had to continue. The bonds between the states remained weak, their legislatures still lacked "the Vigour and self Confidence ... necessary to ensure the safety and promote the happiness of the People," and more Americans had to feel "a Sense of the Obligations to Support" the union and get used to paying taxes. They were not going to be too burdensome.

The Financier questioned whether peace was "really so desireable" and in Philadelphia its likelihood was causing "more general discontent" than he had seen in quite some time, "particularly amongst the mercantile part of the Community";[62] the merchants feared that with the end of the war the government would no longer feel it had to pay them back.

What Rhode Island would have said if it had known about Morris's misgivings concerning the arrival of peace can only be guessed, but his desire that Americans acquire the habit of paying taxes certainly was not shared. The state remained strongly opposed to the impost. Still, up to this time no votes on the impost had actually been cast by Rhode Island legislators. Then, on October 10, Congress decided to wait no longer; it called on the state legislatures of Rhode Island and Georgia to make up their minds immediately.[63]

Howell saw Congress's insistence upon an immediate decision as a "crisis."[64] He wanted "friends of Liberty & a free trade" to stand up.[65] He did not want his legislature to vote for the impost. "Should it be adopted I shall no longer consider myself as the Representative of a Sovereign & free State but wish to be recalled to sink again into retirement on my little farm where I have spent the pleasantest part of my days," he declared. The impost was "but an entring wedge." Once Congress passed this tax, it would then go on to approve others.[66] Thus, "the bond of Union," he and the other Rhode Island delegates sarcastically wrote, "would be complete. And we will add the Yoke of Tyranny fixed on all the states, and the Chains rivettted."[67]

Morris, though, wanted the impost. On the seventeenth he wrote the governors of Rhode Island and Georgia. Enclosed with his letter was Congress's October 10 call for a decision on the impost. "It gives me the most sensible Concern to find that the very important Business of funding the public Debts hangs suspended by the Delay of the States mentioned in the Resolution," Morris began. The impost had to be approved so the deserving creditors and the army could be paid what they were owed. "I would wish to say Nothing on this Subject, but I feel myself irresistibly impelled to observe that the public Creditors are numerous, meritorious and important. It is a Body composed of the most zealous Whigs in America. It contains those who have supplied and those who have composed our Armies under the most trying Circumstances," he stressed. "The Revenues asked for, are to repay the Monies advanced for our Freedom, and the Blood which has been shed in our Cause: And if it were necessary that Pity should come in Aid of Gratitude and Justice, I might observe that the Widows and Orphans of those who have spent their All and lost their Lives in Defence of America, are reduced to the extremest Want by withholding their just Dues. But I will not dwell any longer on these painful Reflections, but merely repeat my Hope that every Ground of Complaint may speedily be removed."[68]

THE SITUATION IN Philadelphia that October troubled Washington. Civilian officeholders were paid when Congress had money, the army had heard, but it was not.[69] Why should the army be singled out for such unjust treatment by the government? More and more the talk was that the officers were going to resign en masse,[70] a move that could end hopes of an imminent victory and render America defenseless. "The patience, the fortitude, and long and great sufferings of this Army is unexampled in History; but there is an end to all things, and I fear we are very near one," the general warned Maryland delegate James McHenry. "[T]his ... more than probably, will oblige me to stick very close to the Troops this Winter and to try like a careful physician to prevent if possible the disorders getting to an incurable height."[71]

Three days after Washington wrote McHenry, on October 20, Secretary of War Lincoln arrived at the encampment to "calm the rising billows." During the week he spent there he met with Washington and members of his high command, listened to officers express their grievances, and assured them that Congress was not going to deprive them of the benefits they were entitled to; it would make some arrangements for them to receive something before they were discharged.[72]

AS LINCOLN WORKED on the soldiers in the Hudson Highlands, a mood of despair prevailed in Philadelphia. Even if Congress got the impost, that alone was not going to provide the Treasury with enough money to fund the debt.[73] Additional taxes were needed, but asking for them while the impost had not yet been approved was a difficult thing for the government to do. Also, every single tax proposed faced certain opposition.

"The Evil presses hard," Morris declared in a letter to Rhode Island's governor. "Public Credit is at the last Gasp, or rather it is expired. Not only are we to expect a formidable Clamor from the abused and injured Creditors, but there is really very little Hope of obtaining foreign Loans: For how can it be expected that a Republic without Funds should persuade Foreigners to lend their Money, while its own Citizens who have already lent theirs can neither obtain the Interest nor any solid Security either for Interest or Principal."

The issue of the impost and public credit was important; it affected every single American. "The critical Situation we stand in has rendered it necessary for Congress to demand a decided Answer," he continued. "No Time is to be lost, for if the Revenues cannot be obtained the public Creditors must be told so in plain Terms. The Efforts to borrow farther Sums must cease … and then the whole Weight of the War must fall on the People in one Mode or the other." Rhode Island's legislature had to decide "whether the little Applause which Individuals may gain by specious Declamations and Publications should over balance every Consideration of national Safety."[74]

In spite of the prevailing mood of despair in Philadelphia, Morris had reason to believe he was going to get what he wanted. The public creditors were "organizing themselves," just as he had advised, and he felt "their Numbers and Influence joined to the Justness of their Cause" were going to ensure success if they remained steadfast.[75] Also, on the thirtieth he had heard from Secretary of War Lincoln, who had by this time returned from the Hudson Highlands, just how upset the army there was about not being paid.[76] Its anger also could help change the minds of state legislators who were reluctant to give Congress funding.

But on November 1 Morris suffered a setback; Rhode Island legislators voted unanimously to reject the impost. Congress was notified by the Speaker, who gave three reasons for the legislature's decision: Rhode Island, as a commercial state, would bear a disproportionate burden of the taxes; having collectors unaccountable to Rhode Island appointed and sent in by Congress was "against the constitution of the state"; and to give the delegates the taxation authority they wanted without specifying limits on the impost's duration and on the size of its duties meant the states were not going to be able to hold Philadelphia accountable for the way it spent the money it collected. Thus, the impost was "repugnant to the liberty of the United States."[77]

Howell and Jonathan Arnold, another Rhode Island delegate, also disingenuously claimed that the impost was unnecessary;[78] John Adams had secured a large loan from Dutch bankers in June, but not so large that the impost was no longer needed.

The state also wanted questions regarding the sale of western lands to be resolved before new taxes were considered. Rhode Island felt that proceeds from their sale should go into the national treasury. Howell felt enough money could be brought in that way to solve the nation's financial problems. Congress had established procedures for selling such territories as a means to obtain needed income, but often boundary disputes between the concerned parties made for slow progress. And Rhode Island's concern over western lands was really nothing more than a convenient excuse to allow it to reject new taxes.[79]

Rhode Island's rejection of the impost was very important. It was one event that helped cause the Newburgh Conspiracy.

Chapter Eight

"No Officer Was More Distinguished"

IN THE MONTHS preceding Rhode Island's vote against the impost, from September through October 1782, the Massachusetts officers had not waited idly for Congress to come up with the funding to make pensions possible. They thought their state might be receptive to assuming responsibility for providing them with half pay or a lump sum payment in lieu of it.[1] In early September Rufus Putnam and Lieutenant Colonels William Hull and John Brooks arrived in Boston.[2] The Massachusetts officers had wanted Henry Knox, a ruddy-complexioned man over six feet tall and between two hundred-eighty and three hundred pounds, with broad shoulders and a bulbous nose, to head the officers' delegation, and he wanted to lead the mission, but "circumstances" beyond his control prevented him from doing so. Knox had to be content with only writing Governor John Hancock to urge his support.[3]

After arriving in Boston, Brooks called on Governor Hancock and gave him Knox's letter, which was received "with great politeness." The three officers then "spent several Days in conversing with different characters" in the Massachusetts General Court. The Senate was favorably disposed towards satisfying them, but most members in the legislature displayed "an extrime degree of reserve," and the officers did not present the petition that Knox and Putnam had drafted in July until September 24.[4]

Opposition to half pay was strongest in the House, where legislators were lined up about four to one against the pension. They represented the more financially distressed rural regions of the state and were less influenced by the mercantile class than senators. The plan, they contended, was going to prove too expensive and taxes would have to be increased. They were frightened to think of an officer receiving half pay for three or four decades, from the age of thirty till his death at sixty or seventy. Officers did not deserve such a generous benefit. A caste of idle retired officers was certain to result.[5]

After the officers presented their petition, the House established a committee to work with the Senate on the matter. Soon thereafter its members started meeting with Putnam and the two colonels, and a report was prepared for the whole legislature. The legislators considered the report, established a joint committee, and referred the officers' address to it. Garnering its support was important because around this time—on October 8—Knox was writing John Lowell, one of its members, to warn him of "the extreme uneasiness of the Massachusetts Line." The army's "only food for years" had been the promises of financial remuneration made by Congress and now with its "patience ... so much exhausted and ... passions so high," it did not want to see delegates in Philadelphia or legislators elsewhere do anything to cause it to lose hope.[6] If the three officers in Boston did not succeed, the army might cease to exist and America would be defenseless against the British.

Success, though, was not going to come soon, if at all. As the legislature established the joint committee, a private letter for Lowell from Samuel Osgood, a Massachusetts delegate to Congress, arrived and was read aloud before the whole body.[7] "The Promise of half Pay for Life ... has occasioned considerable Difficulty," Osgood reported. Some delegates were opposed to providing the officers with the pension, while others supported rewarding them with the benefit. That division was preventing the government from reducing forces.

But lack of agreement in Philadelphia on whether the officers should be so generously compensated after the war did not mean the Massachusetts legislature should take that business up. It was "altogether a national Matter," and some delegates were not going to agree to allow a state that approved "a Compromise for the half Pay" for its officers—without getting approval from Congress—to have its own requisition quotas for pensions cut.

Osgood predicted that the issue would eventually be sent back to the states but anticipated strong opposition to such a referral. Delegates against referring half pay to the states wanted Congress to assume responsibility for furnishing the officers with half pay either because they believed such an action was going to "have a Tendency to cement the Union" or because they did not know how agreeable their state legislatures were going to be to providing the pensions "indiscriminately." Of the two reasons, the second was the one the Massachusetts delegate considered "more probable."

Supporters of the pension had to base their arguments on "the Sufferings & hard Services of the Officers—The Sacrifice ... made in their private Fortunes—and the Injury done to their Constitutions." The officers' "Mode of Life in the Army ... disqualified them for any other Employ."

The certain responses from opponents of the measure were that "no Country ever gave half Pay for Life, which did not maintain a standing Army," and that as it now stood the promised pension was going to prove to be "an exceeding unequal Reward"; not all officers deserved so generous a benefit. "Our Officers are very numerous, & many of them have not performed nine Months actual Service," the Massachusetts delegate elaborated. "In the Distribution of Rewards, equal Justice ought to be a governing Principle—But many of our old & best Officers will receive a much less Reward, than younger Officers. ... What Reason there can be given, why an Officer that left a Family which depended upon him for Support & Protection, & hazarded his Life at the Expence of all his domestic Feelings, should not be, at least, entitled to the equal Favors of his Country?"

Osgood considered himself to be "a very sincere Friend to the Army," but he did not want it to be rewarded with "a special Contract," a costly pension financed by "Taxation beyond what the People will submit to." Yes, the army had suffered greatly but that did not give it the right to place such a heavy burden on the rest of the country's citizenry "as would render it miserable afterwards." The army certainly did not wish to have the pensions if they were going to be seen as "an excessive, as well as an unequal Reward."

More lines followed, the most important of which let Lowell know that Osgood thought Congress was likely to take up the issue of half pay soon after the New Year began.[8] Brooks, who informed Knox of the letter's appearance, understood that that was one reason why the Massachusetts delegate felt "the State ought not to meddle with the matter."[9]

Osgood's letter was used by Massachusetts legislators opposed to half pay and, on October 16, "after long debate," the House voted to delay taking up the issue until the next session. When Brooks wrote Knox the following day, though, he was not altogether pessimistic; all the members of the joint committee supported commuting the half-pay pensions to some other form of postwar compensation, and they and the officers were going to fight to have the question brought up again during the current session. Also, Brooks had received a letter written by Knox on October 8 and had passed on an extract of it to one of the committee members, who planned to use it in his argument for the legislature to reconsider its vote for a delay; the letter, one can safely assume, was identical in content to the one the general sent to Lowell that same day, the one that warned the Massachusetts legislator of the army's impatience and inflamed passions. "We are endeavoring to convince them that a delay, as it respects us, is the same thing as a denial," the colonel reported.[10]

On October 28 the officers' petition was again read aloud to the members of the House. Another committee was established to work with the Senate on a solution, and on November 1 a day and time for "coming to the choice of Gentlemen to settle with the army" were suggested.[11]

But a settlement was not forthcoming. House members preferred not to act until they learned the sentiment of the delegates in Philadelphia. Their support of a postponement, they claimed, was based on their fear that any action taken by the Massachusetts General Court during this session might be later disapproved by Congress.[12]

With nothing to show for their effort, the three officers returned to the Hudson Highlands. If the officers wanted something done, they should first go to Congress.

IN EARLY NOVEMBER a group of officers representing the various Massachusetts regiments stationed in the Hudson Highlands began another effort to have their grievances redressed. The state legislature had treated the Massachusetts officers' appeal in a way that produced "universal discontent," so the members of the delegation, "having conferred together, came to a determination of taking the sense of the army at large." At a meeting on November 16 they established a seven-man committee to meet with officers from other interested state lines eight days later to decide what steps they ought to take to achieve their objective and decided that a petition taking into account lists of grievances prepared by officers from all the Massachusetts regiments should be drafted and addressed to Congress.

The lists were called for immediately and started arriving within two days.[13] They varied somewhat from regiment to regiment, but the officers' main concerns were apparent: the troops' pay arrears, the half-pay pensions, the inadequacy of allowances meant to make up for shortages of rations, the plight of officers involuntarily retired as part of the reduction in forces, and the claims of soldiers who had received small bounties because they had signed up early.

The Massachusetts regiments' responses showed that the officers wanted the petition to be spirited in tone.[14] However, instructions given to Colonel Samuel B. Webb, who was going to represent the Connecticut officers at the upcoming meeting, made clear that the appeal had to be respectful. All the officers could painfully recall "the many and intolerable Grievances" they had endured, and they wanted "the most immediate and effectual relief," but they did not want to behave "with an Intemperate Zeal." In the past they had "exhibited to the World the most Astonishing Spectacle of *persevering Patriotism and Virtue in distress*"; now, as the war appeared to be approaching "a happy termination," they had no desire to do anything that would diminish their reputations. They wished that their actions "be dictated in prudence, and supported with firmness."[15]

When Sunday the twenty-fourth of November arrived, a delegation representing all the lines in the Hudson Highlands met at West Point. There the assembled officers chose Major General Henry Knox, Brigadier General Jedediah Huntington, Colonel John Crane, Colonel Philip Van Cortlandt, and Dr. William Eustis of Cambridge, a twenty-nine-year-old hospital surgeon, to make up "a committee to draft an address and petition to Congress, in behalf of the army." What they came up with would then be presented to the delegation representing the whole army for its consideration when it met again on December 1.[16]

General Henry Knox

THE GRAY-EYED KNOX,[17] the ranking member of the committee, had left school to work at Wharton and Bowes Book Store to support his mother and younger brother when his father died. He was not yet even twelve years old. Years later, before the war, he opened his own establishment in Boston, London Book Store. Making good use of his time there, he became well versed in military warfare by reading extensively and talking with and questioning British officers who walked into his shop. He learned much about engineering and gained an understanding of how to employ cannon in battle.

The Boston Massacre helped turn Knox into a committed patriot. Events during the two years before the war, though, could have kept him out of action or led him to side with the British. In 1773 a hunting accident left him missing two fingers and part of another on his left hand, and the following year he married Lucy Flucker, the daughter of Loyalists and sister of a lieutenant in the British army in Boston.

Lucy's brother wanted Knox to be commissioned as a British officer and he used his influence accordingly, but the young man had other plans. One night not long after hostilities broke out in Lexington, he and his wife quietly rode a chaise through enemy lines in Boston, Lucy supposedly concealing her husband's militia sword in the lining of her petticoat or cloak. Then he became an officer in the Continental Army.

Knox quickly made a name for himself in the army. He participated in the Battle of Bunker Hill and later, in November 1775, was made Colonel of the Continental Regiment of Artillery. The same month he left Cambridge for Fort Ticonderoga. He had proposed to Washington that he go there to collect the artillery that Ethan Allen and his Green Mountain Boys had captured in their victory over the British in May and bring it back to the camp outside Boston; from there the guns could be moved to high ground and used to shell the British in the city below. The proposal was not embraced by many of Washington's advisors; the heavy guns would have to be taken apart and put on barges before Lake George froze and later transferred to sledges drawn by oxen to their eventual destination. Knox, though, got Washington to go along with his plan.

The colonel arrived at the fort with his troops on December 5, identified those guns that were still usable, and had them detached from their mountings. They were then sent by boat and ox cart to an embarkation point at Lake George. There they were placed on flat-bottomed boats, and on the ninth the men began rowing down the lake. The weather, which had been favorable when they were loading the barges, soon decided not to cooperate. Gale-force winds blew and temperatures dropped, eventually turning the surface of the lake to ice. But just before that happened, the men had reached the other end of the waterway.

Knox next turned his attention to finding sleds and draft animals for overland travel. It took a little time, but by the seventeenth of December he had in tow "forty two exceedingly strong sleds"[18] for carrying cannon and "eighty yoke of oxen to drag them as far as Springfield."[19] There he would "get fresh cattle to carry them to camp."[20] His goal was "to be able to present … a noble train of artillery"[21] to Washington in a little over two weeks.

For want of snow on the ground, which the oxen had to have if they were to pull the loaded sleds, the colonel was not able to immediately set out for Springfield. Only when he opened his eyes on the morning of December 25 and saw the earth covered with a thick white blanket was he ready to get his troops and artillery moving again. In fact, too much snow had fallen; their trip was not going to be an easy one.

The difficulty and danger involved in moving the guns was great. This was especially true when the noble train moved downhill. If it gathered too much speed on its descent, it could hit the men in front like an avalanche. So precautions had to be taken to prevent that from happening; ropes were stretched from the artillery and secured to trees in its rear to hold it back, and drag chains and poles were placed under the sleds' runners.

When Knox and his men got to Albany, the ice covering the Hudson was not thick enough to support the heavy sleds. The men tried twice to cross the river, but on both occasions lost one of their cannon. Finally, on the morning of January 8, Knox and his men "went on the ice … and … carefully … before night … got over 23 sleds."[22] They also "were so lucky as to get the [lost] Cannon out of the River, owing to the assistance [of] the good people … of Albany."[23]

They subsequently moved through the Berkshire Hills in western Massachusetts, followed an old Indian path to Springfield and obtained eighty yoke of fresh oxen. With little snow on the ground there, the train of artillery had to halt, but before long temperatures dropped and the convoy started moving again. As they made their way through Brookfield, Spencer, Leicester, Worcester, Shrewsbury, Northborough, Marlborough, Southborough, Framingham, Wayland, Weston, Waltham and Watertown, better roads and more desirable weather made their trip easier.

Knox arrived in camp on January 18, 1776, his men about one week later. They had brought with them about 120,000 pounds of artillery, 2,300 pounds of lead, and one barrel of flints. Historians disagree about the numbers of guns transported from the fort to Cambridge. One, for example, says fifty-two cannon, nine large mortars and five coehorns were brought back from Ticonderoga, while another says forty-three heavy brass and iron cannon, six coehorns, eight mortars, and two howitzers were collected and safely delivered. Whatever the number, the arrival of the men and artillery was greeted with cheers.

The men's achievement was remarkable. In addition to rowing down the thirty-mile long Lake George, they had crossed iced-over rivers, gone up and down snow-covered mountains, and plodded through muddy forests. They had covered more than three hundred miles in all. Their leader, Henry Knox, was only twenty-five years old at the time.

On March 4, 1776, the eve of the sixth anniversary of the Boston Massacre, twenty cannon were quietly moved to the frozen ground on Dorchester Heights by two thousand American soldiers. Wooden frames and fascines—long bundles of sticks bound together—were carried there, hastily assembled, and packed with bales of hay to form a barricade. Large barrels stuffed with rocks and earth were also carried up the hill, arranged in rows, and chained together; a Boston merchant had proposed to Washington that if the British decided to rush up the slope, they could be sent cascading down upon them. And trickery was employed; logs were painted to resemble cannon. When the morning of March 5 arrived, Major General William Howe looked up and was shocked. "The rebels did more in one night than my whole army would have done in one month,"[24] he marveled. The "two posts upon the highest hills of Dorchester peninsula ... appeared more like majick than the work of human beings,"[25] one British officer said. Soon thereafter the British decided to quit Boston.

Little time passed before the action moved to New York. In July 1776 Howe sent two ships, the forty-gun *Phoenix* and the twenty-gun *Rose*, up the Hudson to fire upon New York City and test American defenses. Knox's artillery took aim and fired, but failed to stop the vessels; by the time the British finished, they had sailed forty miles up the river, done damage to several homes, and caused hundreds of panicky New Yorkers to flee their city. One New Yorker managed to maintain his sense of humor through the ordeal, though, noting that the cow he had lost to enemy fire was still going to make "good market beef."[26] Not so funny, however, was the performance of American gunners; six of them lost their lives and several others received bad wounds when their own cannon exploded as a result of their neglecting to use a sponge to put out any sparks inside the guns' barrels between firings. The neglect may have occurred because some of the gunners were drunk.

Not long after that incident, in August, Howe defeated the Americans in the Battle of Long Island and turned his attention to lower Manhattan. British forces landed further up the island in hopes of trapping their foe inside New York City and preventing a retreat northward to higher ground. Although the British had struck suddenly, the Americans escaped capture and made it to Harlem Heights. One of the very last to arrive on the night of September 15 was Knox. His appearance was most welcome, for he was believed to have been caught by the British.

After some fighting there, both sides paused for a few weeks. A congressional committee was considering the merits of establishing a military academy at this time and Knox, in response to a request from John Adams, came up with some "Hints for the Improvement of the Artillery of the United States." Among them was a suggestion that America needed laboratories situated a great distance from the enemy for the production of necessary artillery equipment such as wagons, gun carriages, and ammunition. The laboratories would also have foundries where cannon, mortars, and howitzers were to be cast.

As for the academy, Knox envisioned one where artillery officers were taught the "whole theory and practice of fortifications and gunnery."[27] Academies, though expensive, had to be created if the Americans didn't want to lose the war. In addition to academies, other means of attracting men capable of becoming good leaders had to be found quickly or else the country was soon going to have a shortage of them. "The bulk of the officers of our army are a parcel of ignorant stupid men …. As the army now stands it is only a Receptacle for ragamuffins,"[28] Knox lamented to his brother William.

Later that year Knox again found himself moving heavy guns across an icy river. Washington had decided to cross the Delaware on Christmas night and catch the pig-tailed and mustachioed Hessians at Trenton by surprise. As Colonel John Glover's Marblehead fishermen arrived and departed during the ferrying operation, the nervous Knox barked out directions in a deep voice and paced incessantly by the waterway's bank. Initially the thinking was that the vital crossing could not succeed, but when it was completed about twenty-four-hundred men and eighteen fieldpieces had reached the other side of the river.

The men then advanced towards the Hessian garrison. But by the time they made it there, snow and sleet had left the firing pans of their muskets so wet that they were to a great extent useless. As a result, heavy guns had to play the crucial role in the ensuing battle. Understanding that, Knox placed his cannon at both ends of the small village—at a point where two main streets converged in front of it, and by Assunpink Bridge, which the Hessians had to cross to escape from Trenton.

When the firing began on the morning of the twenty-sixth, a rout became inevitable; the Hessians were in no condition to fight well because they had been drinking heavily the night before to celebrate the holiday. American batteries in the first location quickly mowed down the surprised and sleepy Germans as they came out of their huts, and knocked out their cannon. Meanwhile, at the second location canister shot fired from patriot guns ripped through columns of advancing enemy soldiers and coated the bridge with red. The action did not last long, but more than nine hundred Hessians were captured and another thirty were killed. Among the latter group was the garrison's commander, Colonel Johann Rall. All this was accomplished at a cost of only five casualties to Washington's forces. And the Americans were able to enjoy a breakfast from their foe's Christmas leftovers.

About one week later a large number of troops under Cornwallis advanced on the Americans and almost reversed the results of the twenty-sixth, initially taking much of Trenton. But Knox's artillery eventually drove them back across Assunpink Creek.

By dawn the following day, January 3, 1777, Washington had flanked Cornwallis's army. His vanguard then battled reinforcements heading for the British general but was overwhelmed. Fortunately, Knox's gunners checked the British, buying time for Washington's main body to arrive and lead a rally. When the action finally ended, the Americans had scored another decisive victory.

Knox then spent some time in Massachusetts and from there went to Morristown, where Washington's troops were quartered for the winter. While there, the now Brigadier General Knox—Congress had promoted him even before learning of the victory at Trenton—saw his position as chief of artillery become endangered. Phillipe du Coudray had arrived from France and gone to the delegates to receive a commission as a major general and appointment as Washington's chief of artillery; they had been promised to him by Silas Deane, an American envoy in France. But how could Congress honor that promise without either angering Washington and reassigning Henry Knox or damaging its envoys' chances of getting France to formally ally itself with America in the war effort?

Regardless of Deane's promise, Washington did not want to lose his valuable chief of artillery. So he quickly sent a letter off to Congress. Knox possessed good judgment, had read extensively about the military, and had put the artillery on solid ground. Replacing him with du Coudray would greatly upset the artillery.

Others—Knox, Nathanael Greene, and John Sullivan—also wrote Congress. The delegates had better watch their steps. If they placed the Frenchman with supposed expertise in artillery ahead of them, they hinted, they were going to resign their commissions.

This implied threat, though, only offended the delegates and caused them to demand that the three generals either apologize or resign. Knox, Greene, and Sullivan did not bother to respond and eventually du Coudray's own hubris ended the dispute; he drowned after being thrown into the Schuylkill River by his horse as he vaingloriously rode instead of walked it onto a ferry.

The delegates' insistence that they had the right to make foreigners with good connections high-ranking generals and elevate them above American generals, both in this case and in others, hurt relations between Congress and the army. Our officers were sensitive about their ranks. They had a pronounced sense of personal honor and thought they deserved respect because they were from the better class of society, the landowners. They did not want to be treated like ordinary soldiers, who were from the lower classes.

The delegates, though, often yielded to political pressure and also had a very negative opinion of American officers. They were "Mastiffs, Scrambling for Rank and Pay like Apes for Nuts,"[29] was how John Adams put it. They, like the soldiers they commanded, were to be feared. They were a threat to American liberties.

Knox did nothing to cause Washington, Greene, and Sullivan to regret their championing him. Though the Americans suffered another defeat at the Battle of Brandywine in September 1777, Knox's artillerymen again performed their duty admirably in "most severe action." In a report to Congress, the Commander-in-chief claimed they had fired with greater accuracy than had their British counterparts. Even when British troops swarmed over them, American gunners by and large remained close to their cannon until they met their deaths or were forced to leave their positions. Knox and his regiment had "behaved with their usual coolness and intrepidity,"[30] one newspaper wrote.

At Germantown the following month Knox's artillery was once again active, surrounding and pounding the beautiful stone home of Pennsylvania Chief Justice Benjamin Chew, whose second floor was occupied by British defenders. Though his guns destroyed its windows, knocked in the front door and put a hole in its roof, the large house's thick walls withstood the fire and held up the American advance long enough to turn an apparent victory into a defeat. Nonetheless, Washington did not blame the general for the Americans' lack of success.

Stays at Valley Forge and in Boston followed, and Knox saw more action during the summer of 1778, when the British evacuated Philadelphia and Washington took off in pursuit and caught them near Monmouth Courthouse. During "the hard-fought contest" there the artillery chief flashed back and forth across the battlefield, surveying enemy positions and indicating where guns were to be positioned on his flanks. "No officer was more distinguished than General Knox. In the front of the battle, he was seen animating the soldiers and directing the thunder of their cannon. His skill and bravery were so conspicuous that he received the particular approbation of the commander-in-chief in the general orders issued on the day succeeding the battle."[31]

Knox's last major action, at Yorktown, earned him a promotion to major general. Blasts from his siege guns and French artillery caused homes to collapse and British ships in the harbor to catch fire. "One could not avoid the horribly many cannon balls either inside or outside the city. ... Many men were badly injured and mortally wounded by the fragments of bombs, which exploded partly in the air and partly on the ground, their arms and legs severed or themselves struck dead. ... One saw men lying nearly everywhere who were mortally wounded." The accuracy of the American guns was truly impressive. "You fire better than the French," Lafayette supposedly gushed to Captain Samuel Shaw, one of Knox's aides. "And the progress of your artillery is regarded by everyone as one of the wonders of the Revolution."[32]

By November 1782, Knox's reputation as an effective head of the artillery was well established. He had displayed organizational and administrative skills, selected able officers, trained his men, and developed an extraordinary esprit de corps among the gunners who served under him. And his accomplishments were especially remarkable because throughout the war he had no uniformity of guns and ammunition, and the latter was often incompatible with the former.

But he had also come to believe the army's wartime problems were so great that only a change in the structure of the national government could solve them. He had seen the shortages, the delays in transport, the war profiteering, the depreciating currency, the pay arrears, and the inaction of Congress. The government, he concluded, had to be given more power.

Chapter Nine

"We Have Borne All That Men Can Bear"

ON NOVEMBER 25, 1782, the day after the delegation representing all the lines in the Hudson Highlands met at West Point and established a committee to draft the petition, Knox wrote Secretary of War Lincoln. The Massachusetts officers' petition to their state concerning their postwar pensions had "produced much chagrin." All the wiser legislators supported having the state provide the officers with the promised compensation as long as Congress ultimately approved it, but a letter from Samuel Osgood had convinced a majority of the members to postpone taking up the measure. Consequently, the officers had decided to appeal to the delegates in Philadelphia. They wanted some pay, a settlement of their accounts, and either the half-pay pension or some other form of postwar compensation. "Something must be done to releive their present distress, which is intollerable," Knox emphasized. The officers "must have a full Confidence concerning the execution of the half pay either in its present form, or in some other that may be more agreeable." Almost all of them would prefer the latter, but they were very worried that the appearance of their petition might be used by legislators to abrogate the measure promising half pay—"their only security" for the future. If they did do something like that, the general wanted Congress to recommend "to the different States who dislike the half pay" that they provide the officers with a number of years' full pay after the war.[1]

THE OFFICERS were wise to think about their postwar security. On November 30 the Americans and British reached an agreement on a preliminary peace treaty. When Parliament opened a few days later, King George III made a speech recognizing America's independence; he was going to lose his farms—his colonies.[2] A formal treaty bringing the war to an official end was the only remaining goal for the commissioners in Paris to actively pursue.

THE COMMITTEE'S WORK was read to the officers representing the whole army on December 1 and "voted to be laid before the several lines … for consideration." Additionally, the officers decided that another committee, one comprised of a general officer chosen by "the army at large" and two field officers selected by peers, should be established and sent to Philadelphia "to wait on Congress and execute the business of said address." Money would be raised to pay for their trip, and that committee's members would act according to instructions prepared for them.[3]

RHODE ISLAND'S DECISION to reject the impost could not have pleased Nathanael Greene, if he knew of it when he wrote Robert Morris in early December. "It is hard to conceive what can give birth to that jealousy which prevails in some if not all the States of the growing power of Congress," the general wrote. After all, Congress's power came only from the states and ceased at the end of every year. The jealousy and the feeling that Philadelphia must not encroach upon the individual states' authority existed because "Members of Congress have a permanent interest in the State to which they belong while they have only a transient or temporary standing in Congress." The body was therefore more likely to assume too little authority than too much.

Even "Men of good sense and great information" did not support the Impost of 1781. And the states that had the best reason for supporting it actually were the ones "least willing to delagate the necessary powers for the purpose." That, Greene feared, was "too much the temper of the Southern States." Those states insisted that they were "compleat independent sovereign States; forgetting that the powers delagated to Congress [we]re … retrenchments essential to their sovereignty." Still, a general funding plan could be established. However, it had to "be grounded on obvious principles and conducted with great delicasy."[4]

THE SAME DAY Greene wrote Morris, December 3, Lincoln responded to Knox's letter of November 25. The secretary had recently visited the encampment[5] and upon his return to Philadelphia had "represented to Congress in very strong terms the distresses which really existed in the army from the want of pay," asserting that "the most disagreeable consequences were to be feared if some supply should not be given before the close of the year." He based his assertion not "on the vague whispers of [the] idle and disaffected but on the apprehensions of those who have the best intentions and the best means of information." As for the anxious officers, their greatest concern, Lincoln informed Congress, was half pay. If the body urged the states to provide that promised benefit to the officers of their respective lines, most of them would be happier.

In response to his representations, the secretary continued, Congress had asked Robert Morris to report on the army's pay. He thought the delegates would recommend to the states that they take care of all pay arrears up to January 1, 1781, for men in their own lines, and believed that half pay "might be referred to the several States but so as not to absolve Congress from their promise should the States neglect the settlement." When the three officers chosen to deliver the petition to Philadelphia arrived, he expected them to "have a very easy task in all the matters saving that of procuring the money instantly." But even in regard to that exception, he knew Morris was doing his best, and he had confidence that the Financier would eventually get some immediate pay for the army.

Lincoln then promised to do everything in his power to ensure that the army's accounts were settled and permanent funding for the pensions was established. Success would be greatly determined by the steps taken regarding half pay, he opined, and he knew the delegates were going to let him express his views on that concern.

But he really thought the only way they could get that or any other form of postwar compensation was by having the question "referred for a settlement to the several States." He did not expect Congress to receive the funding necessary to pay for the benefit. Half pay had never been greatly supported, and the impost, which could only be used to pay for that benefit, appeared unlikely to pass anyway. And if that tax—the least objectionable one—was not able to pass, none could.[6]

THE BALLOTS CAST to choose officers to deliver the petition to Congress were opened on Thursday, December 5, at Norton's Tavern. The general officer chosen by the army was Major General Alexander McDougall, a tall man with broad shoulders who loved snuff and spoke with a burr. He was not present for the opening of the ballots and had to be informed promptly of his selection; a meeting for the signing of the petition, which had by now been approved by the various lines, was scheduled for the seventh and his attendance was necessary. The two field officers selected to accompany him to Philadelphia were John Brooks, one of the three colonels who had been to Boston, and Colonel Matthias Ogden.[7]

At around ten in the morning on Saturday the seventh, Knox left West Point for the tavern. There he, a dozen other high-ranking officers—three generals, eight colonels, and a major—and Dr. William Eustis signed the petition and made final preparations for sending it on to Congress. Well over half of the officers who signed were from the Massachusetts and Connecticut Lines. That many were from Massachusetts was natural; more than half the men serving in the Hudson Highlands were from that state's line. Only one officer each signed for the New York Line, the New Hampshire Line, and the New Jersey Line. None of the three officers chosen to deliver the address to Philadelphia were signatories to it.[8]

McDougall, the ranking member of the delegation, received the petition the same day and was given instructions. The general and the two colonels were going to Congress to represent the officers of the army "in matters of the most interesting nature." They were "to inforce our Address in the most modest terms—yet in that Steady manner that is expressive of the Characters of officers, and [of the] justices our requisitions demand." They would be free to make their own decisions during negotiations concerning commutation—the replacement of the half-pay pension with a less objectionable postwar benefit—but the officers in the Hudson Highlands wanted to be consulted "previous to a final conclusion," and the three representatives were not supposed to end their efforts in Philadelphia until the delegates gave "their full determination" on the address.[9]

Although the petition had been signed by the officers and received by McDougall, it still had to be copied. But when Major General John Paterson wrote his fellow Massachusetts native Henry Knox on the ninth, he still had not found someone to copy it for him. His first choice to transcribe it, a captain, was not able to do so because of the "hurry of business," and his second choice, Colonel Philip Van Cortlandt, also was unable to furnish him with a good copy. Consequently, Paterson briefly provided Knox with only "the former copy." Once he obtained a copy he liked and got it signed, he wasted no time in sending it to him.

Knox signed the good copy of the petition, returned it to Paterson and requested that he have the other officers sign it. Paterson said he would do so and then give it to Colonel Brooks.[10]

Were the address and the personal appeals by McDougall and the two colonels to the delegates in Philadelphia going to yield fruit for the army? Lieutenant Colonel Ebenezer Huntington certainly must have hoped so. "The troops are very uneasy for want of pay & have appointed a Committee to wait on Congress to Obtain Pay & some other Matters which they consider themselves as fully entitled to, tho' not in so much need of," he had written on the ninth. "The event of the embassy *must* be agreeable to the Line," he stressed, "or I dread the Consequences."[11]

WHEN KNOX DRAFTED the petition—"the memorial"—he began by noting that the army was experiencing "great distress" because it had not been paid. "We have struggled with our difficulties, year after year, under the hopes that each would be the last; but we have been disappointed," the general lamented. "Our embarrassments thicken so fast ... that many of us are unable to go further." With needs so pressing, he and his companions in arms now had no choice but to petition Congress. All the delegates had to do was look for themselves at the paymaster's records for the last four years to see that they were enduring "hardships ... exceedingly disproportionate to those of any other citizens." And Congress could not claim that the states had settled their accounts by providing the men with "securities for the pay due" because they had little value. Aside from that, the general added, "many have been under the sad necessity of parting with them, to prevent their families from actually starving." Only "shadows have been offered to us," Knox protested, "while the substance has been gleaned by others."

The people could complain about being taxed too much and express surprise that the army received none of the revenue collected, but the army really did never see any of the money collected from them; "numerous [other] demands" always managed to "swallow up the whole" of the revenue collected before its turn came.

Now Congress had to act! The army's complaints could not be ignored any longer. "Our distresses are now brought to a point," Knox reminded the delegates. "We have borne all that men can bear—our property is expended—our private resources are at an end, and our friends are wearied and disgusted with our incessant applications." Philadelphia had to come up with some money for the army quickly. "The uneasiness of the soldiers, for want of pay, is great and dangerous; any further experiments on their patience may have fatal effects," he warned. They were fed up with being made to suffer when the government was unable to find the funds, the will, or the authority to help them.

Lack of pay was not the only problem. Congress had failed to provide the rations, clothing and forage they were due. As a result they were "invariably ... the sufferers, by hunger and nakedness, and by languishing in an hospital." The men and officers should be monetarily compensated as much as possible, and whatever else they were still due the government ought to "put on such a footing as will restore cheerfulness to the army, revive confidence in the justice and generosity of its constituents, and contribute to the very desirable effect of reestablishing public credit."

As for the half-pay pensions that Congress had promised them in the fall of 1780, the officers already involuntarily retired as a result of reductions in forces weren't receiving them and in too many places were being made "the objects of obloquy." That discouraged Knox and his fellow officers and they called for that situation to be looked at and redressed. The pension was "honorable and just recompence for several years hard service" that had left "the health and fortunes of the officers ... worn down and exhausted," and they wanted to believe, "for the honour of human nature," that nobody could be "so hardened in the sin of ingratitude, as to deny the justice of the reward."

Maybe, the public opposed "the mode only." If so, the officers were ready to accept something other than half pay for life in order to preserve "harmony ... throughout the community." One possibility was "full pay for a certain number of years." Another was a lump sum payment at the conclusion of the war.

Knox then turned his attention to others. "The disabled officers and soldiers, with the widows and orphans of those who have expended or may expend their lives in the service of their country," must be covered by the pension plan, as had been promised. And men who had agreed to serve for the duration of the war must be rewarded with eighty-dollar completion-of-service bounties; Congress had agreed to do so on May 15, 1778, and now the petitioning officers wished for the delegates to indicate "some mode ... for the eventual payment of those soldiers."

The general closed the petition by expressing his faith in Congress to take their grievances seriously. No trifling with them! "It would be criminal in the officers to conceal the general dissatisfaction which prevails, and is gaining ground in the army," Knox declared. The army's mood resulted from "seven long years" of "evils and injuries" that often left it in "wretched" shape, and the officers desired that the delegates "convince the army and the world that the independence of America shall not be placed on the ruin of any particular class of her citizens" and that they "point out a mode for immediate redress."[12]

The language in the petition may have been tough, but Washington thought the tone was respectful. Knox later reported to Robert Morris that the Commander-in-chief had "no objection to its presentation."[13]

ON DECEMBER 6, the day after the officers in the Hudson Highlands opened ballots at Norton's Tavern, Congress followed through on a motion by Alexander Hamilton and James Madison and approved sending its own delegation to Rhode Island—"this perverse sister."[14] Recalling some acquaintances from a brief stay in Providence and anticipating that "a train of evils … and many inconveniences" would result from that state's rejection of the impost,[15] Tom Paine spoke with Robert Morris. He too should visit the state; those acquaintances would heed his advice. Morris listened and on the ninth encouraged him to make the trip.

Two days later Hamilton had a letter ready for the delegation to present to Governor William Greene. The impost was "indispensable to the prosecution of the war," and Congress was convinced that once the visiting delegates gave a "just representation of the public affairs," Rhode Island would see that the measure was necessary. Hamilton pointed to "the increasing discontents of the army, the loud clamours [demands] of the public creditors" and one other problem as "so many invincible arguments for the fund recommended by Congress," and asserted that the delegates could not agree on anything better than the impost. If Rhode Island did not approve the impost, "calamities of a most menacing nature" were going to take place, the delegates believed, and it would not be their fault.

One reason for the impost was to make the government's job of securing foreign loans easier. If Philadelphia was not able to obtain revenue, it could not give foreign lenders any guarantee that they were going to be paid back. That made it very difficult to obtain loans. And, Hamilton feared, when Europe learned that Rhode Island had rejected the impost, the news was going to "have a fatal influence on their future progress." Without foreign loans the situation was quite likely to "rapidly hasten to a dangerous crisis" and the states' financial problems were going to become worse than they had ever been, possibly "much more difficult to emerge" from.[16]

The following day, December 9, a letter conveying news of Rhode Island's vote against the impost was read in Congress. David Howell and Jonathan Arnold proposed that the plan to send a delegation to their state now be repealed. Their proposal went nowhere; only Rhode Island voted in favor of it. New Jersey's Abraham Clark then moved that the delegates put off their departure "till the further order of Congress." His motion and the letter announcing the unfavorable vote on the impost were turned over to a three-man committee made up of Hamilton, Madison, and Thomas Fitzsimmons of Pennsylvania.[17]

DURING THE WAR each officer was allowed a servant,[18] and McDougall needed one before he could leave with Colonels Brooks and Ogden for Philadelphia. But by the twelfth he was "destitute a proper waiter" and had to ask Colonel Samuel B. Webb to loan him a soldier to fill that slot. "Some of those allowed me and the family are sick, and all are too rag[g]ed for that service,"[19] he explained.

The general knew that most officers were "reluctant to part with their men," but Webb answered his request by providing him with a soldier a few days later, which was good because the general anticipated leaving soon if the weather permitted, even though he had yet to hear "whether the Commander in Chief had been applied to for his permission to the Committee to go to Phila."[20]

Washington, of course, had already approved the mission.[21] On December 14, as the British evacuated Charleston, he had written Joseph Jones of Virginia to alert Congress that a petition from the officers "on the subject of their grievances" was probably going to arrive within a few days. The Commander-in-chief was not pleased that it had been written, but he knew the officers' discontent was so great that such a step was "just now unavoidable."

As a matter of fact, Washington had been anticipating something even worse. "The temper of the Army is much soured," he alerted his friend, "and has become more irritable than at any period since the commencement of the War. ... The dissatisfactions of the Army had arisen to a great and alarming height," and the decision to write a petition came only after "combinations among the Officers to resign ... in a body, were beginning to take place." His duty was not to tell Congress what to do, but he thought "policy ... should dictate soothing measures." After all, "no part of the community has undergone equal hardships, and borne them with the same patience and fortitude, that the Army has done," he proudly declared.

The officers in his army had up to now remained loyal. They had "in more instances than one, at the hazard of their lives ... quelled very dangerous mutinies." Could Congress be certain they would remain loyal to the government and restore order when their men again rose up and made noise about achieving justice at the points of their bayonets? Washington was beginning to have his doubts. "If their discontents should be suffered to rise equally high [as those of their soldiers]," he reflected, "I know not what the consequences may be."

In the past "the spirit of enthusiasm" alone kept the army going no matter what hardships it endured. Those days, though, were long gone. Now Congress could not expect the army to refrain from complaining about what was going on—Philadelphia making an "invidious distinction" of choosing to pay civilian government officials everything they were due, while military personnel got "no part ... of their pay."[22]

THE POSSIBILITY THAT the officers would resign en masse was real, Washington had to know. Back on May 6, 1779, a day when the New Jersey Line learned that it was going to be part of a campaign against the Six Nations, its regimental officers made such a threat after a petition to their legislature had been ignored. They had wanted something done about their supply and pay problems.[23]

Upon learning of the situation, Washington felt more pained than he had at any other time in the war. He especially feared the consequences if others throughout the army followed their example. The Revolution would come to a ruinous and disgraceful end solely because the New Jersey officers had "*reasoned wrong about the means of obtaining a good end.*" They had "hazarded a step," the general believed, "which has an air of dictating terms to their country, by taking advantage of the necessity of the moment."[24]

When Washington wrote the President of Congress on the eleventh, he said he disapproved of what the New Jersey officers had done but felt disciplining them was out of the question. He knew that they had good reason to be discontent and that the dissatisfaction was widespread. Also, "the ties ... bind[ing] the officers to the service [were] too feeble to admit of rigor."[25]

Some members of the New Jersey legislature, though, wanted to have "the Brigade Disbanded [rather] than ... Submit to the appearance of being bullied."[26] But most did not favor taking that step because they thought America could not win independence if it did not employ a regular army. Eventually a compromise was reached, whereby the legislators would try to obtain new clothing for the New Jersey Line and immediately provide each officer and each soldier with two hundred pounds and a forty-dollar bounty, respectively, in exchange for a withdrawal of the petition. The officers and men were satisfied and marched out of camp for Easton, Pennsylvania, on May 11 to join forces under John Sullivan in the campaign against the Six Nations.

ON DECEMBER 16, 1782, Congress answered Rhode Island's rejection of the impost with a long report drafted by Hamilton. The state's claim that it would be especially hurt because the impost placed the tax burden on the shoulders of importers such as itself was not valid. When it supplied others that could not import commodities from abroad, it would simply pass on the costs of those taxes to them. That principle applied in commerce between states as much as it did in commerce between individual merchants and their customers.

As for Rhode Island's contention that its constitution prohibited the use of congressionally-appointed tax collectors, Hamilton dismissed it. Congress could appoint any number of whatever officials it wanted when that was necessary for "the general welfare." Now the country's general welfare required that Philadelphia have funding, and there was "a common interest in an uniform and equally energetic collection" of the necessary taxes. Therefore the delegates could appoint collectors and send them into the states to ensure that they all paid their fair share of taxes. If they did not do so, justice might not be served; "a very unequal tax" might result.

Hamilton then moved on to Rhode Island's assertion that no indication had been given as to how long the impost was to remain in effect. That was not true, Hamilton retorted; it would only remain in effect as long as necessary to liquidate debt incurred during the war. Congress had no desire to "perpetuate that debt"; the delegates wanted "to discharge it in a moderate time."

He also asserted that the tiny state was incorrect in saying no limits on the size of the taxes in the impost bill had been specified. Rates were fixed and the government was not free to raise them, although they would differ from one good to another "according to the variations in trade."

The strong nationalist next expressed some views certain to anger Rhode Island. Congress's authority to requisition specific sums from the states amounted to a legal authority to raise money by taxing Americans, and the government had "an absolute discretion in determining the quantum of revenue requisite for the national expenditure." The only thing left for the states to do once the amount needed had been determined was to decide *how* they would raise the revenue. "No state can dispute the obligation to pay the sum demanded without a breach of the confederation, and when the money comes into the treasury, the appropriation is the exclusive province of the Foederal government," Hamilton insisted. "The measure in question [the impost] if not within the letter is within the spirit of the confederation. Congress … are empowered to borrow money for the use of the United States, and by implication to concert the means necessary to accomplish the end."

Besides being within the spirit of the confederation, the impost was needed to ensure that foreign and domestic creditors were treated justly. Failure to pay them at least the interest on their loans would be "the deepest ingratitude and cruelty to a large number of meritorious individuals, who in the most critical periods of the war have adventured their fortunes in support of our independence. It would stamp the national character with indelible disgrace."

Later the New York delegate concluded his letter by reminding the state that Congress was responsible for running the war but did not have "any competent means at their command" to do that satisfactorily. The delegates had finally proposed the impost as "the corner stone of ... public safety," but then had watched as it remained "suspended for near two years." Some states had not fully complied with the measure, and Rhode Island had endangered the impost by rejecting it. The delegates were pained by what they were seeing: the government's financial health worsening daily, "the dissatisfaction of the army growing more serious, the other creditors of the public clamouring for justice, both irritated by the delay of measures for their present relief or future security, the hopes of our enemies encouraged to protract the war, the zeal of our friends depressed by an appearance of remissness and want of exertion on our part, Congress harassed, the national character suffering and the national safety at the mercy of events."[27]

"I DESIRED DOCTOR Eustis to inform you that the General [George Washington], had with the greatest readiness consented to your going to Philadelphia, and approved it," Knox wrote to McDougall the following day. The Massachusetts general was enclosing "a long letter from General Lincoln"[28]—almost certainly the one he had written on the third. It would show McDougall that the secretary and the officers were of like mind, and Knox encouraged the Scotsman to see Lincoln after arriving in Philadelphia. The secretary had indicated to Knox that he was anxious to settle the army's accounts and secure half pay.[29]

Three days later, on December 20, Knox wrote Lincoln and meticulously made preparations for Congress to receive the petition. He thought "the accounts up to the present period ought to be settled by somebody" and that somebody in his mind was the states. If nobody did anything to settle the army's accounts, he expected trouble. "The expectations of the army, from the drummer to the highest officers, are so keen for *some* pay," he stressed, "that I shudder at the idea of their not receiving it. The utmost period of sufferance … has arrived. To attempt to lengthen it will undoubtedly occasion commotions."[30]

Captain Samuel Shaw, a well-educated twenty-eight-year-old son of a successful merchant, also expected some commotions. "The uneasiness … in the army" could be seen everywhere. "It pervades every breast, from the major-general downwards," wrote the Massachusetts officer to Reverend John Eliot. "We have experienced for years … the most oppressive treatment that ever an army endured. Could we suppose that the country is unable to prevent or remove the grievances under which we labor … no people under heaven … would support them with greater cheerfulness. But this is not the case. We see the most unequal conduct observed towards us, and, of the enormous sums of money levied for carrying on the war, no part reaches the army. Its distribution invariably among the numerous civil officers throughout the continent, while the soldiery are wholly excluded, aggravates their sufferings, and seems like adding insult to injury."

Shaw was "happy for the country" that McDougall, Ogden, and Brooks were going to Philadelphia to petition Congress because that was the only thing capable of keeping the army quiet. The delegates were now going to become "fully acquainted with the sufferings and the disposition of their troops." They were going to see from the tone of the petition that the army was ready to march off if it were not paid, no matter how bad off that left the country. The captain hoped the petition would produce "the desired effect." If it did not, the consequences were going to be unspeakably bad.[31]

Either the day before or the day after Shaw wrote those words, the delegation set out for

Philadelphia.³² McDougall had expected to leave on the morning of the seventeenth, but the weather apparently did not cooperate.³³ It also had taken some time to make copies of the petition, and he had needed almost two weeks to raise enough money to pay for the trip.³⁴

ONE PERSON ANTICIPATING the arrival of the delegation was Major General Arthur St. Clair. He was in Philadelphia on extended leave to tend to personal matters. He had seen Robert Morris on November 15 to ask when the army was going to be paid and then three days later had written that he was "about four hundred Pounds in Debt, and … not possessed of one Shilling in Money." While serving his country admirably he had been forced to part with "a most valuable Plantation and three Houses" and had never been reimbursed for duty-related expenses. The general was "in absolute Want." He still had valuable property, he admitted, but he was not able to use it as collateral to obtain money. And his family, which was large, depended upon him.³⁵

Though Morris had much sympathy for St. Clair, he could not promise any help. The government's financial situation was "totally uncertain" and the state legislatures were doing "next to Nothing," thus causing "their most faithful Servants to suffer for their Cruelty and Injustice."³⁶

St.Clair understood Morris's predicament and reasoned that nothing might hurt as much as having "to hear of and be witness to Distress without [having the] power of relieving it." Therefore he would not bother Morris with any more appeals. But he did ask that his accounts be settled and that he be given "a Certificate for the Balance."³⁷

Sometime in December the general wrote McDougall, Ogden, and Brooks to advise them; he had some definite ideas on what Pennsylvania troops thought should be done. He noted that Pennsylvania had shown a willingness to provide its line officers who fought for the duration with the half-pay pensions promised by Congress. However, if the state were unable to do so, the national government would still be expected to fulfill its promise. Consequently, the Pennsylvania Line wanted the delegates to have general funds, which were needed to make that postwar compensation a certainty.

As for the army's pay arrears, he did not anticipate the soldiers and officers receiving what they were owed before they were disbanded. What could be done, though, was to make arrangements so they got regular interest payments on securities for what they were owed. To achieve that, a plan uniting the army with the public creditors was "worthy of every serious consideration." Such a union promised to influence the states and increase the army's chances of being paid.

"Congress ought to be informed, in the most express and positive terms, that … without an immediate payment and a certainty of it in the future … the army can not be kept together," St. Clair emphasized, "and that without it there is every reason to expect a convulsion of the most dreadful nature and fatal consequences." No matter how the delegates chose to compensate the soldiers and officers, though, his advice was that "the whole army ... throw themselves upon Congress"; if some lines broke off and went back to their respective states to seek their just dues, there was no guarantee they would receive anything once peace arrived and legislatures were free to look after local interests.

The general then shared his thoughts on the current confederation. Under it Congress was weak and delegates too often followed "the little local policy of their respective States." So what was the solution? Let the issue of army debts "be thrown upon the continent at large," and do not allow the army to be disbanded. Congress would then be able to speak forcefully to any difficult state. That "might be the happy means of procuring justice" and, "by securing the national faith and national character," of establishing and preserving a "great and respectable" nation. Otherwise, all their "best years ... fortunes, and ... blood" would have been spent "to no purpose, or to a very bad one, that of becoming the most abject and despicable people on the face of the earth."

With regard to those states claiming to be opposed only to the mode of compensation for the officers, St. Clair thought they were being disingenuous; they were making such claims "only to cover their dislike to rewarding the men who have made them free." They were guilty of "a horrid instance of ingratitude, which, though a disgrace to human nature, is unhappily not uncommon."

Such skepticism and cynicism was not expressed in the petition, but it certainly existed, and the officers' offer to accept some mode of postwar compensation other than a lifelong half-pay pension would test Congress's sincerity. St. Clair did not say that, but he and the underappreciated officers who were petitioning Philadelphia understood that. Was Congress really opposed only to a lifelong pension?

The general was sure adoption of his plan would not prevent a state and its line from later reaching a compromise. And if a state agreed to commutation for its officers, it should be allowed to pay them and reduce its requisition quota by an amount equal to the payments made.

The general ended his letter by specifying which types of officers and whose corps had no choice but to rely entirely on Congress and noting the aversion of some lines to going back to their states for justice. "Should the army divide, and some throw themselves upon Congress and some upon their respective States, nothing will be done by either," he predicted. "Congress will want the power, and the States, I fear, will want the will."[38]

Chapter Ten

"The Most Intelligent Members Were Deeply Affected"

ON DECEMBER 21, Tench Tilghman, who had been sent to Philadelphia to deliver Washington's letter to Joseph Jones, visited Robert Morris's office. There he shared "some very necessary information respecting the present State and Temper of the army"[1] and likely told the Financier that a delegation was soon going to arrive in Philadelphia to petition Congress.[2]

The next day a congressional committee made up of Thomas Mifflin, Abner Nash, and Samuel Osgood mounted their horses and departed for Rhode Island to lobby the General Assembly there. They planned to "make a full and just representation of the public affairs of the United States," answer the legislators' objections, and "describe in the most pointed Language the unhappy Consequences That would probably result from their Denial of the solicited Impost." All the states except Rhode Island and Georgia had agreed to the impost, but Congress apparently was worried only about the small northeastern state.[3]

The committee members, though, never got a chance to make their case for the impost in person. They had covered only "about Eight or Ten Miles" on frozen roads, when one of the members, Nash of North Carolina, "casually mentioned a private letter from Mr. Pendleton to Mr. Madison informing [him] that the Legislature of Virga. had in consequence of the final refusal of R. I. repealed her law for the impost."[4] Maryland was also supposedly "receding" from its earlier approval of the duties and rumors of such a movement certainly were believable because its ratification was only going to go into effect if all the other states agreed to the measure.[5]

"Convinced ... that it was in vain to go to Rhode Island till the Matter was fully ascertained," the members abandoned their mission and headed back to Philadelphia.[6] In the end only Tom Paine reached their original destination, where from early January to early February he wrote essays for publication in Providence newspapers and was openly attacked in print by other writers for being an agent of Congress.[7]

Not long after the "rather chagrined" committee members returned to the capital, mail confirming the bad news arrived for Congress.[8] The situation was truly alarming. The government now faced the prospect of being powerless to obtain needed revenue from the states. The decision by Virginia was going to strengthen the resolve of tiny Rhode Island. "The most intelligent members were deeply affected & prognosticated a failure of the Impost scheme, & the most pernicious effects [to] the character, the duration, & the interests of the confederacy."[9] Gouverneur Morris believed the only way the union was going to stay intact was if it were ruled by "an absolute monarchy," but he knew the American people were opposed to that form of government. "The necessary consequence," he suspected, was going to be "a separation ... and consequently [civil] wars."

But Morris had not completely given up hope. Greene and his army might be able to influence the southern states, where he enjoyed "very much the confidence" of them. "If the army, in common with all other public creditors, insist on the grant of general permanent funds for liquidating all the public debts, there can be little doubt that such revenues will be obtained,"[10] the Financier's peglegged assistant declared.

For the time being, though, the best way to raise revenue seemed to be by taxing land. The way land was to be evaluated for such purposes had been laid down in the Articles of Confederation, but it was unwieldy. "The difficulties which attend that rule of apportionment seem on near inspection to be ... insuperable,"[11] Madison would later complain. He understood that the richer states were hostile to such taxes because they feared being asked to pony up more than their fair share of the money the government wanted.[12]

Perhaps, the delegates could devise a different system of evaluation agreeable to all. James Wilson suggested that taxes be based on both land and population. He, Madison, and Daniel Carroll were then put on a committee that was to meet with Robert Morris and hammer out an acceptable plan.[13]

BY THE BEGINNING of the 1782–83 winter most of Washington's soldiers were in New Windsor, New York. The cantonment there was just a few miles west of the Hudson, south of Newburgh and across from Fishkill, the longtime home for "the principal Depot of the American Army."[14]

The first soldiers to reach New Windsor had marched out of their summer camp at Verplanck's Point to Constitution Island with "no covering but the heavens" on the rainy morning of October 26, 1782, "crossed the Hudson in boats to West-Point" the next day, wearily marched up the more-than-thirteen-hundred-foot Butter Hill that afternoon, "halted and passed the night on the northern descent of the hill, in the open field."[15] At seven the following morning they started up again. The men "generally marched in the best order and with great regularity," arriving at the location where "they were to build their huts" around 10:30 a.m. The rest of the army soon followed,[16] and eventually the number of men, women, children and camp followers quartered in the area probably reached about seventy-five-hundred or eight thousand.[17]

The area was behind the two-hundred-foot granite Snake Hill, conveniently located where overland routes from New England and the middle and southern states intersected. Its proximity to the Hudson meant that New York City down south and Lake Champlain up north were easily reachable by water. It also was only two miles away from the Red Tavern, where young officers would be able to meet when they were off duty.[18]

After arriving in New Windsor the soldiers began building huts. It was very hard work, and Washington had warned them beforehand that any hut "built irregularly" would be torn down. Besides "*regularity,*" the Commander-in-chief wanted the huts to have "*convenience,* and even some degree of *elegance.*"[19]

Colonel Pickering provided instructions on their locations and dimensions, but a small number of men did not heed the Commander-in-chief's warning and saw their almost completed works leveled. Nonetheless, the men "bec[ame] so adroit and perfect in the Art of Hutting" that both General Gates and Washington could not help but be pleased. Nowhere else "in the Continent" would they "be more comfortable and better Lodged" than in these quarters, Gates believed. More than sixteen hundred acres of what had been woods and meadows only a couple months before were turned into a "regular and beautiful" cantonment with about seven hundred huts for soldiers and officers.[20]

The soldiers' huts varied in size according to regiment. Those built for the New York and Massachusetts men measured thirty-five feet by eighteen feet, while those in which the New Jersey, Maryland, and New Hampshire soldiers lived were twenty-seven feet by eighteen feet. Living space was not great; there were thirty-two men to a hut in the New York and Massachusetts regiments, for example, and they slept in bunk beds. The soldiers' huts had low ceilings and one window each and were arranged "in two regular straight lines." The lines were twenty feet apart from each other.

The officers' huts had two windows and offered their occupants more living space; fewer officers were quartered together under the same roofs. Their huts were located behind those of the soldiers. The structures built for captains and below were forty feet back from the rear of the soldiers' quarters, and those for field officers were another sixty feet further to the rear. All the huts, whether built for soldiers or officers, were partitioned and had Dutch jambless chimneys.[21]

Later the men moved to a nearby low hill in the middle of the camp to begin constructing a large, rectangular, one-story building of wooden logs and crudely cut planks. Its construction had been suggested by the energetic Captain Israel Evans,[22] a thirty-six-year-old Pennsylvanian serving as the New Hampshire regiments' chaplain. The suggestion of "this useful work ... met with the entire approbation of the commander in chief and almost every General, field and regimental officer" who knew of it.[23] The administrative departments of the army in the Hudson Highlands were located a good distance from each other, and the daily task of delivering the many papers they produced to the right addressees consumed too much time. A centrally located headquarters building would solve that problem. Also, Washington realized that the building could be utilized to foster better relations between the officers from the different states and provide a place for worship, celebrations, and special meetings. And its construction was expected to keep soldiers' minds off their troubles.

The Commander-in-chief issued general orders announcing his approval on December 25, 1782, and Gates was put in charge of the work, which was expected to be completed in fifteen days. But it would actually take the men almost two months to finish the job.[24]

Staff officers would call the structure the "Public Building," riflemen the "New Building,"[25] and Captain Evans "The Temple of Virtue."[26]

Chapter Eleven

"Brutus"

McDOUGALL, BROOKS, AND OGDEN reached Philadelphia the afternoon of December 29, 1782.[1] On the way there they had been delayed "by bad and cold weather,"[2] and when they finally arrived their resources were limited, a fact that was subsequently talked about around town.[3]

Those who wanted to strengthen Congress looked forward to receiving the officers' petition. "The representations with which they [McDougall, Brooks, and Ogden] are charged," Madison wrote to Edmund Randolph, "have not been handed in but I am told they breathe a proper spirit and are full of good sense." The petition promised to help the nationalists advance their agenda by providing them with "new topics in favor of the Impost." The officers' grievances, including pay arrears, were certain to be discussed, and Congress was going to have to come up with money for the angry army. The necessity of putting in place a system capable of providing the government with permanent funds would become ever more apparent, and the impost was going to be the most important part of it.[4]

ALEXANDER McDOUGALL[5] WAS born on the Scottish island of Islay in 1732. He, his siblings and his parents, Ranald and Elizabeth, lived in a small two-room cottage with walls made of stone and peat, a straw roof, and an earthen floor. Ranald was a poor, hard-working farmer and his family was very religious.

During the summer of 1738 Ranald and Elizabeth obtained from their minister a letter attesting to the family's sobriety, honesty, and industriousness, visited the graves of their three children who had died in childhood, and departed for America. Later that year they arrived in New York.

As a child Alick spent much time in the streets of New York City helping his father deliver milk and other farm products. He also studied his Bible, and when he became a teenager his father hoped

General Alexander McDougall

the boy would choose to make his living as a minister; the young boy could use words particularly well and demonstrated real feeling when speaking in public, though he stuttered a bit.

The ministry, though, was not for him: what really attracted him was the sea. At the age of fourteen, after trying his hand as an apprentice tailor for a short time, he began working as an ordinary seaman. Eleven years later he was commanding a sloop. By that time, the summer of 1757, he was also a married man and father of three.

The sloop Captain McDougall commanded was a privateer called the *Tyger*. Since England was at war with France, the *Tyger*'s mission was to go after French merchant ships carrying cargo to and from their colonies in the West Indies. Such a mission could bring him much prize money or result in his death from French guns or violent storms. The latter, in fact, did almost end his life: On September 4 a hurricane dispersed the sloop and the small number of privateers sailing with it, drove huge waves over their sides, swept away cargo, and hurled men into the sea. Although McDougall took drastic action—four cannon were thrown overboard and the ship's mast was cut away—many hours passed before he knew whether the *Tyger* was going to survive. It did but with much damage; the captain had to return to New York to have it repaired and refitted.

After a few weeks in port the *Tyger* was again fit for sailing and it headed for the Carribean. If the crew thought all its misfortunes were behind them, they were wrong; in January 1758 an epidemic of smallpox visited the ship and left five dead.

McDougall's luck finally changed during the spring, when he captured a Dutch sloop believed to be carrying cargo for the French. He later became commander of the larger *General Barrington* and in June 1759 captured the *Saint Esprit*. Those two prizes and others left him well off and allowed him to end his career as a privateer and sail back to New York before the year ended.

With the new decade came greater wealth. Alexander made money by shipping goods to and from the West Indies, the southern colonies, and Canada. He acted as an agent for some planters on the island of St. Croix. He collected interest on loans to New York merchants. He had gains from land investments. And he even profited from renting the services of a slave to a brother-in-law who needed a seaman.

But not everything went well for him during the 1760s. He lost his wife in February 1763 and his father less than a year later. He did remarry in 1767, but while that event must have given him great joy, the actions of his mother country had to have worried him. By that year scores of Americans were angry and fearful for American liberty. The Stamp Act had been repealed, but the Quartering Act was still in effect. Many Americans, including McDougall, had already joined the Sons of Liberty to protest British tyranny.

The following year did not bring an end to American uneasiness. Some prominent merchants, upset over the passage of a number of new taxes, including one on tea, had had enough. Feeling that something had to be done to protest the actions of Parliament, they gathered at Fraunces' Tavern and decided not to import British goods.

In the spring of 1769 the New York General Assembly balked at fully complying with the Quartering Act, which required the state to pay much of the cost associated with garrisoning British soldiers in the colony. However, by mid-December the legislators had decided to give in to Parliament's demands.

McDougall, who had watched the legislators debate the issue, was furious. For almost two days he worked on a broadside, which he titled "To the Betrayed Inhabitants of the City and Colony of New York." He thought that "in this day of constitutional light, the representatives of this colony would not ... be so lost to all sense of duty to their constituents ... as to betray the trust committed to them." By agreeing to pay for the billeting of British troops they were "implicitly acknowledging" that Parliament did not need their consent to tax them. Such an action was cowardly and would lead the British to conclude that America was abandoning its cause.

The only explanation for such an action, especially considering the colony was too poor to afford such an expense, was that a corrupt deal between old Cadwallader Colden, the state's former lieutenant governor, and the powerful DeLancey family had been struck. When Governor Sir Harry Moore died, Colden agreed to come out of retirement and become governor. He had received word that the majority in the General Assembly would grant the money needed to pay for the billeting of British troops and assurances that they were going to give him his "full salary" in exchange for his signing a currency bill that Moore had refused to sign. By putting his signature on it Colden was also providing job security for those of his children who held government offices.

New Yorkers had to rise up. The vote on the Quartering Act had been close, so it was not too late to act. "What I would advise to be done is, to assemble in the fields, on Monday next, where your sense ought to be taken on this important point. ... After this is done, go in a body to your members, and insist on their joining with the minority to oppose the bill; if they dare refuse your just requisition, appoint a committee to draw up a state of the whole matter, and send it to the speakers of the several houses of assembly on the Continent, and to the friends of our cause in England,

and publish it in the newspapers, that the whole world may know your sentiments on this matter," McDougall wrote just before concluding his boadside and signing it "A SON OF LIBERTY."[6]

After finishing his call to action, Alexander and a friend went to the shop of a printer named James Parker, who made several hundred copies of it. That night and the rest of the weekend, from December 16 to December 18, a strong man carried a large box at the end of a pole around the city. Whenever he became too tired to continue, he stopped by the side of a building and set his weighty object against it. As he pretended to rest, a small boy inside the box drew back a sliding panel and pasted a copy of McDougall's work on the structure the man had chosen for a resting spot. The boy then went back inside his box and slid the panel closed. This procedure was repeated until much of the city was plastered with copies of the broadside.

Soon thereafter about fourteen hundred people from all over the city gathered at the Fields, elected a chairman for their meeting, and passed a resolution denouncing the legislators' decision to comply with the Quartering Act. A committee of patriots, which included McDougall, presented that resolution to the legislators at City Hall the following morning, the nineteenth, but its demands were essentially dismissed; the time for changing votes had passed.

The legislators' main concern that morning was the inflammatory broadside that had just appeared. After reviewing it, they condemned it by an almost unanimous vote. They also offered a reward of one hundred pounds for information that led to the discovery of its author.

With an eye on the reward and an axe to grind against the man who had fired him, a young journeyman printer named Michael Cummins came forward with the name of the person who had printed McDougall's work—James Parker. On February 7, 1770, Parker and a few of his apprentice printers were brought in and questioned. When the apprentices were threatened with imprisonment, they corroborated what Cummins had said and admitted that McDougall had come into the shop, corrected Parker's proof and departed with some copies of the broadside. Parker also was threatened with the same punishment and the loss of lucrative government contracts, but he initially claimed that he did not know who had written the angry appeal. However, once he was made aware of what his apprentices had divulged and offered immunity, he identified the broad-shouldered Scotsman as the author.

Alexander was visited at his home by Sheriff John Roberts the following morning and arrested. He was then taken to Chief Justice Daniel Horsmanden's chambers. The Chief Justice said McDougall was in much trouble and later added that "there was full Proof" of his having written or published the broadside, "a false, vile, and scandalous Libel,"[7] but McDougall was not cowed; only a jury had any authority to determine whether he was guilty, he insisted. Eventually, when the Scotsman made clear that he was not going to post bail, which was set at two thousand pounds, the Chief Justice had him put in jail.

While he sat in a cell there, his case became something of a cause célèbre. New York Sons of Liberty thought McDougall's imprisonment was like that of John Wilkes, an English legislator who in 1763 had been thrown in jail after his criticism of a speech by King George III appeared in the forty-fifth issue of the *North Briton*. Newspapers debated the Scotsman's case. Committees of correspondence in other cities and radical politicians backed him, while most members of the Chamber of Commerce and conservative politicians did not. So many people wanted to visit or interview him in his cell that he had to schedule appointments; for three hours, from three to six in the afternoon, people were able to see him.

No better proof that supporters saw him as another Wilkes existed than what happened on the forty-fifth day of the year, February 14. That day "forty-five gentlemen, real enemies to internal taxation by, or in obedience to external authority, and cordial friends of American liberty, went in decent procession to the New Gaol; and dined with him, on forty-five pounds of beef steaks, cut from a bullock of forty-five months old,"[8] one Boston newspaper reported. And they were not his only visitors; forty-five "virgins"[9] came and conversed with him, had tea, cakes, and chocolate, and finished their stay with song. The innocent women were said to be "female lovers of liberty."[10]

A grand jury heard McDougall's case in April and judged him to be "a Person of a Turbulent and unquiet mind and Seditious disposition."[11] He had caused Lieutenant Governor Colden, the New York Council and General Assembly to be subjected to "the utmost hatred, Scandal, distrust, and Contempt."[12] His case had to go to a full trial.

Before that trial took place Newport, Rhode Island, began trading with England again and New York businessmen wanted to do the same. The Sons of Liberty denounced Newport's action and warned New York merchants not to follow suit; if the merchants did, the Sons would regard them as their enemies. The city's most prominent merchants, though, thought they alone should decide whether nonimportation continued or ended.

McDougall responded on May 16, only about two months after the Boston Massacre. Believing that he was defending his fellow New Yorkers' freedom, the Scotsman chose to write a broadside under the pseudonym "Brutus" because he apparently saw the slayer of Julius Caesar as a heroic figure. In his "To the Free and Loyal Inhabitants of the City and Colony of New York" McDougall attacked the "mercantile Dons."[13] The question of whether to import British goods or not was something that every New Yorker had a right to voice his opinion on because the issue related to taxes, which affected all Americans' liberties. And since he believed Parliament was acting "tyrannical"[14] by taxing Americans without their consent, he urged New Yorkers to stand firm, to continue to reject trade with England.

Both sides battled for support. On June 2 a city committee supportive of the merchants called for neighboring towns to convene and come up with a concerted plan of action. Less than two weeks later, on June 12, a house-to-house poll was begun to see which side had more support among city residents. When the polling was completed the merchants had twelve hundred New Yorkers on their side and McDougall had only three-hundred-fifty on his.

On July 7, a day when another poll was being taken, the two sides held meetings at different locations. After McDougall and another patriot concluded theirs with a vote for nonimportation, the Scotsman and other Sons of Liberty harassed the polltakers as they went about their work. They then went to a tavern, became fired up from drink, and in the evening marched out of the establishment with a flag bearing the inscription "no importation, but in union with the other colonies" to the accompaniment of music. Some of those at the other meeting, which was taking place in the Merchants' Coffee House, wanted the procession stopped. Eventually the two groups met on Wall Street. When the Sons refused to give up their flag a brief melee ensued. As the participants shouted and cursed, they went at each other with canes and fence slats. When it was over McDougall and the Sons had suffered two defeats; they were sporting black eyes and bloody noses, and the poll results showed that New Yorkers stood with the merchants.

The full trial occurred in December. The Sons of Liberty had done their best to intimidate those who might testify against McDougall—the informant Cummins had been forced first to go into hiding, then to flee the city, and finally to leave for England—but the lawmakers were determined. They demanded that the Scotsman tell them whether he had written the broadside but he refused to do so, declaring that he had already been indicted by the grand jury for writing and publishing it and citing the principle of double jeopardy. What was being done to him was unjust.

Alexander's words angered the lawmakers. One of them even hinted that McDougall could be tortured into confessing. Back and forth the two sides went, the proceedings growing more heated. Finally, the General Assembly ordered the defiant Scotsman, guilty of contempt, to be taken to jail.

McDougall spent a little less than three months there. From the time of his release until early spring 1773 little happened to provoke him. Then, in May, the British passed the Tea Act to save the East India Company from bankruptcy. American merchants were still going to be required to pay the import tax on tea, but the company would be paid back for all the export duties it incurred and therefore be able to undersell honest colonists going through middlemen and smugglers who got their tea in Holland.

The East India Company stood to gain a monopoly, which could not be tolerated. Merchants must not do business with them! In an October meeting the Sons of Liberty thanked captains who had already decided not to carry the company's tea on their ships. In late November McDougall visited a number of agents and persuaded them not to handle the tea, and some "Mohawks" threatened to take care of anyone who assisted in the landing or storing of it in New York. Two days after the Indians had made their threat, the Scotsman and some other Sons disseminated fifteen hundred copies of a paper warning that those who did business with the East India Company were to be considered enemies of the country.

Not all heeded the warnings; the captain of the *London* saw his tea dumped into the East River by some Indians. He supposedly was lucky not to have been killed by the large, angry mob that had gathered at the dockside.

After the Boston Tea Party and the subsequent Boston Port Act, McDougall and others sought the city's help in coordinating a broad boycott of British goods. Many New York merchants feared being ruined by a trade war and quickly worked to calm the situation down. First, on May 16, 1774, the Committee of Fifty was established. Then, three days later, that committee's membership was expanded to fifty-one. Among its members were McDougall and Gouverneur Morris.

The committee did not favor a boycott and sent letters to Boston and Philadelphia proposing that an intercolonial congress be established to deal with the problem. Boston preferred to see each colony come up with its own boycott, though it realized a congress ought to be established when time was not of the essence. Fortunately for the cause of liberty, Philadelphia sided with New York.

The Committee of Fifty-One subsequently selected the five men it wanted for Congress and McDougall was not among the chosen. But on July 6, at a meeting in the Fields that the Scotsman presided over, a large crowd learned that the Sons of Liberty had selected their own slate of five candidates. Theirs was different from the committee's and it included McDougall. Consequently, the people had to vote to decide who was going to represent New York. In the event, the voters accepted three of the committee's choices but not the two others. In place of one of the two whom they had rejected, the voters selected the Scotsman.

The Committee of Fifty-One did not recognize the crowd's vote. Either its slate or the one offered by the Sons of Liberty could be chosen but not a mix from both. McDougall soon thereafter resigned from the committee and withdrew his name as a candidate.

He later served in committees of sixty and one hundred, and in the New York Provincial Congress. Since the latter two were established after Lexington and Concord, they were mainly concerned with war preparations. During his time in the provincial congress McDougall served with Gouverneur Morris on the committee established to question witnesses about the Hickey Plot. The two of them served in more committees than any other members.

New York was asked to provide ten companies for the war. McDougall quickly responded, recruiting men for the 1st New York Regiment and accepting a commission as a colonel and an appointment as its commander in early summer 1775. As such, he had to strengthen the city's defenses so it could withstand a British attack. That task must have looked difficult to him, since he was starting almost from scratch. Defense works had to be built; few of the companies requested had been raised; he had few cannon; he faced shortages of gunpowder, saltpeter, and clothing; and he needed money. So much had to be done that when a large number of his men, including his two sons, headed north to be part of an invasion of Canada, McDougall felt compelled to stay in New York to continue recruiting men and fortifying the city. While he remained behind, one of those sons died from a fever and the other was taken prisoner.

In early August 1776 Congress promoted McDougall to brigadier general. Soon thereafter the Battle of Long Island began. The British and Hessians greatly outnumbered the Americans but chose not to employ a frontal assault; they attacked the flanks. Eventually, they got behind the American left wing and center and those patriots not killed or captured had to flee or retreat to the forts and breastworks at Brooklyn Heights.

The British commander, General Howe, though close enough to storm the forts, instead held back and began siege preparations. Washington realized that enemy forces had his men hemmed in. They controlled the ground to his left, right and front, and the East River and the British fleet were to his back. His best hope was to try to evacuate his troops at night by ferrying them across the river.

McDougall drew the assignment of coordinating the difficult operation. Once assigned the mission, the general energetically carried it out. He sent men back to Manhattan to find sailors, who then set off in sailboats and rowboats for Washington's waiting army. After they reached the other side of the river, the evacuation began. By this time—8 p.m.—the sky was dark and rain was falling. McDougall, organizing the effort without the benefit of a single lantern, pulled one regiment at a time out of its trenches; the men went to the ferry boat landing; and former fishermen serving in the Massachusetts regiments of Israel Hutchinson and John Glover helped them onto the boats and ferried them across the river to the opposite shore. There they disembarked, and Hutchinson's and Glover's men returned to pick up and ferry across more men. For a while it looked as if winds were going to end the evacuation, but when the sun rose the following morning, August 30, Washington's army was gone.

In September the British captured New York City, and the following month they forced Washington to retreat north to White Plains, where he had a supply depot. As Howe slowly advanced over difficult terrain, American soldiers built breastworks.

Washington ordered large contingents of troops to be deployed on the wooded Chatterton Hill, which was close to the general's main positions on the right. McDougall left by horse with his regiment. By the time he arrived, British cannon were already pounding the 180-foot hill and one American regiment had almost disappeared; its men had fled until officers managed to get them to return to their positions.

In order to dislodge the Americans the British had to cross the storm-swollen Bronx River just in front of the hill. As they prepared to attack that sunny Monday, October 28, McDougall directed Maryland and New York troops under Colonels William Smallwood and Rudolphus Ritzema to go down the southeastern slope and take up positions behind some fences and timber. The Marylanders and New Yorkers first drove off Hessians, who were attempting to ford the river with a crude bridge, and then scattered a couple of British regiments that tried to ascend the hill.

However, the tide of battle soon changed. Hessians reinforced the British regiments that had been scattered. The enemy forded the river and ascended the hill by the thousands, turned the American right flank, and beat their kettledrums and blew their trumpets to herald the arrival of light dragoons. Now the artillery fire had ceased and the two sides' combatants slashed, shot, and thrust at each other with their swords, muskets and bayonets. Inexperienced militiamen ran and casualties mounted. Ultimately, McDougall had to withdraw. For much of the battle, which lasted until dusk, they had fought valiantly.

In early December rheumatism brought on by bad weather left McDougall bedridden. Later that month he recovered somewhat, but not enough to hold an active command. Washington, therefore, sent him to the Hudson Highlands to work on American fortifications and ensure that the British did not gain control of the river; if they did so, they could stop trade and sever New England from the mid-Atlantic and southern colonies.

The British attempted to cut the country in half during the summer and fall of 1777, but their three-pronged attack never reached McDougall. The only action he saw while in the Hudson Highlands came on a Sunday in late March; the British landed hundreds of soldiers near Peekskill, forced him and his greatly outnumbered forces to withdraw from the village, and plundered the depot there. The British might have advanced to Fishkill, where more supplies were stored, but on Monday American reinforcements from Fort Constitution arrived and drove them off.

The raid really did not do much damage—only one man reportedly had received mortal wounds—but it did provoke a heated argument between a loud, fist-shaking McDougall and Colonel Henry Beekman Livingston that led to the latter's immediate arrest. The colonel, who had arrived with his regiment late on the first day of action, slandered the general, spoke disrespectfully to his superior while other officers were present, and committed a number of smaller offenses. Such charges must have rankled Livingston, since he was said to have believed that the real "scandal"[15] was the general's order to retreat.

The colonel was eventually tried by court martial and received a reprimand. Not long after the trial concluded, he went on the attack. He sent McDougall a note hinting that they could settle their differences in a duel, and he wrote and had copied for circulation a tract denigrating the general for, among other things, having been the son of a milkman and later a privateer. But fortunately for him, the general largely ignored what Livingston had written.

The last major battle that McDougall participated in was Germantown in October 1777. Washington wanted to strike there because he knew Howe had sent a large detachment of men off to the Delaware River to assist in action against forts in that area and, consequently, would have fewer forces to oppose him. The Commander-in-chief's plan called for four columns, two middle ones to hit the British center and two outside ones to turn the enemy's right and left flanks and envelop him. More than half of Washington's men were to be under the command of Nathanael Greene. McDougall's orders were "to march in front of the troops that compose the left wing and file off to attack the enemy's right flank."[16]

During the battle, as the loud sounds of American artillery trying to reduce to rubble the beautiful stone home of Pennsylvania's Loyalist Chief Justice Benjamin Chew filled the air, Greene and McDougall moved toward the British center in Germantown. So too did Brigadier Generals Charles Scott and Peter Muhlenberg. The American column eventually reached the British center, proceeded to their main camp, and took a large number of prisoners. Victory appeared imminent.

However, a victory was not in the cards for the Americans. Fog was hampering visibility and preventing units from communicating with each other and coordinating actions. Major General Adam Stephen had without authorization removed his men from Greene's column to head off to the battle at the Chew House and had run into the rear of Brigadier General Anthony Wayne's brigade and mistakenly fired on his men, who then returned fire; Stephen was drunk at the time. Major General John Sullivan's men had been attacked and, hearing the awesome sounds of the artillery at the Chew House and concluding that they were surrounded, were now fleeing. And Major General John Armstrong, commanding the American right, had retreated.

With the flight of Sullivan's men, the British who had been fighting them were now free to concentrate on Greene. Unable to get any help from Wayne, Stephen, and Armstrong, the Rhode Island general, realizing he was in danger of being flanked, ordered his column to retreat. As Greene's soldiers left the scene, McDougall's men provided covering fire.

The defeat at Germantown could in no way be blamed on McDougall, and before the month ended he was promoted to major general. He had "from the time of his Appointment as Brigadier, from his abilities, military knowledge, and approved bravery … every claim to promotion,"[17] Washington wrote in his recommendation.

McDougall returned to the Hudson Highlands in late March 1778. While there he assumed responsibility for the construction of the chain across the Hudson and saw it stretched across the important river. Shortly thereafter he learned that he would be losing his command to Horatio Gates, of whom he had a very unfavorable opinion, at least in part because of something called the Conway Cabal.

McDougall's next stops were White Plains and Connecticut, where he did little of note. Then, in late November, he received orders to return to the Hudson Highlands. After assuming command there, he saw his men grow uneasy. They experienced many shortages, including ones of clothing, beef, flour, forage, straw for bedding, and even candles. Also, they did not receive adequate pay and often found it in arrears.

General officers also had good reason to grow restless. By the summer of 1779 Congress had excluded them from a group authorized to receive a subsistence allowance of $500 a month and had referred the half-pay pension to the states. Stung by such neglect, they held a number of meetings in September and decided to send a petition to Philadelphia.

By mid-November one was ready for the generals to sign. It emphasized their sacrifices for the cause of American liberty and spelled out their grievances. They were supposed to pay for their clothing, have horses, and entertain others in a manner befitting their high ranks, but they were unable to do so; depreciation made their salaries and allowances wholly inadequate to the task. Also, soldiers, junior officers, and even colonels were entitled to land grants "beyond the war" but not the generals. They wanted them, though, "not so much … for their pecuniary worth, as for a consideration infinitely superior"—recognition and gratitude from the public for their service and the hardships they had endured. The generals sought "no extravagant advantages,"[18] only higher pay and something after the war to keep them from having to return to their dependent families poorer than when they had left home to join the war effort.

More than two dozen generals, including McDougall and Gates, signed the long petition, but it had little effect on Congress. The delegates were as "Calm and easy as if all things were in the most flourishing and prosperous train," an angry Nathanael Greene informed the Scotsman. They were "determined to keep the General Officers poor, to prevent their obtaining an extensive influence." The generals were losing the best years of their lives to the war and upon being discharged would be "cloathed with poverty and distress." They "ought to have something done, or speak plainer,"[19] Greene believed.

A furious McDougall responded that the officers had long complained about the amount of time Congress spent debating "small matters of Form" instead of things that really mattered. The generals, though, were unable to do anything about that and the situation they found themselves in; they must simply endure the frequent insults, the "Calumny," and the neglect. If the people were responsive to their feelings and showed an inclination "to bear an equal Share of the Burden," the generals would be able to better tolerate their unbearable condition. But that was not the case; the public was insensitive and not inclined to share the burden. "Can the Army or the world expect Justice or gratitude from a nation who have by law robbed the widow & the Fatherless without remors[e]?"[20] the general asked.

The following summer the generals wrote a second petition. They felt an "infinite Mortification" that the delegates were ignoring the army's grievances and they wanted justice. For their patriotism and sacrifices they deserved "the generous rewards of a gratefull people"—immediate compensation for pay losses resulting from depreciation, the right to draw all their rations "or be paid full Value" of those not handed out by the commissary, pensions for widows and orphans, and an allowance "to each General Officer to enable him to Support a Table Suitable to the Rank he holds."

Continue to ignore the army's grievances while it was "expos'd ... to the Rapacity of almost every other Class of the Community," the generals implied, and the officers and soldiers might be forced "to quit the Service." If they did so and America suffered "any ill Consequences" as a result, "they [would] leave to the world to determine who ought to be responsible for them."[21]

Once the petition was signed, the generals gave it to McDougall for delivery to Congress. They hoped their appeal and his efforts in Philadelphia would remove any chance that "Ignorance of the real state of the Army may remain." He was to do everything in his power "to impress upon Congress, and the members individually the necessity of immediate Redress" and emphasize that he was not going to leave until he had "a definitive answer."[22]

When McDougall arrived on horseback in Philadelphia, he insisted that he be allowed to speak before the whole Congress but did not get his way. Instead, he ended up presenting the generals' case frankly but respectfully to a five-man committee and other delegates during daytime and nighttime discussions with them.

After those talks, McDougall provided the committee members with some notes concerning the subjects addressed in the officers' petitions. In the notes he elaborated on why the generals should get a pay raise, emphasizing that they had never received enough to keep up with inflation; even if their pay was increased fifty per cent—as that of all officers below the rank of general had been—they still would earn less than "half the pay and emoluments of a Colonel in the Enemy's Service."

As for half pay, he saw two problems. First, Congress had barred officers holding positions in government, no matter whether they paid well or not, from receiving the pension. That did not make sense, since the pension was supposed to compensate the officers for their service during the war, not for any postwar service. Second, a ceiling of "but half pay of Colonels" had been placed on pension payments. The generals felt that they could not accept such a pension "without dishonoring themselves" and, McDougall added, in civilian life they would be unable to meet the greater expenses associated with past "connections and acquaintances" made when they were in the army if they received only that amount.

The Scotsman also indicated that the officers from New England were willing to accept lump sum payments when the war ended instead of half-pay pensions. They would provide sufficient compensation for their wartime service and their "lost time" and allow them to go into business after the war.

The notes also touched upon such things as the officers' concerns for widows and orphans, the inadequacy of their rations, and postwar land grants. In regard to the last item, the general made the point that the war was being fought "for property as well as for liberty and Empire" and he believed they had "a just Claim on the Community" for some of the land which they were protecting for the people.[23]

The five-man committee submitted a report on its meetings, and Congress reacted by passing many resolutions. The delegates recommended that the states compensate officers and soldiers of their lines for pay losses resulting from depreciation; Philadelphia would take care of those who were not in any state lines. They agreed to postwar land grants for the generals. They voted to provide the officers with two months' pay as soon as possible "to relieve their present wants mentioned in the memorial."[24] They promised that if officers did not receive enough money as compensation for rations not issued, Congress would make up the difference. They urged the states to grant half pay for life to duration officers and some type of postwar compensation to duration soldiers in recognition of "the many Dangers, Losses & Hardships they ... suffered"[25] or decide on some other way to reward them. They approved extending half pay for seven years to widows and orphans. They repealed the clause barring officers holding government positions from receiving pensions. And they acceded to the generals' wish that they not be forced to dishonor themselves by accepting "but the half pay of Colonels";[26] a general would now receive the half pay of a general.

McDougall remained in Philadelphia after Congress passed those resolutions. During his stay in the capital the general appealed to Congress for some of the back pay he was due; he had to support a family and by this time his finances were in extremely bad shape. He succeeded in getting $1,900, but Congress did nothing to reimburse him for expenses incurred in Philadelphia. The money he did manage to obtain was the last he got until the war ended.

On September 19, 1780, McDougall departed for West Point. Soon after he arrived there, he went to Poughkeepsie to meet with Governor George Clinton and New York's legislature. There he learned of his election as one of his state's delegates to the Continental Congress. He went on to serve in that body from January 17 to March 2, 1781 and, while there, voted for the impost. He had already by the previous fall concluded that the government was not able to adequately meet the military's needs without greater taxation authority. And since he believed the state legislatures were unlikely to give it what it needed to prosecute the war effectively, he naturally saw the army as an instrument that might be used to force them to give Congress greater power.

He did not leave Philadelphia immediately after his service in Congress ended. During his remaining time there he learned that the government was not going to reimburse him for loans he had made in 1775 and 1776 to several New York battalions and a couple of artillery companies; they had needed support and he had dipped very deeply into his own resources to help them. "A disposition appears in Congress to get rid of officers and the expence attending them, in a manner I own, which does not altogether correspond with my Idea of Justice to them," he despondently observed in late April 1781, "however *I* may view those subjects thro too partial and inter[ested] mediums."[27]

As time passed, McDougall's situation did not improve. In late March 1782 he again tried to obtain some relief, this time writing to Governor Clinton to ask that New York pay him all he was owed for his service; he had received his pay only twice since August 1776 and both times late. Additionally, the back pay he was owed had to be adjusted for depreciation or it would have no real value.

But how was it to be adjusted? "The legislature thought it just and reasonable to make good the Depreciation of nominal pay received"[28] by issuing interest-bearing certificates to the officers and soldiers. McDougall, however, had almost always *not* received his nominal pay. Did that mean he was not entitled to receive certificates? He thought that that could not be the case, for that would be unjust. The law certainly had not foreseen pay arrears becoming so great a problem. The general believed that to deprive him of pay that had real value was contrary to the spirit of the law. And to have real value his pay had to be adjusted for depreciation; he had to receive not just money but also interest-bearing certificates. By his calculations, with adjustments, the state still owed him a little more than $6,900.

What he wanted was a resolution. McDougall had petitioned the legislature in June 1781 and had brought up the matter again the following autumn but to no avail; no favorable resolution had been passed by the time he wrote the governor. All he had seen was "inattentive Contempt."[29]

Several months went by after he wrote Governor Clinton and nothing happened. When he wrote Washington in late August 1782, the Scotsman's estimate of what he was owed in back pay had risen to "not … less than 12,000 Dollars." His financial health was so bad that he felt he would quickly use up all his hard cash if he continued "to Support Mrs McDougall at distinct Quarters."[30] Consequently, he had her move to West Point, where he was.

JOHN BROOKS,[31] ONE of the two field officers chosen to accompany McDougall to Philadelphia, was the son of a Meford farmer. Though he developed an early interest in military drills, he chose a career in medicine. Since just one medical college existed in America in the mid-1760s, the vast majority of men aspiring to become doctors worked as apprentices for three to seven years to get the necessary education. Brooks had put himself under the wing of Dr. Simon Tufts in 1766, when he was only fourteen. He received seven years of training and then began his own practice in Reading, Massachusetts, in 1773.

When the war began on April 19, 1775, Brooks hurried off to fight the British at Concord. At the time he was a captain, the commander of the Reading Company of Minutemen. Later he participated in the Battle of Bunker Hill as a major in middle-aged Colonel Ebenezer Bridge's Massachusetts Regiment; at Long Island and White Plains as a major in the 19th Continental Infantry; and as a lieutenant colonel of the 8th Massachusetts Regiment at Saratoga.

In that last battle, which took place on October 7, 1777, Brooks played a crucial role in bringing about a great American victory, one that led to France joining the war effort. By that date Major General John Burgoyne's hopes of gaining a permanent foothold in the Hudson Valley had already been dashed. When the British general sent out a large force that day to test the American left wing, General Gates was ready, and eventually the entire British front had to retreat back to Bemis Heights. Not long after that point in the battle Colonel Brooks emerged from some woods and had his regiment deploy in front of Lieutenant Colonel Heinrich von Breymann's redoubt, the last defense covering Burgoyne's right flank. Facing the colonel were well-entrenched Germans armed with muskets and "several brass pieces … guns mounted on three sides."[32] When "the decisive moment"[33] came, Brooks raised his sword high and called his men to follow him and charge the breastwork. A "most violent and bloody conflict ensued,"[34] but the Americans overcame the Germans' fierce resistance and captured the redoubt. Burgoyne had to retreat and ultimately surrender. A historian who served in the army wrote, "The capture of Gen. Burgoyne and his army may be attributed in no small degree to the gallant conduct of Col. Brooks and his regiment, on the 7th of October, in the battle of Saratoga."[35]

Colonel John Brooks

After that battle the colonel's troops marched to Valley Forge for the winter. There he saw uneasiness among the men of the northern army. His "poor brave Fellows living in Tents, bare footed, bare leg'd, bare breech'd &c., &c. in Snow, in Rain, on marches, in Camp & on Duty" were not being supplied with what they needed and he was not able to do anything about the problem. His men also were not being paid; they had "rec'd but 2 Months pay for twelve months past." Their esprit de corps, he admitted, was still good, but he did not expect it to remain that way. Only so long would the army stay intact solely because it loved its country.

Officers, in particular, had to be compensated or else they would not "continue in the Service any considerable time." And without experienced officers "a good Army" was not possible.

That was one reason why Brooks wanted them to receive compensation. Another was that he did not want them to end up in debt, especially at a time when civilians were profiting greatly from the war. He saw "no Reason why one part of the Community should Sacrifice their all for the good of it, while the rest [we]re filling their Coffers."[36]

While he was at Valley Forge the colonel served as an assistant to Baron von Steuben, the newly appointed inspector general. Washington wanted "uniformity of discipline and manoeuvres in the army" and to bring that about men of "character and abilities" were needed to fill subinspector positions. The Commander-in-chief believed Brooks to be such a man and the colonel did not let him down, apparently carrying out his duties so well that Washington on several occasions pointed him out as a fine example for others to follow.

In late June 1778, the energetic colonel served as Major General Charles Lee's adjutant at the Battle of Monmouth,[37] but of greater relevance to his eventual role in the Newburgh Conspiracy is his involvement in events that took place from December 1780 on. Realizing that something had to be done for their line, Massachusetts officers decided that month to send four officers, including Brooks, to Boston to seek help from the Massachusetts General Court. Instructions were drafted for them and signed on January 1, 1781. The most important ones could not have surprised any of them. The officers were supposed to try to get the Massachusetts Line's accounts settled; a partial settlement had been made earlier but the pay of the officers and soldiers was still in arrears. They also were to ensure that soldiers who received enlistment bounties from Massachusetts towns did not have their pay reduced by the amounts of them or, if some had already seen deductions, have their emoluments restored. And they had to see that adjustments for depreciation were fairly calculated so the officers and soldiers did not lose money when they were not paid on time.

The four officers set out for Boston that month and, judging by the memoirs of one of them, Rufus Putnam, spent the rest of the winter and some of the following spring there. They achieved some success, for the Massachusetts Line received some pay in specie, but their efforts probably influenced the legislators less than the mutinies of the Pennsylvania and New Jersey Lines, which also took place in January.

Later, in early September 1782, Brooks would once again be sent to Boston, this time as part of the delegation whose failure led to Knox's petition to Congress and the mission to Philadelphia.

In the Hudson Highlands the thirty-year-old Brooks was head of medicine at the New Windsor Cantonment and at Washington's headquarters. He also commanded the 7th Massachusetts Regiment. Though he was quite young to be commanding a regiment in that state's line, he must have shouldered his responsibilities well; Washington identified his regiment in early June 1782 as having been found "to be in excellent condition" when inspected.[38] He was "So worthy a character" that Rufus Putnam wanted him to be allowed to stay in the army after it was reduced at the beginning of 1783 and pointed out to Washington that his own retirement before the end of the war would open a slot for the lieutenant colonel,[39] who otherwise was likely to be involuntarily retired with the reduction in forces.

MATTHIAS OGDEN,[40] THE other field officer chosen to accompany McDougall to Philadelphia, was born on October 22, 1754. He attended the College of New Jersey but left to join Washington's army in Cambridge soon after the Battle of Bunker Hill. As a twenty-five-year-old major he went marching off with Benedict Arnold to Quebec to fight the British. There he attempted to give the

British his commander's surrender summons, but had to make a hasty retreat when an eighteen-pound shot fired by the enemy landed too close for comfort. Later, early on the morning of December 31, 1775, when the Americans launched an assault that proved disastrous, Ogden was wounded.

He received a promotion to lieutenant colonel in March 1776, but that spring and the early part of the following summer had to have been difficult for him. During that period the army went without pay, withdrew from Canada to Fort Crown Point, left that location because of the poor condition of its wooden walls and went to Fort Ticonderoga, suffered from fatigue and endured desertions, much sickness, and even many deaths. By the second week in July the army appeared to be collapsing.

Only weeks after the appearance of a new commander at Fort Ticonderoga, though, Ogden was able to write of a miraculous improvement in morale. Among other things, the new commander took steps to improve the troops' housing, clothing and water supplies, attacked and eliminated smallpox, tried to enforce discipline fairly, and offered men ten-dollar bounties to sign up for three years of service. The new commander Ogden credited for the improvement was Horatio Gates.

On December 26, 1776, Congress promoted Ogden to colonel, and when the New Year began he took over command of the 1st Regiment of the New Jersey Line. The regiment gave a good account of itself against the British in September 1777 at Brandywine, impeding their advance on "the plowed hill,"[41] but eventually the entire army had to retreat toward Philadelphia. Shortly thereafter the British occupied the city.

Germantown, Monmouth, and General Sullivan's campaign against the Six Nations followed in October 1777, June 1778, and August 1779, respectively, and then Ogden's men encamped at Morristown, New Jersey. There they went without pay and endured "weather … cold enough to cut a man in two,"[42] unimaginable snowfall and blizzards, and hunger-causing shortages of rations. It was the worst winter of the war. In January 1780 an intense three-day snowstorm decimated fences and roads in the area and caused the troops' tents to cave in on top of them. By the time the winter season had ended the troops had endured twenty-eight snowfalls and weeks of freezing temperatures. So low did the mercury drop that even the Hudson River turned to ice. Rather than stay in camp, where as much as six feet of snow lay in spots, and try to survive on such food as "black birch bark" and roasted "old shoes,"[43] the poorly clothed men tried to desert.

The officers understood that they had to keep the army intact and did their best to prevent desertions. They held many courts-martial, and in late February 1780 Colonel Ogden served as the presiding officer in one that resulted in a death sentence for a private in his regiment. More than a few soldiers suffered the same fate.

Later that year, in October, the colonel was taken prisoner at Elizabethtown. He remained in British hands until April 1781, when he was exchanged. Not too much else appears to have happened to Ogden from that time until his arrival in Philadelphia with McDougall and Brooks. In late March 1782 he came up with a plan to kidnap Rear Admiral Robert Digby and Prince William—the future King William IV—who were staying in a mansion in New York City, but the British learned of the plan less than one month after the colonel had submitted his proposal to Washington, and Ogden decided against trying to abduct the two Englishmen.

THE THREE MEN, McDougall, Brooks, and Ogden, appeared to be wise choices for the delegation that was sent to the capital. All had the respect of their peers and knew firsthand what hardships the soldiers and officers had endured. Two of them—McDougall and Brooks—already had experience in politics or with politicians, and all three had relationships with people who were going to become very important in early 1783. McDougall had served with Gouverneur Morris on the committee that had investigated the Hickey Plot, and he was friends with Alexander Hamilton: on July 6, 1774, when McDougall spoke before a large crowd at the Fields in support of the slate of five candidates for Congress that had the backing of the Sons of Liberty but not the Committee of Fifty-One, he had invited the young New Yorker to come forward and speak and had been so impressed by what he said that he became his friend that very day.[44]

Brooks also considered Hamilton to be a friend; both of them had been at Valley Forge, and they corresponded with each other when the New Yorker found himself accused of making an incendiary speech directed against Congress—one in which he said "it was high time for people to rise, join General Washington, and turn Congress out of doors"—in a coffee house in Philadelphia in July 1779.[45] And Ogden probably knew both Gouverneur Morris and Hamilton well; he was a cousin of one of Morris's brothers-in-law and he was friends with Hamilton, possibly having become acquainted with him through his own brother-in-law, Francis Barber, who had been one of the New York delegate's teachers.

Now, at the end of December 1782, all five men—McDougall, Brooks, Ogden, Morris, and Hamilton—were together in Philadelphia. They all wanted to see Congress win real taxation authority so it could obtain the revenue it needed to redress the army's grievances. They all were in the right place at the right time to become involved in what would come to be known as the Newburgh Conspiracy.

Part II

The Plot and the Flame

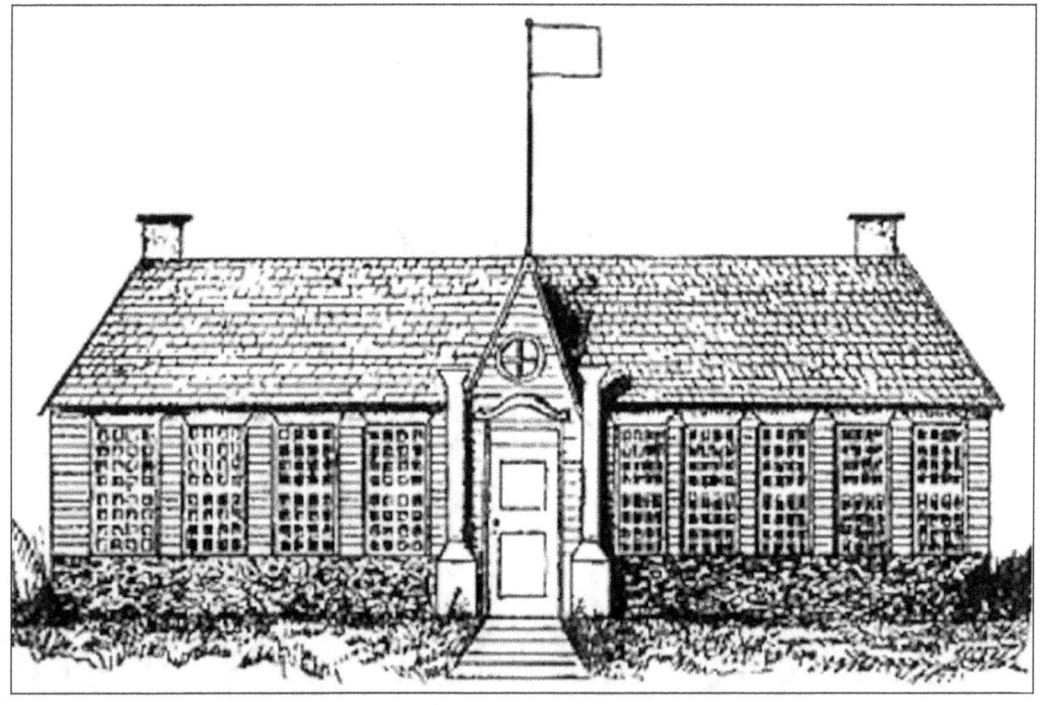

Temple of Virtue

Chapter Twelve

"The Army Have Swords in Their Hands"

WHEN THE THREE officers arrived in Philadelphia[1] in late December 1782, what they saw was the largest city in America, one with between thirty and forty thousand residents. It was a little more than one hundred years old, much younger than New York and Boston. During the decade before the war it had seen rapid growth, and by the beginning of the Revolution it was a wealthy city offering chances for upward mobility and featuring a growing middle class.

It was also an important supply center for the Continental Army. When the war began the belief was that losing Philadelphia to the British would spell disaster for America. "You will consider Philadelphia," Robert Morris wrote, "from its centrical situation, the extent of its commerce, the number of its artificers, manufactures and other circumstances, to be to the United States what the heart is to the human body in circulating the blood."[2] Nathanael Greene felt "she must be preserved at all events."[3]

She wasn't preserved, though. British forces under General Howe took Philadelphia without firing a shot. But their stay was short; they began their occupation of the busy seaport in September 1777, finding almost six hundred vacated houses and more than two hundred closed shops upon their arrival, and evacuated it for New York City in June 1778.

The list of trades and professions represented in Philadelphia was long and diverse. The city had coopers, wheelwrights, and makers of coaches, cabinets, chairs and spinning wheels. It had people who worked with metals—blacksmiths, gunsmiths, coppersmiths, goldsmiths, silversmiths, tinsmiths, and brass founders. It had stonecutters, brickmakers, bricklayers, plasterers, and painters. Skinners, tanners, curriers, and saddlers plied their trades in the city. So too did people who made breeches, stockings, stays, hats, and perukes. Manufacturers of canes and whips worked in

Philadelphia. Distillers, brewers, sugar refiners, victualers, and bakers did business there. Printers, tallow chandlers, clockmakers and watchmakers, potters, tobacconists, and barber-surgeons also thrived.

Two evenings a week all the city's bells rang. The following days were main market days. Much trade took place in the city, and people came from afar in covered wagons to Philadelphia on market days. Philadelphia was, after all, Pennsylvania's only seaport, and whatever they needed could probably be found here. Whether a person was looking for honey, flour, beans, meat, game, dried fish, timber, shingles, rafters, stoves, masts or even ships, he could find them in Philadelphia.

The people of Philadelphia kept their city neat, orderly, and peaceful. A physician inspected ships arriving from Europe and took steps to make sure those on board did not transmit diseases. Sanitation workers swept the city's brick and flagstone sidewalks. Conduits carried water and filth away from tree-lined streets illuminated by whale-oil lamps. Wealthy Philadelphians owned beautiful two-story brick homes with ornate stucco ceilings, grand chimney pieces, fine interior paneling, carving, gilding, mahogany furniture, Franklin stoves, fine carpets, portraits by Charles Wilson Peale, and outdoor gardens.

The city had fire companies, constables, and two jails, the newer of which was the large Walnut Street Prison, near an area where hundreds of soldiers who had died from smallpox six winters before were buried. It had Robert Morris's one-year-old Bank of North America and the large House of Employment, a poorhouse where those less fortunate—the elderly, the indigent, and the physically disabled—were able to work at trades such as knitting and weaving to partially pay for their board and lodging. It had the fine Pennsylvania Hospital and the Humane Society, which had been organized in 1780 to handle medical emergencies where drowning, chokedamp, hanging, or sunstroke had left a person with his "animation … suspended."[4] The University of the State of Pennsylvania, which had formerly been called "The College, Academy, and Charitable School of Philadelphia"[5] and the American Philosophical Society were located in Philadelphia. So too was the Library Company of Philadelphia, the country's first library to lend to the public; it was in its sixth decade. Many places of worship dotted Philadelphia's map; the greatest number of these was for the Quakers, but other religious sects—such as Presbyterians, Lutherans, Roman Catholics, and even Jews—had their own churches, chapels, and synagogue. And the city had a number of newspapers for Philadelphians to choose from.

Outside the city's center stood the brick and wood Southwark Theatre. Built before the war, it may have been America's first playhouse. Oil lamps illuminated its stage when actors performed, but for most of the war nothing happened there; Pennsylvania had decided in March 1779 to ban all theatrical performances and shows to reduce vice and immorality. One evening in early January 1782, however, Washington and others attended a fête in their honor there that included theater, dances, and an illumination of thirteen pyramid-shaped columns bearing his and other generals' last names and the names of their home states.

Even if Philadelphians did not or could not attend theatrical performances, they still did not lack for places to go when they were not at work. Fishing clubs located up the Schuykill were one possibility. The Jockey Club was another. It had been established to promote horse breeding and racing; southern delegates especially liked going to races. The many taverns in the area were a third option. One—the City Tavern—was the best in the colonies for well-bred members of society, according to John Adams. A farewell dinner had been held there for Washington before he rode off to Boston to take command of his army.

Philadelphia was also home for the government of the state of Pennsylvania and Congress. Both conducted business in the two-story Pennsylvania State House, which had been built in 1732 and was used as a hospital during the British occupation.

THE REVOLUTIONARY WAR Congress was quite different from what Congress is today. It was unicameral and "worked behind a veil of secrecy."[6] Its members were chosen by state legislatures and provincial congresses "ignorant of new issues and void of national vision."[7] Delegates from the larger states tended to be the most articulate and influential members, the ones that controlled deliberations and standing committees.[8] Members were limited to serving no more than three one-year terms over a stretch of six years,[9] so the turnover rate was high. That probably lessened the fears of some that nationalist members would conspire to strengthen Congress at the expense of the states' sovereignty,[10] but it also prevented a corps of very experienced delegates from emerging. States were free to recall representatives if they so pleased, which they did. Few delegates stayed long enough to be able to keep track of the army's needs.[11]

Congress suffered from a high rate of absenteeism.[12] Sometimes not even one member of a state's delegation was present,[13] and on one occasion only eight of the body's sixty-five delegates sat in session.[14] Consequently, committees were not filled[15] and the body's general business went undone.

That was just one of the several reasons why delegates often suffered from low morale. They also didn't enjoy being separated from their loved ones. They received little remuneration for their service and living expenses, which were high in Philadelphia. They endured meetings and debates that dragged on without end. And the resolutions they passed were ignored by the states.[16]

Another problem was the little prestige attached to being a member of Congress; service there was seen as an unpleasant patriotic duty that delegates were obligated to perform, a duty that entailed hours and hours of their time every day.[17] Robert Morris, writing in September 1778, grumbled, "The time I have spent in it has been the severest Tax of my life." He wanted "to get out of Congress at the next appointment of Delegates."[18] Gouverneur Morris claimed in January and February 1781 that he had "from the Beginning ... never asked nor sought the public Confidence," that he was serving "by virtue of a *positive Order*."[19] Henry Laurens likened service in the army to "a Bed of Ease, a Pillow of Down" when compared with that in Congress.[20]

Even with a quorum, achieving anything substantial was difficult. Votes were taken by state. Each state delegation was allowed to have anywhere from two to seven delegates, but regardless of its size it had only one vote. And if its members evenly split on an issue, they essentially deprived their state of a say in the matter. To pass something rather minor seven delegations had to say aye. To pass an appropriation of public money nine had to do so. To pass an amendment to the Articles of Confederation all had to favor it.[21] Many members were more loyal to their home states, upon which they depended for their pay, than to the country as a whole; they voted in accordance with instructions from their state legislatures instead of in the best interests of the nation.[22]

In his orders Washington referred to the body as "the Honorable the Congress," but at this time it appeared to be unworthy of such respect.

McDOUGALL WAS NOT able to meet with Benjamin Lincoln upon his arrival in Philadelphia, as Knox had wished, because the secretary had gone to Hingham, Massachusetts, for the winter.[23] So he, Brooks, and Ogden began their stay in the city with a "Visit of Ceremony" to Robert Morris's office. Accompanying them that day, December 31, were two other officers—the general's son and aide, Major Ranald Stephen McDougall, and Colonel Stephen Moylan. Among those also present were Gouverneur Morris and Alexander Hamilton. There the officers had "some Conversation respecting the want of Pay for the Army, etc." and learned of Virginia's decision to repeal its ratification of the impost. They also were made to realize that, no matter how just their claims were, justice alone would not be enough to ensure that they got what they were due.[24]

That month the government had received about $100,000 from the states, a large sum of money compared to what it had received in each of the first eleven months of the year. However, that still did not bring the government close to reaching its goal of $8,000,000. For all of 1782 only $422,000 in tax revenue had been received from the states.[25]

Colonel Brooks began New Year's Day by breakfasting and talking with Massachusetts delegate Samuel Osgood about the matters that had brought the three officers to Philadelphia. The other two officers also paid individual delegates unofficial visits.[26] Now was a good time to begin confronting them, for with the arrival of the New Year the plan to reduce the army went into effect. The Massachusetts and Connecticut regiments were reduced, and many officers still had no guarantee that they were ever going to receive the postwar pensions they had been promised. Some members of Congress had even been saying that the states should be responsible for providing that benefit to the officers of their lines.

And what about the pay they were owed? The accounts of the "deranged" officers—those who were being involuntarily retired because of the reduction in forces—had not been settled.[27]

The officers might have been disheartened, but three strong nationalists who wanted Congress to be granted real power by the states—the Financier, his assistant, and Hamilton—were not. Although they were aware that most of the delegates in Philadelphia did not share their goal, they knew they had something forceful enough to persuade the states and their biggest supporters in Congress to yield—the officers' petition. That document could be used to frighten legislators into giving the government the authority it needed to collect tax revenue. Then creditors would be paid back and Congress would be able to fund its operations without having to come to the states on its hands and knees.

When Gouverneur Morris wrote his friend John Jay, one of the peace commissioners in Paris, on January 1, 1783, he did little to hide his view that the appearance of the angry petition was going to bring a change for the better. "Genl. McDougall, Colo. Brooks ... and Colo. Ogden ... are now here with a Petition to Congress from the Army for Pay," Morris informed Jay. "The Army are now disciplined and their Wants as to food and Cloathing are releived but they are not paid. Their back Accounts are not settled. If settled the Ballances are not secured by competent Funds. No Provision is made for the Half-Pay promised them." Worse yet "some Persons and indeed some States pretend to dispute their Claim to it."

If the three officers succeeded in terrifying Congress, though, the delegates would have no choice but to act. "*The Army have Swords in their Hands,*" Morris declared threateningly in cipher. "I am glad to see Things in their present Train. Depend on it good will arise from the Situation to which we are hastening," he went on, switching from cipher to amazingly clear language. "And this you may rely on ... my Efforts will not be wanting."

Morris then started to make a pledge and switched to cipher once again as he specifically raised the specter of a coup: "*Although I think it probable that much ... Convulsion will ensue ... it must terminate in giving to Government that Power without which Government is but a Name. ... The People are well prepared. Wearied with the War their Acquiescence may be depended on ... and you and I ... know by Experience that when a few Men of Sense and Spirit get together and declare that they are the Authority such few as are of a different Opinion may easily be convinced of their Mistake by that powerful Argument the Halter,*" a hangman's noose.[28]

IF CONGRESS AND the states had to be guilefully terrified into acting, so be it. Gouverneur Morris was not averse to using less than honorable means to achieve what he thought were good ends. Early in the Revolution, when he was anxious to recruit soldiers for his state, a committee he sat on had succeeded in getting a local militia battalion to agree to serve by assuring its men that they were not going to be employed far from New York. But no formal agreement in writing existed, and the committee did not bother to inform the New York Provincial Congress that it had made such a promise, Morris noted to Washington. In other words, the promise could be broken.[29]

FOUR DAYS AFTER Morris wrote Jay to share with him his views on the officers' petition, a Philadelphia businessman named Arthur Clairy visited the three officers and proposed that the army and private creditors join forces. If the claims of both were "thrown upon the continental [Congress] at large," Clairy asserted, "paradoxical as it may appear, the hands of Congress will be strengthened—the army may be kept together, and the continental government take some tone, and be able to speak with proper authority, to any single refractory state, and be sure both of being heard and attended to." Only by the creditors and army working together could a "national faith and national character" be established in the country.[30]

But before that type of union could take place, the officers had to officially present their petition to Congress. That they did the next morning, January 6, in a large room with two fireplaces and high windows on the first floor of the Pennsylvania State House. As delegates sat in eighteenth-century Pennsylvania Windsor chairs and ladder-backs behind tables covered in green cloth, the petition was read aloud. Then, "as a mark of the important light in which the memorial was viewed," they quickly set up a committee to study it, meet with the officers, and prepare a report.[31] The Grand Committee, as it was called, was made up of one member from each state except Georgia, which had no representatives present at the time.[32] Four of its members—Oliver Wolcott, Samuel Osgood, Daniel Carroll, and James Madison—had sat in Congress with McDougall in 1781. One—Philemon Dickinson—had served in the army with him. Another—Richard Peters—had held the top post on the Board of War, which meant McDougall was familiar with him. And Alexander Hamilton had in the past received political lessons and book loans from him. Apparently only Phillips White, Jonathan Arnold, Silas Condict, Abner Nash, and John Rutledge did not know McDougall.[33]

In order for the committee to do anything about the officers' grievances it had to learn exactly what the government's financial health was. When its members gathered that evening they "agreed to meet again the succeeding evening for the purpose of a conference with the Superintendt. of Finance."[34]

At that subsequent meeting the Financier told the committee members "explicitly that it was impossible to make any advance of pay in the present state of the finances to the Army and imprudent to give any assurances with respect to future pay." That could not be done until the delegates were granted real taxation authority capable of producing a reliable flow of revenue from the states to Philadelphia. Morris "observed that even if an advance cd. be made it wd. be unhappy that it sd. appear to be the effect of demands from the army; as this precedent could not fail to inspire a distrust of the spontaneous justice of Congress & to produce repetitions of the expedient."

However, in spite of the American government's inability to provide the army with pay at this time, the situation was not hopeless. Morris had begun taking steps involving a foreign source that were aimed at getting some pay to the army. He did not spell out what those steps were but alluded to a scheme to obtain $500,000 in specie from Havana, saying "he had communicated these measures to Genl Washington under an injunction of secrecy, that he could not as yet disclose them without endangering their success."

Morris considered the state of the government's finances to be "so alarming that he thought of asking Congress to appoint a confidential committee to receive communications on that subject and to sanctify by their advice such steps as ought to be taken." Finally, after "much loose conversation … on the critical state of things the defect of a permanent revenue, & the consequences to be apprehended from a disappointment of the mission from the army," they decided to meet with McDougall, Brooks, and Ogden in three days to discuss the officers' petition.[35]

When Virginia's delegates wrote their governor, they noted the arrival of the three officers and their recommendation that the army immediately receive some back pay and "adequate provision for the residue of their arrears." The delegates, though, realized how difficult that task was. They were "pressed … by justice humanity & the public good to fulfil engagements" for which Congress did not have sufficient funds, and they knew they had not done all that was in their power to improve the situation.[36]

The pint-sized Madison understood that some delegates were certain to work for the adoption of general funding to enable Congress to satisfy the army, while others not wanting to see the government's power increased at the expense of the states' were going to do what they could to prevent the necessary measures from being taken. He had no idea what would happen if Congress failed to give the officers what they wanted, but did "wish the disquietude excited by the prospect" of failure to be felt exclusively by "those who impede the measures calculated for redressing complaints against the justice & gratitude of the public."[37]

IN NEW WINDSOR soldiers were busy preparing the materials needed to construct the Public Building—the Temple of Virtue. Trees were chopped down, trimmed of branches, and cut into logs of different sizes. The biggest and sturdiest were made into framing timber; the rest sawed and split for use as siding, laths, shingles, and ribs.

Each regiment had to provide about 400 timbers and more than 1000 shingles. Since plans to build some regimental hospitals had been cancelled, boards designated for use in their construction were also available for the building. The work crews were supposed to produce 5,120 board feet of timber, 3,000 laths, 21,000 shingles, and 1,000 split ribs. The shingles were not to be brought to the site of the building until needed, but other materials had to be there by the eighth of January in spite of the snow and low temperatures that were making the work in the woods harder. If a deadline weren't enough to motivate them to work hard, a good incentive—extra rations and rum—was.[38]

The plans for the construction of the building had been drawn up by Major Stephen Rochefontaine and Colonel Benjamin Tupper, a forty-four-year-old former schoolteacher and veteran of the French and Indian War. The major had actually chosen the site for the building, but the colonel was responsible for its overall construction. Assisting the colonel and liaising with Quartermaster General Timothy Pickering "for any Demands ... necessary to make" was Captain Israel Evans, the army chaplain who had first suggested the construction of the building to Washington.[39]

ON THURSDAY, JANUARY 9, McDougall wrote Henry Knox to give him an initial report from Philadelphia. He told the general at West Point that "it was judged expedient" to first speak with delegates about the officers' grievances before presenting the petition so "their Minds might be fully possessed of the Nature and importance of the Subject" of his mission. He did not want any delegate antagonistic towards the officers' cause "to give the Matter less Consideration than it deserves." That was done; the petition was received by Congress; a committee was established to consider it; and a meeting with its members was scheduled for Friday night. The delegates whom the officers had already spoken with believed that there was "a great Majority of Congress ... seriously disposed to do every thing in their power ... for the fulfilment of all their engagements to the Army" and that the petition was actually welcome.

But Congress lacked both cash on hand and general funding. It was not able to pay for present needs, erase debts that were "long due," or provide the future compensation it had promised the officers. McDougall questioned whether a number of eastern states would "pass even Vague Laws to recognize those debts." If not, the officers had to worry about their future security. Even if laws recognizing the debts were passed by a couple of the states, the officers had no guarantee that funds to pay them were going to be provided.

"Under these apprehensions, as well as others of general Concern to the Confederacy, what if it should be proposed to unite the influence of Congress with that of the Army and the public Creditors to obtain permanent funds for the United states which will promise most ultimate Security to the Army?" McDougall asked. He wanted General Knox's and General Huntington's opinions on the proposal and felt that later it might be necessary to get the other officers' views.[40]

Congress's lack of cash was also on Robert Morris's mind. When he met with a special committee made up of Madison, Osgood, and Rutledge, the Financier reported that America had overdrawn on funds in France by 3,500,000 livres. But he maintained that the government had to continue drafting bills of exchange regardless, and he requested that the committee give him permission to do so. He also asked that news of its action be kept secret in order to prevent damage to the public credit.

The committee members, as well as Morris, thought bills drawn on France in anticipation of a loan of $4,000,000 would be honored[41] and presented a report to Congress that Thursday. The following day, the tenth, the delegates unanimously approved a secret resolution allowing Morris to make further drafts. However, they did not want him to borrow more than Congress anticipated receiving in loans from Europe.[42]

AS McDOUGALL FOCUSED on his task in Philadelphia, Washington grew bitter about the neglect of his army. After noting in a letter to General Armstrong that they were "now ... in a disagreeable State of suspense respecting Peace or War" and giving his opinion on the British political situation, the Commander-in-chief vented his frustration over how the men and officers were being treated. "The Army, as usual, are without Pay, and a great part of the Soldiery without Shirts," he wrote to his friend, "and tho' the patience of them is equally thread bear, the States seem perfectly indifferent to their cries. In a word, if one was to hazard for them [the states] an opinion, upon this subject, it would be, that the Army had contracted such a habit of encountering distress and difficulties, and of living without money, that it would be impolitic and injurious to introduce other customs in it!"[43]

When Washington wrote his reliable aide Tench Tilghman that same day he did not say anything of the distress of the army. As was the case with Armstrong, he gave his views on British politics and the prospects of peace. Before doing so, though, he thanked the colonel, who was in Philadelphia, for taking care of some "small Commissions" for him and casually added, "I have sent Mr. [David] Rittenhouse the Glass of such Spectacles as suit my Eyes, that he may know how to grind his Christals."[44] He had by this time tried some of his officers' spectacles and found a pair that was just right for his eyes, the lenses of which he wanted duplicated.

Since Washington used his eyes a great deal[45] and was considered old for that day and age, the problems he experienced with his vision were to be expected. What Washington suffered from was presbyopia,[46] a form of farsightedness caused by muscle weakness and decreased elasticity in the eye's clear lens. *Presb-* is of Greek origin and means "old" or "old man."

THAT EVENING THE Grand Committee did not meet with the officers to discuss the petition, as it had planned to do. McDougall was suffering from rheumatism and had spent the day in bed at the Indian Queen Inn. Still, he wanted to meet with the committee members, but when he asked them to hold the meeting in his quarters there, they declined; having the discussion there, they thought, was "derogatory from the respect due to themselves." So they said some of them would be unable to make it because of the bad weather and rescheduled it for Monday evening, January 13.[47]

IN THE HUDSON HIGHLANDS the army was now preparing to lay the foundation of the Temple of Virtue. General Gates had appointed two lieutenants to assist Colonel Tupper[48] and indicated how many and what types of workers were needed. Each regiment was told to have its masons' helpers bring four spades and to "furnish Col. Tupper with one non-commissioned officer and twelve privates, with two hand sleds … to collect stone for [the two] chimneys and underpinning for the Public Building." Gates's orders also noted that the men were to "be furnished with a gill of rum and a half ration on the spot."[49]

For the carpentry and masonry work Gates had directed each regiment to provide the Massachusetts colonel with two carpenters, a mason and three masons' helpers, all of them privates. They were to be supervised by a small number of sergeants and corporals. Each brigade had to provide "one cross-cut saw, one adz, and as many inch-and-a-half augers as can conveniently be spared." Masons were told "to bring their [own] tools with them."[50]

Later, when the building was ready to be erected, eighty artificers[51] would be used to purchase materials and fill in the walls.

THE DAY AFTER Congress authorized Robert Morris to draw more bills of exchange, January 11, the Financier conferred with the French minister, Luzerne. The Frenchman promised to aid the superintendent as much as he could "consistent with his Duty" and asked Morris to explain in writing why America had overdrawn on funds in France, which he subsequently did.[52]

The Financier's situation was not enviable. "At this Moment I am making farther Exertions to bring our unwieldy System into Form, and Ward off impending Evils, but what the Success may be Heaven knows," he wrote to Benjamin Franklin. "Imagine the Situation of a Man who is to direct the Finances of a Country, almost without revenue … surrounded by Creditors whose Distresses, while they encrease their Clamors, render it more difficult to appease them. An Army ready to disband or Mutiny, A Government whose sole Authority consists in the Power of framing Recommendations," an obligation to settle all accounts and make "an honest Provision for Payment" that "becomes next to impossible" to meet because of "Confusions" that are destroying Congress's chances of getting the authority it needs.

Morris needed Franklin's help. "An immediate Command of Money is … necessary to our present Existence and future Prospects," he emphasized. Peace might arrive but America had to be prepared just in case the war continued.[53]

Around this time Hamilton wrote Governor Clinton to inform him of the three officers' arrival in the capital. He and his colleagues could "feel the mortification of a total disability to comply with their just expectations" and he intimated that a plot to employ the army in a scheme to help them broaden the national government's powers was in the air. If the men involved handled the officers' appeal properly, he felt it "may be turned to good account." More and more members were coming to the conclusion that Congress had to be strengthened, and Hamilton, a dark-clothed delegate with a serious countenance, thought Philadelphia might soon be given the authority to tax its citizens to get the revenue it needed to pay the army and public creditors, though he admitted that he was "far from being sanguine."[54]

How the army was going to be used in the scheme Hamilton referred to became clearer when the rescheduled evening meeting between the Grand Committee and the three officers took place on the thirteenth. As the highest-ranking officer, the still-suffering McDougall did most of the talking for his small group. At first he spoke calmly, but his tone became more heated as he continued. Perhaps he even began to stutter, since he had a speech impediment. What he talked most about were "the 3. cheif topics of the memorial, namely an immediate advance of pay, adequate provision for the residue and half pay."

The first of those three he saw as being essential because it was something certain to "soothe the discontents both of the officers & Soldiers." While serving honorably during the entire war, they had suffered greatly and had seen their hopes rise and fall. "If a disappointment were now repeated the most serious consequences were to be apprehended; … nothing less than the actual distresses of the army would have induced at this crisis so solemn an application to their country." With peace now appearing likely and the men worrying that they were going to be "still more neglected when the necessity of their services should be over," Congress's agreement on a soothing measure was even more important.

After the general made that point, the two colonels recited for the committee members "various incidents & circumstances tending to evince the actual distresses of the army, the irritable state in which the deputies left them and, the necessity of the consoling influence of an immediate advance of pay. Col Ogden … wished not … to return to the army if he was to be a messenger of disappointment to them."

When the officers were asked what to expect if no pay were advanced, they presented a terrifying specter. "The Sergeants & some of the most intelligent privates had been often observed in sequestered consultations," and a mutiny or something even worse was a real possibility. And "the temper of the officers, at least those of inferior grades," was such that they might be less likely now than in the past to exert themselves to quash one: They would feel the soldiers had good cause to mutiny because the public's neglect of them was a type of breach of contract between the two parties. The anger of the men in the army had reached such a level that they were in danger of going mad. "They did not reason or deliberate cooly on consequences, & therefore a disappointment might throw them blindly into extremities." One thing in particular that irritated them was that civilian officials were "regularly receiving their salaries" while military personnel were not.

When the second item on the officers' agenda—pay arrears—came up, McDougall and the two colonels "animadverted with surprize and even indignation on the repugnance of the States, some of them at least, to establish a federal revenue for discharging the federal engagements." Americans were well-off enough to sacrifice more of their financial resources. If they did not do so and the army unnecessarily suffered as a result, its patience would be exhausted and the union might even dissolve. "The benefits expected from the Revolution wd. be greatly impaired, and ... the contests which might ensue amg. the States would be sure to embroil the officers."[55]

Madison was not sure whether McDougall meant the officers would no longer stand behind the government if it continued failing the army or that a civil war could result and draw the officers into it. Whichever the case, neither Madison nor his colleagues were able to ask the general to clarify what he meant before he turned his attention to the officers' postwar pensions.[56]

Half pay had been promised by Congress and was "but a reasonable provision for the remnant of those lives which had been freely exposed in the defence of their country, and would be incompatible with a return to occupations & professions for which habits of 7 years standing unfitted them." However, it "had been industriously and artfully stigmatized in many states with the name of pension." Why was this so? The officers "had lent their blood and services to the public" and were therefore as entitled to "receive an annuity thereon, as those who had lent their money" to finance the Revolution. Nonetheless, they had indicated in their petition a willingness to accept some other reward in lieu of half pay.[57]

By the time the officers had finished and departed, the members of the Grand Committee were convinced that they had to take immediate steps to put out the fire. Accordingly, they set up a three-man subcommittee made up of Hamilton, Madison, and Rutledge to meet with Robert Morris to learn what financial resources were available and to prepare a report on the army's grievances for the larger committee. Hamilton was to act as the subcommittee's chairman.[58]

Earlier that day Congress had approved a motion by Richard Peters that, for the sake of the army, America seek more loans from France.[59] When the Financier then met with Luzerne the following day, he explained why he had to draw more bills of exchange in anticipation of a loan though he had already overdrawn on funds there: The officers' delegation was making demands; the army was in dire need; and the creditors who supplied American forces were clamorous. If the merchants who had loaned the government money were not satisfied, the army was not going to receive supplies. Consequently, France had to provide the funds asked for.[60]

As Morris tried to convince Luzerne that France had to lend America more money, Madison worried about what he had heard from McDougall, Brooks, and Ogden. They had provided the Grand Committee with "explanations ... of the most serious nature" and the Virginia delegate hoped they "could with propriety be promulged throughout the U.S." They were certain to "at least put to shame all those who … labored to throw a fallacious gloss over our public affairs," all those who by their actions frustrated the government from taking the steps it had to take to put the country's finances in good order.[61]

ON THE MORNING of the fourteenth, Horatio Gates learned from Colonel Tupper that the men building the Temple of Virtue had finished work on its foundation and had completed much of the framing. In his general orders Gates praised the artificers and laborers who were continuing the work on the building for their "spirit and alacrity," but he was not happy that some of the regiments were "dilatory in furnishing their quota of materials"; that was the only thing that could prevent "the speedy finishing of the business." He had a very high opinion of the army and did not want to have to provide the slow regiments with "another hint on the subject."[62]

At least two reasons could be cited for the delay in furnishing materials. One was that the 2nd Massachusetts hadn't provided the timber asked for because it didn't know how much it was required to furnish.[63] Another, which Washington learned from Colonel Pickering, was that men were "daily cutting wood in the neighborhood of Camp, transporting it to New Windsor on hand sleds and selling it to Inhabitants" instead of delivering it to the construction site.[64]

The day after Gates learned from Colonel Tupper that the underpinning was complete, he ordered "the foreman of the blacksmiths of each brigade to attend at Col. Tupper's quarters tomorrow morning at 9 o'clock to receive nail-rods and directions how to work them up."[65]

IN PHILADELPHIA ON the fifteenth, Robert Morris received a letter from Nathanael Greene. The most important news was that the British had evacuated Charleston, but the Financier also learned that the general had drawn bills on him in order to give the officers of the southern army an advance of two months' pay. Morris disliked that; either the whole army—the men and officers of the northern and southern armies—received pay or nobody did. Greene had forced the Financier's hand; it now seemed that something had to be done for the men and officers of the northern army.[66]

Later that day Morris met with Hamilton, Madison, and Rutledge. They "had a long Conference" and must have discussed Greene's action and what to do about pay for the northern army. The Financier knew roughly how much one month's pay amounted to because the Assistant Secretary of War, Major William Jackson, had provided an estimate the day after the Grand Committee's evening meeting with the officers.[67]

AS THE FOREMEN received the nail-rods, *The New York Packet, and the American Advertiser* reported that the men's huts had been built so well that "the American troops were never so comfortably accommodated with quarters … as at present." This resulted from "the surprising exertion and zeal of the officers and men." They had, "out of the rude materials with timber and stone alone ... in a few weeks built themselves more convenient and decent habitations than a great part of mankind ... ever possessed," the newspaper gushed. "This military site, from its extent, novelty, and perfect uniformity," the paper continued, "is thought to be the most pleasing and beautiful of anything of a similar nature, which has ever been exhibited in the world."[68]

Of course, the soldiers had not stopped working once they finished constructing their huts. They had gone to a nearby hill in the middle of their camp and were "now engaged in erecting a spacious building, of 110 feet long and 30 feet wide"[69]—the Temple of Virtue.

The day after the newspaper made that report, Gates informed the regiments that they were to deliver their shingles and "eighty ribs of round, straight, split out poles, eight feet and a half long, and two and a half inches wide at the upper end" to the building site on the afternoon of the 22nd. Rum and provisions were promised "for every ten ... good and straight, and for every fifty shingles ... well shaved."[70]

AS THE TROOPS in the Hudson Highlands received praise and continued their toils, Robert Morris concerned himself with those who were suffering as a result of Philadelphia's pecuniary problems. On the sixteenth he informed a creditor that he was unable to pay him any of what he was owed because of the terrible condition of the government's finances and the unresponsiveness of the states to his many heartfelt requests for funds, "from whence the public Creditors might receive at least an annual Interest for their Debts." All he could do was promise future settlement of his account and a certificate for the balance due, and express his pain over having to postpone "Payment of well founded Demands ... especially to those virtuous Americans whose personal Services have been attended with long suffering."[71]

The next day he summoned the officers' delegation to his office, but apparently only McDougall and Ogden came. They had "a proper Conversation on the Distresses of the Army &c" and then Morris, alluding to his scheme to get $500,000 in hard currency from Havana, informed them that before they had delivered their petition he "had taken Measures to obtain a Sum of Money for the Purpose of making them Pay." However, events had not yet developed to the point where benefits could be reaped from the measures he had taken. And they might even "frustrate" his measures.

The Financier, though, was "willing to make an Exertion to Advance one Month to the Army." He planned to pay enlisted men "about half a Dollar a Week until ... each received a full Months Pay" and give the officers "Notes of sixty Days Sight" or—if they preferred and were willing to wait until all the soldiers were paid—cash.

The two officers were satisfied and suggested that one member of their delegation in Philadelphia "return to Camp to state this and other Matters to their Constituents."

As for the other items brought up in their petition, Morris continued, "they must have Patience." For them to receive "Substantial Justice, they must give time for Wise Measures &c. &c."[72]

Although McDougall and Ogden were satisfied, a letter written by Brooks to a fellow colonel back in the Hudson Highlands reflected a growing sense of despair. Some of the delegates had "expressed great satisfaction at the army's having taken up their complaint in so spirited a manner, but had to lament their utter inability to give them redress." They knew "their powers were totally inadequate to the great purposes of a general government." Congress "had long since, called on the states for monies without effect—…of the eight millions which were to have been in almost a year ago not one sixteenth was yet received." And the delegates had seen "the impost, upon which they had put great dependence," go down to defeat. The belief was that if Congress did not get general funding, "confusion, disgrace and ruin" were certain. Also, a number of delegates opposed referring the lines to their respective states to seek redress. So the officers were at a loss as to what to do. "With an impotent congress, and unfeeling refractory states," the colonel complained, "we may well ask in God's name, what is to become of us?"

Maybe, one of the three officers in Philadelphia would return soon to the Hudson Highlands to work on a solution. Brooks did not elaborate on what he meant, but he stressed that what he was saying was not to be repeated to just anybody; "Secrecy" was absolutely crucial.

A few paragraphs later, the colonel mentioned that Robert Morris was working on getting the officers "a little pay." They could expect no more than "a month's pay … in notes at 60 days sight," an amount so small that, given their "present distress'd state," news that this was the most they were to expect might "throw them into convulsions which would be dangerous." Therefore, he believed, the news should be kept from them to ensure that they remained unified and better off; "in our union lies our safety,"[73] he opined.

Morris must have believed that he could provide the pay advance by drawing bills of exchange on France. However, he was mistaken. The day after he met with the two officers, Luzerne wrote to inform him that bills of exchange were not to be drawn on France's treasury without his prior authorization.[74]

The Financier had already promised the officers that he was going to advance the army one month's pay, however. And Nathanael Greene had advanced two months' pay to the southern army. Believing that he had to follow through on his promise and that both the northern and southern armies had to be paid equally, Morris provided Paymaster General John Pierce with instructions. Half of the two months' pay to the officers of the southern army was to be counted towards "last Year's Subsistance [allowance] and if the Advances to any Officer should exceed the Whole Subsistance due [for 1782] then a Deduction must be made from the Subsistance of the Current Year."

Morris then informed Pierce that because of the government's difficult financial situation an immediate advance of one month's pay in cash was not possible, and even if that were not so, he worried that "placing so much money … in the Soldiers hands might have ill Effects as to their Discipline and Morals." He explained what the privates and noncommissioned officers were to receive and then moved on to the officers, again ruling out any immediate advance of pay in cash and expressing his belief that the majority of them were going to wait until the government's financial health allowed them to receive that. However, since "many of them may be in immediate Distress," he continued, "I propose that for their Relief you may cause Advances to be made in my Notes payable at Sixty days."[75]

After providing instructions for Pierce, Morris wrote Greene. Enclosed with the letter to him was a copy of those instructions. "In Effect the Sum to be possessed by the Officers will be the same but the Account on which it is received will be different and by that Means the whole Army will be placed on an equal Footing," he said of his plan. "The Mode prescribed for paying the Soldiery is suggested by a Committee of Officers who are now in this City and perfectly coincides with my Opinion of Propriety for I cannot conceive that when Soldiers are well fed and clad they will have much Need of Money and … considering what Kind of Men usually fill up the Ranks of an Army too much would be rather pernicious than useful."

Of greater concern to Morris than the army was the inability of Congress to get funds. Greene's "Apprehensions that other States may like Virginia divert their Revenue to other Purposes than those of the general Defence" were well founded. Morris had "severely felt the Effects" of such diversions of funds and thought they were not seen as being as "infamous" as they really were because they occurred too often. "When the People shall have had their Eyes opened upon the Consequences they may perhaps endeavor at a Remedy but in the Interim we stand tottering on the Brink [of] Ruin,"[76] he mused.

GREENE WAS JUST as concerned as Morris about Congress's inability to get funds. So he wrote the governor of Georgia to urge that his state support at least a small tax. If Congress was unable to defray any of its expenses because it lacked revenue, both the government and the army were finished. The states would claim they could not bear the burden of taxes, but the government had to receive funds. "Cannot they bear a small one better than the Army can live without pay or support?" the general asked. "Had not you better submit to the inconveniences of a small tax than to suffer Government to expire and the Army disband?"[77]

Chapter Thirteen

"Mr. Hamilton Had Let Out the Secret"

AS MORRIS AND Greene worried that Congress was tottering on the brink of ruin, the officers focused on commutation. Colonels Ogden and Brooks visited the Financier on January 21 and consulted with him on that and other matters, and in the evening they apparently met with Hamilton's committee to discuss the same concerns.[1]

The officers could speak with Hamilton or Morris about commutation as often as they wanted, but without funding for Philadelphia nothing was going to happen on that front. And for funding to begin an entering wedge—the impost—was needed. Madison did not like that Virginia had repealed its approval of the impost, but he was not ready to give up on getting it and other taxes. "Congress cannot abandon the plan [the impost] as long as there is a spark of hope," he wrote to Edmund Randolph on the twenty-second. "Nay, other plans [taxes] on a like principle must be added. Justice, gratitude, our reputation abroad, and our tranquility at home, require provisions for a debt of not less than fifty millions of dollars." If Congress allowed each state to act separately, it would not receive the funds it needed. What the delegates had to have was real taxation authority, "revenue laws which operate at the same time through all the States, and are exempt from the control of each." If any state fearful of losing its sovereignty was able to effectively veto tax legislation favored by all the others, both domestic and foreign creditors were never going to be paid back.

Madison mentioned that the three officers from the army were still in Philadelphia, "urging the objects of their mission." The delegates were "thoroughly impressed with the justice of them, and ... disposed to do every thing which depends on them." However, Virginia's delegates had to wonder what they could say to the officers when their own state was claiming it couldn't afford "to make the necessary contributions [comply with requisitions], and [was] unwilling to establish funds for obtaining them elsewhere."[2]

Hamilton was particularly interested in the objectives of the officers' mission. He had begun working on a report for the Grand Committee almost immediately after meeting with the general and the two colonels but only now, after more than a week of discussions, was it ready to be presented.[3] Not much time was spent on the recommendations in his report on the first day of debates, the twenty-third,[4] but the following two days they were taken up with a real sense of purpose.

As the delegates considered Hamilton's suggestions, an angry Robert Morris attempted on the second day of debates to influence events by abruptly sending the President of Congress a letter offering his resignation as superintendent. The government had to have the authority to obtain the revenue needed to fund the debt, but he was losing hope that it was ever going to get it. "To encrease our Debts while the Prospect of paying them diminishes, does not consist with my Ideas of Integrity. I must therefore quit a Situation which becomes utterly insupportable," the Financier announced. In his overly emotional message, which the delegates decided to keep secret, Morris vowed that he would "never be the Minister of Injustice," but did say he was going to stay on "until the End of May" out of a concern that "the Public Measures might be deranged" if he left precipitately.[5]

The announcement "made a deep & solemn impression on Congress. It was considered as the effect of dispondence in Mr. Morris of seeing justice done to the public Credtrs. or the public finances placed on an honorable establishmt; as a Source of fresh hopes to the enemy … as ruinous both to domestic & foreign Credit: & as producing a vacancy which noone knew how to fill & which no fit man wd. venture to accept."[6]

In addition to Morris's resignation, Congress had to consider a report prepared by the Grand Committee.[7] That report, which took into account what Hamilton had written about the army's grievances, included recommendations on how to resolve three of the five issues in the officers' petition. The other two, which related to the inadequacy of their rations and clothing allowances, had to wait until Congress got "more precise information."[8]

The Grand Committee recommended that Robert Morris give the men at least one month's pay "as soon as the State of the public finances … permit."[9] The army's other pay arrears would be taken care of by either the individual states or the Financier; arrears before August 1, 1780, were to be the states' responsibility, those after that time Morris's. Unpaid soldiers whose accounts showed arrears after that date were to receive certificates yielding six percent interest.

Delegates from eastern states objected to that date, though. Hamilton therefore proposed changing it to December 31, 1780, and Congress approved the new date.

The committee also "resolved that the troops of the United States in common with all the Creditrs. … have an undoubted right to expect … security, and that Congress will make every effort in their power to obtain from the respective States, *general* & substantial funds adequate to the object of funding the whole debt of the U.S. and that Congs. ought to enter upon an immediate & full consideration of the nature of such funds & the most likely mode of obtaining them."[10]

Some delegates, however, did not want Philadelphia to have that power. Virginia's Theodorick Bland moved that the resolution be changed to "Congress will make every effort in their power consistent with the Articles of Confederation to obtain from the respective states, *general* & substantial funds."[11] Jonathan Arnold liked his fellow doctor's motion and seconded it, but most of the members grew upset and Congress adjourned for the day without any resolution on the motion. The important issue of how to fund the national debt remained unsolved. The delegates agreed to take up that issue the next time Congress met.

Another recommendation by the Grand Committee was that the officers be given the opportunity to choose between a postwar half-pay pension and commutation. The latter, if chosen, was supposed to come in the form of a lump sum payment in cash or in notes bearing six percent annual interest. Those notes were to be payable one year after the officers had left the army. How many years' pay the lump sum would equal was not specified.

FOR THE MEN at the New Windsor Cantonment the twenty-fourth was the day Gates had set for them to bring "270 laths, split out of shingle timber" to the building site. These narrow, four-foot-long strips of wood were to be used "to complete the filling in the frames." Each regiment was to provide a sergeant and two privates for the job, and masons and their supervisors also had to appear at the site that morning. Gates expected the men to complete the work in two days and again promised rum and provisions for the delivery of "good laths" and the completion of the job.[12]

THE FOLLOWING DAY Congress continued to debate the Grand Committee's report. The delegates approved its recommendation that Robert Morris give the men at least one month's pay once the government's finances were in order. They also changed the date when pay arrears would become Congress's responsibility back to August 1, 1780. A small number of delegates, including Hamilton, had talked with Morris and he had voiced objections to the December 31, 1780 date; he was working to get general funding for Congress and the more debt it was responsible for, the stronger case he could make for it getting greater taxation authority.

The delegates also considered the clause "Congress will make every effort in their power to obtain from the respective States, *general* & substantial funds adequate to the object of funding the whole debt ..." again and eventually decided to shorten its length and scope; now they promised to "make every effort in their power to obtain from the respective states substantial funds, adequate to the object of funding the whole debt ...."

Turning to commutation, Hamilton moved that the officers receive a sum equal to six years' pay. This motion was voted on and rejected, delegates from New England and New Jersey joining forces and casting nay votes to thwart the nationalists. Bland then proposed that the sum be equal to six-and-a-half years' pay, not realizing that Hamilton's motion had been rejected because it was considered too generous. There may have been concern about the number of years and the associated cost, but those opposed to commutation probably were motivated to vote against it for another reason: they saw little difference between it and pensions. Delegates from Connecticut and Rhode Island, where the general public disliked pensions and feared the creation of a privileged class of citizens, had even received instructions to oppose any such benefit. The best that could be done was to toss the issue to a five-member committee headed by Samuel Osgood and including James Wilson, Thomas Fitzsimmons, John Lewis Gervais, and Hamilton.

As for funding the debt, Congress again put off that issue; it would be taken up on the twenty-seventh.[13]

When the debates resumed on Monday, a delegate who possessed a mind that was "one blaze of light"[14]—the tall, muscular, bewigged James Wilson—opened with "some judicious remarks" concerning Congress's need for substantial permanent funds; he understood that now the delegates should focus exclusively on establishing a general funding program to free Congress from its dependence upon the states. The Pennsylvanian who spoke with a burr praised his country for having "displayed both an unexampled activity in resisting the enemy, and an unexampled patience under the losses & calamities occasioned by the war. In one point only … they had appeared to be deficient & that was a cheerful payment of taxes." The reason why Americans had an aversion to paying taxes, why they saw them in an "odious light," was traceable to their troubles with England.

Americans were able to afford taxes and, Wilson asserted, what Congress needed was "some more effectual mode of drawing forth the resources of the Country." Now the government had to have them because it was not able to pay its huge debt, had no funds available to meet future needs, and was still at war. Delegates must, he maintained, level with their constituents about the situation and, if nothing better could be achieved, "come to eclaircissement" on funding. If Congress got general funding, it would be able to make domestic loans again and the value of paper currency would increase. Also, "a public debt resting on general funds would operate as a cement to the confederacy, and might contribute to prolong its existence." When Wilson concluded, he moved for his fellow delegates to resolve that "it is the opinion of Congress that complete justice cannot be done to the Creditors of the United States, nor the restoration of public credit be effected, nor the future exigencies of the war provided for, but by the establishment of *general* funds to be collected by Congress."[15]

After the motion was seconded by Thomas Fitzsimmons, Bland requested that two papers from Virginia be read aloud. One was a resolution by the General Assembly letting Congress know that Virginia could afford to provide the delegates with only fifty thousand pounds in local currency of the amount requisitioned by Congress. The other was the state's repeal of its ratification of the impost.[16]

Virginia's actions struck Connecticut's Oliver Wolcott as being inconsistent and Nathaniel Gorham, a forty-four-year-old Massachusetts moderate, also criticized that state. But he was more interested in Wilson's motion. He worried about how the word "general" was going to be interpreted. He did not want the word "understood to refer to every possible object of taxation as well as to the operation of a particular tax throughout the States." And he believed the states' failure to comply with Congress's requests for funds indicated that "the constitutional mode of annual requisitions was defective." He "intimated that lands were already sufficiently taxed; & that polls & commerce were the most proper objects. At his instance the latter part of the motion was so amended as to run 'establishment of permanent & adequate funds to operate generally throughout the U. States.'"[17]

Hamilton then rose and spoke at great length on funding, specifying two ways for the government to get permanent funds: One relied entirely on Congress to levy taxes on all Americans alike and collect the revenue with its own appointed officials; the other allowed each state to establish its own permanent funds for the national government and to choose to use either its own officials or congressionally-appointed ones to collect the revenue. The program Wilson envisioned used the first way to obtain funding, which in Hamilton's opinion had very discernable advantages over the current system. It offered simplicity, whereas the other program offered complexity; if Congress allowed all the states to establish their own permanent funds for its usage, "difficulties attending the mode of fixing the quotas" were certain to arise. It offered certainty; if Philadelphia allowed the states to choose between their own elected officials or congressionally-appointed ones to collect taxes, they were going to choose their own people, who would not aggressively perform their duties for fear of becoming unpopular with the public. And it offered cost savings; "the [tax] collection would be effected with fewer officers under the management of Congress, than under that of the States."[18]

Hamilton's view was not shared by all the delegates, though. Gorham felt several of the states could be trusted to collect taxes for Congress.[19] Fat, old Eliphalet Dyer of Connecticut strongly opposed having congressionally-appointed officials collect taxes and thought "the States would never be brought to consent to it."[20] Bland believed that even if Congress should have general funding, the states were not going to grant it. He also claimed that the real reason why they were not providing Philadelphia with the funds it requisitioned was not "their inability but ... the inequality of the apportionments." He wanted Congress to abide by the Articles of Confederation, "to ground the requisition on an actual valuation of lands."[21]

And what would happen to the suffering army and the anxious public creditors if Congress did not get general funding? South Carolina's Dr. David Ramsay, who spoke before Bland, thought that if that happened, they were going to have to go to their home states for the money they were owed, which was a bad thing: Some states would bear heavier burdens than others; "rivalships relative to trade wd. impede a regular impost & wd. produce confusions amg. the States; … some of the States would never make … provision for half pay and … the army wd. be so far defrauded of the rewards stipulated to them by Congress."[22]

IN THE HUDSON highlands the smiths were now delivering the nails they had made to the hilltop where the Temple of Virtue was being erected. The men were ready to begin shingling the structure. Engaged in the work would be five carpenters from each regiment, all of whom Gates hoped were highly skilled in shingling because he planned to complete the job while they were experiencing "weather … extremely soft and favorable."[23]

IN PHILADELPHIA THAT Tuesday, James Wilson stood up and defended the use of congressionally-appointed tax collectors "as essential to the idea of a general revenue, since without it the proceeds of the revenue wd. depend entirely on the punctuality energy & unanimity of the States." And the states were sadly deficient in those qualities, which explained why Congress was now in serious trouble.[24]

After Hamilton strongly supported Wilson, Thomas Fitzsimmons brought to the delegates' attention the case of Pennsylvania to illustrate why Congress had to get general funding. The General Assembly there, Fitzsimmons informed them, had been ready to pay its own creditors with money meant for the national government and was stopped from doing so only by the "urgent representations of a Committee of Congress & … the hope that some general system in favr. of all the public creditors would be adopted." If the national government ended up having no chance of getting general funding, the Pennsylvania legislators would promptly go ahead and pay creditors from their state with funds intended for Congress's use.[25]

Madison then offered an amended version of the motion Wilson had made the previous day. Wilson's proposed resolution was bound to provoke protests because it insisted that Congress be charged with collecting the tax revenue it needed in order to pay back the government's creditors and restore public credit. Madison's proposed resolution simply stated that Congress considered "the establishment of permanent & adequate funds to operate generally throughout the U. States … indispensibly necessary for doing complete justice to the Creditors of the U. S., for restoring public credit, & for providing for the future exigencies of the war."[26] It said nothing about who would collect them.

John Rutledge was not satisfied. The word "generally" suggested "a degree of uniformity in the tax which would render it unequal" and the public would not support a "general tax." The South Carolina delegate also apparently wanted no such tax himself "if [it] extended beyond an impost on trade." He favored congressional requisitions based on the value of land.[27]

Arthur Lee of Virginia agreed that the tax "wd. be unequal" and later cited his state's decision to repeal its ratification of the impost as proof of an "aversion to a general revenue." He also did not want Congress to have greater taxation authority; "placing the purse in the same hands with the sword, was subversive of the fundamental principles of liberty."[28] In other words, if the government had the power to fund its own operations by taxing the people directly and had an army behind it, it would be able to trample on the sovereignty of the states. It would use its funds to reward the army and turn it into a privileged body of men different from the rest of the population, thus securing its loyalty and guaranteeing that it became the government's willing instrument for enforcing oppressive laws.

Wilson came to his feet once again and defended himself. His motion of the previous day had been meant as a recommendation that the states vest in Congress the power it needed. The Articles of Confederation had provided the government with too little authority and, as a result, "there was more of a centrifugal than centripetal force in the States." The solution was to have Congress fund the national debt using the method that had been proposed. That "would produce a salutary invigoration & cement of the Union."[29]

Connecticut's Oliver Ellsworth, a thin snuff-loving man with dark brows whose stubbornness had led a friend to say of him that had he written "Godd" instead of "God," it would have taken him three weeks to relent and correct his spelling mistake,[30] was philosophical. Yes, Congress needed general funding, but not all the states would support it. And if some states proved "delinquent," was it appropriate for Congress to use force against them? If so, how much force? If none were used, general funding was impossible. Therefore the best option was to let the states establish their own permanent funds, which would then "be provided at the recommendation of Congs. and appropriated to the discharge of the common debt."[31]

Hamilton did not like that idea. The desired results were not going to be achieved if Congress allowed each state to establish its own permanent funds for the delegates' use. Philadelphia should levy taxes on all Americans alike and, since "the energy of the federal Govt. was evidently short of the degree necessary for pervading & uniting the States … introduce the influence of officers [tax collectors] deriving their emoluments from & consequently interested in supporting the power of, Congress" to collect the revenue.[32]

Hearing such a statement, some delegates might have concluded that Hamilton and others who supported general funding were prepared to sacrifice the interests of the states at the altar of the national government. When he said "introduce the influence of the officers deriving their emoluments from & consequently interested in supporting the power of, Congress," they might have believed he and likeminded nationalists intended to send officials paid by and supportive of Congress into the states to bully them into giving the national government broad taxation authority. That was impermissible! Those delegates remembered how the British army had been used by Parliament to oppress American colonists and they were not going to let themselves and state legislatures be bullied into endowing Congress with excessive powers.

"This remark," Madison later noted when writing about Hamilton's statement, "was imprudent & injurious to the cause wch. it was meant to serve. This influence was the very source of jealousy which rendered the States averse to a revenue under the collection as well as appropriation of Congress" and every delegate in Philadelphia "who concurred in any degree with the States in this jealousy smiled at the disclosure" by Hamilton. "Mr. Bland & still more Mr. L[ee] … took notice in private conversation that Mr. Hamilton had let out the secret."[33]

He had not said *army* officers would pervade the states but he, like the Financier and his assistant, certainly was eyeing the military. And the rumor was that some public creditors believed if the army simply put its foot down, the states were bound to yield to those desiring to see Congress have greater taxation authority.

North Carolina's Hugh Williamson followed Hamilton and then Madison spoke. The blue-eyed, soft-voiced, thirty-one-year-old Virginian chose to address the issue differently, beginning with an appeal to his fellow delegates' sense of public virtue. For him "the idea of erecting our national independence on the ruins of public faith and national honor must be horrid to every mind which retained either honesty or pride." The question therefore was not whether Congress should pay its debts to the creditors, but whether Congress had to have permanent funding to do so.

They all knew the current system, whereby Congress requested the money it needed to reduce the national debt from "13 separate and independent governments," was too unreliable "to satisfy our present creditors, or to tempt others to become our creditors in future." And a system whereby each state established its own permanent fund and provided Congress with money from it to retire the debt was not practicable. For one thing, once one state broke its commitment to Congress and diverted money to local needs, others were sure to follow its example.

The best way to provide Congress with permanent funding was to give it the authority to tax all Americans and collect the revenue with its own appointed officials. Such a system should reduce jealousy between the states by making them realize that everybody was being taxed at the same time. And it should prevent states from diverting funds by having the money collected and sent "directly into the treasury of the U S." Also, it would "become soonest productive" and "give instantaneous confidence & content to the public creditors at home & abroad, and place our affairs in the most happy train."

Madison then reminded the delegates of what Fitzsimmons had said about the Pennsylvania General Assembly and pointed out that if that state chose to pay its troops and creditors with money meant for Congress, other states were sure to do the same. "What then wd. become of the confederation?" he asked. "What wd. be the authority of Congress? wt. the tie by which the States cd.

be held together? what the source by which the army could be subsisted & cloathed? What the mode of dividing & discharging our foreign debts?"

After posing a couple more rhetorical questions, he became an advocate for the army. "It ought to be carefully remembered that this subject was brought before Congress by a solemn appeal from the army to the justice & gratitude of their Country," he began. "Besides immediate pay, they ask for permanent security for arrears. Is not this request a reasonable one? will it be just or politic to pass over the only adequate security that can be devised, & instead of fulfilling the stipulations [promises] of the U. S. [government] to them, to leave them to seek their rewards separately from the States to which they respectively belong?" he asked. "The patience of the army has been equal to their bravery, but that patience must have its limits; and the result of despair can not be foreseen, nor ought it to be risked," he warned.

As for the assertion that Philadelphia would be in control of the sword and the purse if it had general funding, Madison maintained that it already had legal authority over both. Congress had the constitutional authority to determine how much money it needed to requisition. The states were free to determine only how to provide the funds requested. "A requisition of Congress on the States for money is as much a law to them; as their revenue acts when passed are laws to their respective Citizens," he insisted. And if laws passed by Congress are found lacking, they should be changed to allow it to uphold the constitution. If they cannot be changed, Madison explained, "order & justice among the members of the Union" will not be preserved. If Congress chose to obtain funds by taxing the people and having its own officials collect the revenue instead of relying on requisitions from the states, it would not be doing anything unconstitutional or infringing on the states' sovereignty; it would simply be changing the law so its constitutional authority to get the money it needed had "a more certain & equal efficacy."

The contention that the states were so opposed to the impost that "any recommendations of a general revenue [were] hopeless & imprudent" was dismissed by Madison. The five percent duty on imports had been "adopted immediately & in its utmost latitude by several of the States." Others that had given their conditional approval, he added, "have since complied more liberally," and "one of them after long refusal has complied substantially." Now only two states—Georgia and Rhode Island—were holding out, and Madison could not say for sure that the first of those two was strongly opposed to the impost. "On the whole it appears that the necessity & reasonableness of the scheme have been gaining ground among the states," he surmised.

Virginia, though, had repealed its ratification of the impost, thus embarrassing Madison, who admitted a reluctantance to "disregd. ... the sense of Constitnts." But members of Congress weren't just representatives of their states; "they [also] owed a fidelity to the collective interests of the whole." Sometimes they should follow their true beliefs and "hazard the personal consequences" regardless of instructions from their states or the views of their constituents. This was one of those times. And Madison thought if the Virginia legislature knew as much about the state of affairs as he did, it "would not have repealed … the impost & would even now rescind the repeal."

Madison concluded that "it was the duty of Congress under whose authority the public debts had been contracted to aim at a general revenue as the only means of discharging them; & that this dictate of justice & gratitude was enforced by a regard to the preservation of the confederacy, to our reputation abroad & to our internal tranquility."[34]

His appeal did not end the debate. Rutledge complained that those who wanted Congress to have permanent funding did not specify what items would be taxed.[35] Fitzsimmons feared that distrust was preventing them from making "progress … towards the attainment of those ends wch. all in some way or other aimed at" and said "it was a mistake to suppose that any specific plan had been preconcerted among the patrons of a general revenue."[36]

Wilson reassured the delegates that Fitzsimmons was correct. His motion on funding was the result of "the declaration on Saturday last by Congs. that substantial funds ought to be provided; … the memor[i]al of the army … the memorials from the State of Pa. holding out the idea of separate appropriations of her revenue unless provision were made for the public creditors, … the deplorable & dishonorable situation of public affairs which had compelled Congress to draw bills on the unpromised & contingent bounty of their ally, and which was likely to banish the Superintdt. of Finance … from his department." He had not offered specifics on his plan "because he thought them premature." Once the government's right to levy taxes and collect the revenue itself was established, they could work on the specifics.[37]

After Wilson spoke, a motion was made to have his proposal for general funding referred to a committee so "some practicable plan might be reported" and some possible specific taxes suggested. When the motion was voted on, it failed to pass.[38]

Arthur Lee thought "it was a waste of time to be forming resolutions & settling principles on this subject and asked whether these wd. ever bring any money into the public treasury." The best course of action was for Congress to call all the governors together and "lay before them a full state of our public affairs." Lee knew "the States would never agree to those plans which tended to aggrandize Congress; that they were jealous of the power of Congress," and he confessed that he did not think their fear was "an unreasonable one; that no one who had ever opened a page or read a line on the subject of liberty, could be insensible to the danger of surrendering the purse into the same hand which held the sword."[39]

He saw clearly what the nationalists' strategy was: "Every Engine is at work here to obtain permanent taxes and the appointment of Collectors by Congress, in the States. The terror of a mutinying Army is playd off with considerable efficacy," he wrote to Samuel Adams the following day. "It is certainly a great misfortune to any Country that their army should be discontented," he continued, "and the more so when they have reason on their side, as in the present case." But the nationalists' strategy was "neither wise nor safe." The states, he was sure, were not meeting their quotas because their financial health did not permit them to do so. Once peace arrived they would be able to provide Congress with the funds it needed to pay the army and the other creditors what they were owed. Lee then predicted that the nationalists' plot would not succeed: "A majority of the Army at least, will remember that they are Citizens, and not lend themselves to the tory designs, as I verily beleive this is, of subverting the Revolution."[40]

When the debates resumed on Wednesday a committee of the whole was established and several amendments were made to Wilson's proposed resolution. It now read: "It is the opinion of Congress that the establishment of permanent & adequate funds on taxes or duties which shall operate generally & on the whole in just proportion throughout the U. S. are indispensably necessary towards compleat justice to the public Creditors, for restoring public Credit, & for providing for the future exigencies of the War."

The amended resolution passed,[41] but that did not mean the two sides were going to be able to work together to craft a funding program capable of solving the government's financial problems. Bland suggested that all money requisitioned by Congress be used to pay the creditors the interest they were due; that was "the only expedient that cd. produce immediate relief to the public Creditors." No delegate seconded his motion,[42] though.

Wilson estimated the government's foreign and domestic debt, the deficits for 1782 and 1783, the amount of interest that would have to be paid, the annual revenue the government ought to have, and how much the impost and certain taxes could bring in. Salt, land, wine, imported spirits and coffee were all considered by the Pennsylvania delegate to be items worth taxing. When he finished expressing his ideas and throwing around numbers, he admitted that his analysis was "extremely imperfect." He had provided it only out of "a desire to contribute his mite towards such a system as would place the finances of the U. S. on an honorable & prosperous footing."[43]

Gorham found fault with both Bland's and Wilson's ideas. Bland's suggestion, among other things, "could never be admitted because it would leave our army to starve." Wilson's proposal upset him because it placed a tax on salt. What Gorham wanted the delegates to do was focus solely on the impost and "remove the objections which had retarded it, by limiting the term of its continuance, leaving to the States the nomination of the collectors, and by making the appropriation of it more specific."[44]

Rutledge shared Gorham's view that they should focus solely on the impost. The impost, he proposed, could be sent to the states again but with some changes to make it more acceptable to them: Let it remain in effect for no more than twenty-five years; have the tax revenue generated by it go only towards eliminating present and future foreign debt, paying the army what it was owed, and meeting future war-related needs; and allow the money collected in each state to be counted as part of the quota assigned to it under the requisitioning program.

Lee seconded Rutledge's proposed changes, but Wolcott complained that the major importing states were going to pass on the costs of the duties to states that had to purchase almost all their foreign goods from them because they lacked ports. Ellsworth, too, believed the impost favored the big importers; they were going to have their requisition quotas reduced by the amount of the duties they paid, though they actually felt zero-sum affects from them because they were passing on the costs.

The Connecticut delegate also thought the states would not accept the impost if it came with land and excise taxes, agreed that the measure could only remain in effect for a limited number of years, and wanted the states to be allowed to either nominate or appoint the tax collectors. Revenue generated by the measure should first go towards reducing foreign debt.[45]

Hugh Williamson saw good and bad in Rutledge's motion. The impost had to be changed, "particularly in its duration & the appointment of the Collectors. But … crediting the States severally for the amount of their collections was so palpably unjust & injurious that … it should not be persisted in." Though the credits appeared to benefit states that did much importing from abroad, Williamson believed they were better off not receiving them. They traded with states that had few or no ports and under the impost they were certain to pass on the cost of the duties on foreign goods by taxing them. Rather than both paying those costs that were passed on and sending funds to Congress, states with few or no ports would simply choose to stop trading and become self-sufficient.[46]

Ramsay and Bland also did not want the money collected in each state to be counted as part of the quota assigned to it. Bland "indeed … opposed … the whole motion (of Mr. Rutledge)." He did not believe the government would be able to find people or businesses willing to lend it money if Congress had no authority to get the funds needed to make interest payments to the creditors or pay the principal of their loans. "He proposed that the revenue … solicited from the States should be irrevocable by them without the consent of Congress, or of nine of the States." And although he had been a strong supporter of state sovereignty, he wanted no limit placed on the duration of the impost because it was not possible to say how long the debt was going to last. He held these views because "it was trifling with Congs. to enable them to contract debts, & to withold from them the means of fulfilling their contracts."[47]

Arthur Lee came to Rutledge's defense again. He had seconded the South Carolinian's motion "because he thought it most likely to succeed; … the States would not concur in the impost on trade without a limitation of time affixed to it," but "with such a limitation and the right of collection, he thought Virga. R. Island & the other States probably wd. concur."

As for Bland's proposal, it was impossible for revenue solicited from the states to be made irrevocable because the states still could repeal any of their acts. Lee, though, "thought there wd. be no danger of a repeal."

On letting a state's collections count towards its requisition quota, he was ready to make a concession to those opposing Rutledge's motion. He knew the delegates had to do something "in the present alarming crisis," so he "was willing to strike out the clause crediting the States for their respective collections of the revenue on trade, as it was supposed that it wd. impede the measure."[48]

Hamilton's concern was that some creditors might be given priority over others when relief was provided. He did not want Congress to decide that foreign creditors and the army had to be paid what they were owed before domestic creditors. The delegates should do everything in their power to fund the entire debt, as they had promised on the twenty-fifth. If they now adopted a plan that put the foreign creditors and the army first, "the domestic Creditors would take ... alarm ... [and] withhold their influence from any such measures recommended by Congress." Such an action on their part was very undesirable because their lobbying effort was the key to getting general funding for the government.[49]

Rutledge's motion containing proposed changes to the impost was not appreciated by Wilson; it ignored the public creditors in his state. On Thursday he went on the attack and charged some of the delegates with displaying too little concern for Pennsylvania's creditors. If the government did not address their concerns, his state would take the money that was supposed to be sent to Congress and use it to pay them what they were owed.[50] It was not a threat that Wilson must have enjoyed using, for he and his fellow nationalists did not want creditors going to their home states to be paid back. They preferred having the moneyed men go to Congress because that bound them to the national government.

As the month came to an end the impost appeared to be dead. Where was the government going to get money to pay the army and the public creditors what they were owed? Only about $420,000 of the $8,000,000 requisitioned from the states for the following year had arrived and just $833,000 in loans from Europe had been obtained.[51] Even without taking into account interest payments that had to be made to creditors, the government expected expenses the following year to be more than $5,700,000.[52]

The delegates had to find a way to obtain revenue that they all agreed was legal under the Articles of Confederation. The requisitions they had been making were legal but problematic; they were based on the values of states' lands and the buildings and improvements made on them. As Hamilton knew, if the states made the assessments they would deliberately undervalue their lands and buildings so as to lessen their tax burdens. The logical alternative would have been to have congressionally-appointed assessors determine the values, but there was much opposition to that idea.[53]

NATHANAEL GREENE was still hoping Georgia would ratify the impost and levy a tax on its people when he wrote Secretary of War Lincoln and the Financier in early February. He had been to that state and had told the legislators there and in South Carolina, which he also planned to visit, that if they did not approve those measures, the northern states were not going to support Congress and keeping the army intact was going to become impossible. "They were already tired of living on promises," the general warned, "and ... the Moment the Officers are convinced that Congress cannot make good their engagements they will leave their service."[54]

ON TUESDAY, FEBRUARY 4, the officers' delegation visited Robert Morris's office to inform him that Colonel Brooks was going to be returning to the Hudson Highlands soon. The three officers wanted to know when the process of providing the army with one month's pay would begin and had questions on how the army's accounts were to be settled. Regarding the one month's pay, the Financier replied that he was "not quite ready" yet but promised an answer the following morning. As for the settlement of accounts, Morris asked that they write their questions down and allow him time to study them so he could give the officers precise answers.[55]

Meanwhile, the delegates took up a report they had received the day before from the five-man committee tasked with doing something about the officers' request for commutation. Commutation, a substitute for the half-pay postwar pension, was important to the officers because they felt that when Congress had resolved to provide them with that benefit, it had concluded "a solemn contract" with them. That contract, which had been approved by the delegates "at a most critical juncture ... [as] the only expedient left to prevent the dissolution of the Army," they were honoring by their "faithful and painful Performance." The nation had to now hold up its end of the bargain and honor that agreement because "an attempt to abridge them in their expectations would not only be dishonorable but dangerous."[56]

What the committee recommended was approval of commutation. Remembering that Hamilton's recommendation to provide the officers with six years' pay had failed when voted on back on the twenty-fifth, the delegates started at five-and-a-half years' pay. When that failed to pass, they proposed five years' pay. It didn't matter; the votes for commutation were not there. Massachusetts delegates supported it, but other members from New England and New Jersey remained opposed, and though the ayes outnumbered the nays six to five, seven votes in favor were needed. Hamilton and Wilson had pointed out that commutation would cost the government less than the half-pay pension, but delegates lined up against it probably could never have been swayed by that argument. When Hugh Williamson proposed five-and-a-quarter years' pay, some members who disliked commutation and half pay reminded their fellow delegates that they had instructions from their states to oppose such a measure and "queried the validity of the act of Congs. which had stipulated half pay to the Army, as it had passed before the [Articles of] Confederation [were ratified], and by a vote of less than seven States."

A surprised Madison countered that the act had been approved in accordance with what were then the accepted rules and since the officers had served faithfully under them, they were entitled to the compensation promised as a matter of justice. And commutation had been offered in place of the pension "because of objections agst. the half pay" from the very states that were now opposing commutation.

Wilson also acted surprised; he wondered why a state would tell its delegates to oppose laws passed by Congress. If the states proved strong enough to continue opposing absolutely binding and legal obligations of Congress, the authority of the United States was doomed.

Rhode Island's Jonathan Arnold then asked that the report be set aside until he heard further from his state, and the delegates eventually agreed not to make any decision on it at this time.

Before they made that decision, though, New Hampshire's John Taylor Gilman had suggested that "it wd. be best to refer the subject of ½ pay to the several States to be settled between them & their respective lines." He would make this suggestion again a few weeks later, and others besides Gilman favored that idea.[57]

On the fifth, Robert Morris issued written authorization for the soldiers to receive their one month's pay in weekly cash payments of fifty cents and for the officers to get theirs in notes.[58] Authorization of the pay was possible because loans from Holland and France were anticipated, though they were still being negotiated. The Financier informed McDougall and Ogden of the action when he saw them, accepted some questions on the settlement of accounts that they had written at his request, and "promised a speedy Answer."[59]

THE FOLLOWING DAY, February 6, was the anniversary of America's alliance with France. Colonel Tupper had been anxious to have the Temple of Virtue ready for a reception that the Commander-in-chief wanted to hold there, so General Gates had set a deadline of 9:00 a.m., Thursday, January 30, for regiments that were behind in filling their quotas for shingles, laths, and ribs. Because the weather had eased in late January the colonel felt that the shingling could be finished, but as the month ended he found himself complaining about "a want of nails," and he worried that the building wouldn't be finished in time for the celebration. Those who were holding up the shingling, he thought, might consider it "so trifling a matter" as to be not worth noting, and he did not want to be blamed for their actions since "in this case [he was] only a servant."[60]

By February 4, though, the delay in shingling was a thing of the past. That day Gates directed each regiment "to make and deliver to Colonel Tupper or his assistant ... four benches" for the building's large central hall. The benches, which had to arrive in time for the anniversary celebration, were to be "eight feet four inches long, eleven inches wide, eighteen inches high, with two substantial legs exactly one foot from each end, with a supporter in the middle."[61]

When the important day arrived the building was ready. "The troops having been reviewed by the Commander-in-chief on their brigade parades, formed two lines, the first in front and a second on the heights in the rear of the cantonment of the right wing." Then, "at a given signal," from right to left and in turn, each soldier fired his musket. After that, each cannon boomed. This *feu de joie*—fire of joy—"exhibited a beautiful appearance to a great number of gentlemen and ladies who had previously assembled at the new public building; —to which place the officers of the whole army repaired as soon as the exhibition was finished, after hearing an oration suitable to the pleasing occasion pronounced by the Rev. Mr. [Israel] Evans, chaplain of the New Hampshire Brigade, and partaking of a cold collation (at which not less than five hundred gentlemen and ladies were present)."[62]

AWAY FROM THE *feu de joie*, Congress appeared to have resigned itself to obtaining funds through requisitions based on land assessments. The committee of Wilson, Madison, and Carroll had prepared a report, and a resolution directing the various legislatures to pass laws to divide their states into districts so the values of their lands could be accurately estimated was ready. The estimations were to be made by officials appointed by the states and given to the governors, who would send them to Philadelphia.[63] Since neither those officials nor the governors had any incentive to set them high and thus increase their residents' tax burden, the delegates had no reason to believe the land assessments they received were going to be accurate. For that reason, Hamilton made a motion to have them postponed. The process of evaluating lands would be costly, and Congress should wait until it had the money needed to do it with its own appointees, using the same rules in all the states. That ensured accuracy and fairness, which were necessary for "the harmony and welfare of the United States."

The New York delegate's motion to delay the assessments was seconded by Fitzsimmons, but when all the members voted, it did not pass. Congress then called for ayes and nays on the resolution requiring the legislatures to pass laws to divide their states into districts, and that too was rejected.

Hamilton really thought taking another look at land assessment methods was a waste of time;[64] the government was going to get permanent funding only if it had greater taxation authority. But too many members of Congress did not want to hear anything about giving it such authority, so ardent nationalists now had to employ others outside Philadelphia to ram through the financial program they thought was needed.

Chapter Fourteen

"Guide the Torrent"

ON FEBRUARY 7, 1783, Gouverneur Morris wrote Henry Knox. After noting that Colonel Brooks would soon be returning to the Hudson Highlands, Morris got down to business, emphasizing how pained he was "to see the Army looking wildly for a Redress of Grievances to their particular States." The officers of the different lines were not going to find any real security if they appealed to them, he felt, "for any Laws which they can repeal they will repeal as soon as they find it expedient." Once the war ended and the army was no longer needed, its grievances were sure to be ignored; the states would seek "to get rid of" the army and let it "starve rather than pay a six Penny Tax." Even "the best Legislature on the Continent," he believed, would "do things which the worst Man among them would in his private capacity be ashamed of."

The only way the army could receive what it justly deserved was to join forces with "the public Creditors of every Kind both foreign and domestic and unremittingly urge the Grant of general permanent Funds." The time to act had arrived! "The Army may now influence the Legislatures,"[1] Morris proclaimed.

The following day McDougall and Ogden prepared a letter for Knox. No important decisions on the army had been made yet. After arriving in Philadelphia, they had talked with the delegates for a week before presenting the petition to Congress "to prepare them for the Reception of it before it was Read, least [lest] a want of information Should Retard a favourable Resolution on it." Once the delegates read it, they appointed a grand committee which subsequently met with the three officers and listened as they "communicated the condition of the Army ... dilated very diffusely all the Subjects Stated in the Address" and explained in fine detail why they were asking the government to decide on some mode of compensation other than the postwar half-pay pension.

The general and the colonel informed Knox what pay the soldiers and officers could expect and then elaborated on commutation, reporting that to deal with the issue the Grand Committee had established a subcommittee, which had presented Congress with a recommendation calling for the officers to be given six years' full pay instead of the half-pay pension; the determination had been based on the assumption that the officers' life expectancy after the war would be twelve years. The delegates, though, considered six years' full pay too great a sum and tossed the issue to another committee, which reduced the compensation to five years' full pay. But the opposition was still too great. "We advised our Friends not to Press for a Determination, if they could not carry the Question," the two officers continued, and eventually the delegates decided "to keep [put] off the question, to give them time for more consideration." McDougall and Ogden still had hopes that commutation might gain additional support and pass.

Next, they brought up general funding. Many in Congress were displaying a "Zeal ... to get Continental Funds" in order to settle the army's accounts and pay for commutation, but only a small number of members "wished to have us Referred to the States." The officers really did not care who gave them those things—Congress or the states; they just wanted results and they realized that they could not afford to alienate either side in the debate, so they did not commit themselves one way or the other. They understood what the political situation in Philadelphia was like and did not make their wishes and expectations known because they feared that if they declared their preference, they "might Retard a Settlement of our Accounts, or a Determination for the equivalent for half-pay." Once they got commutation, they could specify what type of funding they preferred.

The two officers ended their report to Knox with, among other things, a referral to Colonel Brooks, who would be able to provide the general with more details on the army's prospects when he returned to the Hudson Highlands, and an expression of their belief that McDougall should continue his efforts in Philadelphia.[2]

With copies of Congress's resolutions concerning the army's grievances, some of the pay the men were to receive—three kegs of silver coin with an estimated value of $10,000, and cash and notes payable worth more than $11,000, instructions for the paymaster general, Gouverneur Morris's letter, and the report by McDougall and Ogden, Colonel Brooks departed for the Hudson Highlands. Now he and Knox had to garner support from the officers up north for the nationalists' plan of having the army and the other public creditors join forces to win general funding for Congress.[3]

When the Virginia delegates wrote Governor Benjamin Harrison on the eleventh they, unlike him, did not appear to be too worried. The governor, in a letter to them at the end of January, had expressed his fear that the petition to Congress and its delivery in person by such high-ranking officers would "be attended with very serious consequences" both in America and abroad.[4] But the delegates, even if capable of acknowledging that the officers' demands were "distressing," appeared unconcerned. The officers would remember that they were "Citizens as well as Soldiers" and not "be dissatisfyd with the best provision that can be made for them, during the distress of the war."[5]

They should have been less confident. Since the officers' arrival in Philadelphia, "Brutus"—McDougall—wrote to Knox on the twelfth, a feeling had been growing that the army was not going to and should not allow itself to be disbanded until it received justice. In fact, "Some of the Sensible members of Congress" feared the army was certain to declare that that was its intent and "disgrace the national Character" by making "the Cause of it [their declaration] … apparent to the whole world." Congress would therefore likely preempt the army by proposing that it not be disbanded until its grievances were redressed. The plan was just in its embryonic stage, though, so Knox was supposed to say nothing about it until an announcement was made or he was contacted again. McDougall wished America did have "So much sense of Justice and Policy left as [to] do justice to the army without any violent declaration on their part," but he advised that "the Army … not … loose a moment in prepareing for events—and for the worst that may happen to them."[6]

Meanwhile, Congress adopted the resolution approved by the Committee of the Whole on January 29, which essentially said that general funding was necessary. Having agreed on that point, the delegates formed into a committee of the whole again and focused specifically on the impost, unanimously deciding that it had to be changed. Virginia's John Francis Mercer, who strongly opposed giving Congress general funding, "observed that the liberties of Engd. had been preserved by a separation of the purse from the sword; that until the debts sd. be liquidated & apportioned he never wd. assent in Congs. or elsewhere to the scheme of the Impost."[7] He was so alarmed by Madison's earlier assertion that states were essentially bound by law to comply with congressional requisitions that he vowed to "crawl to R____d [Richmond] on his bare knees" to keep his state from reversing its recent decision to repeal its ratification of the bill.[8]

Theodorick Bland proposed limiting the impost to "25 years, or until the requisition of Congs. according to the Articles of Confedn. shall be found adequate." In other words, if the requisitions were still inadequate after the limit had been reached, the impost would continue to remain in effect. That was unacceptable and, consequently, his proposal was rejected. The committee then voted in favor of the strict twenty-five-year limit and, finally, resolved to allow the states to appoint the collectors. But they would be "amenable to & under the Controul of Congs."[9]

Some time that day a ship brought news of great importance to Philadelphia: During a speech to Parliament in December, King George III had announced that he intended to sign a preliminary peace agreement and declare America independent.[10] Congress was very pleased, but "the most judicious members," Madison noted the following day, "suffered a great diminution of their joy from the impossibility of discharging the arrears & claims of the army & their apprehension of new difficulties from that quarter."[11] Peace, they knew, was going to lead many to conclude that an army was no longer necessary, and without angry officers and soldiers hanging over legislators' heads like a sword of Damocles, the states and their supporters in Congress would casually dismiss the nationalists' calls for greater taxation authority. The plotters had to get moving immediately, before the discontented army was disbanded, the creditors were forgotten, and any chance for justice was lost.

Hamilton sensed the urgency of the situation and wanted to find out how receptive Washington was to the nationalists' plan. But the two of them had not communicated with each other ever since a small incident back on February 16, 1781, at New Windsor: The then Lieutenant Colonel Hamilton had kept his Commander-in-chief waiting at the top of the stairway of his headquarters after the general had asked to speak with him; that was a sign of disrespect, Washington said. Hamilton did not feel he had done anything wrong and expressed that view "without petulancy, but with decision." The colonel's reply did not please Washington, but they quickly parted.

Within an hour after the two had parted, Lieutenant Colonel Tilghman arrived on behalf of Washington to inform Hamilton that the Commander-in-chief thought highly of him and wanted to have "a candid conversation to heal a difference which could not have happened but in a moment of passion." Hamilton preferred not to meet with Washington, though, and made that known to Colonel Tilghman.[12]

The "open rupture"[13] between them ended on February 13, 1783,[14] when Hamilton wrote for Washington a carefully worded letter filled with observations that were meant to be kept secret. He felt "the temper and situation of the army" had made "the present juncture ... a very interesting one" and thought "the stat[e] of our finances was perhaps never more critical." What they really needed now was "wisdom and decision in Congress," but he did not think those qualities guided the delegates in their actions. They would not do what was right, thereby soon causing "an embarrassing scene" regardless of whether peace arrived or not.

If they had peace, Hamilton was sure the army would not disband. The majority in the army believed that as soon as they disarmed, they lost their "means of ob[taining] justice," and he regretted that outward indications provided "too much ground for their distrust."

He then went on to recommend a course of action for the general: "The claims of the army urged with moderation, but with firmness, may operate on those weak minds which are influenced by their apprehensions more than their judgments; so as to produce ... the measures which the exigencies of affairs demand. They may add weight to the applications of Congress to the several states. ... But the difficulty will be to keep a *complaining* and *suffering* army within the bounds of moderation." That was where Washington had to use his influence; he had to ensure that the army did not go too far. He should not show his disapproval of "their endeavours to procure redress, but rather by the intervention of confidential and prudent persons ... *take the direction of them*." One such person the Commander-in-chief could use was Henry Knox, someone the army trusted. Washington must do this maneuvering behind the scenes, though, because to do so openly might cause the general public to lose confidence in him. If both the public's and the army's confidence in Washington remained strong, he would even "in case of extremity" be able "to guide the torrent, and bring order perhaps even good, out of confusion."

After recommending a course of action to take, Hamilton intimated that Washington was falling out of favor with the officers, informing him, "An idea is propagated in the army that a delicacy carried to an extreme prevents your espousing its interests with sufficient warmth." He did not have such misgivings about the general's leadership, but the whispering could not be ignored: Though the impression of Washington that the whisperers were propagating was false, it tended to lessen Washington's ability, "should any commotions unhappily ensue, to moderate the pretensions of the army and make their conduct correspond with their duty."

As for Congress, it now needed to get general funding. That was the only thing that could "do justice to the Creditors of the United States (of whom the army forms the most meritorious class), restore public credit, and supply the future wants of government." That was what "all men of sense" sought, and Hamilton believed "the influence of the army, properly directed," could help bring it about.[15]

The picture drawn by Hamilton would stun Washington, who had been counting on funds from Europe to help with pressing concerns, and his warning had to be taken seriously. After several months in a volunteer militia company, Hamilton had served in the Continental Army as an officer from 1776 to 1782 and he was perceived to be one of the two leading authorities on its affairs, opinions, and mood. The other was Pennsylvania delegate Richard Peters,[16] who had served as the Secretary of the Board of War from 1776 to 1781.

Although Hamilton had warned Washington that trouble was brewing, his primary motive for writing the letter was to manipulate the general. He wanted the Commander-in-chief and his army to become his cat's-paw in the battle to win general funding for Congress. If his purpose in writing the letter had been to warn Washington of a dangerous situation, there would have been no need to try to convince him to take charge of the movement and guide the torrent.

While Hamilton attempted to manipulate Washington, Secretary of Foreign Affairs Robert Livingston despaired over Congress's financial problems. In a letter to John Adams he noted its increasing "distress for money" and the growing unrest within the army and among the creditors, and said nothing would change even if peace arrived. He knew the government's "exhausted situation" was going to prevent it from getting the domestic loans or the funding needed to relieve them.[17]

Madison's words about the army were more ominous than Livingston's. After congratulating Edmund Randolph "on the dawn of peace," he became more somber and even switched to cipher from time to time: "I will not damp your joy by dwelling on prospects which have that tendency; but it will not be improper to hint to you, that there is much reason to believe that the *cloud, which has been some time lowering on* the *North River will not be dispeled by the rays of peace.* The opinion seems to be *well founded that* the *arms which have* secured the *liberties of their country will not* be *laid down until justice* is *secured to those who have wielded them and that dangerous convulsions* would be *hazarded by orders* for that purpose."[18]

The secretary and the Virginia delegate were not able to see firsthand what was happening with the army when they wrote those letters, but their apprehension was justified, for that day Colonel John Brooks was arriving in the Hudson Highlands with the February 8 report from McDougall and Ogden and the February 7 letter from Gouverneur Morris. He was expected to see Knox and provide him with more details on the happenings in the capital and let the other officers there in on the nationalists' plot.[19]

Alexander Hamilton, a New York delegate to Congress at the time of the Newburgh conspiracy

The following day, as Congress moved away from the issue of general funding to look at the question of commutation,[20] Hamilton expressed his concern over the grave situation in a letter to Governor Clinton. The belief was that the army planned to refuse to disband until it received justice, and he feared Philadelphia would not make the "solid arrangements" needed. So, wanting his state to think about how to best protect "its safety and interest" in case the union broke up, he proposed that New York's legislature "set apart a tract of territory, and make a liberal allowance to every officer and soldier of the Army … who will become a citizen of the State." He hoped that the country would remain united but was not optimistic; he saw that the bonds between the states were very "Feeble."[21]

ALEXANDER HAMILTON[22] WAS born in 1755 to a beautiful woman of French descent and a handsome but lazy Scottish fortune-seeker, James Hamilton, on the tiny mostly slave-inhabited island of Nevis. His red hair, blue eyes, and pale skin may have betrayed his Scottish blood; but it was known that his birth was illegitimate, which made it a "subject of humiliating criticism."[23] When the woman's legal husband, Johann Levine, moved to divorce her, three witnesses were brought forward to say she had "given herself to whoring with everyone."[24] True or not, she continued to bring up Alexander and his older brother James from the time of the divorce proceedings in 1759 until 1768, when she died from yellow fever. By that time they had already been without their father since 1765, the year he left them behind on the island of St. Croix, where he had gone to collect a debt owed to the mercantile house that employed him.

Alexander worked for a few years in a counting house of a major New York-based import-export concern and then left for America in October 1772 to further his education. He arrived in Boston the same month and left for New York a short time later. There he saw a friend from his days on St. Croix and was introduced to a number of people, including the author of "To the Betrayed Inhabitants of the City and Colony of New York," Alexander McDougall. Upon learning of the Scotsman's imprisonment for writing the broadside and of the subsequent clashes between the Sons of Liberty and the British, Hamilton could not help but look up to the zealous patriot.

Hamilton studied at Elizabethtown Academy in New Jersey for one year and, if he had had his way, would have then attended the College of New Jersey. The president there, Dr. John Witherspoon, examined him, and he appeared set to enter the college. But when he made it known that he wanted to be free to complete his studies at his own accelerated pace, the trustees rejected his request.

So Hamilton looked to King's College in New York City. There he encountered no opposition when he said he wanted to spend a year studying at his own pace with tutors before matriculating as a sophomore. He had planned to study medicine but upon matriculation in May 1774 gave up on that plan.

By that time Hamilton had already become active in the patriot cause. In April he first attended a rally that followed the arrival of the tea ship *Nancy* off Sandy Hook and then, when the *London* attempted to deliver tea, helped post "invitations" from the Sons of Liberty to attend a "tea party" throughout Manhattan. They wanted the ship's captain to "see with his own eyes their detestation of the measures pursued by the Ministry and the [East] India Company to enslave this country."[25] The party that followed, though, was not to Hamilton's liking. The angry crowd that gathered could not be held back; it not only broke open cases of tea and threw it in the river, but was so unruly that the captain and his crew were fortunate to have left the scene in one piece. Hamilton was so aghast that he later tried to deny any involvement in the affair.

McDougall was also present when the *London* tried to deliver tea, but his friendship with Hamilton probably did not begin in earnest until July 1774. The Sons of Liberty wanted the tall Scotsman and a lawyer friendly to their cause to be two of New York's delegates to Congress, but the Loyalist-controlled legislature refused to allow their names to be advanced. So the Sons held a protest on the sixth in the Fields that large numbers of workers attended. At the rally, McDougall, who had come with a large entourage, spoke from a makeshift stage. Hamilton and some friends stood well away from most of the crowd. As the Scotsman railed against "the numerous vile acts used by the enemies of America"[26] and put forth a number of resolutions opposing Parliament, Hamilton quietly told others just how dangerous the situation had become. Suddenly he was encouraged to take the stage, but the surprised young college student apparently drew back, content to be nothing more than an inconspicuous listener. Without any warning, though, McDougall summoned him to the platform.

The general thrust of the speech Hamilton gave was recalled much later by a friend who had been present with him that evening. At first he appeared affected by the noisy taunting that his youth occasioned, but as he proceeded he spoke with more assurance. The Boston Port Act was his target. It was responsible for the great "suffering ... of these colonies."[27] The country should be united in its opposition to the unconstitutional taxes the British had imposed on them, and he supported Boston's nonimportation of British goods, which, he believed, would "prove the salvation of North America and her liberties."[28]

The Scotsman was impressed and the friendship that developed shortly thereafter would last a lifetime. In early 1781 McDougall would be nominated by Hamilton to be America's first head of the Department of Marine, and during his lifetime the Scotsman would speak with him often and lend him many of his books, journals and pamphlets, some pertinent to the Revolution but others on subjects such as philosophy and Latin.

After the opening exchange of fire at Lexington on April 19, 1775, Hamilton joined a volunteer militia company. Their first taste of battle came on the night of August 23-24. While coming under British musket and cannon fire from a barge and a man-of-war, they and men from two other companies hauled away twenty-one of the twenty-four cannon that made up the Grand Battery beneath Fort George to the Liberty Pole outside City Hall. The slight New Yorker personally dragged one cannon away, a feat that no doubt served as an example to the others.

The following January the New York Provincial Congress decided that the colony needed an artillery company for its defense. Hamilton wanted to be its commander and took steps to boost his candidacy for the position. He had his mathematics teacher at college attest to his knowledge of trigonometry and an artillerist certify that he had tested him and found him qualified. He also got McDougall, now a New York provincial congressman, to recommend him for the position and two other important politicians—William Livingston and John Jay—to support him. As a result, in March 1776 he received a commission to be the captain of his colony's independent artillery company.

In the little less than a year Hamilton commanded the company, he and his men performed their duties well. In mid-April 1776 they earned praise from Washington for the fine job they had done constructing Fort Bunker Hill, the highest-placed redoubt in New York City. In October at the Battle of White Plains his gunners inflicted heavy casualties on the British while helping repulse an initial bayonet charge by Hessians up Chatterton Hill before being driven back. One month later, fire from cannon that Hamilton had placed on the west bank of the Raritan River kept a large force of pursuing British and Hessian grenadiers at bay as Washington's men escaped to Princeton. In the second week of December the captain's artillery did much the same from the western bank of the Delaware as the Commander-in-chief's army crossed the river into Pennsylvania, and two weeks later it performed admirably in the face of fire when the general launched a victorious surprise attack on the small Hessian outpost at Trenton. Then, in early January 1777, Hamilton forced two hundred British to surrender at the Battle of Princeton; after being surrounded, the enemy troops had run into Nassau Hall and subjected American soldiers to fire until the captain came to the rear of the building with two cannon.

After the victories at Trenton and Princeton, large numbers of Americans decided to fight for independence, and Washington had to add another aide to his staff. Hamilton was approached and, on March 1, made a private secretary and aide to the Commander-in-chief with the rank of lieutenant colonel. Soon his energy and competence earned him the nickname "the Little Lion," and still later that year one delegate in Philadelphia was writing that "he had a penetrating intellect that flies like an arrow from a bow."[29]

Hamilton would fill those positions for four years, performing a variety of tasks for Washington. That much of what he did was through correspondence did not mean he no longer exposed himself to personal danger. At Brandywine in September 1777 the sword-wielding colonel rode back and forth among soldiers to rally them as they endured heavy fire from British guns, and helped pull Lafayette out of harm's way after he had fallen from his horse with a wound in the thigh. At Deviser's Ferry his horse and two oarsmen were shot by fast-approaching enemy dragoons just as his men were leaving the scene by flat-bottomed boat, after having set fire to the flour mills there. Shortly before the British moved into Philadelphia he went there and removed munitions and other military stores "with so much vigilance that very little public property fell ... into [British] hands."[30] At the Battle of Monmouth he was injured when his old gray horse was shot and fell on him as he was attempting to rally troops and check an American retreat; one officer credited him for changing the course of the battle and said he had "seemed to court death."[31]

During the winter of 1777–78 Hamilton concluded that Congress was the cause of the army's hardships. While looking into abuses at Valley Forge, a committee that included Robert Morris and his future assistant arrived to see what the conditions there were like. Hamilton had already been corresponding with Gouverneur Morris for more than a year, periodically giving him and Robert Livingston his opinions on political and military matters. Now, for the first time, he had a chance to meet with him face to face. He listened to Morris, who also had a negative opinion of Congress, and before winter ended was having him forward to Governor Clinton letters in which he complained of the emergence of a faction in Philadelphia and of the low quality of the delegates. "Folly, caprice, a want of foresight, comprehension and dignity characterise the general tenor of their actions," he charged, and "their conduct with respect to the army especially is feeble indecisive and improvident. ... We are reduced to a more terrible situation than you can conceive."[32] Officers were becoming apathetic because the delegates had not made arrangements to provide them with postwar pensions; foreigners were being given preferential treatment in promotions; and soldiers were complaining about inadequate rations and deserting.

The problem was that the states did not put their best men in national offices; they put them in local ones. That "most pernicious mistake"[33] they had to correct; local offices caused those men to become "more provident for the particular interests of the states to which they belonged, than for the common interests of the confederacy,"[34] thus making America weak—especially in its dealings with Europe.

For the country Hamilton wanted the best delegates the states were capable of providing, for himself a post as a diplomat somewhere or a field command. An aide's work, much of which was done behind a desk, did not excite him. So in April 1781 he forcefully made known to Washington his wish to be given a field command. The general offered him a commission in the line but without any regiment to go with it; to put him in command of a regiment over other officers also worthy of such a position would be resented. Washington acknowledged that he had the right to make Hamilton a commander and that the slight New Yorker deserved to be one, but he felt it was risky "to push that right too far ... at a time so critical as the present."[35] This was not the first time Hamilton had requested a field command and come away disappointed and, as a result, on July 8 he effectively resigned.

By the end of the month, though, Hamilton was persuaded to return, and he got what he had wanted so badly; he would command a new battalion made up of light infantry companies from two New York regiments and two other companies. On August 19 a couple of companies from the Connecticut Line were added to that battalion.

Meanwhile, four articles appeared in *The New-York Packet*. They had been composed as a letter and then serialized by the newspaper. The author, disguising his identity by using the pseudonym "The Continentalist," was Hamilton. His goal was to point out how "A WANT OF POWER IN CONGRESS" imperiled the American cause. To ensure that American liberty proved lasting the body needed to be given just enough authority to function effectively; history had shown that too much power in a government's hands "leads to despotism, too little leads to anarchy."[36] The latter could result when states were not "strongly united under one government." When such a situation existed, the individual states making up a union quarreled with each other and eventually sought to leave it. "A schism once introduced, competitions of boundary and rivalships of commerce will easily afford pretexts for war," Hamilton warned.

He already saw "SYMPTOMS OF THE EVILS TO BE APPREHENDED" appearing in America. "In the midst of a war for our existence as a nation; in the midst of dangers too serious to be trifled with, some of the states have evaded, or refused, compliance with the demands of Congress in points of the greatest moment to the common safety. If they act such a part at this perilous juncture, what are we to expect in a time of peace and security?" he asked.

However, most people were not worried about the possibility of the states later becoming rivals and eventually belligerents. Too many other problems were drawing their attention now. "Our whole system is in disorder," Hamilton lamented, "our currency depreciated, till in many places, it will hardly obtain a circulation at all, public credit at its lowest ebb, our army deficient in numbers, and unprovided with every thing, the government, in its present condition unable to command the means to pay, clothe or feed their troops."[37]

The solution to America's problems was to give Congress more power; it had to have the authority to raise revenue independently. As long as Congress had to beg for funds from the states to finance its operations, it was not going to be able to pay its creditors what they were owed.[38]

Hamilton's last article appeared on August 30, 1781. Two-and-a-half months later, on October 14, 1781, Hamilton saw his last action of the war at the Battle of Yorktown. Two especially key British redoubts—nine and ten—"about 300 yards in front of their principal works"[39] had "enfiladed our intrenchment and impeded our approaches."[40] Redoubt ten, the Rock Redoubt, was "on the left of the British garrison, bordering on the banks of the river."[41] It was "well secured by a ditch and picket, sufficiently high parapet, and within were divisions made by rows of casks ranged upon end and filled with earth and sand. On tops of parapet were ranged bags filled with sand."[42]

Lafayette was responsible for taking the redoubt, and he selected a fellow countryman to lead the initial charge, but Hamilton argued to Washington that he was actually senior to the officer the French general had chosen and was therefore entitled to the assignment. Though he did not have any experience leading infantrymen into battle and the Frenchman whom Lafayette had wanted did, Hamilton won the argument and was assigned to lead four hundred American soldiers against probably sixty or seventy British and Hessian soldiers.

The attack on the redoubt began "shortly after dark"[43] that Sunday. When the men heard a prearranged signal—a short series of mortar blasts coming one after another—"the word 'up, up' was … reiterated through the detachment"[44] and they "immediately moved silently on toward the redoubt"[45] with bayonets fixed but muskets empty; any accidental discharge, Hamilton feared, might be heard and correctly interpreted by the British. The ground across which they moved had "holes sufficient to bury an ox in" and occasionally men fell.[46]

When the first Americans reached the abatis—a barricade made from long, sharpened, pine branches and tree tops—they found it had been little damaged by earlier allied artillery blasts. Pioneers, sappers, and miners wanted to attack it with their axes and explosives but were impeded by the body of soldiers massed in front of them. A British sentry issued a challenge, which went unanswered, and a volley of shots followed. The Americans "broke silence and huzzaed"[47] so loudly that one Hessian likened the yelling to the howling made by the god of the dead and his subjects during their "wild hunt" at the beginning of winter.[48] Soon the Americans found themselves under heavy fire. Not waiting for the pioneers to chop through the abatis, they wriggled through it.

Hamilton ordered long bundles of bound branches brought forward and placed in the ditch in front of the redoubt, but the men in their eagerness did not wait for their arrival. They crossed the ditch and began climbing up the redoubt, first breaking off the sharpened ends of sticks that the enemy had planted in its wall and then using what remained of them as steppingstones. The British the whole time continued to subject them to intense fire and hurled so many grenades into the trench that the Americans thought firecrackers were going off around them.

The colonel ordered a bigger soldier to drop down, climbed onto his back and propelled himself over the side into the redoubt. As he yelled and waved his sword, his men entered right behind him, overcoming yet another obstacle—undamaged parts of a wooden palisade built on the top of the redoubt's wall. The two sides engaged each other with bayonets but the Americans had moved so rapidly and with such skill that the British soldiers never had a chance. The redoubt was taken and most of its defenders chose to flee rather than end up being casualties or prisoners of war. The number killed on both sides was not great.

The allies then dug trenches to connect the Rock Redoubt to the other redoubt and form a link with their second parallel so they could bring their guns forward, shell the enemy's positions with impunity, and "convince his lordship … that submission must soon be his only alternative."[49] The British later attempted a counterattack, but it failed to reverse the allies' gains or even delay their eventual victory.

Washington had much praise for Hamilton. "Few cases have exhibited stronger proofs of intrepidity, coolness, and firmness," he asserted, and he wanted others to emulate the brave, frail colonel[50] with a quiet voice.

Just before the New Year arrived Congress expressed its satisfaction with his performance, voting to keep the now exhausted and ill colonel in the army till the end of the war and deciding to let him retain his rank and receive the pay, pension, and land that came with it. Hamilton, though, some time later asked Washington to place him on the inactive list. He promised to return to service if needed, but voluntarily gave up the benefits he was entitled to receive because he did not expect another field command. Since one of those benefits that he surrendered was the postwar pension, he obviously was not acting out of self-interest when he later supported using the angry army to get the funding for Congress that would make half pay or commutation a reality.

Only one day after asking Washington to put him on the inactive list, on May 2, 1782, Hamilton started studying law. While doing so, he accepted an offer from Robert Morris to become New York

State's receiver of Continental taxes. During his stint as a receiver he again wrote for *The New-York Packet* under the pen name "The Continentalist," recommending some import duties as a source of revenue for the government, and talked the New York General Assembly into passing a number of resolutions calling for a national convention to strengthen Congress and make changes to the Articles of Confederation. Soon after those resolutions passed, in July 1782, he was appointed to serve as a delegate in Philadelphia; one of those who had urged him to join the legislative body was Robert Morris. In late autumn he took his seat there to begin the new term.

AROUND THE TIME that Hamilton urged Washington to guide the torrent, Gouverneur Morris wrote Nathanael Greene. Morris knew the onetime Rhode Island Quaker and he were "actuated by the same principles of justice, and the same sentiments of policy," so he felt he could express himself with "a freedom of communication which, to most men, would be imprudent."

Peace was coming, which was sure to "give very serious thoughts to every officer and soldier of the American army." If the government kept the promises it had made to the army, this would be "of beneficial importance." But if the government did not, the promises would prove to be "extremely injurious." The issue of whether they were going to be kept was making the army anxious. Morris was not about to "pretend to guess, precisely, at their sentiments," but he implied that their grievances could not be ignored. "I am convinced," he declared, "they will not easily forego their expectations. Their murmurs, though not loud, are deep; and I do not think that the committee they have sent hither will ... allay the apprehensions which were excited."

He then directed some criticism at the three officers in Philadelphia: "They were precipitating themselves in the road to ruin ... by pursuing a recommendation to the several states for compensation, &c." If the veterans split up "into thirteen different parts" and went to their respective legislatures back home instead of to Congress for their just dues, the states would find it "easy to elude the force of their applications" or take back "grants made in consequence of them" after their disbandment.

The best course of action for the army was to unite with the public creditors. If they both demanded "the grant of general permanent funds for liquidating *all* the public debts," Congress was likely to get enough revenue to provide them with "a solid security." Both groups, though, had to support one another, and the army had to stay together and be "*determined in the pursuit*" of its goal because Morris expected that, barring any "miracles," nothing else would get the states to give Congress permanent funding.[51]

Although Morris did not specifically request that Greene help the plotters carry out their plan, he clearly wanted to know if the general was willing to do so. Whereas Hamilton had been so bold as to ask the Commander-in-chief to guide the torrent, Morris had only tossed out a feeler to the southern army's top officer to determine how receptive he was to the nationalists' scheme. If Washington responded favorably to Hamilton's letter, great. But if he did not, which must have appeared likely, another influential general had to be found to take charge of the movement.

ON FEBRUARY 14 Washington announced the rates at which privates and noncommissioned officers were to be provided their one month's pay. Aware that Brooks had not brought enough money from Philadelphia to pay all the men in the Hudson Highlands, he ordered Deputy Paymaster General Hezekiah Wetmore not to begin disbursing weekly cash payments until he was sure the process could be completed without interruption.[52]

While that process had yet to begin, another one—the construction of the Temple of Virtue—was proceeding nicely. By the fifteenth the one-story building with a triangular cupola, a broad shingle roof, two chimneys, and high windows[53] was "so far finished as to admit the troops to attend public worship." The benches requested by Gates for the hall had been made, and beginning on February 23, church services were supposed to be "performed there every Sunday by the several [Protestant] Chaplains of the New Windsor Cantonment, in rotation." Separate services were to be held for each brigade and the chaplains were urged to work with the brigade commanders to arrange a suitable schedule. In his orders Washington made clear that he felt "public homage and adoration" were owed to God for having "through His infinite mercy, brought our calamities and dangers (in all probability) very near to a happy conclusion."[54]

The following day, the sixteenth, Washington wrote David Rittenhouse. The new spectacles the Pennsylvania scientist had made for the general had arrived. "The Spectacles suit my Eyes extremely well," Washington reported, "—as I am perswaded the reading glasses also will when I get more accustomed to the use of them—At present I find some difficulty in coming at the proper Focus—but when I do obtain it, they magnify properly & shew those objects very distinctly which at first appear like a mist blended together & confused."[55] Washington could hardly have known at the time that almost one month to the day those glasses were going to play an important role in American history.

IN PHILADELPHIA ON February 18 the delegates again focused on the impost. John Rutledge and John Francis Mercer proposed that all funds from any impost go towards paying the army what it was owed. Such an appropriation was "the most likely to be obtained as their merits were superior to those of all other Creditors, and as it was the only thing that promised what policy absolutely required" they receive—"some satisfaction."[56]

James Wilson agreed that if anybody deserved preferential treatment, it was the army, "but that no such discrimination was necessary, that the ability of the public was equal to its whole debt." Congress should first make "the most vigorous efforts" to fund all the public debt, to pay back all the creditors. Only as a last resort, if they saw that they were not going to have enough funds, should they allow preferential treatment.[57]

Nathaniel Gorham also did not like the idea of "an exclusive appropriation to the army." If revenue went towards paying back only the men in uniform, the states that had the biggest creditors of the United States government were not going to approve the impost. They "would even be interested in frustrating the measure" if no funds from it went towards paying back the creditors.[58]

Mercer responded. The only way the states would approve the impost was if the revenue from it was used solely to pay the army what it was owed. The army had an unquestionably greater right to be paid back than the public creditors who, the Virginia delegate slyly suggested, by virtue of their "speculations ... in loan office certificates," were war profiteers. And Congress could not ask the states to pay back both the army and the other public creditors because "if too much were asked from the States they would grant nothing."

Also, those who "alledged that the large public debt if funded under Congress would be a cement of the confederacy" were wrong. If Congress took over the funding of the huge public debt, "it would hasten its dissolution; as the people would feel its weight in the most obnoxious of all forms that of taxation."[59]

When the proposal to use revenue from the impost to pay only the army was voted on, it failed to gather enough ayes for passage; only South Carolina voted to give the army preferential treatment.[60] Nationalists did not like the proposal because they wanted Congress to have broader funding authority, and their opponents disliked it because they feared giving the national government greater powers at the expense of the states. When guardians of state sovereignty like Rutledge and Mercer proposed that all revenue from the impost be used to pay the army, they were simply playing obstructionist politics; they knew the nationalists would never go along with separating the army from the other public creditors.

Before the day's debates came to an end, Hamilton and Wilson decided that public pressure could change the minds of members who were opposed to having Congress fund the whole debt. Accordingly, they moved that "when the subject of finances was under debate the doors of Congs. should be open."[61] They wanted them opened, Madison speculated, because they thought "the presence of public creditors numerous & weighty in Philada. wd. have an influence & that it wd. be well for the public to come more fully to the knowledge of the public finances."[62] This idea, though, was "generally disrelished" and the delegates decided to adjourn.[63]

WASHINGTON HAD ANOTHER matter on his mind that Tuesday: Colonel Walter Stewart, the inspector general of the northern army, still had not returned from sick leave in Philadelphia. Two months earlier the Commander-in-chief had asked for his return, noting that his assistant, Major William Barber, was not able to manage "the business of Inspecting and Mustering the Troops

Monthly" without help. Washington hadn't heard from him since that time and he now wanted the colonel "to repair to Camp without one Moment's loss of time" or a replacement was going to have to be named.[64]

Stewart would not return to camp until the second weekend in March, and it might have been better for Washington if he had not returned at all. Having ties with angry creditors in Philadelphia and restless officers back in the Hudson Highlands, the colonel was someone who could act as a liaison or even an agent provocateur. If he got both groups to join forces, the nationalists would have a powerful tool to use in their fight to achieve general funding for Congress. If state legislatures and their ardent supporters in Philadelphia had a sword of Damocles hanging over their heads—angry creditors and army officers demanding that they be paid what they were owed—they would have to yield to the nationalists and grant Congress real taxation authority.

Chapter Fifteen

"The Political Pot in Philadelphia Boils"

IN PHILADELPHIA ON Wednesday, February 19, 1783, Congress began its work by soundly voting down the previous day's motion to open its doors; only Pennsylvania favored it. Alexander Hamilton then moved to have the twenty-five-year limit on the impost postponed. Theodorick Bland seconded the motion, pointing out that the creditors were looking to Congress to pay them back and since the Virginia delegate saw no proof that Philadelphia would be able to discharge the debt within twenty-five years, he did not think its duration should be limited. When a vote was taken the motion did not pass.[1]

Undaunted by the setback he had suffered the previous day, John Rutledge again proposed that the revenue generated by the impost be used only to pay the army. Arthur Lee seconded his motion.[2]

That proposal provoked Hamilton. "As a friend to the army as well as to the other Creditors & to the public at large he could never assent to such a partial dispensation of Justice." The states, he was sure, would never agree to any funding for Congress but to that intended for discharging the whole public debt. Although he apparently did not say so, he understood that a state like Pennsylvania, which had a very large number of creditors of the national government, was not going to support the impost if none of the revenue generated by it was used to pay them back. Also, the delegates were "impolitic to divide the interests of the civil & military Creditors, whose joint efforts in the States would be necessary to prevail on them to adopt a general revenue."[3]

Hamilton then veered away from Rutledge's motion and spoke about Rhode Island's and Virginia's opposition to the impost. Devotion to liberty was not what motivated them to be against it, he charged. Rhode Island benefited from Connecticut's not having any important seaports of its own. When the people of Connecticut wanted foreign goods they had to go through Rhode Island and pay extra to get them. That helped Rhode Island commercially. But once the impost was approved, Rhode Island would start paying taxes on those goods it imported and then sent to Connecticut. And it was not going to get tax refunds later to make up for that new added cost of business, for no provision was made for them in the impost.[4]

Virginia's real reason for objecting to the impost was different. Neither the state nor its residents had been major creditors of the national government, so when Congress paid its debts with revenue from the impost they stood to receive little.[5]

John Francis Mercer shifted the debate back to Rutledge's proposal to have the revenue from the impost be used only to pay the army. He differed with Hamilton. The provision Rutledge had offered was "necessary to satisfy the army & to avert the consequences which would result from their disappointment on this subject." If the delegates failed to appease the army, it would refuse to disband. What Rutledge proposed was "the only attainable provision," and the claims of the army and those of the other public creditors should not be lumped together because "the latter were not supported by justice."[6]

Siding with Hamilton, Thomas Fitzsimmons did not favor giving priority to the army's claims. If only the army's debts were funded, that "wd. be unjust & impolitic: … the States whose Citizens were the chief creditors of the U. S. wd. never concur in such measure." The major Pennsylvania creditors had used their influence to get their state to approve the impost. If Congress decided not to use revenue from the impost to pay them back, he expected them to withdraw their support for it and the Pennsylvania General Assembly to repeal its ratification of it.[7]

Lee responded. None of the states would object to an impost whose revenue went only towards satisfying the army's claims; "eve[r]ybody felt and acknowledged the force of the demands of the army." And besides having "more merit" on their side, soldiers and officers were not as likely to be able to support themselves in the business world after peace arrived as the public creditors,[8] so they would really need the money generated by the impost.

Madison considered Rutledge's proposal "premature"; the delegates should decide where they were going to get their funds from before designating recipients for the various appropriations. Once they did that, they were likely to conclude that it was best to use revenue from the impost to pay back foreign creditors and revenue from other taxes to satisfy the claims of American creditors. While the impost "wd. be … little felt," the other taxes would be "obnoxious" and therefore it made sense to have the revenue from them go to people Americans could sympathize with, the American creditors.[9]

The last two delegates to express themselves were Hugh Williamson and James Wilson. Neither man liked Rutledge's proposal, although both wanted to see the army get what it was due. Williamson, a forty-seven-year-old European-trained physician with a receding hairline, "did not wish the army to disband untill proper provision should be made for them; … if force sd. be necessary to excite justice, the sooner force were applied the better."[10] And Wilson thought "by dividing the interest of the civil from that of the military Creditors provision for the latter would be frustrated."[11]

When the delegates finished voicing their sentiments, they voted down Rutledge's motion. Then they sustained one of the Committee of the Whole's decisions of the twelfth and rejected another, allowing the states to appoint the collectors but having them "be amenable to & under the Controul of Congs." and voting against the twenty-five-year limit.[12]

AS CONGRESS ARGUED over general funding, a depressed "Brutus"—McDougall—wrote Knox. In Philadelphia they had learned of the King's speech—the one he had given when Parliament opened in early December—and "Brutus" thought peace was likely. He expected most people to be happy because with its arrival they were going to be able to make more money. But forgotten would be "the wretched condition of the Army." People really could not care less about the army except "when some of its [Congress's] members remind them of it," the general continued.

He now found his stay in Philadelphia "irksome." He could say nothing more to the delegates and some were so refractory that to get them to be more accommodating was as difficult as producing "a Courser's motion in an old Continental Hors." Still, he saw fit to "patiently wait for an answer" from them until it appeared that none was forthcoming.[13]

WHEN DEBATES RESUMED on Thursday the proposal to limit the impost to twenty-five years was again taken up, and when the time to vote came it received enough ayes to pass.[14]

Sometime in the evening Fitzsimmons had Madison, Hamilton, Gorham, Peters, and Carroll come to his home for dinner and a discussion on the matters before Congress. When they finished discussing the subject of revenue, all but Hamilton agreed that they faced an "impossibility of adding to the impost on trade any taxes that wd. operate equally throughout the States, or be adopted by them."[15]

Of greater concern was the state of the army. Hamilton and Peters, the leading authorities on the army, asserted that the men "had secretly determined not to lay down their arms until due provision & a satisfactory prospect should be afforded on the subject of their pay" and told their three colleagues "there was reason to expect that a public declaration to this effect would soon be made." Already "plans had been agitated if not formed for subsisting themselves after such declaration." What the army planned they did not say, but both men must have envisioned armed soldiers plundering the countryside. Even if the army felt wealthy creditors were capable of purchasing the food the officers and their men needed for their subsistence, Hamilton and Peters must have realized that such an idea was delusional.

As talk turned to Washington, Madison took more detailed notes. "The Commander was already … extremely unpopular among almost all ranks from his known dislike to every unlawful proceeding." Furthermore, his "unpopularity was daily increasing & industriously promoted by many leading characters." Some of these characters believed Washington guilty of surrounding himself with "unfit & indiscreet persons," others simply made the charge as a "pretext" for their actions. What they really wanted was "to displace him from the respect & confidence of the army in order to substitute Genl. _____ as the conductor of their efforts to obtain justice."

Hamilton claimed that "he knew Genl. Washington intimately & perfectly, that his extreme reserve, mixed sometimes with a degree of asperity of temper both of which were said to have increased of late, had contributed to the decline of his popularity; but that his virtue his patriotism & his firmness would … never yield to any dishonorable or disloyal plans into which he might be called; that he would sooner suffer himself to be cut into pieces; that he [Mr. Hamilton] knowing this to be his true character wished him to be the conductor of the army in their plans for redress, in order that they might be moderated & directed to proper objects, & exclude some other leader who might foment & misguide their councils." Therefore he had written Washington to let him know what was happening and to advise such a course of action.[16]

IN NEW WINDSOR that day Horatio Gates wrote Peters. "The Political Pot in Philadelphia Boils so furiously," he declared, "that I suppose, as a Stranger rides through this Town, They Cry Scaldings, as they do on Ship board, when the Tea Kettle is Lugging For and Aft, what a Blessed Prospect we Republicans have before us!" He then switched subjects, signed his letter, and added a telling postscript: "The Financier has the Prayers of the Army."[17]

With the letter, Gates enclosed "On the Prospect of Peace," a poem he had written as an allegory for what was going on in Philadelphia. As hostilities between the Americans and the British and the Indians were ending, the "Debate" was on "How they [the delegates] shall save the Sinking States,/ And Gratify the Army." The two sides in the debate were "The Tories" and "The Whiggs." The Tories were losing the debate, "looking like the restless Dam'd." Down, they "Would lick the Hands that beat them."

The Whigs, though, were not in a forgiving mood. They were determined that "nor George, nor all his Crew" would "ever more … cheat them." Their victory in this "Famous Battle" was going to save the country's liberties, cause America to be "with Glory Crown'd" and force other nations to respect her.[18]

In Gates's poem the Whigs were not just the nationalists fighting for general funding but also the officers aligned with them. After all, the officers did not want Congress to "cheat them" by failing to pay the army and not providing for their pensions. The Tories were those opposed to general funding, since they were the ones "Dam'd" by the officers and all the delegates anxious to pay back the army and the creditors.

IF HAPPENINGS DOWN south were any indication, though, the Whigs were not likely to win their fight for funding. Nathanael Greene expected South Carolina to repeal the impost and feared Georgia, which he had visited and where he "wrote and said every thing [he] could think of to induce them to tax and to adopt the duty," also might reject it. "The Southern States in matters of Government are really in a deplorable situation," he declared in a letter to Robert Morris, "and I fear there is little prospect of their mending. The Continental expences are growing great in this department ... and the revenue arising here little or nothing at all."[19]

IN ORDER FOR the Whigs—the nationalists—to win their fight for funding, John Brooks had to get Henry Knox to pledge his support for their plan and get the army in the Hudson Highlands to follow him. Knox's backing was essential for a variety of reasons: First, he had been actively supportive of the disgruntled officers' cause, trying to get back pay and a postwar pension since the middle of 1782. Second, he was friendly with most of the key officers and close to Washington. Third, he shared the nationalists' goal of strengthening Congress.

Though Knox had by now read the letter from Gouverneur Morris and the report by McDougall and Ogden that Brooks had brought with him from Philadelphia, his support could hardly be considered a certainty. He was being pulled in two different directions; the officers' dissatisfaction with their situation was very evident, but he was in no way anxious to involve the army in anything calling into question its loyalty.[20]

Which direction he really wanted to go in became clear only on the twenty-first, when he wrote to McDougall. Copies of the February 8 report by the Scotsman and Colonel Ogden "ha[d] been distributed to the different parts of the Army," he told the general, and the army was further from a resolution of the issues of pay and commutation now than it had been before the officers presented their petition to Congress. "The complex System of Government," was presently working "against the army, who certainly deserve[d] every thing in the power of a grateful people to give."

The army happened to be "in an unhappy predicament indeed not to know who [we]re responsible ... for a settlement of accounts." When people later looked back on these times they would "hardly beleive that an army contended incessantly for eight years under a constant pressure of misery to establish the liberties of their country, without knowing who were to compensate them or whether they were ever to receive any reward for their service." With peace imminent they should know who—the individual states or Congress—was going to reward them for their services.

He knew of all the talk "about the influence of the Army being united with the influence of the other public creditors to procure a General System of Finance or permanent continental funds," but he did not see how that union might be brought about and "how & in what manner the influence of the Army" could be applied. The army's influence, he warned, "can only exist in one point, that to be sure is a sharp point, which I hope in God will never be directed but against the Enemies of the liberties of America. Rhode Island and Virginia ar[e] refractory and will not grant the impost of five per cent. I do not ... see how the influence of the Army can work any conversi[o]n of those States." If Congress was "really defective and inadequate to the purposes of its institution," the solution was to have the states convene and make the changes needed to allow the government to be more effective.

"That the Army should ... be the imediate sufferers" and not have its accounts settled until those changes were made was difficult. However, the idea of it making a violent declaration not to disband until it received justice was abhorrent. "I consider the reputation of the American army ... one of the most immaculate things on earth, and ... we should even suffer wrongs & injuries to the utmost verge of toleration rather than sully it in the least degree," the hefty Massachusetts general declared.

Still, he knew the army's capacity to endure sufferings was not limitless. He did not want to see the breaking point passed.[21]

The Massachusetts general also wrote Gouverneur Morris on the twenty-first. Remembering Morris's letter of the seventh, Knox reassured him that the officers were not anxious to be referred to their respective states for a settlement of their accounts; "the Army generally ... always, reprobated being thirteen Armies." What they really wanted was "to be one continental body, looking up to one sovereign." By going to Congress they would spare themselves of "much heart burning at the partialities ... practiced by the respective States."

Congress's weakness particularly concerned Knox. If the government did not get general funding, it was not going to be strong enough "to preserve the peace," and all the fighting and bloodshed would be shown to have served "little purpose." And since the Articles of Confederation were "so defective" as to prevent the government from getting those funds, he proposed that the people be called together and told "to have a convention of the States to form a better constitution." That seemed, in his and others' "superficial view ... to be the most eff[icacious] remedy." They certainly had to do something before peace arrived or else they were going to be worse off than they were when the war began.[22]

The general's view of the Articles of Confederation, the new American government's first constitution, was correct. Although they allowed the government to run the war, negotiate treaties, and handle issues concerning western lands, they did not give the government any means to force the states to provide it with troops or funds. The government was able to ask for those things, but the states were free to ignore Congress's requests.

IN PHILADELPHIA the delegates again looked at funding and clashed on the question of how much power the Articles of Confederation gave them. Some members saw Congress as "merely an Executive body; and therefore ... it was inconsistent with the principles of liberty & the spirit of the Constitution, to submit to them a permanent revenue which wd. be placing the purse & the sword in the same hands."

Madison, however, thought otherwise. He considered Congress to be more than just an executive body when it came to revenue issues; it also had legislative power. And even if its power was that of an executive body, giving it the authority to raise permanent funds so it could discharge its debts would not be "inconsistent with the nature of an Executive body, or dangerous to the liberties of the republic."

Repeating the opinion he had given in earlier debates, he maintained that Congress had the constitutional authority to both determine how much money it needed and get that amount from the states. The relationship between the two parties was like the one between each state and its inhabitants. Just as someone living in a particular state had to obey its laws, so too did that state have to obey the laws of the national government. "Nothing could justify the States in disobeying acts warranted by it, but some previous abuse or infraction on the part of Congs." The states were bound by law to provide requisitioned funds. Each of them had to provide Philadelphia with the requested amount, which was based on the value of the land it owned. As defined by the Articles of Confederation, Congress had "a right to borrow money indefinitely, and emit bills of Credit ... for repayment & redemption of which the faith of the States was pledged & their legislatures constitutionally bound." Could any Congress with such powers be just an executive body?

Madison was realistic, though. He was not going to get a funding plan that put everything under the control of Congress; he knew the delegates had to "limit the call for a general revenue to duties on commerce." Whatever funds were still needed after that had to come from "a revenue established within each State & appropriated to the Common Treasury." His guiding principle on this issue was "to concur in every arrangement that sd. appear necessary for an honorable & just fulfillment of the public engagements." He did not want to do anything that gave Congress power it really did not need.[23]

Madison's last words failed to reassure Arthur Lee. The former doctor thought his views on government were "pregnant with dangerous consequences to the liberties of the confederated States; that notwithstanding the specious arguments that had been employed it was an established truth that the purse ought not to be put into the same hands with the Sword." As for the assertion that Congress had to have more funding authority to meet its obligations and establish public credit or it would be "nothing more than a rope of sand," it was clearly better to "see Congress a rope of sand than a rod of Iron." He offered as an explanation for "why some States would not & ought not to concur in granting to Congress a permanent revenue, that some States as Virga, would receive back a small part by paymt. from the U. S. to its Citizens [creditors]; whilst others as Pena. wd. receive a vast surplus; & consequently be enriched by draining the former of its wealth."[24]

Madison's words also upset John Francis Mercer. "If he conceived the foederal compact to be such as it had been represented he would immediately withdraw from Congress & do every thing in his power to destroy its existence." The onetime student of law under Jefferson did not think "Congs. had a right to borrow money as they pleased and to make requisitions on the States that wd. be binding on them." If it did have that right, then "the liberties of the States were ideal [not real]." Congress should make frequent requisitions and provide all the necessary information, but "the States must be left to judge of the nature of them, of their abilities to comply with them & to regulate their compliance accordingly."[25]

Returning to one of his themes of the eighteenth, Mercer made some "remarks on the injustice of the rule by which loan office certificates had been settled"; he thought some revision of it was necessary. In essence he was insinuating that public creditors profited unfairly from speculation in the certificates.[26]

After Massachusetts delegate Samuel Holten and Hamilton came out against and for permanent funding, respectively,[27] an irritated Gorham responded sharply to Lee's and Mercer's remarks about the public creditors. He believed that "the Union could never be maintained on any other ground than that of Justice; that some States had suffered greatly from the deficiencies of others … that if Justice was not to be obtained through the foederal system & this system was to fail … it was time this should be known [so] … some of the States might … [form] other confederacies adequate to the purposes of their safety."[28]

When the debates concluded, Congress relieved the Committee of the Whole of the responsibility to come up with a program to fund the debt and restore the government's credit. That task was assigned to a five-man committee made up of Gorham, Hamilton, Madison, Fitzsimmons and Rutledge.[29]

As February entered its last week the situation appeared bleak. Congress was able to do little and the gridlock only increased the officers' frustration. When McDougall, Pelatiah Webster, and William Judd visited Robert Morris to ask that officers involuntarily retired as part of the reduction in forces at the beginning of 1781 receive some pay, they spent much time talking and arguing, but the Financier said he thought it would not be possible to pay them because of a "Want of Money."[30]

SAMUEL SHAW HAD his doubts about the government and the country's citizenry. "No money, no funds, and what is worse, no disposition in the people to establish funds," he moaned to Reverend John Eliot. "The certain consequence … must be the death of public credit."

Who was shackling the government? Rhode Island. "It is astonishing with how much obstinacy ... Rhode Island has opposed the impost, and by its non-concurrence defeated a measure which seemed so essential to the public welfare," the captain exclaimed. Forgetting or ignoring Virginia's decision to repeal its ratification of the impost, Shaw expressed disbelief that "the smallest State in the union should thus counteract and annul the proceedings of the other twelve." That was "an awful defect in the Confederation." An individual state should not be allowed to block measures seen by all the other states and the national government as certain to improve the overall health of the nation.

The solution was to have "power vested in some supreme head, sufficient to enforce a compliance with such regulations as are evidently calculated for the general good." That supreme head with enhanced authority had to be the national government. "Thirteen wheels require a steady and powerful regulator to keep them in good order, and prevent the machine from becoming useless," Shaw declared.

The chances that the army would receive the compensation it was due did not look good. "The expectation of a speedy peace has greatly lulled the discontents of the army," Shaw informed Eliot, "and is a reason why so little redress has been granted by the country. On this account our application to Congress did not answer our intention. The mountain has brought forth a mouse," just a promise from the delegates that the army was going to get one month's pay. Nothing had been decided concerning pay arrears and opposition to both half pay and commutation existed in spite of the officers' "sacrifice of time, health, and property."[31]

KNOX AND SHAW saw Rhode Island as refractory and obstinate, but the General Assembly there viewed things differently. During its February session, the body passed a resolution praising its delegates in Philadelphia for their "meritorious Services rendered to this state, and to the Cause of Freedom in General," and for their "firmness and patriotic conduct ... particularly in their strenuous Exertions to defeat ... Measures ... dangerous to the public liberty." Among the services Howell had performed for his state was the forwarding of copies of passages from Congress's journal and correspondence concerning foreign loans; Robert Morris had deliberately understated how much aid America had been receiving in order to make it appear that without approval of the impost the war effort would be imperiled, but Howell had always felt that the country was securing sufficiently sizable loans to make the measure unnecessary.[32]

ON TUESDAY, FEBRUARY 25, John Taylor Gilman again proposed that the officers be sent back to their home states to get half pay or commutation. Too few delegates supported Gilman's motion, however, and when it was voted on it failed to pass. One of the arguments made by delegates opposed to referring the matter to the states was that if officers were referred to their home states, some—

those from "States who objected to half pay"—were not going to receive the postwar compensation they had been promised. That "would increase the present irritation of the army." Above all, though, what Gilman suggested was unconstitutional. The Articles of Confederation required that requisition quotas be based on *land values*, and that could not be changed without the approval of all thirteen states. But under the plan Gilman supported, apportionment for half pay was to be based on *"the number of officers belonging to each line"* and the states that agreed to compensate their officers were free to start executing it immediately, before all the states had approved the change.[33]

Sometime that Tuesday James Madison wrote Edmund Randolph. After devoting much of his first paragraph to the issue of funding the public debt, the conscientious Virginian got down to what really troubled him—the words he had heard at Fitzsimmons's home on the evening of the twentieth. "The *discontents and designs of* the *army are every day takeing a more solemn form,"* he wrote mostly in cipher. "It is *now whispered* that *they have not only resolved not to lay down their arms ti*[l]*l justice shall be done them* [but] *that to prev*[en]*t surprize a public declaration will be made to that effect*. It is *added and I fear with too much* certainty, *that the influence of General* [Washington] is *rapidly decreaseing in the army insomuch that* it is *even in contemplation to substitute some less scrupulous guardian of their interests."*

The concerned tone then disappeared for two paragraphs but returned in his fourth paragraph. The actions taken by Congress and the states over the next six months, Madison opined, are going to determine "whether prosperity & tranquility, *or confusion and disunion* are to be the fruits of the Revolution. The seeds of the latter are so thickly sown that nothing but the most enlightened and liberal policy will be able to stifle them." Writing mostly in cipher again, he related what had happened during the debates on the twenty-first, when Gorham, "a little *chafed* by some *expressions of Masters Lee and Mercer* unfavorable *to loan office creditors* said that if *justice* was not to be *obtained thro* the *general* confederacy, *the sooner* it *was known the better* [so] that some *states* [could leave the union for the purpose of] *forming other confederacys adequate to the purpose."*

What Gorham had said concerned Madison. "However erroneous these ideas may be, do they not *merit serious attention?"* he asked. "Unless some amicable & adequate arrangements be speedily taken for adjusting all the subsisting accounts and discharging the public engagements," he warned, "*a dissolution of the union* will be *inevitable."* And to avoid a civil war, "*alliances* would be *soug*[h]*t"* by the states, and "this country [would] be made *subservi*[ent] *to the wars and politics of Europe."*[34]

Madison's letter shows that he recognized the need for compromise. When he wrote that "nothing but the most enlightened and liberal policy" would prevent "confusion and disunion" from resulting, he was essentially saying that the delegates in Congress had to move away from their hardened positions. He did not want the nationalists to use the angry army as a sword of Damocles to get their way because he understood that that threatened the existence of America's developing republic. Rather, he wanted the delegates to realize that sometimes they had to put the whole country's interests above their own or those of the states they represented. That was necessary if they wanted to preserve the union and ensure harmonious relations between the states. Now each of the states jealously guarded its sovereignty, so the bonds between them were too weak; they could easily break even after a victorious end to the war.

In this case the enlightened thing for delegates to do was support the impost. If the states gave up some of their sovereignty and allowed Congress to directly levy taxes, they would be enabling the government to pay back the creditors and the army what they were owed and save its reputation at home and abroad. Once it was saved, Congress would be able to tempt other lenders to provide it with funds. With the government able to count on a regular flow of tax revenue and loans it would be able to fund its operations and provide the country with a degree of stability.

If, on the other hand, Congress did not get the impost and the other taxes that were sure to follow, creditors would lose faith in the American government. Instead of going to one body—Congress—to get what they were owed, they would head in thirteen different directions to the various state legislatures. Some states might satisfy their demands, while others might not. The situation would be chaotic and nobody would really be bound to the national government. Ultimately the states, which Madison thought were really acting more like thirteen separate and independent nations, would also go their own ways, each likely being played off against the other by the European powers. If that happened, all of them would essentially lose the independence they had fought for and the union would break apart.

THE ONLY THINGS the army was talking about at this time were "the news of Peace" and its own situation. "The better Patriots are alarmed at the situation of Congress," Baron von Steuben informed Henry Knox in the second page of his four-page letter. The army was not going to allow itself to be disbanded or reorganized in any way until it received justice, and "the People at large" did not expect promises to suffice; the only way to satisfy the army was to establish funding so the officers and soldiers could be paid. Discussions on how to establish funding were taking place, but to decide what needed to be done was going to take some time.

Steuben worried about what might happen in the meantime. What would the army do if Congress did disband or reorganize it without paying it or establishing funding for that purpose first? And how was the general public likely to react if the delegates decided to keep the army completely intact with no force reductions until funding was established?

Those concerns were why he wanted Knox to consider an idea put forward to him by some men who thought in terms of "the honor & dignity of the nation" and desired justice for the army. The army, they advised, should appeal to Philadelphia after peace was firmly established. It should express its "great confidence in the Justice of Congress & of the people," its certainty that the delegates were going to pay the officers and soldiers once they were able to do so. But since some time was needed to make the necessary arrangements, the army would "supplicate Congress & the people to continue their Subsistance & their emolument" and allow them to "remain on their present footing without being reformed dismembered or changed in any manner whatever" until a plan was effected.

"This demand," they believed, "ought to be made by the army through the Commander in Chief to Congress." If it was written "in terms respectfull, but firm," Philadelphia would acquiesce and use it to protect itself "from the unjust clamors of the people," Steuben added.

The general had already informed McDougall of the plan and assumed the Scotsman was going to contact Knox and say more on the matter.[35]

ON WEDNESDAY, FEBRUARY 26, the report by the five-man committee tasked with doing something about commutation was again debated. Hamilton moved that Congress approve five-and-a-half years' pay. Peters seconded his motion, but most members opposed it. Gorham then made a motion for five years' pay, which Bland seconded. The delegates then voted and enough of them said "aye" to pass the measure.[36] However, that did not really mean much; the only thing they had agreed upon was a specific number of years. If they wanted to actually appropriate funds to pay for the five years' pay, they needed a total of nine votes, and Gorham's motion had garnered only seven.

That same day Congress gave its consent to lifting the injunction of secrecy on Robert Morris's offer of resignation. Though he had offered to stay on until the end of May, he wanted to notify the many people who had contractual arrangements with him some time before he actually left office.[37]

"Nothing would have induced me to take this Step but a painful Conviction that the Situation of those to whom the Public are indebted is desperate," the Financier explained to Washington. The vast majority of the delegates wanted to treat the creditors and the army justly, he believed, but he doubted they would "adopt the necessary Measures" to improve their situation because the delegates were "afraid of offending their States."

Morris had vainly anticipated being able to provide the army with its just dues and had "labored to make their Situation as tolerable as Circumstances would permit." To the general, who had been kind to assist him, and to the officers, who he knew held "just Sentiments" towards him in spite of the "unwearied Pains ... taken to give them disagreeable Impressions," he said thank you. He wished for his successor to have better luck and wanted to see "our glorious Revolution ... crowned with those Acts of Justice, without which the greatest human Glory is but the Shadow of a Shade."[38]

As the Financier wrote to Washington, so too did Virginia delegate Joseph Jones. He had received the general's letter of December 14 long before but because of illness had not gotten around to answering it until now.[39] Congress had been spending much time trying to come up with a funding plan, and the impost's chances for eventual approval looked good, but most of the other specific duties that had been considered probably were not going to be adopted.

The delegates had "the purest intentions towards the public creditors" and were going to do their utmost "in obtaining from the States the means to do them speedy and complete justice." And they had "such ... opinion of the merit and services of the army, that did it not wound the sense of justice," they would be inclined to give it preferential treatment. Jones understood that Congress's "delay in complying with their requests" was one reason why the army was discontent and suspicious of the delegates' intentions, but they must understand that "so mixed a body as that of Congress" was bound to reach decisions only after much deliberation. Also, "every class of public creditors" had to know that Philadelphia could not pay them unless it got funds from the states. Efforts to get funding from them were being made, but so far had not been successful.

Jones then became cautionary, informing Washington that the existence of "dangerous combinations in the army" was being openly reported around the capital. They supposedly were soon going to make a declaration amounting to a refusal to disband until their demands were met. He hoped such reports were unfounded, though, and wanted the army to continue to "exercise awhile longer at least, that patient forbearance which ... so honourably distinguished them." If a complete loss of trust "between the civil and military authority, by intemperate conduct or an assumption of improper power, especially by the military body," occured, they would be passing "the Rubicon." Therefore "every worthy officer" needed to do what he could to prevent "the adoption by the army of any hasty and rash measure."

The possible presence in the army of some designing men and an inevitable claim by them that Congress did not intend to do it justice worried Jones. If such men were present, they would "gradually endeavor to hurt the reputation of those averse to their projects, and by sinister practices lessen their weight and influence among the soldiery." That meant going after Washington. "I have lately heard," Jones reported, "there are those who are abandoned enough to use these arts to lessen your popularity in the army in hopes ultimately the weight of your opposition will prove no obstacle to their ambitious designs." If they succeeded, peace was not going to bring with it "its usual blessings to America," he feared. Washington would have to decide "whether to temporize, or oppose [them] with steady unremitting firmness."[40]

The letter was important. Washington would later take it with him to an important meeting of the officers and read part of it aloud, thinking the delegate's words might soothe their feelings and prevent the army from taking any action that it might later regret. Jones was known to be a friend of the army and his assurances of Congress's sincerity might help.

Another attempt to refer the officers to the states for half pay was made the day Jones wrote Washington. Mercer was pleased the issue was being reconsidered. Although he recognized that the divisions within Congress and its inability to decide what to do were causing alarm and knew that the body had to do something, he worried that "the commutation proposed … with the funding of other debts" would help "establish & perpetuate a monied interest in the U. S.[and] that this monied interest would gain the ascendance of the landed interest, … resort to places of luxury & splendor, and, by their example & influence, become dangerous to our republican constitutions."[41] In essence he was voicing the fear so common in New England that the officers were going to become a privileged class and an instrument of an oppressive and tyrannical government. Lest the officers become bound to the national government, have them return to their home states, which could then look after them.

Madison responded sharply. Commutation had been advanced to please those who found "the idea of pensions … obnoxious." Now opponents of the measure were making it "no less obnoxious than pensions by stigmatizing it with the name of a perpetuity."

The state of the government's affairs "was truly deplorable." It was not able to pay back the principal on the loans it had received and if someone proposed funding for Congress so it could do that and make interest payments on its debt, "it was exclaimed agst. as establishing a dangerous monied interest, as corrupting the public manners, as administering poison to our republican constitutions."

But the delegates had to somehow fund their debts. Even if the consequences of doing so were bad, they could not be more unrepublican than "a violation of the maxims of good faith and common honesty."[42]

After Madison had had his say, commutation was set aside for the following day so Connecticut's delegates would have a chance to express their opinions regarding the issue. A report by the five-man committee tasked with establishing a funding program for Congress was then reviewed. The committee had recommended, in addition to the impost, specific duties on imported salt, wines, rum and brandy, and the delegates voted for duties on only the first two.[43]

It was while the duties were being debated that two delegates who had opposed general funding for Congress now indicated a willingness to accept it. Since its opponents "appeared to have formed no plan adequate to the public exigencies, and he was convinced of the necessity of doing something," John Francis Mercer decided to "strike in with those who were pursuing the plan of a general revenue." Also joining their ranks was Samuel Holten.[44]

As the debates went on, McDougall wondered in a letter to Knox what would happen to the army once peace arrived. The delegates could not accept a plan seen by the states "as a design in Congress to Establish a Force to awe" them, and they feared the army might refuse to lay down its arms until it received justice. "An attempt … to split the Army [in the Hudson Highlands] into detachments" and remove the regiments to different locations around the country "to prevent their being formidable" was a possibility for the near future. If the delegates really did do that, the officers stood no chance of getting half pay and perhaps even the back pay they were owed; the states were far too inclined "to cancel all the public debts on a Peace, Especially those due to their own people."

Also, although the officers had made clear in their petition that they understood half pay was not very popular and indicated a willingness to accept something less objectionable, commutation's prospects did not appear to be good; the army could count on no more than seven states to vote for it.

The general then said he needed to find out what the army's mood was before giving advice on "measures they ought to take to obtain Justice," declared that peace was very likely, signed his letter "Brutus," and later added a postscript to urge that Knox "put into careful hands" the letters he was sending to Philadelphia.[45]

Friday was the last day of the month. Connecticut delegates Eliphalet Dyer and Oliver Wolcott moved that the issue of half pay be sent to the states. Their motion, which "specified 5 years whole pay as the proper ground of composition with the Officers of the respective lines," was overwhelmingly voted down.

The more important issue, though, was whether Gorham's motion that half pay be commuted to five years' pay should be considered a proposal to appropriate funds. When that question was posed by Bland and Madison and a vote was taken, the answer was a resounding "aye." So the Wednesday vote, which had seemed favorable, had actually been lost by two states.[46]

THE ONE MONTH'S pay intended for the army was, of course, a more immediate concern than commutation. Although Washington had already announced the rates at which the soldiers were to be paid, no weekly payments had yet been made; Deputy Paymaster General Wetmore still had too little hard currency at his disposal to guarantee that the process could be completed without interruption. But the Commander-in-chief, sensing how uneasy his army was becoming, decided on the second of March to allow payments "to commence this week and to be kept up so long as the supply of Cash shall be furnished." Wetmore planned to make the first payments on the fifth but was uncertain if he would have enough cash to make all the subsequent payments. If it should happen that he got no cash, he planned to give the soldiers notes payable that were redeemable in cash or merchandise.[47]

Around this time, on March 3, Knox wrote McDougall to tell him that in the Hudson Highlands they were "impatiently waiting the result" of his efforts in Philadelphia. The Massachusetts general really hoped for a better result than what now seemed likely and had no doubts that the Scotsman was doing everything in his power "to bring the matter to an happy termination."

After making clear that what the army desired most was justice, not gratitude, Knox turned his attention to the Scotsman's letter of February 12. Their "friend B_____ [Brutus]" had written that "a resolution ... might be obtained," one that he hoped for because "it would releive us from the apprehensions of … great commotions uncertainty and chagrin."[48] Perhaps the army's greatest desire was going to be fulfilled before it was disbanded, he must have been thinking.

Later that day, after receiving two letters from McDougall, Knox decided to write him again. What the Scotsman had written can only be surmised, since the letters appear to have been lost. However, one of them—dated February 28—must have included the results of that day's debates and a report of the support for five years' full pay, for the Massachusetts general told McDougall that the army in the Hudson Highlands had been pleased by what it had learned and that Washington had ordered "the Several lines to Signify their acceptance as required after 15 April, when all the officers will have returned from furlough."

But to the "pain and chagrin" of the army the chances of getting funding for that compensation had not improved. "Certainly we ought to have some object either State, or continental, to rest our hopes upon, previous to our being disbanded,"[49] Knox remarked in his conclusion.

Knox also wrote four letters to Secretary of War Benjamin Lincoln, the general who had visited the New Windsor Cantonment in late fall 1782 and, on returning to Philadelphia, had reported the severe distress that the army there was experiencing as a result of its not being paid. In one of his letters he urged the secretary to look into the complaints of company officers attached to a corps of artificers assigned to build carriages for the artillery. They had been serving since the beginning of the war and deserved praise for the "exemplary manner" in which they had performed their duties, but they were suffering "for want of pay and provisions." They felt they deserved higher commissions and believed they were "entitled to the same emoluments after the War as officers of the same grade in the line of the army."[50]

His greater concern, though, was the army as a whole and McDougall's efforts in Philadelphia. He wanted the secretary "to urge that every thing respecting the Army be decided upon before peace takes place," and since an end to the war was now a certainty, "no time ought to be lost." In the Hudson Highlands they were "anxiously waiting the result of General McDougalls mission." If it were not successful, trouble was to be expected. "Let the public only comply with their own promises, and the Army will return to their respective homes, the lambs & bees of the Community," he reassured the secretary. "But if they should be disbanded previous to a settlement, without knowing who to look to, for an adjustment of accounts & responsibility of payment, they will be so deeply stung by the injustice & ingratitude of their country as to become its tygers & wolves."[51]

Chapter Sixteen

"The Old Leven"

WHEN GEORGE WASHINGTON wrote Alexander Hamilton on March 4, he began by subtly criticizing Congress for not keeping him adequately informed; he had not realized that the government's financial situation was "so deplorable." He had been under the impression that Holland was going to provide enough money to enable the government "to rub along." Only information gathered from newspapers and Hamilton's earlier letter had enlightened him.

The general did not want to see "a political dissolution [of the army] for want of subsistence." Such an action would "be productive of Civil commotions & end in blood," and Washington feared possible army involvement.

He was facing a difficult problem and had to perform a careful balancing act. He was not just a soldier but also a citizen. The soldier in him saw "the sufferings of a complaining army on the one hand, and the inability of Congress and tardiness of the States on the other" as omens of bad things to come, "events which are more to be depricated than prevented," but the citizen in him had not yet given himself up to despair; "if there is such a disposition shewn as prudence & policy dictates to do justice, your apprehensions, in case of Peace, are greater than there is cause for," he told Hamilton.

If, though, Hamilton had not been exaggerating the danger when he wrote in February, and the extent of the plot and the discontent in the army with his leadership were great, then he suspected "the old leven," Horatio Gates, was the cause. Washington could not prove that Gates was behind the plot, but that was what he was hearing. And Gates's "mask of the most perfect dissimulation & apparent cordiallity" did not fool him; he still distrusted Gates.

Whatever the case, Washington wanted to have nothing to do with the plotters' scheme to frighten reluctant delegates and states into giving Congress greater authority by hanging a mutinous army over their heads. He planned to "pursue the same steady line of conduct" that he had pursued in the past, "fully convinced that the sensible and discerning part of the army" was well aware of how much he had done for them. Even though he knew most of those in uniform believed their chances of getting their just dues were going to come to an end when peace arrived, the general did not worry much about his army "exceeding the bounds of reason & moderation."

Washington wished to believe that the states would provide Philadelphia with the funds to satisfy the army's "just claims" if the delegates lobbied their legislatures. They were not "so devoid of common sense, common honesty, & common policy as to refuse their aid on a full, clear, & candid representation of the facts from Congress; more especially if these should be enforced by members of their own body; who might demonstrate what the inevitable consequences of failure must lead to." The army should not be used as an instrument to achieve that end, though; that was "impolitic" and might "excite jealousy, and bring on its concomitants."

What the delegates should do, he advised Hamilton, is explore the possibility of "an adjournment of Congress for a few months." If they did do that, they might go back to their states and "fully & boldly" lay out for them "the great defects of their Constitution. ... Such a measure would tend to promote the public weal." Congress had to have "powers competent to all *general* purposes." If it did not get them, nothing would be gained from "the distresses ... encountered, the expences ... incurred, and the blood ... spilt in the course of an Eight years war."[1]

General Horatio Gates

HORATIO GATES'S[2] MEN called him "Granny Gates."[3] His forehead receded; his hair was thinning and gray; his cheeks were ruddy; he had a double chin; and he relied on a pair of thick wire-rimmed glasses that rested on his long, pointy nose to see. He was short, heavy-set, and his shoulders stooped a bit. Burgoyne thought he resembled an "old midwife."[4]

The supposed bastard son of Robert Gates and the Duke of Leeds's head housekeeper, Horatio began his military career in 1749, but did not see his first real action until Major General Edward Braddock's expedition against the French at Fort Duquesne in 1755. When the general's army neared a dangerous ravine at Turtle Creek that July 9, Captain Gates's company and one other unit secured fords above and below the point where the creek flowed into the Monongahela, enabling an advance force to successfully cross and recross the river. But not long after the double crossing was accomplished the British got caught in an ambush by the French and Indians. Under heavy fire, they started to retreat. Braddock, hearing the gunfire, sent a detachment to help but it collided with the retreating troops. In the event Gates was wounded and had to be removed to safety.

Years later Gates helped organize a victorious invasion of Martinique. He was then chosen to convey the good news to England and given a letter for the Earl of Egremont that praised him as "a very deserving officer."[5] After arriving in London in March 1762, he received a commission as a major in the 45th Regiment in Nova Scotia.

When he arrived in New York, Gates learned that someone else already had the commission. Now he was not on any regiment's payroll. He remained in America, hoping his situation would change before the war ended, but it didn't and he later returned to England. There he was able to collect some back pay and receive his regular salary.

A major's commission with the Royal American Regiment came in late 1764, but he did not want to return to America and could not afford a better commission. Eventually he exchanged the one he had for another that offered only half pay in a deactivated regiment, and later he left the British army altogether.

In part because he was upset that his low birth had prevented his promotion, Gates left for America during the summer of 1772; he had already written Washington, whom he knew from Braddock's expedition, to explore purchasing an estate in America. After his arrival he bought a 659-acre Virginia plantation in Berkeley County, which he named "Traveller's Rest."

When war broke out Gates was made a brigadier general and the army's first adjutant general. A promotion to major general came in May 1776, and command of the army in Canada came in June.

But before Gates even left New York the army had withdrawn from Canada to Fort Crown Point, and it would soon move to Fort Ticonderoga. The men were "dispersed, some few in tents, some in sheds, and more under the shelter of miserable brush huts."[6] They were "but a mob ... ruined by sickness, fatigue and desertion, and void of every idea of discipline and subordination."[7] Death and discouragement were everywhere. The soldiers were "without pay ... and altogether reduced to live from hand to mouth."[8] They also did not know who their real commander was; Major General Schuyler was claiming Congress had made him the army's commander.

Gates was undaunted. He took steps to improve the housing, clothing, and water supplies. He had latrine areas covered daily. He used huge bonfires and extra rum to warm fever-stricken men. He eliminated smallpox as a problem. He attempted to enforce discipline fairly and to curb inflation in the camp. He offered ten-dollar bounties to encourage three-year enlistments. He gave chaplains more attention.

Also, he had a fleet built. The foot of Lake Champlain had to be protected, and Congress did give

Gates command of all the troops in that area, though it confirmed that Schuyler was the commander of the northern theatre.

The men saw that he was concerned for their well-being and responded. "Our worthy and well-esteemed General Gates ... is putting the most disordered Army ... into a state of regularity and defense," Matthias Ogden wrote to Aaron Burr. "If our friends in *Canada* ... will wait a few days, we will give them a very proper reception."[9]

However, no proper reception did take place. The British did rout the American fleet and occupied Crown Point, but they realized Fort Ticonderoga could not be taken before winter and decided in early November to return to Canada. Gates then left the fort in early December and marched south to reinforce Washington, rejecting the urgings of the New York Committee of Safety, which wanted him to disobey orders and have his forces become part of an independent army in the Hudson Highlands.

Later, in March 1777, he was directed by Congress to return to Ticonderoga to assume command of the army there. Schuyler, angered by the decision, rode off to Philadelphia, and the delegates there established a committee to determine how much authority Gates should have. When it finished considering the matter, it decided he could remain at the fort but only as a subordinate to Schuyler. That did not sit well with him and he went to the capital and protested, but to no avail.

But he did not remain below Schuyler for long. In July Schuyler lost Ticonderoga and, as a result, Philadelphia decided to replace him with Gates.

When he took over the army in August it was in a "miserable state of despondency and terror."[10] While Gates improved their fighting spirit, General Burgoyne advanced towards Albany, where he planned to link up with Colonel Barry St. Leger and General Howe. As Burgoyne did so, Indians under his command disobeyed orders and killed some women and children in raids, giving Gates some atrocities he could use for propaganda purposes. Burgoyne—"in whom the fine Gentleman is united with the Soldier and the Scholar"—had employed "the savages of America to scalp Europeans and descendants of Europeans" and paid "a price for ... each scalp so barbarously taken." A "young lady lovely to sight," Jane McCrea, had been "scalped and mangled in a most shocking manner" while waiting for her fiancé. No mention that her lover was a Loyalist officer and that she was of like sympathies; instead she was said to be of "virtuous character and amiable disposition."[11]

Hoping to keep Burgoyne from reaching Albany, Gates led his men north to Bemis Heights. There they waited, their forces augmented daily by militiamen.

Finally, on the morning of September 19, the British general arrived in front of the American position, his forces arranged in three greatly spaced columns. When they burst through woods into a clearing at Freeman's Farm, two American units located well in advance of Gates's left wing met them. As the day progressed, both sides poured men into the battle. At one point the enemy's defenses between its center and right appeared ready to collapse. Benedict Arnold galloped off to his commander's small headquarters in the rear and implored him to send reinforcements. After much hesitation an additional brigade was sent, but by the time it arrived German reinforcements had saved Burgoyne's center. Finally, nighttime arrived and the Americans withdrew, leaving the battlefield "covered with dead almost for several acres."[12]

In the days that followed what was to be called the First Battle of Saratoga, Burgoyne's supply situation deteriorated, and officers and men were shot or captured by American snipers and raiding parties. Morale suffered and desertions increased. With no relief in sight, the British general decided to launch another attack.

In the meantime, Arnold had had a heated argument with Gates; he had learned that Colonel Daniel Morgan's troops were no longer going to be under his command and that neither he nor his men had been mentioned in his superior's report to Congress on the battle at Freeman's Farm. The northern army's top officer did not recognize Arnold as a major general and informed him that Benjamin Lincoln would take over his command upon his return. Infuriated, Arnold sent Gates a long letter: he wished to leave and rejoin Washington's army.

About two weeks later, on October 7, Burgoyne's large force arrived to test the American left wing. Gates was not caught unawares by the British general's decision to attack; "despair may dictate to him to risque all upon one throw,"[13] he had speculated a few days before. Accordingly, he responded by launching a three-pronged attack. The British right began to buckle; and soon thereafter the entire front had to retreat.

Arnold, who had changed his mind about leaving camp, heard cannon and muskets and paced about his quarters. Finally, late that afternoon, he mounted a small bay mare and raced off to the battlefield. Arriving to cheers, he waved his sword and urged the troops on. Eventually Breymann's redoubt, the last defense covering Burgoyne's right flank, was captured and the weakened British army withdrew under darkness, torching "all the Houses before them as they retreated."[14] Gates pursued Burgoyne and on the seventeenth forced him to surrender. Almost fifty-nine-hundred men laid down their arms.

Instead of immediately informing his Commander-in-chief of the victory, Gates wrote directly to Congress to convey the news. An irritated Washington, with fresh memories of his own recent defeats, let the general know that he was not pleased that he had done so.

That, though, was not what really caused Washington to grow hostile towards Gates. What did was something called the Conway Cabal, a case of intrigue that took place mostly during the fall of 1777. Thomas Conway, a Frenchman of Irish descent who had not waited long to volunteer to fight for America, considered himself Washington's superior and expected to be recognized as such. He let Congress know that it should rely on his expertise, which would make up for the Commander-in-chief's obvious shortcomings. He wanted to make good use of the experience he had gained under Frederick the Great and receive the recognition he believed an officer of his caliber deserved, a promotion from brigadier general to major general. If he did not get one, he might resign.

When Washington heard from Richard Henry Lee of Virginia that the delegates were going to grant Conway his wish, the Commander-in-chief became furious. The Frenchman didn't deserve a promotion. "General Conways' merit … as an officer, and his importance in this Army, exists more in his own imagination than in reallity,"[15] Washington scoffed. Other officers were more deserving, he believed, and of the army's twenty-four brigadier generals the Frenchman did rank last in terms of seniority.

Promoting him ahead of them would deal "a fatal blow to the existance of this army." At a time when many financially strapped officers were leaving the army to look after their families, Washington feared the effect such an undeserved promotion would have on those still remaining. He had been able to keep the army together in the past but he was unsure about the future. "It will be impossible for me to be of any further survice if such insuperable difficulties are thrown in my way,"[16] the Commander-in-chief wrote in an apparent attempt to frighten Congress into believing that he might also walk away from his commission and abandon the war effort.

What caused trouble between Washington and Gates was a very brief letter Conway sent to the latter in October 1777 to explain why the Americans had lost at Brandywine. In it the Frenchman referred to the Commander-in-chief as "a weak General" and lamented that he and "bad Councellors would have ruined" America.[17] The disparaging characterization of Washington was heard and supposedly seen by one of Gates's aides, Colonel James Wilkinson, who was unable to keep his mouth shut. After drinking too much at the headquarters of Lord Stirling on the evening of October 28, he repeated Conway's inappropriate remarks to Lord Stirling's aide, Major William McWilliams, who relayed what had been said to his superior. Lord Stirling then reported the disparaging remark to Washington. Soon afterwards, on November 5, the Commander-in-chief wrote Conway a short letter to make him aware that he knew what was going on.

The Frenchman received it that day and immediately admitted that he had sent Gates a letter somewhat critical of "several Measures pursued in this army." But he praised the Commander-in-chief as "a Brave man, an honest Man, a patriot, and a Man of great sense." The problem was not Washington's judgment; it was the men who "influenc'd" him. He started to deny having called the Commander-in-chief a "*Weak General*" and then hedged a bit, saying that if he had written such a thing, it was used only in connection with Washington's "excess of Modesty" and faith in those who were "Much inferior … in point of judgment and Knowledge" to the Commander-in-chief.

As he continued, his tone became more hostile. He referred to Washington's "inquisition in Letters," but expressed a willingness to turn over what he had written to Gates to prove his innocence. He then concluded with what could certainly be construed as a veiled threat to rehash all of the Commander-in-chief's missteps at Brandywine, saying that after his return to France he would come out with "an impartial account" of what he had seen during his campaign in America.[18]

Soon thereafter Conway decided to resign. He sent his commission and a long explanation of his actions to Congress, citing the letter to Gates that had the remark about Washington and the failure of the delegates to promote him. He informed the Commander-in-chief two days later, on the sixteenth, and expressed his desire to be allowed to leave the service so he could "return to france as soon as possible,"[19] but Washington promptly replied that the general's resignation was a matter for Philadelphia to decide. However, neither Congress nor the Board of War, to whom Conway's letter was referred, chose to act on it.

On November 28 Thomas Mifflin wrote Gates to tell him Washington was no longer in the dark; "an Extract from General Conway's Letter ... had been procured and sent to Head Quarters." It was "a Collection of just Sentiments" but not ones that he ought to have shared with his staff officers. "My dear General take care of your Sincerity & Frank Disposition," Mifflin cautioned Gates. "They cannot injure yourself but they may injure some of your best friends."[20]

A short time after hearing from Mifflin, Gates finally answered the letter Conway had sent him in October. The Frenchman's words had pained him, but his "judicious observations" made him "sensible of the difficulty ... in remedying the evils ... retard[ing] ... success." However, even if Conway's criticism of Washington was justified, replacing him with another general would not bring about an immediate solution to the army's problems: "The perfect establishment of military discipline ... is not only the work of Genius, but of time," Gates pointed out.

After urging Conway not to resign and affixing his signature, the general added a postscript to inform him that Washington had obtained an extract of his letter and to urge him to find out "which of the letters was copied off." He had to learn the identity of "the person ... guilty of that act of infidelity."[21]

Five days later Gates also wrote Washington to seek his help in finding the guilty party. He did not know which papers had been "stealingly copied," but the author was "a Wretch," someone capable of betraying him and doing great harm to military operations. Not knowing whether the disloyal individual was a delegate or an officer, Gates intended to send the President of Congress a copy of his letter to Washington; that would enable the delegates and the Commander-in-chief to work together to "obtain, as soon as possible, a Discovery" that he felt greatly affected "the safety of the States." He suspected someone from Washington's staff had committed the act while he was out of sight and felt "Crimes of that magnitude ought not to remain unpunished."[22]

By this time Lee and Mifflin had begun weakening the Commander-in-chief. Responsibility for supplying the army had been transferred from temporary congressional committees to the Board of War for the sake of stability, which was in accordance with Washington's wishes, but the president of the board had been given authority over all of the Commander-in-chief's orders and actions. And the man chosen to be its president was Horatio Gates.

About two-and-a-half weeks later, on December 13, 1777, Conway was made inspector general. Washington had wanted a qualified foreign officer to assist him in establishing standards for drill and maneuver and instilling discipline in the troops, but he certainly would not have selected Conway. As inspector general, the Frenchman was not subordinate to Washington; he went straight to the Board of War with his reports.

When Conway showed up at Valley Forge soon after his appointment and tried to exercise his new authority, the Commander-in-chief essentially dismissed him. The Frenchman took offense. Washington told Congress that Conway "was received & treated with proper respect to his Official character" but admitted that he had not welcomed him as if he were a friend: "My feelings will not permit me to make professions of friendship to the man I deem my Enemy,"[23] he explained.

On January 4, 1778, the Commander-in-chief answered Gates's letter of December 8. He did not understand why Gates found it necessary to send Congress a copy of the letter he'd sent him. Since the general had chosen that course, Washington now unhappily had to "answer through the same channel" in order to ensure that no delegate suspected that he had "practiced some indirect means, to come at the contents of the confidential Letters between you [Gates] & General Conway."

He told Gates that he had found out about Conway's disparaging remarks from Lord Stirling and had written the Frenchman to make him aware that he "was not unapprized of his intriguing disposition." He had not known that Gates and Conway were corresponding with each other and, he continued, "much less did I suspect that I was the subject of your confidential Letters." As a matter of fact, Washington thought Gates had been the original source for the information concerning the disparaging remarks and had just passed them on "with a friendly view to forewarn, and consequently forearm me, against a secret enemy … a dangerous incendiary—…Genl Conway."[24]

About one week after Washington had deemed Conway his enemy, the Frenchman wrote the Commander-in-chief. He was still in a tiff. He understood that Washington's hostility towards him resulted from the disparaging remarks he had made in his letter to Gates, but saw nothing wrong with expressing an opinion on another general or on the army. "Must such an odious and tyrannical inquisition beginn in this country? Must it be introduc'd by the commander in chief of this army rais'd for the Defence of Liberty?"

No, Washington must not have had such a thing in mind. Even if the Commander-in-chief thought of himself as "an absolute King," which Conway knew was not the case, he would be better off directing his antipathy towards the "officious sycophant" guilty of reporting what Conway had written than towards the Frenchman himself. "It Would be more Generous, more to your Glory and interest" to do so, Conway told Washington.

"I Do not pretend, sir, to be a consummate General," he continued, "but … as an old sailor Knows more of a shipp than admirals who have never been to sea, Long experience and constant practice make me think that I could in some Measure be a helping hand in putting your army upon a Better footing, and in correcting the many abuses of Which no one is more sensible than you are."

The Frenchman did not stop there. He charged Washington with being against his promotion, receiving him coldly at Valley Forge, turning other officers against him, and then announced that he would leave and go wherever Congress directed if the Commander-in-chief so despised seeing him in camp. He was even willing to return to France,[25] he declared shortly before signing his letter.

About two weeks later, Gates defended himself in a reply to Washington's letter of the fourth. The remarks in Conway's letter were very moderate rather than extreme. The letter was actually completely innocuous and the part disparaging the Commander-in-chief and his advisors "was in Words as well as in Substance a wicked Forgery." Wilkinson had insinuated that Colonel Robert Troup and Hamilton were involved in the affair, but he had not listened to such talk.[26]

Washington knew Gates was lying and the following month he sent him a letter saying so. He had not learned of the disparaging remarks from Hamilton.

By that time Congress had woken up and Conway's star had faded. The government had received a petition from nine brigadier generals alarmed at the prospect of his promotion and letters from Washington that showed what was happening. The delegates understood that the Frenchman was far from being a military genius and they had no desire to take any action on his behalf that might cause the generals to resign en masse and Washington to follow through on his threat to walk away from his commission.

From there things only went downhill for Conway. He was named by the Board of War to be the second in command under Lafayette of an expedition to Canada, but when Washington's tall friend arrived in Albany in mid-February to lead the men north, Conway's behavior disturbed him; he behaved "like a man sent from heaven for the liberty and happiness of America."[27] So Lafayette refused to accept him as his second in command; he wanted either Alexander McDougall, if he was well, or Major General Johann Kalb.

Lafayette got his way and Kalb was appointed to be the second in command, but Conway was still supposed to be part of the expedition. Lafayette thought "the actual scheme" was to have him replaced as commander of the expedition with Conway, "under the immediate direction of general gates."[28] To prevent such a thing from happening he relegated Conway to doing paperwork. The move was not necessary; soon after Lafayette wrote Washington, Congress decided against invading Canada.

Conway was not the only guilty party. The Board of War had deliberately bypassed Washington when it appointed Lafayette to command the expedition to Canada. Gates, Mifflin, and others unfriendly to the Commander-in-chief supposedly wanted to draw Lafayette from Washington's side to theirs. If that was their plan, it failed.

Not long before Lafayette reported on Conway's behavior, Gates had written another letter to Washington. He was not a member of any faction opposing the Commander-in-chief, and he claimed to "have no personal Connection with [Conway], nor … any correspondence, previous to his writing the Letter" that had offended Washington. The only letter he had written to the Frenchman was one to corroborate "the contents of the letter" as he knew them. He apologized if anything in his letters hurt Washington.[29]

Washington replied to Gates's apology four days later. The two of them were then able to put the matter behind them.

As his troubles with Washington over Conway's letter were coming to an end, Gates found himself having to deal with the seemingly hurt Colonel Wilkinson, who claimed the short general was casting aspersions on his honor. The two exchanged letters, Gates explaining in his how the Commander-in-chief had learned of the Frenchman's offensive letter and expressing his shock at Wilkinson's trying to insinuate that Robert Troup was the real culprit when the colonel himself had actually repeated the damaging remarks to McWilliams. Still refusing to admit his own guilt, Wilkinson responded by challenging Gates to a duel.

Though Congress did not allow commissioned officers to settle their differences in duels, Gates was prepared to stand up to the colonel's challenge. But on the morning of February 25, the date set for the duel, they were able to make peace. Gates received a letter from Benjamin Stoddert, a mutual friend of the two antagonists, urging him not to go through with the duel. Stoddert claimed Wilkinson maintained his love for the general and was hurt that he had fallen out of his favor. Also, he appealed to Gates's patriotism: "If nothing else will stop you—this consideration must—Your life is not your own, it belongs to this Country."[30] The solution was for the two of them to come to some understanding. Gates, heeding his friend's appeal, sent word to Wilkinson that he wanted to meet with him. When they did meet at a field near York, the two officers took a long walk along a back street and repaired relations enough to end all thoughts of a duel.

In late April, after Congress had decided to place Conway under McDougall's command in Peekskill, the Frenchman complained in a letter to Gates of the treatment he had received and asked to be allowed to resign if he could not get a field command. He then had a change of heart and galloped off to catch the courier, but by the time he reached York—Congress could not sit in Philadelphia because of the British occupation—the delegates had already accepted his resignation.

The whole affair probably should not have been called the Conway Cabal. The Frenchman certainly disparaged Washington, but no real sinister plot against him appears to have taken place. Whatever the case, though, the Conway Cabal led Washington to wrongly believe that Gates wished to supplant him as Commander-in-chief. "It appeared in general, that General Gates was to be exalted, on the ruin of my reputation and influence,"[31] he had declared in a letter to his fellow Virginian, Governor Patrick Henry, in late February. He remained apprehensive about that possibility for a number of months, and one can understand why the Commander-in-chief harbored such suspicions even if he was wrong to do so. At the time of the affair Gates was quite popular with New England politicians, and memories of his victories on the battlefield were still fresh in the minds of many, while Washington's lack of success—the American loss at Brandywine Creek in September, the subsequent British occupation of Philadelphia, and another defeat at Germantown in October—led some to wonder whether he was the right man to lead the army. Dr. Benjamin Rush, who had left Congress before the Conway Cabal, and Massachusetts delegate James Lovell even spoke openly about replacing Washington.

However, assurances from then President of Congress Henry Laurens and two other members—Jonathan Bayard Smith and Eliphalet Dyer—that no plan to replace Washington existed, have to be believed. Washington himself would write in May 1778 that there had never been even a "whisper ... heard in Congress" about replacing him with someone else.[32]

Less than a year after Washington wrote those words, in March 1779, Gates further displeased Washington by declining to lead an expedition against Indians in the Mohawk Valley, claiming he lacked the necessary youth and vigor. The offer "merited a different answer from the one given to it." The Commander-in-chief recalled the "symptoms of coldness and constraint in General Gates behavior" towards him that he had seen "very early in the war," which had worsened with time, and the "direct breach"[33] in relations between them because of the Conway Cabal.

Another chance for action in the field came when Gates was offered the southern army in the spring of 1780. "I fear your laurels may wither if you accept the command,"[34] Robert Morris presciently warned him. But the general did accept the command. It was an unenviable one: "an Army without Strength. A Military Chest without Money. A Department apparently deficient in public Spirit, and a Climate that encreases Despondency."[35] His men would have to travel great distances with no depots to draw supplies from and no money coming from the states of Virginia and North Carolina. "I have before me the most unpromising Prospect my Eyes ever beheld,"[36] Gates wrote from Hillsboro, North Carolina, on July 20.

The general joined the main army at Coxe's Mill, North Carolina, on July 25. Soon, "as though actuated by a spirit of great activity and enterprise, he ordered his men to hold themselves in readiness to march at a moment's warning." The order produced "great astonishment," but Gates was determined to reach his objective—Camden, South Carolina—before the British could be reinforced, and he assured his men that "plentiful supplies of rum and rations were on the route, and would overtake them in a day or two."[37]

The route he took was direct; however, it passed through Loyalist country and woods and forced his men to use roads either soaked with swamp water or dense with sand. Still, by August 13 they had covered more than one-hundred-twenty miles and had arrived at Rugeley's Mill in Clermont, South Carolina. Brigadier General Edward Stevens's Virginia militia joined them the next day and then, at ten o'clock on the warm night of the fifteenth, Gates's army quietly advanced towards Sanders Creek, not many miles from Camden.

Unbeknownst to the American general, Cornwallis already knew of the Americans' earlier arrival at Rugeley's Mill. Hoping to catch them by surprise there, the British general had his army quietly march out of Camden at exactly the hour Gates had chosen to begin his advance. About four-and-a-half hours later the two armies ran into each other, the initial action beginning with a British cavalry charge that failed to break the American front.

By daybreak both sides had reformed their lines; they were now separated by only a few hundred yards. Gates's forces outnumbered Cornwallis's, but almost two-thirds of them were inexperienced militiamen who would be defending much of the long front against mostly tested and proven British regulars. Not only were they tired from having endured the Carolina heat and humidity; they were malnourished as well. The plentiful supplies of rum and rations promised by Gates had not materialized. The men had been forced to subsist on a miserable diet of soup made from lean beef and green corn that was thickened with officers' hair powder, unripe peaches, and—before their nighttime departure on the fifteenth—a good-sized portion of cornmeal mush mixed with molasses that gave them diarrhea.

Both sides opened with heavy artillery fire, adding smoke to the morning haze. Hoping to catch the British before they completed their redeployment, Gates ordered Stevens's militia on the left to attack and another brigade to advance slowly. Soon after Stevens's men began advancing, the Americans realized they were not going to be able to surprise the British; their right wing was already in line. Some forty to fifty volunteers were led forward to a point close to the British and ordered "to take to single trees and thus annoy the enemy as much as possible";[38] they supposedly would provide some cover for the attacking militia and reduce their initial horror.

Cornwallis saw what was happening in front of his right wing and decided to land the first blow. British troops advanced, subjecting the Americans to heavy fire. As they drew nearer and nearer, they maintained good order. Suddenly the Virginia militia panicked and "generally threw down their loaded arms and fled." Their "unworthy example ... was almost instantly followed by the North

Carolinians; only a small part of the brigade commanded by Brigadier General [Isaac] Gregory, made a short pause."³⁹

Joining them was Gates, who fled sixty miles to Charlotte on a famous Virginia racehorse, the offspring of a stud with the ironic name of Fearnaught. There he changed horses and continued another one-hundred-twenty miles to Hillsboro. "Was there ever an instance of a General running away as Gates has done from his whole army?" Alexander Hamilton derisively asked. The distance he had covered was quite remarkable for a man of his age.⁴⁰

Congress asked Washington to replace Gates until a court of inquiry into his actions could be held, and on December 3 the disgraced general turned over his command to Nathanael Greene. He then retired from the army and went home.

But for several reasons his retirement would not last long: Robert Morris corresponded with him and urged him to end his retirement; he experienced financial difficulties; and during the summer of 1782 Congress decided not to hold a court of inquiry and returned him to the army, making him the immediate commander of the New Windsor Cantonment. Gates arrived there in October.

WHY DID GATES become part of a plot that promised to increase Congress's authority? He had believed that power should reside with the states and had never opposed the idea that the military must be subordinate to civilian officials. He had seen the delegates at Philadelphia eventually back Washington during the Conway Cabal and relieve him of his own command after Camden. He probably was not friendly towards Hamilton; the New York delegate's father-in-law was Schuyler, whom the general had angered when he assumed command of the army at Fort Ticonderoga earlier in the war. Hamilton had, in fact, back in September 1780, called Gates "his enemy personally, for unjust and unprovoked attacks upon my character." And Gates and Robert Morris had not always been friendly towards each other, although their relationship might have completely mended after the Financier loaned him large sums of money.

However, by the time the general returned to the Hudson Highlands he must have been eager to restore his damaged reputation. Looking after the troops' daily needs, supervising the construction of the Temple of Virtue, and serving on courts-martial would not do that. Leading the officers and other creditors in an effort to get their grievances redressed might.

That was one reason for him to participate in the plot. A second reason was that by this time his support for a small central government had diminished somewhat. Others were his record of regularly staying in touch with the restless officers in the Hudson Highlands, his contacts with Philadelphia creditors like Robert Morris, his ambition, and his lack of devotion to and admiration for George Washington; he would not be likely to voice strong objections to any plan placing himself at the head of the army.

Nationalists like Hamilton, Robert Morris, and his peglegged assistant probably were wary of employing Gates in their scheme. But they had to have a top general on their side, and as the second in command he was in a high enough position to have some influence. Perhaps they could guide or manipulate him, even if they did not entirely trust him.[41]

Chapter Seventeen

"Faith Has Its Limits"

WHAT, MY DEAR sir, could induce the State of Virginia to rescind its assent to the Impost Law?" Washington asked Governor Harrison in a letter written on March 4, 1783. How were the many creditors and the army to be paid if the government had no way of obtaining general tax revenue? Rhode Island certainly would not help since it also had rejected the impost and was making great noise about "the danger of entrusting Congress with the Money," noise that the Commander-in-chief thought was "too selfish and feutile to require a serious answer." But Philadelphia had to be given the authority to obtain general tax revenue. If it did not get that, "the Blood ... spilt, the expence ... incurred, and the distresses ... felt" by the country were going to be for naught; the fragile bonds between the states were going to soon break and America would be plunged into "anarchy and confusion."[1]

AS IF WASHINGTON did not already have enough to worry about, that day's issue of the *Pennsylvania Packet* included Robert Morris's letter of resignation. It was actually old news; the *Independent Gazetteer* had published the letter earlier, on the first.

Although Morris had indicated in his letter of resignation that he intended to stay on until the end of May, the reaction to the news was hardly going to be favorable. Washington wanted Morris to continue in his post regardless of the difficulties he faced. Madison, though supportive of Morris's goals, regretted the Financier's announcement. Congress had consented only to allow Morris to notify his creditors that he would be resigning; it had not known that he planned to publicly announce his decision in the newspapers.[2]

The following day Arthur Lee wrote Samuel Adams. The Financier's resignation and the way he had made it known were "a great shock to public credit." His action was "a manouvre to force the system of funding upon the States." Morris and likeminded nationalists wanted funding so badly because it would allow them to become rich from their speculation in loan office certificates, which they had bought at "infinitely low" prices resulting from currency depreciation. They were even willing "to hazard the distruction of this Country" to get it.[3]

Another critic—or possibly Lee using a pseudonym, "Lucius"—attacked Morris in the *Freeman's Journal*. He did not believe the Financier when he claimed Congress had no hope of funding the public debt. But if Morris was being truthful, he was especially wrong to have made his claim public. The American government would not be trusted here and in Europe if that were true. And who would be willing to become the new superintendent if the job required him to "be the *minister of injustice*?" By leaving the country "without character, without credit, without justice, without resource," Morris had so prostrated the country that a worse situation might not be imaginable.

"Lucius" felt Morris's wisdom and virtue had to be questioned. Should the Financier "substitute the danger of civil commotions for that from the common enemy?" How sad for America; she was certain to face yet more "trials" because of Morris's action.

Had the Financier done what he had been asked to do in his post? Were the government's finances in better order? Had he found new sources of revenue so it could continue to prosecute the war? No, he had not. He had made the situation worse.[4]

No matter what the state of the government's finances was, something had to be done to satisfy the officers. When Richard Peters answered Gates's letter of February 20, he acknowledged that the general was correct in likening the political situation in Philadelphia to a boiling pot. Though "not yet ... scalded by it," Peters did not seem to be optimistic about his prospects for remaining so. The delegates had spent much time working on getting general funding, but in spite of their "good Disposition" they were experiencing "many Difficulties." Still, he hoped they would survive these perilous times and the many misfortunes they had suffered and eventually be able to render justice to those who deserved it.

One thing he felt optimistic about was commutation. It had not been approved, but the Pennsylvanian expected it to soon be "revived and from an Alteration of Sentiment in some Gentlemen who voted against the Measure ... carried"; they needed just one more state's approval. The proposal being considered called for each officer to receive an amount equal to five years' pay. The state lines would have the right to choose between that and the half-pay pension.[5]

AS PETERS WROTE Gates to reassure him that justice was going to be done to the army, "the old leven" had another concern—the health of his wife, Elizabeth. Earlier in the year a friend had notified him that she was very sick, and she had written to ask him to return to Virginia to comfort her; she was in pain from rheumatism and feared dying. The general, though, got assurances from doctors that his wife's condition was not that serious, so he decided to stay with the army in the Hudson Highlands. But another letter from her made him have a change of heart, and on March 5 he wrote to tell Elizabeth he was going to come home to be by her side. He intended to leave camp once the roads allowed him to travel, but in no case later than ten days hence—March 15.[6] The fifteenth would be an important date for Gates, but not for any reason related to his wife's sickness.

CONGRESS, MEANWHILE, WAS thinking about Robert Morris's resignation. His action had provoked much criticism, but that did not relieve the members of their responsibility to do something to solve the government's financial problems. So they had set up a committee to decide what steps needed to be taken because of his move.[7]

Around this time the five-man committee of Madison, Hamilton, Gorham, Fitzsimmons, and Rutledge submitted a funding plan. It began with a recommendation that the states give Congress the authority to levy the agreed-upon five percent impost on foreign imports and captured ships and cargo. Congress would limit the impost to twenty-five years and the states were to be responsible for appointing the tax collectors, although they would be accountable to Congress and could be removed only by that body. If any states did not make their appointments in a timely manner, Congress was allowed to do so.

The states were also called on to provide the government with annual supplements of $2,000,000. And various specific duties on imported salt, wines, rum, brandy, different types of sugar, and some teas were envisioned. The revenue obtained from the duties was to go only towards paying off the government's war-related debts.

The portion of the government's war costs that each state had to bear was to be based on its population instead of on the value of its land. To ensure that the states accepted how war-related expenses were apportioned to them, the plan recommended that they "enable Congress to make ... equitable exceptions and abatements" when they were in need of them. Accordingly, any previously unauthorized but demonstrably "reasonable expences ... incurred by the States" in offensive or defensive actions would become the national government's responsibility.

The plan took into account each state's likely responses to the recommendations and offered some provisions to make them palatable. One example was its call for states owning western lands to complete the cession process. Ceding them to Congress was expected to speed up the reduction of the public debt and, more importantly, help establish harmonious relations between the various states. Small landless ones feared large ones with western lands because some of the big states felt that charters granted long ago by the King of England gave them claim to territory stretching to the Pacific Ocean, which was then believed to be not far beyond the Blue Ridge Mountains. Virginia thought its claim amounted to an almost "boundless empire" and landless Maryland, its neighbor, thought she could bankrupt her. Virginia, Maryland believed, could simply sell some of her western land when she needed income and escape having to tax her inhabitants. Marylanders would then leave their state for Virginia to enjoy freedom from taxes. As Maryland's population decreased, the tax burden on those remaining stood to increase. Eventually Maryland, with no western land and a very small population, would be financially ruined.[8]

AT TEN O'CLOCK on the morning of Friday, March 7, each brigade delivered two lime burners to the Temple of Virtue. They were to be used "in erecting a kiln and burning lime for finishing the building."[9]

Of greater concern in the Hudson Highlands was the plight of the officers, whose wants Deputy Paymaster General Wetmore thought to be "exceedingly pressing." Little had been done to provide the officers with the one month's pay they had been promised in January, and Wetmore had only enough notes for furloughed officers, so he asked Paymaster General Pierce to send more.[10]

ON SATURDAY MARCH 8 Robert Morris suggested to the President of Congress that the states be given an ultimatum: They would either provide Congress with the requisitioned funds for their shares of the national debt by some specified time or comply with any plan adopted by Philadelphia imposing the taxes and tariff duties needed to erase it. The delegates already had the authority to decide how and when the national debt was to be met without the states' approval; it was a power implied by the Articles of Confederation. "The Right of Congress is perfect and the Duty to pay is absolute,"[11] he asserted.

The ultimatum made sense because that same day the Financier received a letter from Nathanael Greene making clear that something had to be done. The general had gone to the very poor and suffering state of Georgia and urged the legislators there to approve the impost and a tax, and he planned to do the same in South Carolina. He was worried. If the officers became convinced that "the States would take no measures to support the Servants of Congress in their engagements," he was not going to be able to keep his army together "a moment longer."[12]

WASHINGTON HAD BY now received Morris's letter explaining his decision to leave his post and was ready to respond. "Very painful Sensations are excited in my Mind by your Letter," he began. He was sorry to hear that Morris had resigned and that he was unable "to do that Justice to the public Creditors, which their Demands require" because of the states' "Negligence." His hope was that Morris's resignation might "sound the Alarm to their inmost Souls, and rouse them to a just Sense of their own Interest, honor, and Credit." But he was not optimistic; it was no easy matter to get rid of "mutual Jealousies, local prejudices, and misapprehensions."

The general had wanted Morris to stay on as superintendent until the end of the war or even longer. Now, though, with Morris determined to leave the post, he wanted him to know that he considered his departure "one of the most unfortunate that could have fallen upon the States." He feared "sad Consequences" from the Financier's resignation. "The Army, I am sure, at the same Time that they entertain the highest Sense of your Exertions, will lament the Step you are obliged to take, as a most unfortunate Circumstance to them,"[13] the general concluded.

ELSEWHERE, NATHANAEL GREENE was writing Governor Benjamin Guerard of South Carolina to provide some information that he felt the legislature had to have to make a sound decision on the impost. After admitting that he wanted Congress to be strengthened, which meant it had to be given permanent funding, and emphasizing that delegates were too likely to put the interests of their respective states ahead of the interests of the nation as a whole, he made his case for the measure.

"The Financier says the affairs of his Department are tottering on the brink of ruin; The Army to the Northward are in the highest State of discontent; and the same may be expected to the Southward," he began. Up to this time the soldiers had virtuously and patriotically borne "almost every species of distress and suffering," accepting arguments that "the distresses of a suffering Country" prevented them from receiving justice at the present time and believing that they would ultimately receive it. But eventually those arguments were not going to be able to influence them.

Now, with peace, the legislature had an opportunity to permanently fund Congress. The army was watching the states and it expected them to do that. What steps they took would "determine the conduct of the army." Promises alone no longer sufficed. "Nothing short of permanent and certain revenue can or will keep them subject to authority," Greene warned. "I think it my duty to be explicit, because I know the sentiments of the army. Men will suffer to a certain degree, beyond which it is dangerous to push them."

If troubles arose in the future, he would do everything he could "to promote the tranquility of Government"; he was unable to picture himself turning his back on his country. But he knew his influence was certain to be of "little weight when opposed to the Demands of an injured soldiery." And what would the hurt soldiers do if South Carolina rejected the impost, which promised to provide Congress with the revenue it needed to meet the army's claims? Well, they might disband themselves and leave the state with too few men to defend itself. Should they do that, and if the war then continues and the British invade the state, it would be ruined.[14]

ON THE WEEKEND of the eighth and ninth Colonel Walter Stewart finally returned from sick leave in Philadelphia to the Hudson Highlands. Earlier in the war he had attended meetings of disenchanted officers. More recently he had met with Blair McClenechan, Benjamin Rush, Charles

Petit, John Ewing, and other prominent members of Philadelphia's public creditors' committee. The meetings' purpose was to line up support for the plotters' scheme, whereby the government's lenders and the unpaid army would unite and pressure state legislatures and their supporters in Congress to give the government the taxation authority it needed. With that enhanced power, the government would be able to pay them what they were owed and provide the officers with postwar pensions. Stewart had large holdings in public securities and considered these men to be close friends and natural allies. Now, having gained their backing, he was ready to turn to a general whom he also considered a close friend—Horatio Gates.

Before seeing Gates, though, Stewart first called on Washington at his Newburgh headquarters in order to find out if there was any chance that Washington would agree to lead the angry officers and creditors in their plot to force Congress to pay them what they were due. There the colonel apparently asked the general some indirect questions and judged that they "should meet with the most decided opposition from the Commander in Chief."

Stewart, whom Gates later described as "a kind of agent from our friends in Congress and the administration," then went to that general's beautiful stone and wood headquarters, John Ellison's house. There Dr. William Eustis, Lieutenant Colonel James Miles Hughes, Major John Armstrong, Jr., Major T. Stewart, a Major Moore, Major Nicholas Fish, and three or four junior officers listened to the handsome colonel report on the situation in Philadelphia. Peace was almost a certainty. Congress, which hadn't shown any inclination to answer the officers' calls for back pay and a pension, intended to disband the army soon. They had to do something to force Congress not to renege on its promises. The time to set their plan in motion was near. Robert Morris was with them; an after-the-event account of the troubles, which may be apocryphal, says that he supposedly had responded to a question about how the army could be fed if the country opposed it by declaring that he would feed it. The public creditors were also with them.

The conspirators agreed to call the officers together. Before the day they were to convene arrived, an address "setting forth the objects of the meeting, and preparing them to act in unison" had to be written. It was decided that its writer should remain anonymous.

The task before the plotting officers was clear: They had to spread the word throughout camp that the creditors and some important members of Congress supported the army and that now was the time for them to act. They must stir things up. The army had to stay intact and fight for what it believed in until it received justice. Civilian creditors would even join them in the field, if necessary; they understood that their grievances were more likely to be redressed if they stood side by side with the army.[15]

On the afternoon of Monday, March 10, Washington got his huge hands on a brief, anonymously written notice that had appeared shortly after the dawn muster.[16] All general and field officers, an officer from each company, and a delegate from the medical staff were being called to meet the next day at eleven o'clock in the morning at the Public Building—the Temple of Virtue—"to consider the late letter from their representatives in Philadelphia [Ogden and McDougall's report that Colonel Brooks took with him from the capital on February 8] and what measures (if any) should be adopted to obtain redress of grievances which they seemed to have solicited in vain."[17]

Washington had not authorized the meeting and that certainly must have troubled him, but by the end of the day he still had not issued orders canceling the gathering; the general was not yet aware that only hours after the appearance of the call for a meeting, an incendiary address to the officers had also surfaced.[18]

The address had been written at Gates's headquarters by Major John Armstrong, an aide and friend of the short general. After the address had been finished, it was copied by Captain Christopher Richmond—another of Gates's aides and a friend. On Monday morning a number of the copies were taken along with the announcement of the meeting to the adjutant general's office by Major William Barber, Stewart's assistant in the inspector's department. There officers of the different lines who assembled early each day for general orders were able to see the address. Sometime later that day copies of it were distributed at the camp, ensuring a wide circulation among all the state lines.[19]

AT TWENTY-FOUR, Armstrong[20] was an arrogant young man who possessed more than a few enemies. But he also was very bright and wrote exceptionally well, though he had abandoned his studies at the College of New Jersey when war broke out between the mother country and the colonies.

The major had close ties to Horatio Gates. Gates had first seen Armstrong in Carlisle, Pennsylvania, in 1760, when John was just a toddler of about the same age as his own son—Robert. The French and Indian War was still going on and Gates and the boy's father, John, Sr., were officers in the British army.

Many years later, in 1777, Gates and young Armstrong became reacquainted in Esopus, New York. Armstrong was looking for a position. Earlier, at the battles of Trenton and Princeton, he had served as a brigade major and aide-de-camp to Brigadier General Hugh Mercer. But when Mercer received a mortal wound at Princeton and what was left of his command joined up with forces under General St. Clair near Morristown, Armstrong was not offered a position. So he left the camp, thinking he might have better success if he reached the northern army. After he left the camp, though, his father, who was a friend of George Washington, arrived there with a letter of introduction to General Gates. When Gates met with Armstrong at Esopus he liked what he saw in and heard from the young man and that, coupled with the letter of introduction, led him to offer Armstrong the rank of major and a position as an aide-de-camp. Armstrong did not hesitate to accept the offer.

Armstrong served with Gates at Saratoga. There he received an order to recall the defiant Benedict Arnold, who had galloped off towards Burgoyne's right flank. He was unable to overtake Arnold before the general had broken through the British line, driven a number of Canadians and Indians from some cabins, captured Breymann's redoubt, and been shot in the thigh. The major was with Gates in early September 1778 in a field near Harrison, New York, for the duel with Colonel James Wilkinson that eventually was cancelled. And Armstrong almost saw action with Gates at the Battle of Camden during the summer of 1780. Armstrong had become a deputy adjutant general with a rank of brevet lieutenant colonel, but soon after arriving in North Carolina, he contracted a very severe fever and Colonel Otho H. Williams was chosen to replace him. Consequently, he saw no action in the battle. When he was well enough to be removed, he was taken to Richmond, Virginia. His recovery there and later at home in Carlisle, Pennsylvania, was very slow.

Later that year, Robert Gates—the general's only child—died at the age of twenty-two. That Armstrong was one of his son's friends certainly helped strengthen his ties with the senior Gates: Long after the Revolution had ended, Armstrong and his wife would name a son Horatio Robert.

What started as an acquaintanceship between Gates and Armstrong had by now become a real friendship. In a letter that Armstrong sent to Gates from Carlisle in early 1781 he wrote, "If I know my own heart, I can well assure you that parting from you in Carolina was among the most painful incidents of my life."[21] Not only his parting from Gates was painful, but also the knowledge that his friend had lost his command and reputation because of the disaster at Camden. In April he and Gates went to Philadelphia to request that Congress examine the general's actions in that recent campaign, but the delegates showed such a lack of interest that Armstrong came to view them as "bankrupt in credit, sense, honesty and spirit."[22]

THE "FELLOW-SOLDIER," Armstrong, began his address to the officers by underscoring how much he had suffered in the past and saying that his future prospects might be as bleak as theirs. He and many of them had been sorry to leave civilian life to fight "the enemies of his country, the slaves of power, and the hirelings of injustice." They had struggled and faced dangers together and he knew what it was like to bear "the cold hand of poverty without a murmur" and observe "the insolence of wealth without a sigh."

Yet "till lately, *very lately*," he had "believed in the justice of his country." What he wished for was that when "the clouds of adversity scattered, and … the sun-shine of peace and better fortune broke in … the coldness and severity of government would relax, and that, more than justice, that *gratitude* would blaze forth upon those hands which had upheld her in the darkest stages of her passage, from impending servitude to acknowledged independence."

However, he warned, "faith has its limits, as well as temper; and there are points beyond which neither can be stretched, without sinking into cowardice, or plunging into credulity." The officers, he felt, were on "the very verge of both." They were only a hairsbreadth from "ruin … for ever." They had to stand up for themselves! Now was not the time for patience: "To be tame and unprovoked when injuries press hard upon you, is more than weakness," he emphasized. "To look up for kinder usage, without one manly effort of your own, would fix your character, and show the world how richly you deserve *those chains* you broke."

Having urged the officers to take action, Armstrong then posed a number of rhetorical questions intended to provoke feelings of resentment. How was the country rewarding them, the men whose courage had made likely an independent America? Was it "willing to redress your wrongs, cherish your worth, and reward your services?" Was it "courting your return to private life, with tears of gratitude, and smiles of admiration?" Was it "longing to divide with you that independency which your gallantry has given, and those riches which your wounds have preserved? … or [wa]s it trampl[ing] upon your rights, distain[ing] your cries, and insult[ing] your distresses?" Armstrong knew how the officers would answer and who was to blame. "Have you not, more than once, suggested your wishes, and made known your wants to Congress? Wants and wishes which gratitude and policy should have anticipated, rather than evaded. And have you not lately, in the meek language of entreating memorial, begged from their justice, what you would no longer expect from their favour? How have you been answered?"

And how would they be treated after disbandment? Now they had their swords and numbers. Later they would have neither. "What have you to expect from peace, when your voice shall sink, and your strength dissipate by division?" Armstrong asked. The officers would be left with only their "wants, infirmities, and scars!" Could they "consent to be the only sufferers by this revolution, and retiring from the field, grow old in poverty, wretchedness, and contempt?" Could they "consent to wade through the vile mire of dependency, and owe the remnant of that life to charity, which has hitherto been spent in honor?"

Yes? Well, then "GO—and carry with you the jest of tories, and the scorn of whigs—the ridicule, and what is worse, the *pity* of the world. Go, starve, and be forgotten!"

If the officers could not consent to that, though, and if they had "spirit enough to oppose tyranny, under whatever garb it may assume; whether it be the plain coat of republicanism, or the splendid robe of royalty," then now was the time to act! "Awake!—attend to your situation, and redress yourselves," Armstrong exclaimed. "If the present moment be lost, every future effort is in vain; and your threats then will be as empty as your entreaties now. … If your determination be in any proportion to your wrongs … [c]hange the milk and water style of your last memorial; assume a bolder tone—decent, but lively—spirited and determined; and suspect the man who would advise to more moderation and longer forbearance."

Congress would be given only one more chance to redress the army's grievances. "Let two or three men, who can feel as well as write, be appointed to draw up your last remonstrance," Armstrong directed, "in language that will neither dishonour you by its rudeness, nor betray you by its fears." The delegates would be reminded of "what has been promised by Congress, and what has been performed; how long and how patiently you have suffered; how little you have asked, and how much of that little has been denied."

And Congress had to know that "despair … may drive you from the field: that the wound often irritated, and never healed, may at length become incurable; and that the slightest mark of indignity from Congress now, must operate like the grave …: that in any political event, the army has its alternative." Should the war between England and America be brought to a peaceful end, the army could still refuse to disarm. And should the war continue, "courting the auspices, and inviting the direction of your illustrious leader, you will retire to some unsettled country, smile … and 'mock when their [the delegates'] fear cometh on'" with the approach of British troops.

Not wishing to close the address with the threat, Armstrong finished by telling the officers that their last petition should point out how happy they would be made by a positive response from Congress and how the delegates would be made "more respectable." Proper action by Congress was also certain to ensure the officers' continued performance of duty during the war and their return to "the shade of private life" after its end. That would "give the world another subject of wonder and applause—*an army victorious over its enemies—victorious over itself.*"[23]

The address was about twelve hundred words long. Armstrong had written it at "the solicitations of his friends, in a few hours." His goal was to "touch with some ability the several chords of sympathy and feeling that belonged to the case." If he accomplished that, the address would "secure to the deliberations [of the officers' meeting] and their result, that tone and energy, without which, they would be a dead letter."[24] In other words, it was necessary to arouse the officers before they met and planned further action.

Judging by what Armstrong's contemporaries later wrote, the address certainly was effective. One colonel said it was embraced "with admiration" and "rapture" by the officers,[25] but another wrote that it "Caused much Uneasiness especially at Head Quarters."[26] General Heath described it as being "couched in very firm and decided language."[27] Washington maintained that it, "in point of composition, in elegance and force of expression, has rarely been equalled in the English language."[28] Colonel Pickering felt it was no less deserving of praise than the letters of "Junius,"[29] who from 1769 to 1772 had used a London newspaper to assail the King and his ministers for their refusal to allow the American colonies' friend John Wilkes to take his seat in Parliament. William Peartree Smith of New Jersey wrote, "The writing … was well done, shrewd, sensible, & artful," but also "perfectly calculated to blow all up into a universal flame."[30]

The writing also seemed calculated to "sap the influence of the commander in chief."[31] That was what the historian Reverend William Gordon thought. Armstrong was certainly alluding to Washington when he urged his fellow officers to "suspect the man who would advise to more moderation and longer forbearance." And he implied that they no longer *had to* follow Washington's orders; they only had to seek his support and "*invite*" him to lead them if they turned their backs on the war and went on to "retire to some unsettled country."

ARMSTRONG CERTAINLY DID not intend for Washington to see the address. If Washington learned that an officer was urging the army to threaten not to disarm or to turn its back on its country and let the British march on Congress, he would perceive that action as treasonous or something bordering on treason. He would realize that a meeting of officers inflamed by the major's words might lead to actions imperiling the young American republic. He would take all the steps necessary to put an end to their nefarious plan.

Chapter Eighteen

"The Most Anxious Moment of His Life"

IN PHILADELPHIA ON the tenth of March, Congress was to vote again on commutation, the substitution of some form of postwar compensation for the officers that the general public would find more tolerable than a half-pay pension for life. McDougall appeared somewhat optimistic; with the recent arrival of Delaware's delegates, the general counted on eight states to support the army. And now Eliphalet Dyer's opposition to the measure looked less certain; he would yield if his negative vote was the only thing preventing passage, he had promised. He had kept Connecticut from voting for it, so his capitulation would move that state to the supporters' side and give the army the nine states needed for its approval.

When the votes were cast, though, only eight states came out it in favor of commutation; Dyer had not budged and Connecticut's delegation was split on the issue. Three other states—New Hampshire, Rhode Island, and New Jersey—had voted against the measure. McDougall would make one final attempt to get Dyer to switch sides, but if he failed again the general vowed he would leave Philadelphia and rejoin the army in the Hudson Highlands.[1]

ON TUESDAY MORNING, March 11, 1783, George Washington was given a copy of Armstrong's address.[2] He realized that the situation was turning into a real powder keg. One author says that Washington felt on this occasion the way he had after learning of Benedict Arnold's betrayal in September 1780 and that his aides, after giving him the address and other papers, eased away from him because they could sense the intensity of his anger from the way his hands shook and his face wrinkled from apprehension.[3] Whether Washington really reacted that way is uncertain, but he was worried. "This was the most anxious moment of his life,"[4] one eyewitness to the events claimed.

Washington's reaction indicates that he was shocked at the appearance of the anonymous address, though he had warned Secretary of War Lincoln the previous October that both the soldiers and the officers were upset. And others probably were shocked. Lincoln felt that the main army was "quiet"[5] at this time. Samuel Shaw thought likewise, later writing that "the certainty that we were on the eve of a general peace, kept the army quiet,"[6] that it was "in this state of patient expectation"[7] until March 10, the day Armstrong's address appeared in camp. The rejection of commutation by Congress was a cause for dissatisfaction, but not enough to outweigh the belief that an end to the war was imminent—or the other news conveyed to the various state lines by General Knox from McDougall and Ogden's report: that Congress had resolved to give the men one month's pay and the remainder of what they were owed as soon as possible.

Neither Washington nor any of the officers at his headquarters suspected that Armstrong was the author of the address. They believed that Gouverneur Morris had written it. Stewart had then brought it with him from Philadelphia to the Hudson Highlands, Washington thought.[8]

In any case, who wrote the address did not matter at this time. What did was the unauthorized meeting scheduled for this day. The general knew that the officers could not be allowed to attend it. So he reportedly "rode up to Col. Brooks … to ascertain how the officers stood affected" and, "finding him … to be sound … requested him to keep his officers within quarters, to prevent them from attending the insurgent meeting."

Brooks replied, "I have anticipated your wishes, and my orders are given."

Washington was probably pleased, but it is highly unlikely that he, "with tears in his eyes, took him by the hand and said, COLONEL BROOKS, THIS IS JUST WHAT I EXPECTED FROM YOU," as one of the Massachusetts officer's descendants claims in a memoir of him.[9]

The general also quickly issued orders, noting the call for the officers to meet at the Temple of Virtue "by some unknown person" and expressing his dissatisfaction. He was "fully persuaded that the good sense of the officers would induce them to pay very little attention to such an irregular invitation" but felt "his duty as well as the reputation and true interest of the Army" made it obligatory for him to disapprove "such disorderly proceedings."

In place of the unauthorized meeting, Washington proposed one for the fifteenth at noon at the Temple of Virtue. "The General and Field officers with one officer from each company and a proper representation from the Staff of the Army" were asked to attend. They would listen to an officer read the report sent by McDougall and Ogden from Philadelphia and "after mature deliberation … advise what further measures ought to be adopted as most rational and best calculated to attain the just and important object in view." The highest-ranking officer at the meeting was to "preside and report the result of the deliberations to the Commander in Chief."[10]

Although his orders made it appear that he was not going to be able to attend, Washington actually planned on showing up at the Temple and catching the officers unawares. He had learned from his experiences in the French and Indian War the usefulness of deception and secrecy[11] and especially liked employing the element of surprise.[12]

Surprise was fine, but the Commander-in-chief also knew he needed the support of some key allies if he wanted to snuff out the conspiracy. He summoned Henry Knox by letter from West Point to Newburgh that morning, but the general was unable to come see him; the Hudson was too full of ice for boat use. If the Hudson was less icy the following day, he wrote Washington, he would come see him. He knew what Washington wanted to speak with him about because copies of the unauthorized call for a meeting of the officers and the anonymously written address had been dispatched to him, and he realized that what was going on was highly irregular. However, he expected no officer from West Point to answer the call by attending the meeting.[13]

BEING IN PHILADELPHIA, James Madison knew nothing of the appearance of the address that Armstrong had penned. He was writing Edmund Randolph. Peace, Robert Morris's resignation, and the funding plan that the five-man committee had recently submitted were on his mind.

Madison understood why negotiations were taking a long time, but he was astonished that none of the parties involved were passing on progress reports. It had been more than three months since they had learned of the speech given by King George III to Parliament, and the last time they had received any official news was almost five months ago. They were now in a state of "suspence" waiting for information.

When the Virginia delegate moved on to the subject of Morris's resignation, he chose to write mostly in cipher. "The peremptory style and publication of Mr. M's letters ha[d] *given offense to many*" who were not members of Congress and "*to some within Congress.*" And "*enemys of both* descriptions [we]re *industrious in displayin*[g] *their impropriety.*" Madison could only "wish *they had les*[s] *handle for* the *purpose.*"

He then switched out of cipher and summarized the funding plan the five-man committee had presented. "The fate of this plan in Congs. is uncertain, & still more so among the States," he opined. "If the substance of it is rejected, and nothing better introduced in its place," he declared, "I shall consider it as a melancholy proof that narrow & local views prevail over that liberal policy & those mutual concessions which our future tranquility and present reputation call for."[14]

Later in the day Congress debated the funding plan and some remarks that Robert Morris had made concerning it. Among other things, the Financier wanted the list of imported goods subject to duties expanded to include pepper, molasses, cocoa, and coffee. As a result, the delegates voted to send the first three paragraphs of the plan and Morris's letter back to the committee for further revision.[15]

Not to be revised were the twenty-five-year limit on the impost and clauses defining who would appoint and remove the tax collectors. When Hamilton and Wilson made motions to replace those clauses with ones to allow the impost to remain in effect as long as the debt existed and to give Congress the power to nominate the collectors, the votes were not there for passage. In regard to their motion concerning tax collectors, the states essentially had to accept or reject the men nominated by a certain date or else they would be considered appointed.[16]

"HIS WISDOM AND judgment are considered adequate to the most trying experiences. He rises in the midst of distress," Dr. James Thacher had said of Washington at Valley Forge.[17]

Immediately after receiving a copy of Armstrong's angry address to the officers, and over the next few days, Washington proved the doctor right, moving on a number of fronts to end the conspiracy. The general knew that the plotters' ideas posed a great danger to America, and he had to do something to stop them before the situation got out of control. He did not want to see the angry army in the heat of the moment involve itself in a political plot that might cause the new American republic to fall and the country to end in ruin. He had to stop them, but to do so was not a simple matter. He needed to get and share up-to-date information from those whom he could count on to support him. He had to regularly take the pulse of the army units at the cantonment to determine their moods. And he thought it imperative to convince the officers that the suggestions made in the address were ill-considered; if they decided on extreme measures, they might damage the army's reputation, prevent America from achieving a lasting peace throughout the country, and destroy its hopes of becoming a prosperous nation.

So he wrote letters to and had private meetings with key delegates and high-ranking officers whom he trusted, hoping they would understand that they needed to nip the disgruntled officers' plot in the bud. Colonel Philip Van Cortlandt, commander of the New York Line, was present at one of the meetings with the brigade commanders and wrote that he was "happy to find a unanimous determination to support order and agreed with Genl. Washington to Suppress Every attempt at disorderly conduct."[18] Colonel Pickering wrote decades later that the general had spoken to him "with much solicitude of their [Armstrong's suggestions'] dangerous tendency, and of the necessity of counteracting it."[19] William Gordon wrote that Washington's words even made several of those he saw teary-eyed.[20]

The words of support from brigade commanders did not tell the whole story, though. What Washington saw at the New Windsor Cantonment on days when he went there on horseback indicated that some type of underlying tension existed beneath the surface calm.[21] Officers removed their hats in his presence to afford him the respect he was due, but eye contact was not established and smiles did not cross their faces; they gave the impression that they were uncomfortable with his being there.[22]

ON THE MORNING of Wednesday, March 12, Robert Morris's packet ship *General Washington* arrived at Philadelphia from France with news of a provisional peace treaty recognizing American independence and 600,000 livres. The provisions of the treaty, which had been signed on November 30, 1782, did not give Washington great assurance that "a general pacification" was imminent, however, so he advised that the army remain "in a hostile position."[23]

Morris at this time was being excoriated for his resignation. "This day ... appeared a virulent Attack on my Publick and private Character signed Lucius in the Freemans Journal, replete with the most infamous Falsehoods," the Financier noted in his diary. They were "Assertions without the least Shadow of truth to support them, and insinuations as base and infamous as Envy and Malignancy could suggest." Morris believed he knew the identity of the writer and if correct, that man was "of that baneful Character which brings dishonor to those whom he means to befriend and the reverse to whom he opposes."[24]

This baneful character had indeed launched a virulent attack. Morris was like Macbeth. He had "murdered public credit as she slept." He had shown himself *capable of betraying the high secrets of his office.* From now on nobody would "trust a single shilling to the United States of America." Seeing that America had lost her credit, the British might take advantage of the situation.

Additionally, Morris was not being truthful when he faulted the states for forcing him to resign. The states were contributing more funds "as their abilities increased." They could not meet the quotas established for them only because of "the pressure of the war, and the almost total abolition of commerce."

Why was Morris so interested in having the debt funded? To "Lucius" the answer was obvious: Morris wanted funding because he was speculating in loan office certificates. He had bought low when depreciation raged, and when the government got funding and its financial situation improved he would sell high.[25]

THAT SAME DAY Washington wrote Knox again. He did not anticipate much improvement in the Hudson's condition on this day but if the river was sufficiently free of ice on Thursday, he wanted Knox to come to his quarters to see him and have dinner. He also wanted to see General Huntington; he was a friend, a signatory to the officers' petition, and Connecticut's highest-ranking officer. The invitation was considered private and the Commander-in-chief wanted both of the generals to arrive early.

Washington told Knox that his general orders of the eleventh would show him how matters stood with the meeting of the officers. There was no need for details concerning his action now, for he would explain when he saw Knox and Huntington on Thursday.[26]

With the gravity of the situation in the Hudson Highlands becoming more apparent, Washington also wrote a long letter to Joseph Jones. "The temper of the Army, tho. very irritable on acct. of their long-protracted sufferings has been apparently extremely quiet while their business was [pending] before Congress until four days past," he informed the Virginia delegate. He had heard about the formation of "dangerous combinations … in the Army" and was surprised that that was happening "when there was not a syllable of the kind in agitation in Camp." The troubles appeared to have begun with "the arrival of a certain Gentleman from Phila. [Colonel Walter Stewart] in Camp," after which certain "sentiments … were immediately and industriously circulated." The first was that "it was universally expected the Army would not disband until they had obtained Justice." The second was that "the public creditors looked up to them for redress of their [own] Grievances, would afford them every aid, and even join them in the Field, if necessary." The last was that "some Members of Congress wished the Measure might take effect, in order to compel the Public, particularly the delinquent States, to do justice."

Where then did the idea of threatening Congress with a restless army come from? Washington indicated that most thought "the Scheme was not only planned, but also digested and matured in Philadelphia." Another common belief was that agitators were active at the cantonment and in Philadelphia. And once "the Minds of the Army were thought to be prepared for the transaction, anonymous invitations were circulated, requesting a general Meeting of the Officers next day." Meanwhile, "many Copies of the Address to the Officers of the Army was scattered in every State line."

Washington told Jones that once he had learned about these events, he "issued the order of the 11th … in order to rescue the foot, that stood wavering on the precipice of despair, from taking those steps which would have lead to the abyss of misery while the passions were inflamed, and the mind trimblingly alive with the recollections of past sufferings, and … present feelings." He was guided by "the principle that it is easier to divert from a wrong to a right path, than it is to recall the hasty and fatal steps which have already been taken."

Washington's rescheduling of the meeting would give the officers the time they needed "to view the matter more calmly and seriously." They then might "adopt more rational measures, and wait a while for the settlemts. of their Accts." The general recognized that back pay was what they wanted and that its postponement caused them "more uneasiness … than any other thing." Although they knew Congress was broke, they were still asking why it could not just "one and all, liquidate the Accts. and certifie our dues?" Were they "to be disbanded and sent home without this?" And then were they supposed to go to Philadelphia or their home states to get what they were due? When they made their applications, were they going to be sent to one board after another and be put off, only to "loose the substance in pursuit of the shadow?" The officers were uneasy when they thought about those questions, and many "insidious characters" were saying that the public had no plans to give them what they were due. It would put off the settlement of their accounts, using "one pretext or another till Peace … and a seperation of the Army takes place when … a generl settlement never can be effected and that individual loss, in this instance, becomes a public gain."

Congress had to act. "However derogatory these ideas … with the dignity, honor, and justice of government," Washington understood why they existed. The issue of pay was important to his men and action could easily be taken, but Congress kept putting off settling their accounts for no evident reason. So "in a mind soured and irritated" such ideas could be expected to dwell. "Let me entreat you therefore," the general requested in closing, "to push this matter to an issue, and if there are Delegates among you, who are really opposed to doing justice to the Army, scruple not to tell them, if matters should come to extremity, that they must be answerable for all the ineffable horrors which may be occasioned thereby."[27]

Another delegate whom Washington had to inform was Hamilton. In an unofficial letter to him the general related what Jones had written at the end of February and, for the most part, essentially repeated what he had written in his reply to the Virginia delegate, alluding to Stewart and reporting that a threatening "storm" had all of sudden gathered on the horizon in the Hudson Highlands. It had been "diverted for a moment," but had "not yet blown over."

What was going on struck him as being "very mysterious." The plot had been "managed with great art"; the call for a meeting of the officers and the address had been circulated at just the right time, immediately after the officers' minds had been prepared to receive them. He had issued orders "to rescue them from plunging themselves into a gulph of Civil horror from which there might be no receding," but he still had to worry about the "designing men" who were saying to the officers that the public had no plans to give them what they were due.

Washington found the officers' situation to be "distressing beyond description." Many of them would end up in a debtors' prison "if they [we]re turned loose without liquidation of accts. and an assurance of that justice to which they [we]re so worthily entitled." Therefore, Hamilton had to persuade the delegates from the states that were making life hard for them to treat them justly. "If any disastrous consequences should follow, by reason of their delinquency … they must be answerable to God & their Country for the ineffable horrors which may be occasioned thereby," the general warned, essentially repeating what he had written in the conclusion of his letter to Joseph Jones.

In a postscript Washington then mentioned that he had just learned about the appearance of a second anonymously written address to his officers. "The Contents, evidently prove that the Author is in, or near Camp," he added. The address, he now realized, was "the illegitimate offspring of a person in the army."[28]

That person was Armstrong. Again using the third person, he claimed to have been "aware of the coyness with which his last letter would be received" and was "neither disappointed nor displeased with the caution it … met." The first address "spoke a language, which till now, had been heard only in whispers" from the grousing men and officers in the army. It "contained some sentiments which confidence itself would have breathed with distrust."

Readers of the address might be suspicious of him, but that was not a bad thing. Suspicion, though "detestable … in private life," was in his mind "the loveliest trait of political characters." Suspicion "prompts you to enquiry, bars the door against design, and opens every avenue to truth," he explained. "It was the first to oppose a tyrant here, and still stands centinel over the liberties of America." He was not about to "stifle the voice of this honest guardian," one "who … has herself given birth to the address you have read, and now goes forth among you with a request to all that it may be treated fairly; that it may be considered before it is abused, and condemned, before it be tortured."

Armstrong then moved on to misrepresent Washington's recent action, making it appear that the Commander-in-chief supported their plan. "The General Orders of yesterday which the weak may mistake for disapprobation, and the designing dare to represent as such," he declared in his letter, "wears in my opinion a very different complexion, and carries with it a very opposite tendency." Washington's "ostensible silence" signified that he approved of the officers' meeting and, Armstrong assured them, the general's "private opinion has sanctified your claims." If that were not the case, "would not the same sense of duty, which forbade you from meeting on the third day of the week, have forbidden you from meeting on the seventh?" he asked. By allowing the officers to hold a meeting for the same purpose but on a different date, wasn't Washington affixing a "seal of office" to it? Wasn't his decision meant to be received with "all the solemnity of an order?"

The Commander-in-chief's stamp of approval on the meeting "will give system to your proceedings, and stability to your resolves," Armstrong told the officers. "It will ripen speculation into fact; and, while it adds to the unanimity, it cannot possibly lessen the independency of your sentiments."[29]

Before the day closed, Washington sent a report to the President of Congress, Elias Boudinot. Enclosed were copies of the call for a meeting of the officers, both of Armstrong's addresses, and the Commander-in-chief's general orders of March 11, all numbered.[30]

The general felt an "inexpressible concern" as he wrote the report. The anonymous writer's call for a meeting of the officers and the first address had been "handed about in a clandestine manner" and immediately after learning of them, Washington had issued the enclosed orders "to prevent any precipitate and dangerous resolutions from being taken at this perilous moment, while the passions were all inflamed." Congress, he hoped, would approve of the steps he had "taken to dissipate a storm, which had gathered so suddenly and unexpectedly." The delegates should know that he was "in every vicissitude of circumstances, still actuated with the greatest Zeal in their Service." He was going to continue to do everything in his power for the good of America while putting his faith in the delegates to provide "ample justice to the Army" once they were able to do that.[31]

One historian has written that Washington felt it necessary to reassure Congress that he was "in their Service," that he was loyal to the government, because disturbing rumors about him were circulating around the capital and elsewhere. He reportedly was going to carry the banner for his angry army and be at its head when it moved on Congress. He would be made a dictator of this country.[32]

The reasons why such rumors existed were obvious: Washington was physically present with his angry army in the Hudson Highlands; his correspondence to Philadelphia proved that he wanted to see the army receive justice from Congress; as Commander-in-chief he was in a position that allowed him to lead his army in a march on Philadelphia and make himself a dictator; and in America distrust of officers and standing armies was strong enough to make such rumors inevitable regardless of Washington's sense of virtue.

Just as Washington felt a need to let some key members of Congress know what was happening, so too did Knox feel a need to let McDougall know what he was seeing. When he last wrote from West Point "the officers were … quiet." Now, though, the lack of progress in Philadelphia was making them uneasy and unhappy. They had been called to a meeting that was later postponed until Saturday by Washington and had seen Armstrong's anonymously written addresses, and they appeared to have reached a breaking point. They wanted "to do something to obtain that Justice," the general reported, "which they have hitherto from a variety of causes been denied." Knox did not know what the result would be, but he hoped the army would not be driven to do anything that might be diametrically opposed to what they had been fighting for all these eight years. "The men who by their illiberality and injustice drive the Army to the very brink of destruction, ought to be punished with severity," he declared.

But how could the army get its grievances redressed? "The measures we can take to remedy our evils are not known to me," the Massachusetts general despaired. "I know not how by any violence we can obtain a settlement of accounts, and have the half-pay placed upon proper principles, except by the applications we have made." All he could do was urge McDougall to continue his efforts "to convince the obdurate of the awful evils which may arise, from postponing a decision on the subjects of our address."[33]

Knox also wrote Secretary of War Lincoln to update him on the situation in the Hudson Highlands. The officers' call for a meeting, Washington's postponement of it, the incendiary address, and the impatience of the officers were again mentioned. The latter was now "almost heightened into despair." Consequently, "Congress ought not to lose a moment in bringing the affairs of the army to a decision," and the secretary had to "push the matter instantly," giving it everything he had.[34]

IN PHILADELPHIA, MEANWHILE, a New York delegate named William Floyd informed his governor that Congress had been trying "to restore public credit, and to fall on some plan for doing justice to, and satisfying ... our Army." However, for now the best that could be done was to obtain funds sufficient only to pay the interest on the debt.

The delegates were considering whether to accept the alternative to the half-pay pension that the officers had proposed—commutation to full pay for a fixed number of years. Although he had to report that the measure had "lost by the vote of one single person [Eliphalet Dyer of Connecticut]," Floyd remained confident of eventual success. "I believe that it is a matter of so much consequence to the Army, that the person (after consideration) will bring on the matter again and give his assent to it; in that case it will be carried by nine States," he predicted. "And if the Army agree to accept it, it will be funded and the interest yearly paid if the States will make the provision for that purpose."[35]

ON THE THURSDAY before the meeting at the New Building—the Temple of Virtue—Washington included with his general orders news of recent resolutions by Congress concerning the army's present pay, its arrears, and funding.[36] They might reassure the officers that the delegates would finally give them what they were due, though they did not give any specific date for redress.

THE FOLLOWING DAY Robert Morris wrote Nathanael Greene about his resignation. He expected the general to learn about it from the newspapers before his letter arrived, but he could at least explain why he had decided to take such a "painful" step.

While everybody agreed that the debt had to be funded, "no efficient Measures would be adopted for the Purpose." So Morris, feeling he had to remain honest to his principles, resigned. He acknowledged the negative consequences of his action, but did not believe he should be held accountable for them. The adverse affect on public credit, "the probable Derangement of our Affairs," and the difficult situation that the man succeeding him was certain to face were "to be attributed to the Opposers of just Measures." Morris anticipated being subject to "much ... Obloquy" for his action because that was "the Reward for any Conduct whatever which is right." But neither "slander" nor denigration of his services concerned him. His concern was for the officers, including Greene.

The delegates were considering "a due provision for the public Debts," but Morris did not know when they would finish their work and what it would ultimately look like. "If it is such as in my Opinion will do Justice," the Financier declared, "I shall stay somewhat longer in Office to know the Decisions of the States[.] [A]nd if their Proceedings are what ... they ought to be[,] I shall spare no Labor and regret no Time in compleating this Business so that my Successor may receive it from my Hands as clear and simple as it was confused and embarrassed when it was undertaken. But if these things do not happen[,] you and every other Good Man will I hope acquit me for leaving a

Post in which I am totally unsupported and where I must be daily the Witness to Scenes of poignant Anguish and deep Injustice without the Possibility of Administering either Releif or Paliation."[37]

GEORGE WASHINGTON WAS not a naturally gifted orator. Though he served a long time in both the military and government, he did not deliver many memorable speeches, and when he did speak in public he tended to use a minimum of words to make his points. "In public, when called on for a sudden opinion," Thomas Jefferson recalled many years after the general had passed on, "he was unready, short and embarrassed." That is why he always felt more comfortable speaking with a text in front of him.[38] Therefore, on Saturday, March 15, 1783, he would bring prepared statements with him to the Temple of Virtue for his address to the officers.

The speech that Washington prepared shows that he feared for both his army and the new government. He almost certainly chose his more than sixteen hundred words with care as he sat in his headquarters and slowly composed the speech. Whether Jonathan Trumbull, Jr. helped him write it, as historian Douglas Southall Freeman believes,[39] is not known. One particularly cautionary part of it, a section urging the officers to be patient with Congress because such large bodies always need time to make decisions, is essentially a reworded version of something Joseph Jones wrote in his February 27 letter to Washington. By the time it was finished, the speech was several pages long, each written on a large sheet of paper.[40] It was then given to aides to be copied. They knew that their Commander-in-chief's eyesight had been worsening, so they made sure to copy his words large enough so he would not struggle to read them. And Washington also had his new reading spectacles, which had been sent to him in February by David Rittenhouse. He had already tested them in private.[41]

Washington knew he had to cool down the angry officers. "In all Causes of Passion admit Reason to Govern"[42] was part of one of the "Rules of Civility & Decent Behaviour In Company and Conversation" that the teenage Washington had copied into the back of a notebook from Francis Hawkins's *Youth Behaviour*, a book based primarily on a sixteenth-century manual that French Jesuits had prepared for the training of young noblemen. On the day of his speech it would be the most important of Washington's one-hundred-ten rules. He knew it well and almost lived by it, a result partly of having been brought up in a society that placed a great deal of importance on restraint. To dampen the disgruntled officers' ardor he would reason with them at key points in his speech, appealing to their sense of "honor," a word that was then synonymous with "reputation" and something that was always very important to Washington.

One of those disgruntled officers was Colonel Pickering. He had planned to take a ten-day trip to inspect some stores of supplies in Albany, Schenectady, Saratoga, and perhaps, Burlington, Vermont, beginning on the twelfth or thirteenth.[43] But because of the officers' meeting at the Temple of Virtue the trip was put off. Although he was unaware that Washington planned to give a speech there, he clearly understood the importance of the meeting. The officers would "consider ... a representation they shall make to Congress for the purpose of obtaining such decisions as will secure the settlement of their accounts and the ultimate payment of their debts," he informed his wife. "If the business is conducted with prudence it may have the best effects in promoting the success of those salutary measures proposed & proposing by Congress for the purpose of establishing such permanent revenues as will insure the payment of the army and other public creditors: In this view the meeting has my hearty concurrence," the colonel continued. "But should Rashness govern the proceedings, the consequences may be such as are dreadful even in idea. God forbid the event should be so calamitous!"[44] he exclaimed.

Pickering's fear was understandable. That Washington had chosen to move the officers' meeting from March 11 to March 15 should have seemed portentous to anyone who knew Roman history; on March 15 in the year 44 B.C. Julius Caesar was assassinated by Brutus. The Roman Republic, which was more than four-and-a-half centuries old at the time, would die within two decades of Caesar's assassination.

Part III

The Hero and Advocate

"George Washington, Esq.
Americanischer Generalissimus"
(The most exalted American general)
1777-1778

Chapter Nineteen

"Almost Blind in the Service of My Country"

ON SATURDAY, MARCH 15, 1783, the Ides of March, McDougall wrote Knox to inform him of the disappointing vote on commutation that had taken place on the tenth. He was especially upset with Dyer, who claimed to want the measure to be unanimously accepted by all the officers in the army so the states would then have to support it. But the Scotsman saw no way of getting all the officers together to vote, and even if someone knew a way of doing so, only one vote against commutation was needed to defeat it. He suspected that Dyer was being disingenuous, that he really did not want commutation at all. Some believed Dyer could be persuaded to support commutation, and McDougall, though pessimistic about his chances for success, promised to try again to get Dyer to change his vote. He planned to let him know "in plain terms, in what light the Army, and all honest Men must consider his conduct, if he persists in it." And if nothing came of his efforts, he would leave the capital in late March and return to the Hudson Highlands.[1]

THE SNOW LINGERING on the mountains in the Hudson Highlands this chilly day[2] made everybody aware that winter still had not really come to an end, but the immediate concern for Washington was not the cold weather; it was the fervor of his officers. Rufus Putnam, who had been promoted to brigadier general in January, was answering the anonymous addresses to them. Yes, the army's "sufferings, patience, and perseverance" are unparalleled and "*their virtues*" are beyond description, he began. And yes, they "deserve *every thing their Country* can give. *Nay, with reverence, everything* Heaven can bestow." So what they had to do at their meeting was determine how to get that or decide on "the best mode to be pursued in order to *obtain justice.*"

If the officers coerce Congress into meeting their demands by threatening not to disarm in the event of peace or refusing to fight if the war continues, then once the army lays down its guns, "not only the States, but even Congress may then declare, not only our half Pay, and the Debts they owe us, forfeited, but our lives also, for having levied War against the Community."

To prevent that from happening the army would have to keep its arms until it actually received all the money it was owed. That meant a long wait, Putnam implied, and the soldiers were not likely to remain by their officers' sides.

And what if Congress still refuses to give in to the officers' demands even after being told that the army was not going to lay down its arms? The officers cannot simply admit failure and surrender their weapons. If they do so, they "must be subjected to *disgrace* and *mortification* ... must then *submit* to be disbanded with a *lost reputation*, and *forfeited honor*." But if they do not do so, and if they persuade their soldiers or others to stand with them, then they will "involve our Country in the *horrors* of a Civil War."

No, the anonymous author should know that civil war is not an option. If Congress discharges the soldiers who signed up for three years and announces that they have to end their allegiance with the officers immediately or face being charged as traitors, will they leave? Putnam asked. Are the officers sure the duration men will not hesitate to leave them "an hour after Peace takes place, and Congress declares them discharged?" And suppose they persuade the soldiers to wage war with them. "How long will they serve *without pay*?" Are the officers able to pay or support them? No? Well, "how are they to be fed?" The officers certainly cannot get what they need from creditors "to support an Army, designed to *subjugate*, or overturn the present Constitution of America." The only way the officers can provide for their troops is by plunder.

"No, Horrid alternative this!" cried Putnam. It is impossible to believe that officers "under any circumstances *whatever* ... can adopt the measure." Even if "*designing Men*" are able to convince the officers that most of the creditors and the soldiery will follow them, the general continued, their scheme is bound to fail. "For if we have no means of subsisting an Army but by *plunder*, if we are to have no supplies but what are to be obtained by the point of the Bayonet, I leave *you* to determine, *how long* you will persuade this, or any other Army to follow your fortunes. And when the Soldiery forsake you, what will be your situation? *despised* and *insulted*, by an *enraged* populace, *exposed* to the *revenging* hand of *justice—You* will then flee to *Caves* & *Dens* to hide yourselves from the *face* of *day* and of Man—you will then *truly* be, 'the jest of Tories, and the scorn of Whigs.'"

The charges leveled against Congress in the first address were not warranted, Putnam believed. The officers had not "been *abused*, and *insulted* by Congress as ... pretended." Based on Ogden and McDougall's report, which the officers would see at the meeting, and the resolutions that the delegates passed on January 25, he understood that Robert Morris had been told to give the officers "all the cash in his power." Their accounts were to be settled and they were going to receive "the same securities as other public Creditors." And Congress was going to do its utmost "to obtain from the respective States substantial *funds* adequate to ... Funding the whole debt."

Wasn't that enough to satisfy the officers? They could not ask the delegates to accomplish things they were not capable of accomplishing. And though Congress might approve commutation, it was not obligated to do so. If it did not approve the measure, the officers would have no cause to complain. They could, he felt, do no more than present "a warm & affectionate address to our *Illustrious Chief*—pointing out the disadvantages that will arise to the Army if they should be disbanded before their Accots. are settled, or in case the War continues, that justice & policy require there should not be a moments delay," and imploring him to "use his influence" to get Philadelphia to act at once.[3]

Whether copies of Putnam's answer to the anonymously written addresses were ever made and posted or circulated is not clear. His reply might have been prepared as a fallback option should Washington's speech at the Temple of Virtue fall flat.

Officers representing all the units stationed near Newburgh were going to be listening to that speech. They did not know that, though, when late in the morning they marched up the hill not far from the soldiers' huts to the spot where the newly constructed building was located.

If the drawing made by a Massachusetts soldier named William Tarbell is accurate, a walkway led to the front entrance of the Temple of Virtue, and the building itself was only one story high. By each side of its front door stood a vertical column and above the entrance was a triangular cupola with an attached flagstaff. The Temple's windows extended all the way from its stone foundation to the eaves of its broad shingle roof and had sixteen-pane upper and lower sashes. At each end of the large wooden building was a fieldstone chimney.[4] In addition to the room where the meeting was to take place, the Temple had four small rooms for "the issuing of the general orders, for the sitting of Boards of Officers, Courts Martial, etc. and an office and store for the Quarter Master and Commissary's departments."[5]

When the officers reached the Temple they entered its "spacious [central] hall."[6] The rectangular room was "sufficient to contain a brigade of troops on Lord's days, for public worship,"[7] and well-suited for large meetings and dances, but it did not have enough benches for all those who were going to attend the meeting. As more and more men arrived, places to sit became fewer and unoccupied spots had to be found in the aisles, by the room's plastered walls, or in doorways. Eventually, the hall was packed with officers; by this time all but a small number—those down south—were stationed in the Hudson Highlands.

General officers, field officers, commissariat officers from all the companies, and a member of the medical staff were present. Among the first group was the forty-four-year-old Putnam, one of the best engineers in the Continental Army. Tall, gout-ridden, forty-nine-year-old Philip Schuyler of New York, a large landowner and Alexander Hamilton's father-in-law, was in attendance.[8] He had retired from active service as a general in 1779 but since then had often met with Washington to provide counsel. Thin-faced and long-nosed Colonel Timothy Pickering was there; he was standing not far from the dais.[9] He was going to be all ears on this day, ready to record exactly what was said. He shared Armstrong's view that the officers had been treated abominably and thought Congress was going to disband the army and renege on its promises to provide them with the back pay they were due and the postwar pensions they had been promised. The Newburgh Addresses and the meeting this day, he believed, could produce a number of forceful resolutions, letting Philadelphia know that it would be unwise to break up and send home the army to avoid the costs of keeping its promises. Armstrong was there.[10] Massachusetts Captain Samuel Shaw, a twenty-eight-year-old aide-de-camp to Knox, was at the meeting. Washington considered him intelligent, energetic, and courageous.[11] His journal later became a prime source of information for historians interested in the Newburgh Conspiracy. Lieutenant Robert R. Burnet was there. He was in command of redoubt number three at West Point.[12]

Their minds were filled with a mixture of hostility and hope. Some of them thought of the past. Others considered the future. They all anticipated the beginning of the meeting.

Shortly before it was to commence, George Washington arrived on horseback with Henry Knox; he might have met with the general and had some food or drink with him before setting out for the meeting and, perhaps, revealed to him at that time what he planned to say to the officers. After dismounting, the Commander-in-chief secured his large bay horse to a long hitching rail there as many before him had done this day. Then he headed for the hall where the officers had gathered.[13]

Horatio Gates, previously designated to act as the presiding officer, stood under the arched vault on a small dais by a lectern at one end of the room. A low and narrow door behind the dais was closed and the room was now full of officers. The general called them to order to begin the meeting at noon. Officers who had been standing around and conversing with one another suddenly quieted and took their seats. "The matters they were called to deliberate upon were of the most serious nature."[14]

Then the door opened and George Washington walked towards the dais. Officers got to their feet, disturbing the benches they had been sitting on. The sounds of boots hitting and scuffing the floor and scabbards being repositioned replaced the buzz of conversations that had just ended. Moments later a veil of silence settled over the hall, the noisy movements generated by the Commander-in-chief's surprise entry coming to an end. A new atmosphere was evident.[15] Washington, Captain Shaw felt, had "heightened the solemnity of the scene" by making such an unannounced appearance.[16]

WASHINGTON'S PHYSICAL PRESENCE alone was likely to work to his advantage as he addressed the officers. He was much taller than the average soldier; John Adams even remarked once that people always chose Washington to be the leader because he stood above everybody else in the room.[17] Lafayette was similarly impressed by the general's height, recalling in his memoirs Washington's "tall form" and claiming he had no trouble identifying him when they first met.[18] The French nobleman also was struck by the size of his hands, reportedly saying to George Washington Parke Custis long after his death, "I never saw so huge a hand on any human being as the general's."[19] And he could have added that the general had large feet—he wore a size thirteen shoe[20]—long limbs, a handsome face, a strong nose, and a firm chin. Washington also had good posture and a dignified gait. He had an aura about him. "He looks like a hero,"[21] said Count Axel Fersen.

Another thing likely to work to his advantage was Washington's own financial situation during the war, if the officers knew about it. The general accepted no pay for his service during the war, got no rental income from tenants on his vast tracts of land, received paper currency of negligible value from those who were in debt to him and, as a result, saw his net worth decline by about half.[22]

If knowledge of Washington's financial sacrifices were not enough to sway the officers, the fact that he constantly took up the cause of his neglected army should have been. For years he had pleaded with the delegates to redress the grievances of his men. He had seen with his own eyes the shortages of shoes, blankets, bread, and meat. He knew that their pay was months, if not years, in arrears. He too was apprehensive about Congress's willingness or ability to honor its promises to reward the officers with pensions after the war.

WASHINGTON TOOK A seat for a short time and then quietly asked a surprised Gates to let him speak to the officers gathered in the room. His second in command promptly complied and stepped aside. The Commander-in-chief walked directly towards the lectern, neither bowing nor acknowledging his intended audience as he did so, and mounted the low dais.[23] As he was about to begin, "every eye was fixed upon the illustrious man, and attention to their beloved General held the assembly mute."[24] He was, as usual, dressed in a clean blue and buff uniform and his hair was neatly brushed back from his forehead, tied in a small queue, and slightly powdered; every morning during the war his mulatto servant, Billy Lee, arranged his hair that way.[25] His demeanor was sober; "Let your Countenance be pleasant but in Serious Matters Somewhat grave" was number nineteen in the "Rules of Civility & Decent Behaviour In Company and Conversation."[26]

Before beginning his prepared statements, Washington apologized for appearing at their meeting[27] and asked them to be seated. He had originally not planned to attend, but after seeing the efforts made to circulate the two anonymously written addresses in camp he decided he had to let the officers know how he felt about them, and the meeting this day would afford him the opportunity to do that. To ensure that his views were made especially clear he had put them down in writing and now was asking them to allow him to read what he had written.[28]

He removed the speech that he had prepared and his aides had copied from his tunic, nervously unfolded and pressed it flat in front of him, held it in his left hand, and slowly turned his head to look out over the audience. Some of his officers appeared pleased to see him there, but most wore expressions of anger and suspicion or discomfort on their faces, which made him become "sensibly agitated." Washington, probably believing this would be the most important speech of his life, breathed in deeply and then began to read the large script on the paper before him.[29]

He did not deliver his opening remarks with any sense of drama, but the quality of his voice quickly changed.[30] "How inconsistent with the rules of propriety, how unmilitary, and how subversive of all order and discipline" it had been to call for a meeting of the officers without his authorization was something that could be decided by "the good sense of the Army."

As for the first anonymously written letter, it "addressed more to the feelings and passions, than to the reason and judgment of the Army." Its author deserved "much credit for, the goodness of his Pen" but less "for the rectitude of his Heart." He ought to "have had more charity, than to mark for Suspicion, the Man who should recommend moderation and longer forbearance," Washington believed. "But he had another plan in view, in which candor and liberality of Sentiment, regard to justice, and love of Country, have no part." He sought "to effect the blackest design," one meant to serve "the most insidious purposes." He wrote "to impress the Mind, with an idea of premeditated injustice in the Sovereign power of the United States, and rouse all those resentments which must unavoidably flow from such a belief." He planned "to take advantage of the passions" of the officers who read his address and were "warmed by the recollection of past distresses, without giving time for cool, deliberative thinking."

If the officers were to be warmed by any recollections, they should be warmed by those of someone who had demonstrated time and again his concern for the army—George Washington. "If my conduct heretofore, has not evinced to you that I have been a faithful friend to the Army, my declaration of it at this time would be … unavailing and improper," the general continued. "I was among the first who embarked in the cause of our common Country. … I have never left your side one moment, but when called from you on public duty … I have been the constant companion and witness of your Distresses, and not among the last to feel, and acknowledge your Merits," Washington reminded the assembled officers. He always looked out for his army. He was not "indifferent to its interests."[31]

Still unable to assuage the officers' anger at this point in his speech,[32] Washington again went after "the anonymous Addresser." How will he advance the interests of the Army? If the fighting continues, he will have the men abandon the war effort, "remove into the unsettled Country … and leave an ungrateful Country to defend itself." What will become of their families? Will they be left behind on their farms or will they follow their men "to perish in a Wilderness, with hunger, cold and nakedness?"

If, on the other hand, peace arrives, he will have the army not disband until it gets "full and ample justice" from Congress. Justice at the point of a bayonet!

"This dreadful alternative, of either deserting our Country in the extremest hour of her distress, or turning our Arms against it, (… unless Congress can be compelled into instant compliance) has something so shocking in it, that humanity revolts at the idea," an appalled Washington declared. "My God! What can this writer have in view, by recommending such measures? Can he be a friend of the Army? Can he be a friend to this Country?" the general asked. "Rather is he not an insidious Foe? Some Emissary, perhaps, from New York, plotting the ruin of both, by sowing the seeds of discord and separation between the Civil and Military powers of the Continent?"

Washington was not going to dwell on the two options presented by the anonymous addresser. They were "impracticable,"[33] he told the still upset officers,[34] and he had not yet given up on Congress. It was an "Hon[ora]ble Body" that took great pride in what the army had done and fully understood "its merits and sufferings." It would "do it compleat justice." In the past it had worked tirelessly to get funding so it could do just that, and it was not going to quit until its labors were crowned with success.

True, "like all other large Bodies, where there is a variety of different Interests to reconcile," it took its time in acting. But Washington did not want the officers to doubt Congress. If they did so, they might "adopt measures, which may cast a shade over that glory … so justly acquired … tarnish the reputation of an Army … celebrated thro' all Europe, for its fortitude and Patriotism," and greatly hurt their chances of achieving their objective.

In recognition of their fine service to him "under every vicissitude of Fortune" and out of a "sincere affection" for all those under his command, Washington was ready to do everything in his power to help them achieve "compleat justice for all [their] toils and dangers" and get everything they desired, if they requested his help.

But they could not do anything that when "viewed in the calm light of reason" was sure to be seen to "lessen the dignity, and sully the glory" that they had achieved. They had to trust America and wholeheartedly believe "in the purity of the intentions of Congress." It was going to pay them before the army was disbanded, as promised. They were going to receive "ample justice" in recognition of their "faithful and meritorious Services." If they cherished their "sacred honor," held in "respect the rights of humanity," and were concerned for "the Military and National character of America," then they were "to express … [the] utmost horror and detestation of the Man who wishes, under any specious pretences, to overturn the liberties of our Country, and who wickedly attempts to open the flood Gates of Civil discord, and deluge our rising Empire in Blood."

By following his advice, Washington assured the officers, they were going to be on a "plain and direct road" to getting what they wanted, to thwarting "the insidious designs of our Enemies, who are compelled to resort from open force to secret Artifice," and to providing "one more distinguished proof of unexampled patriotism and patient virtue, rising superior to the pressure of the most complicated sufferings." They, by acting in a dignified manner, were going to "afford occasion for Posterity to say, when speaking of the glorious example … exhibited to Mankind, 'had this day been wanting, the World had never seen the last stage of perfection to which human nature is capable of attaining."'[35]

If Washington did not deviate much from the text that has been handed down throughout history, he spoke for anywhere from ten to fifteen minutes. Whether he read it with his spectacles on or off depends on which eyewitness accounts one believes, but since the script was large he likely did not have them on. What is not in doubt is that when he also read from a friend's letter that he had brought with him, he used the glasses—and used them with great dramatic effect.

According to the most accepted version of the story, once Washington finished reading his prepared statements he noted an absence of applause and sensed that his words had failed to soothe the disgruntled officers. He shifted his papers and, realizing something else had to be done to strike a more responsive chord with them, reached into his inside coat pocket and slowly removed and unfolded a "private letter,"[36] the one he had recently received from Joseph Jones. He then cleared his throat to put an end to the sounds being made by his restless officers[37] and, holding the letter in only one hand,[38] began to read. Naturally, he did not read what Jones had written about the plot.[39] What he read was "corroborating testimony of the good disposition in Congress … from a worthy member of that body, and one who on all occasions had ever approved himself their fast friend."[40] It had been "written with calmness & great good sense."[41]

Something was wrong, though. Washington's pauses and his handling of the letter—moving it to and fro in a seemingly futile attempt to make out what Jones had written—betrayed a kind of awkwardness or uncertainty. As he struggled, the officers tried to get better looks.[42] They expressed their increasing dissatisfaction in low voices and wondered why their commander was having trouble with the letter. Was the script too small? Was there insufficient space between the letter's lines?[43] Or was Washington experiencing some type of physical problem? Pickering, who claimed to be "but a small distance from General Washington," thought the Commander-in-chief was "finding some embarrassment in his sight."[44] Finally, after only a few sentences or perhaps a paragraph,[45] the general lowered his hand and stopped reading.

The break in the performance, though, did not last long. At this point, according to some but not all of those who were present, he removed a spectacles case from his waistcoat pocket. Inside were his new reading glasses with the little circular lenses that Rittenhouse had made for him. He slowly took them out of the case, unfolded them, wiped them off and began to clumsily don them.[46] What he said next cannot be ascertained, but most historians cite quotes in letters from Shaw and Lieutenant Colonel David Cobb to Reverend Eliot and Pickering, respectively. Speaking in an uncharacteristically sad voice, Washington supposedly "begged the indulgence of his audience while he put them on"[47] and drove away with one memorable line all the storm clouds that had gathered: "Gentlemen, you will permit me to put on my spectacles, for I have not only grown gray, but almost blind in the service of my country."[48]

Other versions of what he said exist, but appear to have been rejected or simply forgotten. Some of them have Washington putting his spectacles on either before or soon after beginning his prepared statements, and all quote him differently. Two depict the general as the embodiment of patriotism by having him express his faith in America: One from an early biography has him saying, "My eyes have grown dim in my country's service, but I never doubted of its justice!"[49] Another, from an old history of Newburgh, has him declaring, "These eyes, my friends, have grown dim, and these locks white in the service; yet I have never doubted the justice of my country."[50]

Three works attribute to Washington almost the same line as Shaw did. *Washington at Temple Hill* tells us he said, "You see, gentlemen, that I have not only grown gray, but blind in your service."[51] An old history of the Revolution claims the Commander-in-chief was smiling shyly as he announced, "You have seen me grow gray in your service. Now I am growing blind."[52] In a biography of one of Washington's aides the general is quoted as saying, "You see, Gentlemen, that I have grown grey in your service, and now find myself going blind."[53] Historian John Ferling uses that quote, but has Washington facing the officers and putting on his spectacles to read from Jones's letter just before he is about to conclude his prepared statements.[54]

Washington's "mode & manner of delivering" the sad words, not the actual meaning, overwhelmed the officers' animosities and evoked feelings of sympathy.[55] They turned and hugged each other.[56] Some, if not all, started to cry or at least became choked up.[57] And the general himself faltered as he tried to continue reading.

Apparently unable to get the better of his emotions and sensing that he had succeeded in swaying the officers, he decided that now was the time for him to leave the scene. He removed his spectacles, which had been resting near the end of his nose, carefully and slowly refolded the letter, and put them in his waistcoat pocket. The officers, who had just been made more sympathetic towards his plight than their own, gathered near him or got to their feet dazed and looked on quietly without leaving their places.[58] As they did so, Washington acknowledged them by bowing his head slightly,[59] turned away, and quickly departed from the hall. A few moments later he mounted his horse and, as some officers gazed fixedly at him through the windows, slowly rode off and passed from sight.[60] A general stillness had settled over the room, interrupted only by the sounds produced by tearful officers.[61]

Samuel Shaw saw "something so natural, so unaffected, in his appeal, as rendered it superior to the most studied oratory."[62] Many other officers in attendance also must have thought that the performance with the glasses was unaffected. Washington was fifty-one and no doubt appeared comparatively old to many of the younger officers in the room. Though he had remained quite healthy during the war, they had reason to believe him when he said he was going blind. The reddish brown color in his hair had disappeared; his face had grown more lined; his gums and teeth had caused swelling in January; and he had suffered from a variety of ailments earlier in his life. A bout with rickets had left him with a sunken chest. Smallpox had "strongly attacked" him when he was nineteen and left his long face permanently pitted with pockmarks. Acute pleurisy resulting from exposure to tuberculosis had caused suffering soon thereafter, and dysentery was a persistent problem for him. So too was malaria, for which he received quinine treatments that later left him with impaired hearing. Also, only those who were very close to Washington had seen him wear spectacles; he never wore them in public. At that time people were less willing to be seen wearing glasses, feeling a sense of shame similar to what someone with a clubfoot or hunchback might have experienced.[63] Although they could not have known much, if anything, of Washington's medical history, their impression that they were witnessing their Commander-in-chief's health—and more specifically his eyesight—failing before their very eyes was understandable.

But historian Richard Norton Smith maintains that the general's performance was not unaffected, that it was a case of great acting, and notes that the general had relied on spectacles long before the day he spoke at the Temple of Virtue.[64] Other historians would probably agree with him. James MacGregor Burns and Susan Dunn observe in their biography of Washington that theatrical metaphors, such as "theatre of action," "public theatre," "stage," and "actors on a most conspicuous theatre," appear with great frequency in his letters.[65] Richard Brookhiser points out that Washington was a theater lover during a period in our history when acting was seen by Congress as a contributor to immorality.[66]

IF WASHINGTON'S ACTIONS and speech were theater, Joseph Addison's *Cato: A Tragedy* must have influenced the general. It was his favorite play and he knew it well. He had seen it with the Fairfaxes at their Virginia plantation, Belvoir, when he was young, and he saw it often in later years. He borrowed language from it when he wrote letters and he had sat in attendance when his younger officers performed it for the troops in the bakehouse at Valley Forge, even though Congress would hardly have approved at that time or even later, after the soldiers had left camp; in 1774 the delegates had resolved to "discountenance and discourage every Species of Extravagance and Dissipation," including stage performances, and in October 1778 they urged the states "to take the most effectual measures for ... suppressing theatrical entertainments" and decided that any government official who chose to "act, promote, encourage or attend such plays" should be fired.[67]

The play, which made its first appearance in 1713 in London, gave common folk an understanding of ancient Rome. It was often performed throughout the colonies, beginning in the 1730s and continuing until after the war.[68] That was only natural because patriotic Americans associated Cato, a senator, with republican government and liberty.[69] He and those who stood with him were like the delegates in Philadelphia and the American soldiers and officers fighting for independence from England. Julius Caesar, on the other hand, was like George III; he was no friend of liberty.[70]

The play begins during the Roman Civil War, shortly after Julius Caesar's victory at Thapsus in 46 B.C. Cato, who sees Caesar as a threat to Roman liberty and believes that the virtuous thing to do is resist him even if his doing so will cost him his life, is in the North African city of Utica. In the final act, when Caesar's forces near that city, Cato will not surrender; to abandon his cause would be to betray his sense of Roman virtue. Consequently, he even rejects the call of one of his own sons, Portius, to give up, and ultimately takes his own life by sword.[71]

Many themes run through *Cato*. The most obvious ones are the need to control passions, personal betrayal, the desire to protect liberty and, especially, the importance of virtue. These themes also show up in Washington's speech.

The first of those four themes appears in *Cato* when the senator advises one of his colleagues, Sempronius, who is anxious to dispense with debates and just do battle with Caesar, to "Let not a torrent of impetuous zeal/Transport thee thus beyond the bounds of reason," because he fears a war with Caesar may result in great bloodshed and ruin for the Roman Empire. They must check their passions.[72]

Like Cato, Washington wants his colleagues—his fellow officers—to check their passions. In his speech at the Temple of Virtue he lashes out at the author of the First Newburgh Address for having "addressed [the officers] more to the feelings and passions than to the reason and judgment of the Army" when what they really need is "cool, deliberative thinking." He does not support the plot to frighten reluctant delegates and the states into enhancing Congress's powers so it can tax the people and raise the revenue needed to redress the officers' grievances, because he understands that it might end in ruin for America. He sees that this plot is the result of "passions ... inflamed" and realizes that passion is too closely associated with anger which, as Washington's favorite philosopher—the Roman Seneca—had warned, causes a person to lose his ability to reason.[73] Passion has to be stifled; otherwise, inappropriate, regrettable behavior results.[74]

The second theme in *Cato*, personal betrayal, shows up when the senator learns that friends of Sempronius and a general named Syphax are working to increase the "discontents among the soldiers." The realization that these soldiers will side with his enemies and "follow Caesar's banners" hurts Cato greatly because he believes that he has borne more hardships than anybody else during the war.[75]

The Commander-in-chief conveys the same feeling of having been personally betrayed when he addresses his officers. After condemning the author of the Newburgh Addresses for appealing to the officers' passions, he defends himself as a friend of the army and a leader who has shared the hardships of those under him. His defense is about one-hundred-fifty words long.

The third theme, fear for Roman liberty, is expressed in many parts of the play[76] and does not need to be enumerated. It is the reason why Cato opposes Caesar.

Washington, of course, fears for American liberty. He makes this most apparent shortly before he concludes his prepared statements to the assembled officers, when he wants them "to express ...

utmost horror and detestation of the Man who wishes, under specious pretences to overturn the liberties of our Country."

The most prevalent theme in the play is the importance of virtue. The word "virtue" and the various forms that derive from it are uttered almost ad nauseam. Throughout the play Cato is portrayed as a virtuous leader and he himself sees the Roman as "a friend of virtue."[77]

The word "virtue" does not appear often in Washington's prepared statements. But the Commander-in-chief makes his officers understand that virtue is very important. As he concludes his speech, he asks them to follow his advice and rely on Congress to do them justice. If they do so, they will "give one more distinguished proof of unexampled patriotism and patient virtue, rising superior to the pressure of the most complicated sufferings."

The virtue Washington had in mind when he concluded his speech was a kind of public virtue, not a private one. The general knew that for republican government to succeed each person had to believe he must put his country's interests before his own. In the 1700s that was what people meant when they talked of "public virtue." If such a thing did not exist, there could be neither order nor government by the people.[78]

Besides sharing themes, Addison's play and Washington's speech often share words and phrases. For example, while one of Cato's sons urges his brother to "look on guilt, rebellion, fraud, and Caesar,/*In the calm lights* of mild philosophy,"[79] Washington pleads with his officers not to do anything that when "viewed *in the calm light* of reason" would be seen to damage their reputations. Similarly, one of the play's characters wants to "unravel all/This dark *design*,"[80] and Washington seeks to prevent the plotting politicians and officers from effectuating the "blackest *design*." Where one of Cato's colleagues warns that "dire effects from *civil discord* flow,"[81] Washington essentially calls on his officers to denounce the writer of the Newburgh Addresses for trying "to open the flood Gates of *Civil discord*, and deluge our rising Empire in Blood."

Even when Washington and the playwright's characters do not use the same words they sometimes create similar images. While Syphax emphasizes how he has aged by observing that his "*locks are grown white*/Beneath a helmet *in … battles*,"[82] Washington says, "I have not only *grown gray*, but almost blind *in the service of my country*."

WITH THOSE FIFTEEN words, Washington had ended his performance at the Temple of Virtue and left the scene. What would happen in the central hall now that he was gone? Had the officers' anger really been assuaged? Was the image of their gray-haired Commander-in-chief struggling to read a letter because of his failing eyesight strong enough to make the officers forget their own hardships for good? Or were the officers' bitter memories of shortages of food and clothing, and of having gone without pay so long, bound to cause yet another storm cloud to form over the Hudson Highlands?

Chapter Twenty

"A Conduct Truly Admirable"

THE INTENSE DISSATISFACTION that had been present before Washington's arrival was now gone, and a sense of calm permeated the room. Gates, who had remained seated and utterly silent until Washington left the hall, resumed his position as the presiding officer, but any desire to discuss the nefarious plan that had been hinted at in the first anonymously written address was almost entirely forgotten. Knox proposed a resolution thanking the Commander-in-chief for his statements and "assuring him that the officers reciprocated his affectionate expressions with the greatest sincerity of which the human heart is capable."[1] Putnam seconded the motion, and all the officers present voted in favor of it, although Pickering apparently made it known that he was against it.

A brief review of the petition McDougall had delivered to Philadelphia, his and Ogden's report, and Congress's resolutions of January 25 followed. Then, acting on a proposal from Putnam that was seconded by Brigadier General Edward Hand, a committee of three officers—Knox, Brooks, and a Captain Howard—was created to come up with some resolutions and return thirty minutes later to report to the assembly. Knox was to chair the committee, and whatever they proposed was supposed to be "expressive of the business before us."[2]

The three officers left the hall for a corner room, deliberated, and came back to report their resolutions, which were then amended and unanimously approved by the gathered officers. First, the officers declared that they were still "engaged in the service of their country from the purest love and attachment to the rights and liberties of human nature ... and that no circumstances of distress or danger" would cause them to behave in a way that might "tend to sully the reputation and glory ... acquired at the price of their blood and eight years' faithful service."[3] Second was an avowal of the army's "unshaken confidence in the justice of Congress and their country."[4] They were sure the delegates would have "their accounts ... liquidated, the balances accurately ascertained, and adequate funds established for payment" before the army was disbanded or sent off in various directions. And they expected that "the half-pay, or commutation of it, should be efficaciously comprehended."[5] Third was actually a request of Washington. They wanted him "to write to his Excellency the President of Congress, earnestly entreating the most speedy decision of that honorable body on the subjects of our late address, which was forwarded by a Committee of the army." If Congress's decision pleased them, it would "produce immediate tranquility in the minds of the army, and prevent any further machinations of designing men, to sow discord between the civil and military powers of the United States."[6]

After they had approved those resolutions, they passed another to thank the three officers who had gone to Philadelphia and presented their petition to Congress; the general and the two colonels had displayed "wisdom and prudence" in their dealings with the delegates.[7] The assembled officers then asked that "a copy of the proceedings of this day be transmitted by the President to Major General McDougall; and that he be requested to continue his solicitations at Congress" until he achieved success.[8]

Logic would have suggested that they conclude the meeting after making that request of McDougall, but they did not do that. Presumably feeling they needed to do more than just blame some designing men for trying to plant the seeds of discord between the army and Congress, the officers passed another resolution, one to show that they "view with abhorrence, and reject with disdain, the infamous propositions contained in the late anonymous address ... and resent with indignation the secret attempts of some unknown persons, to collect the officers together in a manner totally subversive of all discipline and good order."[9]

For a half hour the officers had debated the resolutions amongst themselves but without much rancor. The only officer who had apparently harbored any bitterness about what was going on was the thin-faced Colonel Pickering. The final resolution, the one damning the author of the Newburgh Addresses, was one "the army will be ashamed of,"[10] he later opined. But realizing that none of the other officers would second him if he rose to voice his opposition, he had stayed seated. He also had abstained from voting on the motion.

Pickering thought the suddenly virtuous officers had "damned with infamy two publications which during the four preceding days most of them had read with admiration, & talked of with rapture!" He did not know who had written the addresses, but he did not believe the anonymous author had intended "to draw the army to revolt and sedition." The author was "an enlightened spirit," someone with a "keen sensibility—who had sustained the toils & dangers of seven campaigns." He had shed blood for his country, while others had stayed home and grown rich. And now, as he witnessed "sweet Peace with her attendant blessings dawning on the land which his sword had contributed to save," he was able to see only "indigence & wretchedness" awaiting him. At a time "when Gratitude should have spread her joyful arms to embrace him," he "saw even Justice barring the door against him." Treated in such a way, Pickering wanted to know, was this officer supposed to just remain patient and tamely submissive?

No, he wasn't! "The army (the most deserving of all public creditors)" had good reason to be alarmed. The officers and soldiers "had seen the obstinacy of a single petty state defeat the wise and salutary measure of the impost." And they had seen the "great & upright" Robert Morris threaten to quit his office because he thought that Congress was never going to get the funding it needed and that he would never be able to pay the army what it was owed.

"Was it manly then implicitly to believe the suspicions against the writer?" Pickering asked. "Was it wise to adopt a resolution that would brand with infamy the man, the brother officer, whose watchful eye & able pen might discover and save them from the evils which ingratitude and injustice might bring or to suffer to fall upon them?"[11]

Whatever Pickering's true feelings were, he likely did not evince much anger at the meeting. Hand refers only to "some grumbling from old Pennsylvania,"[12] and it should be noted that the colonel never overtly supported the plotters' plan; several decades after the event, responding to a charge by Armstrong that he had "opposed the course recommended by Washington," he even wrote, "I did not open my lips in opposition."[13] Another after-the-event account asserts that "Pickering, who was not in the conspiracy, & who was not partial to the Commander in chief, spoke with firmness concerning the wrongs of the Army, but disapproved the Address."[14]

In any case, the meeting ended quietly. The officers then slowly exited the building and headed back to their posts, many still greatly affected by Washington's performance. Two of the officers—Schuyler and Knox—rode off together to the latter's quarters "in absolute silence, because of the solemn impression" it had made on them.[15] By the time all the officers had left the building support for Gates and his followers had virtually evaporated.

Though the meeting had not gone as Gates must have hoped it would go, he did sign the minutes. Washington a short time later forwarded them to Congress.[16]

The Newburgh Conspiracy was now really over, but the identity of the officer who had written the Newburgh Addresses had not been determined. Since the matter was "generally allowed to be a partnership affair" there were many suspects,[17] Samuel Shaw wrote in a letter to Reverend Eliot less than two months after the officers' meeting. "On the very day of the meeting I heard the letters ascribed to not less than five different persons," Armstrong claimed more than four decades after the event. And even by the end of the war there would be no agreement on who had penned them. One person who was a prime suspect—and suffered greatly as a result—was Dr. William Eustis.[18]

PRAISE FOR WASHINGTON would pour in from many quarters. "Never through all the war," Schuyler later wrote, "did his Excellency achieve a greater victory than on this occasion—a victory over jealousy, just discontent and great opportunities. ... I have no doubt that posterity will repeat the closing words of his Excellency's address,—'Had this day been wanting, the world had never seen the last stage of perfection to which human nature is capable of attaining.'"[19]

Knox thought the unexpected outcome of the meeting was certain to reflect well on the American military. "If the people have the most latent spark of gratitude this generous proceeding of the army must call it forth," he would declare. He wanted Secretary of War Lincoln to arrange for the publication of the meeting's proceedings and to then "forward some hundred copies to the Army." Washington had given "a masterly performance."[20]

Lieutenant Colonel David Humphreys of Connecticut, a clergyman's Yale-educated son who often wrote poetry while serving as an aide to the Commander-in-chief, called it "a proud day for the Army," one that should always have a place in America's history. In the eyes of the officers who had watched Washington lead men in battle, he had, on March 15, 1783, "appeared unspeakably greater ... than ever ... before."[21]

Major Joseph Allen Wright told Colonel Samuel Blachley Webb that the general had "made a most excellent address."[22]

Captain Shaw also felt the general had never appeared as great as on that day. In the past the Commander-in-chief had been buttressed "by the exertions of an army and countenance of his friends; but in this [case] he stood single and alone. There was no saying where the passions of an army, which were not a little inflamed, might lead; but it was generally allowed that longer forbearance was dangerous, and moderation had ceased to be a virtue. Under these circumstances he appeared, not at the head of his troops, but ... in opposition to them; and for a dreadful moment the interests of the army and its General seemed to be in competition!" However, when he delivered his speech, "every doubt was dispelled, and the tide of patriotism rolled again in its wonted course." The words Washington had used to praise his army could "with equal justice be applied to his own character. 'Had this day been wanting, the world had never seen the last stage of perfection to which human nature is capable of attaining.'"[23]

William Peartree Smith, who did not witness Washington's performance but learned about it and the troubles that had prompted him to act from an account in the *Freeman's Journal*, gushed that his conduct was "truly admirable[,] [s]uperior to what the common principles of Human Nature would have dictated to a Soaring Genius. ... Had an Oliver [Cromwell] commanded a republican army at such a delicate and critical Juncture, his towering brain would have traced out instantaneously a very different Line of Conduct." Washington, though, had proved that he was "the Patriot of Patriots ... too good for an ingrate, base, degenerate world." Smith could not put into words how deeply he respected the general, especially after his actions at the Temple of Virtue—"the finishing stroke." He believed that "Each State ought to erect a Statue to him" with the inscriptions "Patriae Liberator. Humani Generis Amator. Humanistati Laudibusq[ue] Superior."[24]

George Benet wrote his mother in Scotland that if not for Washington, "the Army would have long since left Congress. … He had as difficult a Task as any in the whole war—the Army was ready for revolt—One speech which he delivered to them in a building called the Temple of Virtue at Camp, reconciled them … from the worst humour which a body of men could be in" to one where they were "unanimous in their duty."[25]

WASHINGTON'S ACTION WAS timely. The British in New York had learned of the discontent of his officers; on that very same day when the American general spoke to his officers at the Temple of Virtue, March 15, 1783, Sir Guy Carleton was sending Thomas Townshend, a member of the House of Lords, a dispatch that included copies of the officers' petition, the instructions for the three officers in Philadelphia, and minutes of meetings and correspondence from that city. The British government would have a clear picture of the restlessness of the Continental Army and know that McDougall, Brooks, and Ogden looked "to be as much alarmed with the idea of peace as any other class of people" because they feared that Congress intended to "immediately disband the army" without settling its accounts in order to save money. The army, though, was vowing not to give up its arms until it received its pay. "Congress is now become so very contemptible a body, that whether it is peace or war, I think the army is ripe for annihilating them,"[26] the writer of a letter dated February 18 reported.

Two days later someone, probably the same writer, noted that "the limited powers of congress" were being talked about and those in the know did not think the government was strong enough to bring about a peace. They believed "the union must either be dissolved or the powers of congress enlarged."[27]

The government was on the verge of collapse, yet another letter proclaimed. The three officers had arrived "to settle a peace between congress and the army," but based upon what its author had seen of the officers' petition, their demands were going to be "as impossible for them [the delegates] to do … as to make bread of stones."

He hoped to see a new form of government for his country. He wanted it to have two separate branches—a legislative one and an executive one. The head of the latter had to have great power in order to prevent the union from breaking up "into innumerable divisions, and becoming the wretched prey of ravenous and designing harpies." This transformation should be brought about before the war ended because the threat of "the enemy and their own army" promised to "check a wanton and riotous spirit." Yes, "wretched must be that government which is formed and established under the influence of an army." However, "the worst government is better than the want of government."[28]

More ominous in tone was a letter dated March 7. "A most violent political storm is gathering," its writer announced. "Whether dependence or independence, whether peace or war" was going to result he could not say, but he was certain "it must and will produce an overthrow of our republican constitution." That should come as no surprise in light of, among other things, the reaction to Robert Morris's resignation, the "poverty" of the government, and "the uneasiness of the army." Just one day ago "he had a long conversation with an important member of congress," during which the delegate "very candidly declared … that it was not in the power of congress to satisfy the public creditors; that their powers were unequal to the business; that the people must delegate more power to them, or create some other power quite new."[29]

Chapter Twenty-One

"An Advocate for Their Rights"

ON SUNDAY, MARCH 16, Washington sent Philadelphia some good news: The result of the officers' meeting had evinced "that good sense and steady Patriotism of the Gentlemen of the Army, which on frequent Occasions" he had witnessed.[1]

The next day, though, "alarming intelligence"—Washington's report of the twelfth, the unauthorized notice calling for a meeting of the officers on the eleventh, the general orders rescheduling it to the fifteenth, and Armstrong's two addresses—reached Philadelphia. "There appeared good ground for suspecting that the Civil Creditors were intriguing in order to inflame the army into such desperation as wd. produce a general provision for the public debts." Though "the steps taken by the Genl. to avert the gathering storm & his professions of inflexible adherence to this duty to Congress & to his country, excited the most affectionate sentiments towards him," the papers helped produce a "peculiar awe & solemnity ... & oppressed the minds of Congs. with an anxiety & distress which had been scarcely felt in any period of the revolution."[2]

The President of Congress, Elias Boudinot, worried that the army might "dishonor themselves, and forfeit that Glory" they so deserved, glory "supported with so much dignity to themselves and advantage to their Country." If it resorted to violence, providing the soldiers and officers with pay and pensions or commutation was going to become more difficult.[3]

Hamilton thought the "steps of so inflammatory a tendency ... taken in the army" were very regrettable but not surprising. Washington had "acted wisely" because "the best way is ever not to attempt to stem a torrent but to divert it."

However, the New York delegate was not entirely dissatisfied that the army had grown so discontented. As long as it committed "no excesses" when it made its demands, he would not be sorry. He had "urged in Congress the propriety of uniting the influence of the public creditors, & the army," planning for them to use their "personal influence ... connections ... and a sense of justice to the army as well as the apprehension of ill consequences" to create what "might form a mass of influence in each state in favour of the measures of Congress." If the states saw that the creditors and angry officers were united in their support for giving Philadelphia more power, they would yield to the nationalists' wishes. "The discontents of the army might be turned to a good account," Hamilton had believed.

Of course, force was not an option; "it could only be productive of the horrors of a civil war, might end in the ruin of the Country & would certainly end in the ruin of the army."[4]

ON MARCH 18, George Washington made his pleasure with the actions of his officers known in his general orders,[5] and followed up on the short announcement he had made on Sunday by sending Boudinot a long letter with an official report on the proceedings of the meeting at the Temple. Included with the letter were the resolutions the officers had passed, and a copy of the speech he had made on the fifteenth. He lauded the officers for deciding to abandon their plans to use the threat of military force to make the government honor its promises and saw the results of their meeting "as the last glorious proof of Patriotism which could have been given by Men who aspired to the distinction of a patriot Army." Their actions were going to "not only confirm their claim to the justice, but ... encrease their title to the gratitude of their Country."

They had "so long, so patiently, and so chearfully suffered & fought" for Washington that he felt he had to do his duty as "an advocate for their rights." As such, he asked Congress to recall past instances when he had lobbied for "a future adequate provision for the Officers of the Army" and requested permission to forward "an Extract from a representation made ... to a Committee of Congress so long ago as the 29th of January, 1778—and also the transcript of a letter to the President of Congress—dated ... Octr 11th 1780." At "the critical & perilous moment when the last mentioned communication was made, there was the utmost danger a dissolution of the Army would have taken place unless measures similar to those recommended had been adopted." And what had been recommended by Washington then, and had contributed to a dramatic improvement in the condition of the Continental Army after Congress approved it, was the half-pay pension.

Now he recommended "the establishment of funds, and security of the payment of all the just demands of the Army." Those steps were "the most certain means of preserving the National faith & future tranquility of this extensive Continent."

As he moved on to the final third or so of his letter, Washington emphatically implored Congress to do the right thing:

"For if, besides the simple payment of their Wages, a farther compensation is not due to the sufferings & sacrifices of the Officers, then have I been mistaken indeed—If the whole Army have not merited whatever a grateful people can bestow, then have I been beguiled by prejudice & built opinion on the basis of error—If this Country should not ... perform every thing which has been requested in the late Memorial to Congress, then will my belief become vain, and the hope that has been excited void of foundation—And 'if ...the Officers of the Army are to be the only sufferers by this *revolution*: if retiring from the Field they are to grow old in poverty wretchedness and contempt—If they are to wade thro' the vile mire of dependency and owe the miserable remnant of that life to charity, which has hitherto been spent in honor,' then shall I have learned what ingratitude is ... realized a tale, which will imbitter every moment of my future life."

Washington, though, did not fear that those worst case scenarios were going to come to pass. He could not believe that "a Country rescued by their Arms from impending ruin" would ever "leave unpaid the debt of gratitude."[6]

While that letter essentially called for the officers to receive justice, one written to Joseph Jones emphasized the urgency of the situation. "The storm ... gathering with unfavourable prognostics" had broken up and the situation in the Hudson Highlands was again calm, but Congress could not be fooled into relaxing its efforts "to bring the requests of the Army to an issue." Jones had to understand that Washington's officers were "too much pressed by their present wants, and rendered too sore by the recollection of their past sufferings to be touched much longer upon the string of forbearance, in matters wherein they c[ould] see no cause for delay." And Philadelphia should not expect the general to be able "to dispel other Clouds if any ... ar[o]se."

The general believed those wanting the best for Congress, the army, and their country intended to "exert themselves to the utmost to irradicate the Seeds of distrust, and give every satisfaction that justice requires." The government had it within its power to make sure that that was done. The army knew it would not get everything it was owed immediately, but the delegates could at least determine the amounts the soldiers and officers were due before discharging them and issue them certificates to be redeemed sometime in the future. If the fighting men were to get nothing at all before being disbanded, it "would be to sett open the doors of the Goals (sic) [gaols, or debtors' prisons], and then to shut them upon Seven Years faithful and painful Services."

Those not in favor of compensating the army might believe the officers knew they were not able to use force to get what they thought they deserved, and the general acknowledged that "no good could result from such an attempt."[7] But, as he observed the following day in a letter to his cousin Lund Washington, if with the end of the war the states decided that they need not take care of those "who ... rescued them from the jaws of danger and brought them to the haven of Independence and Peace" while enduring sickness, "hunger, cold and nakedness" throughout the conflict, they would learn that the army's patience had its limits. "Well may another anonymous addresser step forward, and with more effect than the last did, say ... 'You have arms in your hands, do justice to yourselves, and never sheath the sword, 'till you have obtained it.' How far men, who labour under the pressure of accumulated distress, and are irritated by a belief that they are treated with neglect, ingratitude, and injustice in the extreme, might be worked upon by designing men, is worthy of very serious consideration."[8]

Upon receiving Washington's appeal, Jones would go to Madison and let him read the letter. Understanding the gravity of the situation, Madison approached fellow delegates again to urge approval of his blueprint for strengthening the government.[9]

THE SAME DAY Washington wrote his letter to Jones, Tuesday, March 18, the delegates in Philadelphia unanimously agreed on a list of specific dutiable imports for Congress's funding plan. Jamaican rum, all other distilled liquors, some wines, tea, various types of sugar, molasses, cocoa, and pepper were to be taxed in proportion to their quantities. The wishes of Robert Morris had been granted.[10]

Two days later Washington's short March 16 announcement concerning the successful conclusion of the officers' meeting arrived and was read aloud to the delegates. Also, the sixty-one-year-old Eliphalet Dyer finally surrendered and made a motion to pass commutation; the only delegate still opposed, until that moment, to granting the officers either half pay or commutation, he had been acting in accordance with instructions from Connecticut, where much opposition to providing the officers with pensions existed. McDougall and nationalists in Congress had hounded the recalcitrant representative into supporting the measure, which was more acceptable to the public than the half-pay pension and was the only thing that "would quiet & pacifye the Army." As Madison later wrote, Dyer's change of heart had been "extorted from him by the critical state of our affairs."

Either one or two days later he, Hamilton, and another delegate presented a report urging Congress to give officers who served for the duration of the war lump sum payments equal to five years' pay. Then, on the twenty-second, the entire body approved their recommendation.[11]

Although the Commutation Act allowed the government to pay the officers in securities or money, the latter was not a real option because of its poor financial health. The officers would receive certificates offering six percent annual interest immediately upon leaving the army. They weren't the ideal form of payment, but they could be sold for something to speculators. In theory the officers could choose to get lump sum cash payments from their home states; however, in practice they faced obstacles making that route virtually impossible to take: Officers from a state line had to vote collectively for payments from their state, and applying for them was difficult.[12]

Chapter Twenty-Two

"A Dangerous Instrument to Play With"

ON MARCH 22, the day Congress approved commutation, Washington's official report of the eighteenth arrived.[1] The following day Boudinot wrote the general to convey to him how pleased the delegates and "every friend to the army" were to hear about the favorable results of the meeting, and to inform him that they had approved commutation the day before. More important, though, was another bit of information Boudinot included in his letter: The French sloop *La Triomphe* had brought news of the signing of "the definite treaty of peace" by the British, French, and Spanish on January 20 in Paris. The dispatches brought to Congress were not official, but Boudinot had "no doubt of the event." The preliminary articles signed by the Americans and British on November 30, 1782, would now go into effect. The belligerents were supposed to cease hostilities on the twentieth of April.[2]

OVER THE NEXT two days, March 24 and March 25, Hamilton wrote three letters to Washington. In the first he quickly congratulated him on the preliminary peace agreement and then moved on to their last unfinished business—"to make solid establishments within to perpetuate our union." He wanted Congress strengthened so the United States would not become just "a ball in the hands of European powers bandied against each other at their pleasure." Strengthening the government, though, was going to be very difficult because inside the states the forces were far more "centrifugal" than "centripetal" and "the seeds of disunion much more numerous than those of union." Therefore he wanted Washington's help. The general's efforts had been crucial in winning the war and they promised to be no less so now.

As for the conspiracy, the delegates had been very pleased by the actions taken by Washington to snuff it out. And the steps his officers took were just the ones he could have hoped for; they were going to "add new lustre to their character as wel[l] as strengthen the hands of Congress."[3]

In the other two letters Hamilton wrote—one official, one private—the New York delegate focused more on the army. He informed Washington that it expected not to be disbanded before its accounts were settled and funding was established, but he knew Congress could not do both. Although the delegates might be able to settle the army's accounts, they had no legal authority "to *demand* funds." And if the delegates tried to keep the army intact after the arrival of peace to force the states to give Philadelphia funding, they "would excite the alarms and jealousies of the States, and increase rather than lessen the opposition to the funding scheme."

One idea was to send the soldiers and officers home to the states of their respective lines. That promised to "facilitate the settlement of accounts, diminish present expense, and avoid the danger of union."[4]

As much as he wished it were not so, Congress was naturally inclined to be ungrateful and to distrust the army. "Republican jealousy has in it a principle of hostility to an army, whatever be their merits, whatever be their claims to the gratitude of the community," he pointed out. "It acknowledges their services with unwillingness, and rewards them with reluctance." Based on what he saw, "too many … if they could do it with safety or color, would be glad to elude the just pretensions of the army."

Still, the army should not refuse to disband after peace arrived. It had to "submit to its hard fate." To not do so would be ruinous. "The army would moulder by its own weight, and … the soldiery would abandon their officers; there would be no chance of success, without having recourse to means that would reverse our revolution." For those reasons he could not "enter into the views of coercion, which some gentlemen entertain." However, if force could be of use, he "should almost wish to see it employed," since he had "an indifferent opinion of the honesty of this country, and ill forebodings as to its future system."[5]

IN HIS ORDERS for the twenty-eighth Washington included "for the satisfaction of every brave officer and soldier under his command" an extract from a letter the French minister had sent him. A peace treaty had been signed! This news was not official, but the "certainty of that event" filled him with joy.[6]

The following day's orders gave the army more cause for joy; an extract from Boudinot's letter to Washington provided the officers and soldiers with additional confirmation that peace was certain, and it announced Philadelphia's decision to offer commutation. The officers in the various state lines had two months to collectively decide whether they were going to accept or reject the offer.[7]

As March came to an end, Washington wrote Hamilton. He was happy the war was ending, but he knew Congress still had to be strengthened. "The defects ... & want of Powers in Congress" caused the war to be protracted and, as a result, expensive. "More than half the perplexities" Washington had endured during his time as Commander-in-chief and "almost the whole of the difficulties & distress of the Army" were caused by Congress's weakness.

He wanted the nation to be "a great, a respectable, and happy People," but that could not happen unless "State politics, and unreasonable jealousies & prejudices" were cast aside. If they were not, the American people would become "instruments in the hands of our Enemies, & those European powers who may be jealous of our greatness in Union."[8]

GREENE ALSO WAS bothered by Congress's want of power. That is why Gouverneur Morris had thought he might be willing to take charge of the nationalists' scheme to unite the army with the public creditors and demand general funding, and in February had sent out a feeler to him.

But when Greene wrote Morris on April 3, he made clear that he would never go along with the nationalists' plot. Though the mood of the southern army was now "much the same" as that of the northern army—bad enough to make him admit that he was "afraid of both"—he did not like the idea of using the angry army as a sword of Damocles to terrify state legislatures into granting Congress more power. Such a plan could unleash some unforeseen chain of events and before they knew it cause the whole matter to spin violently out of control. "When soldiers advance without authority, who can halt them? We have many Clodiuses and Catilines in America, who may give a different direction to this business, than either you or I expect," he cautioned Morris. "It is a critical business ... pregnant with dangerous consequences." Congress was "fast declining" and stood to become impotent unless it got "more effectual support," but the general was content to just wait and see what happened rather than try to force the states to give the government more authority.[9]

Greene's decision, coming less than a month after Washington's actions at the Temple of Virtue, was probably the last nail in the plotters' coffin. Without any support from either the top general in the north or the top general in the south, what high-ranking officer would dare try to revive the Newburgh Conspiracy?

ALTHOUGH THE CONSPIRACY appeared to be dead, Washington did not downplay the importance of making a real effort to redress the officers' grievances when he wrote Theodorick Bland on the fourth. He believed that their plan to not disband was less "extensive" than Armstrong's first address had seemed to suggest, and he said that they knew hanging a sword of Damocles over the heads of the delegates was no longer practicable. But the accounts of all his men needed to be "compleately liquidated and settled" and the balances that each of them were due "ascertained" before they were disbanded. The soldiers and officers must not be sent to their home states to have their accounts settled. The army had to stay intact and seek settlement from one body, Congress, under "one general System" of funding. Having the whole army go to Philadelphia, rather than having each line go to its respective state, would save time and money and, among other things, reduce the army's uneasiness and leave his men "better prepared, with good Opinions and proper Dispositions to fall back into the great Mass of Citizens."

One thing was of even greater importance. Congress had to give the men some of their back pay so they would be able to return home with at least a small portion of what they were owed. If Congress didn't have enough funds to give them at least three months' pay, one month's pay and a solemn promise to soon come up with the rest would suffice. "To be disbanded ... without this little pittance ... like a Sett of Beggars, Needy, Distressed, and without Prospect will not only blast the Expectations of their Creditors, and expose the Officers to the utmost Indignity and Worst of Consequences, but will drive every man of Honor and Sensibility to the extremist Horrors of Despair," the general warned. "On the other Hand to give them this Sum, however Small in Comparison of their Dues ... by fulfilling their Expectations, will sweeten their Tempers, cheer their hopes of the future, [and] enable them to subsist themselves 'till they can cast about for some future Means of Business," he predicted.

Washington thought the states might send Congress the money it needed if they received from the delegates "a spirited, pointed, and well adapted Address." The amount promised to be "small ... compared with the large Sum of Arrears ... due." Anticipating that some would not want the debt to the army to be given precedence over that to the other public creditors, the general stated that even the greatest lenders, if honest, would "be forced to yield to the superior Merit and Sufferings of the Soldier, who for a Course of Years, has contributed his Services in the field, not only at the Expence of his Fortune and former Employment, but at the Risque of Ease, domestic happiness, Comfort and even Life." The soldier, in fact, demands little if, "instead of the Pay due him for four, five, perhaps Six Years hard earned Toil and Distress, he is content for the present with receiving three Months only, and is willing to risque the Remainder upon the same Basis of Security, with the general Mass of other public Creditors."[10]

While the words Washington used in his letter to Bland were those of an advocate for the army, the words he used in his response to Hamilton's private letter of March 25 were those of a wise leader reprimanding his former aide. The general had read the onetime colonel's letter "with pain, & contemplated the picture it had drawn with astonishment & horror." Although he was perfectly aware that the officers and men had not been dealt with fairly, he felt that using the restless army to terrify reluctant representatives into giving the nationalists what they wanted was not sensible. "The idea of redress by force is too chimerical to have had a place in the imagination of any serious mind in this army," he chided Hamilton.

Some top officers had already begun to suspect some members of Congress were using them as "mere Puppits" to get a system of funding for the government and if it came to choosing between doing justice to the army and achieving their objective, "they would make a sacrifice of the Army and all its interests." One person "suspected to be at the bottom of this scheme" was Robert Morris. Thinking of those mistrustful officers and the possibility that such use of them was risky, Washington reproachfully observed, "The army ... is a dangerous instrument to play with."[11]

Part IV

The Sad End

"View Near Hudson" at Newburgh, NY

Chapter Twenty-Three

"Like a Rope of Sand"

ON APRIL 6, 1783, the *Prince William Henry*, a British packet from Falmouth, arrived in New York's harbor with news that a cessation of hostilities had been declared by royal proclamation on February 14.[1]

TWO DAYS LATER Hamilton wrote Washington. Among the subjects he drew the general's attention to was the division within Congress. The body was made up of two groups, "one attached to state, the other to Continental politics." The first group strongly opposed general funding for the government and only "the clamours of the army and other public creditors" were forcing its members to take up measures needed to fund the debt. The second group "blended the interests of the army with other Creditors" because it saw no other way to ensure that all those who were owed money would be paid back.

Hamilton wanted the public creditors to get what they were due. The officers and soldiers were not the only ones suffering because of the government's impotence, and he felt that it would be useless "to tell men who have parted with a large part of their property on the public faith that the services of the army are intitled to a preference." To do so would make the creditors feel resentful, and cause them to be less likely to show an interest in the soldiers' grievances. Also, some of those who had proposed that the army be given preferential treatment were insincere; their proposal that revenue generated by the impost be used to pay only debts to the officers and soldiers was just an attempt "to play off the army against the funding system."

As for how to pay back the army and the public creditors, Hamilton saw just one option; he had to pressure the states into giving Philadelphia greater authority. To that end "the necessity and discontents of the army presented themselves as a powerful engine."

Later the onetime colonel took up the contentious issue of half pay. Congress was divided between those who wanted the officers referred to the states for compensation and those who wanted Philadelphia to pay for it. Hamilton was in the latter group. One problem was that if Congress sent the lines back to their states, the officers stood to receive "commutation far short of an equivalent" to half pay for life. A second problem was that some states were going to be less generous than others in compensating their officers, producing "a new source of discontent." A third problem was that referral to the states would have continued the "old wretched ... system" of requisitioning. That system had already left "the ties between Congress and the army ... nearly dissolved" and facilitated a wasteful diversion of funds away from Philadelphia.

Hamilton concluded his letter by again defending the delegates suspected of trying to use the army to achieve their own ends. They were "in general the most sensible the most liberal, the most independent ... the most respectable characters ... the most unequivocal friends to the army ... the men who think continentally."[2]

IN NEW YORK at noon on the ninth of April, the mayor stood on the front steps of City Hall and read the royal proclamation declaring a cessation of hostilities. Many people attended the event, but not all of them liked what they heard; the large number of Loyalists present groaned and hissed at the mayor and heaped "bitter reproaches and curses upon their king for having deserted them in the midst of their calamities."

Their bitterness, though, could not reverse the results of the war. Soon after the event at City Hall ended Sir Guy Carleton informed Washington of the British declaration.[3]

A FORMAL TREATY ending the war was a certainty but pay for the army still was not. When Hamilton, Fitzsimmons, Osgood, Gorham, Peters, and Bland met with Robert Morris that same day to discuss the ideas Washington had included in his April 4 letter to Theodorick Bland, the Financier said that he considered "three Months Pay ... most reasonable," but wondered about the states' willingness to cooperate. Their help was necessary because there was not enough money in the Treasury "to Compleat the Months pay already engaged" and $500,000 from a French loan would have to go towards paying bills of exchange that had been drawn in anticipation of it.[4]

On April 11, two days after the six delegates consulted with Morris, Congress responded to the British declaration of a cessation of hostilities by declaring its own cease-fire. The following day Elias Boudinot wrote to George Washington to congratulate him.[5]

ALTHOUGH CONGRESS HAD declared a cease-fire, disbandment of the army had to wait; the delegates wanted the army's accounts to be completely settled first. Accordingly, Washington wrote a circular to states with soldiers in New Windsor to inform them, mentioned that the paymaster general was already there, and asked the governors to immediately send the information he needed; this was extremely important "both for the ease and quiet of the Army, as well as in point of Oeconomy to the Public."[6]

MEANWHILE, ROBERT MORRIS reported to Hamilton's committee that the army's accounts were being settled satisfactorily and he thought they did not have to wait until they had finished the process before beginning to disband the army.

If Congress planned to give the men three months' pay, it would need an estimated $750,000. Where was Morris, whose resignation was scheduled to go into effect at the end of May, going to find the money? Neither Congress nor the Bank of North America was capable of providing that sum. And Morris was pessimistic about obtaining the money through the sale of public property and taxes.

So the best available option was to issue notes in anticipation of a loan. This promised to be "an Operation of great Delicacy," Morris remarked, which would require that his personal credit "be staked for the Redemption" of them. And he was reluctant to take that risk; he felt that if he issued notes for the amount needed on his personal credit, he was going to "[be answerable] personally for about half a Million" by the time he stepped down as superintendent. "I would sacrifice much of my Property," he said with resignation, "yet I cannot risk my Reputation as a Man of Integrity nor expose myself to absolute Ruin."[7]

THE FOLLOWING DAY Congress ratified the preliminary peace treaty and the main army promptly received official notification, but Washington still had his concerns. In a letter written to Hamilton on April 16 he recalled what the New Yorker had said about the delegates being divided into two factions and pointed out that "there were different sentiments in the Army as well as in Congress." There were those inclined to see the states rather than Philadelphia as being financially responsible for paying them what they were owed and, Washington cautioned, "if an idea should prevail generally that Congress, or part of its Members or Ministers, … should *delay* doing them justice, or *hazard* it in pursuit of their favourite object; it might create such divisions in the Army as would weaken, rather than strengthen the hands of those who were disposed to support Continental measures—and might *tend* to defeat the end they themselves had in view by endeavoring to involve the Army." Whereas Hamilton had called the restless but necessary army a "powerful Engine" that could be made good use of, Washington called it "a dangerous Engine to work with," one that "would, more than probably, throw its weight into that Scale which seemed most likely to preponderate towards its immediate relief, without looking … to future consequences with the eyes of Politicians."

Washington's words of caution to the New York delegate, though, were not to be taken as an indictment of him. Most of the blame for the plot was being assigned "to Mr. G.__ M__ [Gouverneur Morris]" and the Commander-in-chief felt that the army generally regarded Hamilton "as a friend, Zealous to serve them, and one who ... espoused their interests in Congress upon every proper occasion."

What Hamilton and other delegates who espoused the army's interests could do now was assure the officers that Congress intended to refer them "to their respective States for payment" if they could not get general funding. Although the general really did not like that idea, he wanted his officers' "feelings ... attended to & soothed." One way or the other, the officers had to receive justice.[8]

TWO DAYS AFTER Washington wrote that letter to Hamilton, the delegates in Philadelphia made justice for the officers possible, approving the impost and the additional specific duties they had agreed upon in mid-March. The impost was to expire after twenty-five years and the states were allowed to appoint officials to collect the tax revenue, though Congress would have jurisdiction over them. The money collected, which according to Madison's notes was expected to be $1,000,000 a year, could be used only to pay off debts. The annual supplements to the impost that the states had to provide Congress with were set at $1,500,000 instead of the $2,000,000 that had been proposed earlier. These were to be based on their populations instead of on land. Slaves were to be included in the population counts, which would be conducted every three years. And the states with western lands were still being called upon to cede them.

Robert Morris did not like the plan and Hamilton, who along with the Financier and Madison had earlier argued for an impost, was one of several delegates who voted against it. He wanted more than just taxes on imports; he did not favor the twenty-five-year limit on the impost; and he thought the collectors should be appointed by Congress rather than by the states.

However, he did ask Washington to write the states and make clear that the impost should be approved, and he recommended that New York vote for the revenue plan; without some type of plan, he feared, the union might not last.

The question now was whether all the states would ratify the plan. Madison was not optimistic, admitting that he was afraid it offered "no bait for Virginia," which was going to be displeased by the decision to call upon states to cede their western lands.[9]

ON APRIL 19, 1783, exactly eight years to the day since shots were fired at Lexington, the men lined up on both banks of the Hudson "with burnished arms and proudly floating banners." Soon thereafter Fort Putnam's cannon produced a series of booms that echoed throughout the hills, and soldiers fired their muskets, in turn, "from West Point to the utmost limits of the camp." After that, high-pitched trills from fifes and the beats of drums "called the host of freedom to the place of prayer," the Temple. There, at noon, Congress's proclamation of a cessation of hostilities was read aloud, posted on the building's door, and welcomed with three loud huzzas. A reverend then offered a prayer to God and "an anthem [titled 'Independence'] was performed by [hundreds of] voices and instruments."

Once the services there ended, the soldiers headed back to their quarters but continued to mark the occasion in a similar manner. That evening the proclamation was read again to all the regiments and corps; brigade chaplains gave invocations; the cannon at Fort Putnam boomed; the soldiers lit up the dark sky with thousands of musket shots—"vivid flashings of lightning"; and, finally, "the Beacons [giant piles of timber that had been set afire] on the hilltops ... lighted up the gloom and rolled the tidings of peace on through New England and shed their radiance on the blood-stained field of Lexington."[10]

Knowledge that the preliminary peace treaty had been ratified heightened the army's restlessness. The soldiers wanted their discharges now! Neither Congress nor the officers, Washington believed, would be able "to hold them much, if any, longer." More guards had to be employed "to prev[en]t rioting" and to discourage the soldiers from insulting the officers when they tried "to hold them to their duty." And the Connecticut noncommissioned officers had even sent Washington a petition asking for half-pay pensions. The general had returned it "without appearing to Understand the Contents, because it did not come through the Channel of their Officers," but he was concerned that more petitions might appear. So he wanted soldiers who did not plan to wait for the settlement of their accounts to be immediately discharged. Otherwise, they were going to become noisier and the situation would grow more difficult.

He also worried about what would happen if the soldiers and officers were not given adequate pay. Thinking of their likely angry reaction, he stressed to Hamilton that "it would not be more difficult to still the raging Billows in a tempestuous Gale, than to convince the Officers of this Army of the justice or policy of paying men in Civil Offices full wages, when they cannot obtain a Sixtieth part of their dues."

And the general remained in the dark as to whether the delegates had taken up "the Lands, & other gratuities ... promised to the Army." But he did not want to waste time exchanging letters in an attempt to take care of those matters; he wanted Congress to send a committee to the New Windsor Cantonment to make arrangements. "Unless something of this kind is adopted, business will be delayed & expences accumulated—or the Army will break up in disorder, go home enraged, complaining of injustice—& committing enormities on the innocent Inhabitants in every direction,"[11] he predicted.

The Commander-in-chief was anxious to leave Newburgh but he did not know when he would be able to do so. "The distresses of the army for want of money, the embarrassments [financial difficulties] of congress and the consequent delays and disappointments on all sides, encompass me with difficulties, and produce every day some fresh source of uneasiness," he despondently wrote to Tench Tilghman on April 24. The states had to make the changes that would justify having fought for independence. They had to adopt a spirit of "liberality ... [in] place of prejudice, and unreasonable jealousies" and surrender some of their power to Congress to make it "competent to the general purposes of government, and of such a nature as to bind us together." Otherwise, the country was going to "be like a rope of sand," something that could be "easily broken" and quickly made "the sport of European politics."[12]

ON APRIL 26 Congress unanimously approved an address to the states that had been produced by a committee made up of Madison, Hamilton, and Ellsworth. The delegates told the states that Philadelphia was responsible for paying the war debts and anticipating the means needed for "obviating dangers which may interrupt the harmony and tranquility of the Confederacy." Those debts were so great and the government's resources were so limited that completely liquidating them anytime soon was impossible, and experience had shown that Congress could not receive funds promptly from the states under the present system. Therefore "some departure ... from the foederal constitutions"—the funding program just passed by the delegates—was necessary.

The government had to have both the impost and the specific duties in order to pay its debts, and those revenue provisions had to be lumped together into "one indivisible and irrevocable act." If they were not lumped together, "a single State out of the thirteen might at any time involve the nation in bankruptcy" and prevent it from establishing credit.

Who were the people the government had to pay back? Among those the delegates mentioned were men who had lent the government money and "that illustrious & patriotic band of fellow Citizens, whose blood and ... bravery ... defended the liberties of their Country," the officers. Although the delegates urged the states not to discriminate against certain types of creditors, they were especially sympathetic towards the second of those two groups. The officers had been deprived of their pay and now wanted just enough to "enable them to retire from the field of victory & glory into the bosom of peace & private citizenship." Also, they had displayed "their superiority to every species of seduction from the paths of virtue & of honor" by rejecting Armstrong's call for them to either refuse to disband if the war ended or refuse to fight if it did not.

Finally, the delegates reminded the states that Americans had always boasted they were fighting for something bigger than independence—"the rights of human nature." For that boast to be proven true, American liberty had to produce "justice, good faith, honor, gratitude & all the other Qualities which enoble the character of a nation, and fulfil the ends of Government." If those were "the fruits" of independence, America would serve as a model for other nations and "have the most favorable influence on the rights of mankind."

But if the states did not display "these cardinal and essential Virtues," the delegates warned, "the great cause ... will be dishonored & betrayed." America's attempt at "unadulterated ... Republican Government" will have failed; it will have been "the last & fairest experiment in favor of the rights of human nature" and the supporters of man's rights will stand "exposed to be insulted & silenced by the votaries of Tyranny and Usurpation."[13]

The address, which was sent out to the states in pamphlet form, included eight appendices. Madison knew Washington's name would add weight to their case, so the general's correspondence with Congress, which recorded the whole sequence of events in the Hudson Highlands, and his address to the officers at the Temple of Virtue, were among the eight. So too were the officers' petition, the Newburgh Addresses, and the proceedings of the officers' meeting.[14]

With the proclamation of a cease-fire and the passage of the funding plan, Congress was eager to break up the army. The longer the army was maintained, the more the government's debt grew. Also, unpaid domestic creditors might want to resuscitate the conspiracy by turning to soldiers still hanging around camp.

Chapter Twenty-Four

"Compelled to Leave the Army"

CONGRESS WAS RIGHT to be itching to break up the army. Although by early May Robert Morris had been persuaded to stay at his post,[1] and the officers had received their one month's pay in notes,[2] all was not yet well. Connecticut's sergeants were still upset that only the officers would get five years' pay after the war and had now gone through their top officer, General Huntington, to petition Washington. They and the privates, especially those who had to provide for families, were "very impatient."

The Commander-in-chief responded by permitting Huntington and Knox to grant furloughs to any noncommissioned officer or soldier who seemed ready to mutiny for as long as he wished. He felt they were "better [off] without them than with them."[3]

ON THE MORNING of the fifteenth, Morris, Secretary of War Lincoln, and Secretary of Foreign Affairs Livingston met with Hamilton and Gorham to discuss disbandment and the government's financial situation. Later the same day the Financier sent the latter two and Richard Peters a letter and five enclosures showing the Treasury's receipts and expenditures. Morris's resources were not sufficient to provision the army any longer. "If your Army is kept together they will consume as much in one Month as the Taxes will produce in two and Probably much more," Morris observed. "To make them three Months Pay will require I suppose at least six hundred thousand Dollars and every Day they continue in the Field lessens the practicability of sending them Home satisfied." The army had to be "disbanded immediately" or else the government would not be able to pay it "even with Paper."[4]

Much had changed in just two months. From the beginning of the year until mid-March Robert

Morris, Gouverneur Morris, and their allies had been intent on keeping the army intact to force recalcitrant delegates and states to give Congress greater taxation authority, but now they could not disband it fast enough. Now nobody was conspiring, and when Gouverneur Morris wrote Nathanael Greene a few days later, he even tried to reassure him that he had not had any despotic aim when he suggested that the discontented army be employed to get funding for Congress. He understood "the Consequences which must follow from any unconstitutional Procedure of the military" and realized that the line between "their humble Petitions and their most forcible Demands" was fine. What Morris had hoped for was that the army's "*Influence*" would lead Congress to approve the "*manly and decisive Measures*" needed to make the country "united and happy."[5]

BUT CONGRESS HAD not taken manly and decisive measures, and for that reason Gates was skeptical that the officers would ever get what they were promised. He asked Pickering if most of the officers found commutation acceptable and wondered whether there was "the smallest probability of the Assemblies of all or any of the States confirming it to the Officers" if they did. "If not how basely, & Ungratefully, are we Treated," he snapped. "I can live, it is true, without it, but I feel as Poignantly for the Distresses of the poor fellows who have been Our Faithful Companions through the War, as if those Distresses were also my Own—Perdition take the Catifs who have deceived Them."[6]

When Pickering answered Gates on May 28 he said he felt commutation was "universally accepted by the army" but not by the states. He wanted to believe that most states were going to approve it, but thought some would never do so. One of those states unlikely to agree to it was Connecticut. "While the army was necessary to their safety," he added, "they were willing the officers should believe in the justice of their country, & that the promised compensation for their extraordinary suffering, & services should never be denied them." Now with "the hour of danger … past," though, the officers were "already forgotten." Now "avarice & meanness have usurped the places of gratitude & justice,"[7] he groused.

Walter Stewart also appeared pessimistic. "The People to the Eastward are Crying out loudly Against this Commutation, or … any thing which has the most distant tendency to give that Common Justice to the officers which they are Entitled to," he whined to Gates. Officers were talking of not disbanding, but the colonel understood that the army as a whole was not to be relied upon to support such a step and the officers' sense of honor and reputations could not be risked.

He felt for the men who would soon leave the army. They had been "deluded" and now were to "return Home the ridicule of their Neighbors." With "their present Plumage" gone, they had to go back to work and "recollect with Poignant Grief that they themselves … work'd the mighty change."[8]

WHEN ARMSTRONG WROTE Gates on the thirtieth, his mind was on Congress's action four days before, when it had given Washington the authority to grant furloughs to the duration men and had directed that they be discharged upon conclusion of "the definitive Treaty of Peace."[9] The major knew that "a proportionable number of commissioned officers of the different grades"[10] were also going to get furloughs and would have to accept them, but he felt the policy was unjust. Though Congress was pointing to "the necessities of the States" as the reason for the action, he was not fooled. By furloughing most of the army Congress was making it impossible for the officers to have their grievances redressed: "The meaning is evident—wrest the instruments of Redress from the hands of the Officers—by removing the old Soldiers from about them and then discharge the obligations to both with a dash of the pen. Admirable policy!"[11]

The resolution regarding furloughs and discharges bothered not only Armstrong. When Washington included it in his general orders for June 2[12] the officers grew concerned and soon thereafter sent a petition to the Commander-in-chief bearing the signature of General Heath. They had expected to be paid "previous to ... being dispersed or disbanded" and had been gratified when Congress indicated that that was going to be done. But now the government was ordering immediate furloughs before it had even started settling its accounts with the soldiers and officers. If they were "compelled to leave the army without the means of defraying the debts ... necessarily incurred in the course of service," their distress would be "complete." They had not been able to "support and comfort" their families during the long war and they feared that after departing they were going to be "deprived of the ability to assist" them then, too. Seeing no sign that they would receive something for their military service, and "consequently without the least prospect of obtaining credit for even a temporary subsistence" to hold them over until they were able to "get into business," they asked whom they were to turn to.

Washington! Could he suspend or modify the order to ensure that nobody was furloughed before Congress was "apprized of the wretched situation into which the army must be plunged by a conformity to it?" Could he "on the principle of common justice ... insist that neither officer nor soldier be compelled to leave the field" before accounts were settled and notes for the remaining balances due, "including the commutation of half pay to the officers, and the gratuity of 80 dollars to the soldiers," were issued?

The officers wanted to leave "the field of glory with honour" and enough money to bring "credit to our country." They loved America and were still hopeful that she would "never look with indifference to the distresses of those of her sons who ... so essentially contributed to the establishment of Freedom, the security of property, and the rearing of an empire."[13]

Washington responded on June 6. He assured the officers of his trustworthiness and said he was aware of "the past merits and services of the army." Nobody could be more affected by "their present ineligible situation, [and] feel a keener sensibility at their distresses, or more ardently desire to alleviate or remove them" than he.

He did not mention what he had done and was continuing to do on their behalf, but he was confident that his labors were going to bear fruit, for he understood that if the states failed to provide the delegates, who had "done every thing in their power to obtain ample and compleat justice for the army," with the funds Congress had requested, "national bankruptcy and ruin" were sure to follow. The delegates' main goal now was "to enable the Financier to make the three months' payment to the army," for everybody concurred that that was "absolutely and indispensably necessary."

The general then drew their attention to an extract from a letter Morris had recently sent him, in which the Financier had indicated his intention to send notes payable in six months to the army, and added, "Three days ago, a messenger was dispatched ... to urge the necessity of forwarding these notes with the greatest possible expedition."

A couple of paragraphs later Washington let them know that he could liberally interpret Congress's orders of May 26; nobody was going to be sent home before he wished to go, and only enough officers to lead men who had accepted furloughs back home were to be released. He was bound to obey orders but furloughs were a discretionary matter, and he knew Congress was disposed to satisfy the army.

Satisfied that what he had just written would reassure the officers, Washington returned to the notes payable. He hoped they would "arrive soon" and that the army's accounts could be completely settled "in a very few days." While waiting for the notes to arrive, he would forward the officers' views to Philadelphia. They had been "expressed in such a decent, candid and affecting manner," that the delegates were certain to give them their "every mark of attention."[14]

The following day the general wrote the President of Congress and enclosed with his letter the officers' recent petition and his response. He informed him that the army's two biggest complaints were "the delay of the three months' pay ... and the want of a settlement of accounts," told him he had assured the officers that "Congress had and would attend particularly to their grievances," and notified him that he had "made some little variation respecting the furloughs, from what was at first proposed."

His report finished, he once again became the army's top advocate. "The temperate and orderly behavior of the whole Army, and particularly the accommodating spirit of the officers" designated to remain behind to command reorganized battalions, pleased him, and the delegates should "recall to mind all their former sufferings and merits" and promptly approve "their reasonable requests."[15]

ON JUNE 7 the first batch of notes reached Paymaster General John Pierce. Slowly but surely the rest would be issued.

Most of the soldiers, though, had already departed from camp or would do so very soon—

before more notes arrived.[16] The exodus began with the Maryland Battalion on the fifth. Then more soldiers from that state and ones from New Jersey and New York left on the sixth and eighth. The New Hampshire Brigade and men from two of the Massachusetts regiments also left on the eighth, but most of the latter state's regiments had to wait one to five days; their numbers were great and departure dates were arranged by county.

When the day of departure arrived, soldiers appeared with their arms and personal belongings at the grand parade ground by the Temple of Virtue early in the morning. There they were given provisions for the initial stage of their homeward march. Officers then led them out of camp and wagons carrying additional provisions and baggage rolled along behind them. When the furloughed New Englanders reached Newburgh, small boats were used to ferry them across the Hudson to the other side as sloops at the dock were loaded with the officers' belongings and gear. Some of what they had was put in crates and trunks, some was not. Once across the river, the men embarked for home using designated routes.[17]

Washington, who watched the goings-on from his headquarters, drew satisfaction from the way the disbandment was carried out. He acknowledged that the furloughs were "extremely distressing to the Officers on acct. of their want of pay," but believed that they "ha[d] been effected without any disorder and with less discontent than could possibly be expected."[18]

With the war now essentially over, Washington focused on his nation's future. The weakness of the government and the willingness of a small state like Rhode Island to cry that its sovereignty was being taken away when Congress sought greater powers had caused the troubles in the Hudson Highlands. The states had to decide whether they wanted to be one united nation or to go their own ways. They could, he stated in a circular, now "give such a tone to our Federal Government, as will enable it to answer the ends of its institution" or begin "relaxing the powers of the Union, annihilating the cement of the Confederation." If the states chose to take the latter route, they were sure to "become the sport of European politics …." The choice that states made promised to determine whether they were to "stand or fall." Only after that choice was made, were they going to be able to answer the question of "whether the Revolution must ultimately be considered as a blessing or curse …."

If the states wanted to stand, they had "to forget their local prejudices and … make those mutual concessions … requisite to the general prosperity, and in some instances … sacrifice their individual advantages to the interest of the Community." They had to allow the delegates to use the powers that they were authorized to exercise or else "every thing must very rapidly tend to Anarchy and confusion." They had to faithfully comply with Congress's "late proposals and demands" and let it "regulate and govern the general concerns of the Confederated Republic" if they themselves wanted to be happy and not see the union fall apart.

After urging the states to yield some of their authority to Philadelphia for the sake of the whole country, the general praised Congress's most recent efforts "to render compleat justice to all the Public Creditors." The general funding program adopted on April 18 was, "if not perfect, certainly the least objectionable of any that could be devised." Failure by the states to immediately ratify it would lead to "a National Bankruptcy, with all its deplorable consequences."

Debts incurred during the war had to be paid. "Let us ... as a Nation," Washington entreated the states, "be just, let us fulfil the public Contracts, which Congress had undoubtedly a right to make for the purpose of carrying on the War, with the same good faith we suppose ourselves bound to perform our private engagements."

Individuals had to sacrifice some of what they had for the common good. Weren't those who had defended the country entitled to something? "Where is the Man to be found, who wishes to remain indebted, for the defence of his own person and property, to the exertions, the bravery, and the blood of others, without making one generous effort to repay the debt of honor and of gratitude?" he asked. Where in the country could they "find any Man, or body of Men, who would not blush to stand up and propose measures, purposely calculated to rob the Soldier of his Stipend, and the Public Creditor of his due?" If "such a flagrant instance of Injustice could ever happen," Washington went on, "would it not excite the general indignation, and tend to bring down, upon the Authors of such measures, the aggravated vengeance of Heaven?"

He had given his word to the officers that "their Country would finally do them compleat and ample Justice," and he considered "the Resolutions of Congress [concerning half pay and commutation] ... as absolutely binding upon the United States, as the most solemn Acts of Confederation or Legislation." The postwar benefit was "a reasonable compensation offered by Congress, at a time when they had nothing else to give, to the Officers of the Army, for services then to be performed. It was the only means to prevent a total dereliction of the Service, It was a part of their hire. ... It was the price of their blood, and of ... Independency. ... It [was] more than a common debt. ... It [was] a debt of honour." The postwar benefit could "never be considered ... a Pension or gratuity, nor be cancelled until ... fairly discharged."

Once the general finished acting as the officers' advocate, he again focused on Congress's lack of power. He pointed out that America might still have won independence and at a lesser cost "if the resourses of the Continent could have been properly drawn forth." Too often "the distresses and disappointments" endured during the war "resulted more from a want of energy, in the Continental Government, than a deficiency of means in the particular States." Congress did not have "adequate authority." That and "a partial compliance with the Requisitions of Congress in some of the States, and ... a failure of punctuality in others" were the reasons why the government was not able to pass effective measures. And when the government could not do what had to be done, that "tended to damp the zeal of those ... more willing to exert themselves," increase "the expences of the War, and … frustrate the best concerted Plans." Washington believed that "any Army, less patient, less virtuous, and less persevering" than the one he commanded would have soon dissolved if it had had to endure such "complicated difficulties and embarrassments."

When Washington finally concluded his letter, he prayed that God "would incline the hearts of the Citizens to cultivate a spirit of subordination and obedience to Government, to entertain a brotherly affection and love for one another, for their fellow Citizens of the United States at large, and particularly for their brethren who … served in the Field."[19]

Chapter Twenty-Five

"A Foundation to Enslave This Free People"

ON JUNE 20, 1783, one day before hundreds of mutinous troops from Lancaster and Philadelphia would surround the Pennsylvania State House to demand from the state's Supreme Executive Council the pay they were due, a disgusted Walter Stewart was still thinking about events in the Hudson Highlands. "I can Assure you had you been a Spectator of the Scene," he wrote to Gates of the main army's disbandment, "your Heart would have bled for the Poor fellows who were in so disgraceful a manner turn'd off." The officers and soldiers were being sent home to save the government money and he understood that the army had to allow itself to be disbanded, but he thought the action was "Villainous."

"It was propos'd that the officers Should meet and have a general Dinner together" before they departed for home, Stewart continued, "but this Step was Oppos'd, The officers declaring they thought the present Period more Adapted to Sorrow, than to Mirth, And as Wretchedness & distress must Inevitably be the fate of many of them Shortly, they wish'd to move from their present Situation as quietly as Possible."[1] The colonel did not mention that Washington would have been the guest of honor and that perhaps some of the officers voted against having the farewell dinner because they were angry with him.[2] Stewart was not surprised by the officers' decision and was pleased that they had decided against having the dinner.[3]

TWO DAYS LATER Captain Israel Evans delivered his last sermon at the Temple of Virtue. The topic was peace.[4]

At five o'clock the following morning, a Monday, drums began beating and those men of the Massachusetts regiments who still remained at the New Windsor Cantonment began an eight-mile march over Butter Hill to West Point, where they would hereafter be stationed. The cantonment was being closed.[5]

A LITTLE MORE than a month thereafter, Alexander McDougall wrote to Henry Knox to explain how he thought the officers could get commutation, the postwar lump sum payments equal to five years' pay that the delegates had agreed upon as a substitute for half-pay pensions. Though the Scotsman had already invested much time in selling commutation to Congress, it appeared to be going nowhere in the states and he feared they were not going to provide Philadelphia with funds for it. Knox too had been actively working for commutation, getting letters and pamphlets friendly to the officers' cause into the hands of friends in Boston.

McDougall now suggested a campaign to educate the public in the eastern states. A closely tied network of correspondents and supportive printers stretching from New Hampshire to New Jersey would be set up to publish all articles that could help win commutation and general funding. The people had to be told that the officers' cause was a just one. There was no other way to secure general funding, he believed. And what if in the end Congress was not able to get the funding to pay for commutation? Well, the officers could ask their respective states to provide the benefit and the educational campaign would then have served some purpose. A number of friendly articles had already been published by *The New-York Packet* and more were yet to come, McDougall promised.[6]

The Scotsman knew that he faced great obstacles. "There are too many uninformed, and too many, who wish to bury our Claims and Services in oblivion. ... It is a little hard ... that when we have done warring with the Sword we must continue it with the Pen, against those ingrates whom we have made Kings & Princes," he complained to General St. Clair. But he was confident that they were eventually going to be successful, if they did what they were supposed to do during the campaign,[7] because "the sensible and honest part of America" supported them. If they did not get justice, they would be at fault.[8]

In the event, McDougall put a great deal of effort into making his plan work. On one occasion he asked a printer to produce in pamphlet form thirteen thousand copies of the circular letter that Washington had written to urge the states to approve the general funding plan. And when he realized that his officers' delegation had not expended all the money set aside for their stay in Philadelphia, he wanted to use the unspent sum—more than $100—to pay for additional publications. As a result of such efforts, so much material was churned out in favor of commutation that opponents of the compensation were unable to compete; articles backing their stance rarely appeared.

The publications sought to do several things. They wanted to make the general public and politicians understand that the national government was not to be feared. They hoped to convince them that the impost ought to be approved. And, most of all, they wanted the people to realize that the country was well-off enough to afford commutation and that it had to be provided to the officers as a matter of national faith.[9]

IN EARLY SEPTEMBER the Temple of Virtue and the huts once occupied by the soldiers were sold at a public auction at the building. One New York officer bought 252 huts for only a dollar apiece.[10]

By that time Washington had left Newburgh; in mid-August he had gone up and down lines of soldiers assembled before his headquarters and said good-bye.[11] Then, two months to the day of the auction, while at Rocky Hill, New Jersey, the general wrote his final orders. Though not present when they were read the following morning at a farewell ceremony before his former headquarters, he once again urged that the states put the country's interests first and provide Congress with the funds it needed. By doing so they would, among other things, assure his officers and soldiers that they were to receive "considerable assistance in recommencing their civil occupations." But if the states did not do as he wished, he still wanted his men to be good citizens no matter how aggrieved they felt.[12]

The officers who remained in the Hudson Highlands appointed a committee of three—McDougall, Knox, and Pickering—to draft a reply to Washington's farewell address. New York had already rejected commutation, so at this time they did not expect to get "the promised rewards of their long, severe and dangerous services" and therefore were bitter. However, they did not blame Washington. The officers knew he had made "exertions in favor of the troops" and really did not have the power to ensure that they received the compensation they were due.

Although they were very disappointed by the "ingratitude of the people," they planned to remain patriotic and wait to receive justice in the future. They were not going to do anything dishonorable. They regretted that not everybody supported the "salutary measures" devised by the government, but still hoped that time might erase "the prejudices of the misinformed" that prevented them from receiving their just rewards. They did not want to see "the reputation, the honor and dignity of the great and respectable majority of the States" stained because of "the disingenuousness of a few."[13]

During the rest of November and December the brighter day that Washington had anticipated continued its inexorable approach. On November 25 the last British troops left New York and American regiments moved into the city. Soon thereafter, on December 4, a farewell dinner for the general was held in the long dining room on the second floor of the fine Fraunces' Tavern. Finally, at twelve o'clock, December 23, 1783, Washington resigned as Commander-in-chief of the Continental Army.

Knox assumed command and continued the disbandment. On January 3, 1784, he reported that he had fewer than seven hundred men. Less than two weeks later Congress ratified the final peace treaty and then, in June, it decided to reduce his army to a skeleton force, just enough soldiers—eighty privates—and officers to guard supplies.[14]

MANY NEW ENGLAND town meetings and newspapers, meanwhile, had been denouncing the Commutation Act,[15] and state ratification of the impost would continue to lag. The public had not been told about the grant of half pay until two or three years after the fact. Commutation could not become law because not enough state delegations had voted for it. The officers had attempted to extort money from Congress. They were guiltier of war profiteering than civilians and had suffered fewer hardships. They wanted to sit on their duffs and be supported by hardworking citizens. The government had rewarded the officers because it wanted them to be on its side when it started acting despotically. Those were only some of the charges.

Massachusetts was one state where much opposition to commutation and the impost existed. After its delegates voted in favor of postwar lump sum payments to the officers, the disapproving Massachusetts legislature changed the makeup of its representation in Philadelphia and, on July 11, 1783, informed Congress that the benefit was causing unrest in the state. It would be difficult for officers returning to their state to feel welcome; commutation was seen by their fellow citizens as "more than an adequate reward for their services and inconsistent with that equality which ought to subsist among citizens of free and republican states ... a measure ... calculated to raise and exalt some citizens in wealth and grandeur, to the injury and oppression of others."[16] The state in no way wanted to see the union dissolve but "the extraordinary grants and allowances which Congress ... thought proper to make to their civil and military officers ... produced ... effects in their commonwealth ... of a threatening aspect."[17] And because of commutation the impost could not be adopted, although the legislature would consider it again the next time it met.

Eventually, though, opposition to commutation and the impost subsided. Robert Morris personally intervened to help convince the legislature to ratify the impost, forwarding to Governor Hancock in September passages from two of John Adams's diplomatic dispatches that stressed how crucial sufficient funding of Congress was for America's ability to endure as a strong and just nation.

By late October Rufus Putnam, who had been meeting daily with people from around Boston, sensed that opposition to commutation was diminishing. Still, in many rural towns that fall and during the winter the measure remained unacceptable. At town meetings people offered essentially the same arguments against it as had been made in the past, though in different forms, and instructed their representatives to do what they could to bring about its repeal and revocation of or changes to the impost.

But opposition was not really quelled until May 1784. Boston can be credited with playing a big role in ending it. In February it and all the other Suffolk County towns had been invited to convene in Dedham. There the towns opposed to the measures would decide what action to take. Boston, however, was not interested in attending such a convention, and in a letter sent in response to the invitation made that perfectly clear; its town meeting did not favor taking any actions against commutation and the impost. The proposed convention was a "fruitless design of disturbing the tranquility of the State,"[18] and because commutation and pay arrears were being settled by issuing certificates that had little real value in specie, the cost was not great.

One patriot who played a key role in bringing Boston and Massachusetts around was Samuel Adams. Congress, he said, had the right to adopt the Commutation Act and they had to honor their commitment to pay the soldiers who had fought for liberty. This was a matter of public faith.

Connecticut residents were the harshest critics of commutation. A strongly held view was that it rewarded the officer at the expense of the common soldier. The latter, a "Constant Customer" of the *Connecticut Courant and Weekly Intelligencer* had complained in May 1783, would "be obliged to labor the remainder of his life for the support of his officer in ease and affluence."[19]

Throughout the state that summer one meeting after another took place. Wherever townspeople gathered, they blasted commutation. It did not matter whether they met in Canaan, Winsted, Wethersfield, Simsbury, Hartford, Southington, or New London. In the hill towns, the valley towns, and the coastal towns the measure was unwelcome.

At an August town meeting in Farmington attendees called commutation "unjust, impolitic, oppressive to the people, subversive to the principles of a republican government, and exceedingly dangerous when drawn into precedent."[20] That the officers had forced Congress to promise them pensions by threatening to resign en masse when the American cause appeared to be in the greatest peril showed that they were hellbent on "making their fortunes, whatever distresses it might occasion to the people."[21] And some people claimed that a pension or commutation promised to turn the officers into "idle drones in the state hive ... (and) lay a foundation to enslave this free people."[22]

By September the situation was said to be approaching "general anarchy."[23] In Wethersfield a colonel observed that "business [was] conducted in Town-Meeting by passion prejudice without light, reason, or common decency." Everything was "clamor hubbub noise and confusion."[24] The people of Connecticut, another observer reported, were "growing turbulent and ungovernable," ignoring laws and insulting public officials. "The constitution [was] tottering to the foundation." The state was "in more danger now, than when General Howe landed upon Long Island with 30,000 men," he believed. So he appealed to the officers to "do much ... do all that is necessary to save us from ruin," to compromise, to give up commutation. If they did not, he predicted, Connecticut would become "a poor, contemptible state." She would be "without credit ... reputation ... [and] law." She would be "torn with factions [and] distracted in her councils." She would, "like Carthage of old, too jealous of power ... banish her supporters and defenders and finally fall a prey to her own intrigues or the ambition of her neighbors."[25]

Eventually, seeing that what was happening in Farmington and Wethersfield basically amounted to mob rule and understanding that frightened investors were moving their cash and certificates out of the state to New York, some in the General Assembly who stood against commutation reluctantly accepted it. By late September, when the Grand Convention met in Middletown, the Assembly was divided; the Senate favored commutation and the impost, while the House opposed them.

The biggest news coming from that convention was Governor Jonathan Trumbull's decision not to serve beyond the end of his current term. In his announcement the governor made clear, without specifically saying so, that he wanted members of both houses to do right by the army and the nation, calling on them to "pay the strictest attention to all the sacred rules of justice and equity, by a faithful observance and fulfillment of all public as well as private engagements." An accepted truth was that "virtue exalteth a nation, but sin and evil workings are the destruction of a people."[26]

In December representatives from twenty towns assembled again in Middletown to consider overriding commutation and the impost; however, they took no substantive action. Arguments against commutation continued to be made after that, but a steady decline in the intensity of the opposition became apparent, and in the spring of 1784 quiet prevailed as people saw that neither their state nor Congress could or would take any significant steps to stop it. And no matter how much people at town meetings in Massachusetts and Connecticut expressed their ire over commutation, Robert Morris was making their arguments moot; he and others were settling accounts and issuing certificates to the soldiers and officers.

IN ORDER TO pay for commutation Congress had to have money. Some of the money could come from the impost, if all the states ratified it. The delegates believed that all would vote for it, and most of them did do so without undue delay. Connecticut, though, held out until the spring of 1784; Rhode Island did not give in until 1785; and Georgia waited until 1786.

New York then remained the only state preventing the impost from becoming law. The Senate had voted against it in 1785, but the state finally agreed to go along with the measure in 1786; however, attached to its approval were such tough conditions that Congress turned down the state's support. As a result, Pennsylvania was relieved of any pressure to drop the conditions it wanted met before giving its okay to the tax bill; that state and Delaware had agreed to ratify the impost, but only after all the others had approved it. Any reason for Congress to be optimistic about getting the impost ratified by all the states had disappeared within four years of the war's end.[27]

Those opposed to the impost generally feared that if they granted greater taxation authority to Congress, the people's liberties would be endangered. New York's opposition, though, was the result of bitterness. In one case, the bitterness was personal; New Yorker Abraham Yates, Jr., had been rejected by Robert Morris for a position as receiver of Continental taxes for his state, so he took out his anger on the Financier by producing essays that effectively attacked the desired impost. In other cases, the bitterness was directed towards the government or the country; Congress had not helped the state reclaim Vermont, and many New York officials, including Governor George Clinton, felt that their state had made greater contributions to the Revolution than had the other twelve.[28]

ACCORDING TO THE Paymaster General, 2,480 officers were found to be eligible for the half-pay pension or commutation. They did not benefit much from their eligibility, though. Congress delayed greatly in making any provision for redemption of the commutation certificates they received and, as a result, the officers were not able to redeem them until the beginning of 1791. By that year most of the certificates were already in the hands of speculators; they had quickly depreciated after they had been issued to the officers, and from 1784 to 1791 many were sold at only a fraction of their face value.[29]

The issue of pensions for Revolutionary War veterans was not really totally resolved for a long time. In the fall of 1789 Congress relieved the states of their responsibility for invalid pensions, and subsequently it expanded the rolls of veterans who could qualify for them.

Later, in March 1818, the delegates passed legislation to enable veterans other than invalids to also apply for pensions. These were lifelong pensions that both officers and soldiers who had served in the Continental Army could apply for, provided they had served for nine months or until the war's conclusion *and were in need of assistance*. The number of applicants for these pensions, which were also available to men who had served in the navy, was great, and charges were made that some of those pleading poverty did not really need help. Consequently, in 1820 Congress passed additional legislation requiring applicants to provide the secretary of war with proof that they were in need.

The result of the delegates' action was that too many names were removed from the list of those scheduled to get benefits. So in 1823 more legislation was passed to ensure that truly needy veterans who had been rejected for pensions got what they were entitled to receive.

That would not be enough to satisfy many of the still surviving officers, however. In January 1826 a congressional committee reported that officers from five states had met in Philadelphia and decided to petition Congress. The officers believed their country owed them a "reward for their services and sacrifices." They had been waiting "for a period … long and unreasonable" and now were "far advanced in their old age, the youngest among them being within a year or two of seventy."

Despite the petition they had to wait some more. Finally, on May 15, 1828, at President John Quincy Adams's urging, Congress approved a pension for those who had served in the Continental Army for the duration of the war. Eligible veterans stood to get full pay for the rest of their lives. But officers were limited in how much they could receive; none would be entitled to collect more than what a captain was paid. Veterans did *not* have to prove they were in need of assistance. By the end of that year, though, only about eight-hundred-fifty duration veterans were still alive to draw pensions.

Four years later Congress passed another act that allowed anyone who had served for two years or longer to receive the same full-pay lifelong pension. If a veteran had served at least six months but less than two years, he received a less generous pension. This act covered not only those who had served in the Continental Army and Navy, but also members of state militias and voluntary military organizations. Once again a veteran did not have to demonstrate need to be eligible for a pension.

Additional acts were passed the following decades, but the emphasis then was to extend benefits to the widows of Revolutionary War veterans.[30]

THE TREATMENT THE officers received during the war, and in the years immediately following its conclusion, proved that the country needed a strong national government—something the Articles of Confederation did not provide for, but the Constitution later did. Under the Articles of Confederation the power of the purse resided in the state legislatures. That situation changed once the states ratified the Constitution: they granted the national government—Congress—the right to raise revenue by directly taxing the American people.

The ratification of the Constitution in 1788 and the government's assumption of all Revolutionary War debts from the states in 1790 should have improved the officers' chances for receiving justice but, as Washington had noted in his speech on March 15, 1783, large legislative bodies are slow in acting. As one congress replaced another from 1790 until mid-1828, when the legislators approved a pension for all duration men, former officers in Washington's army grew old or died. In the end more than a few of the officers must have considered their country ungrateful and, to borrow Washington's words, seen themselves as "the only sufferers by this revolution ... retiring from the Field ... to grow old in poverty wretchedness and contempt."[31]

One officer who actually benefited from his participation in "this revolution" and certainly never became the object of "contempt," though, was George Washington. Americans will always remember him most for his victory over the British in the war and his ascension to the presidency, but he also deserves to be honored for his role in ending the Newburgh Conspiracy. If he had not appeared unexpectedly at the Temple of Virtue on March 15, 1783, read some prepared statements, taken out a letter from a delegate who was friendly towards the army, struggled to make out what was written in it, removed a pair of small reading glasses from his inside coat pocket, and apologetically informed the assembled officers that he was growing blind in the service to his country, evoking their sympathy and breaking up a storm that might have brought on a period of "Civil horror" for America, the new American republic might have died soon after it had been born.

From that day forth there have been no assaults on the principle of civilian control of the military. Benjamin Lincoln, speaking in 1798 about Washington's actions to end the Newburgh Conspiracy, supposedly remarked about that difficult period that "*then* he trembled for his country" and that "no other man could have saved it."[32] Former aide David Cobb, writing in 1825 of the events that had transpired more than four decades earlier, paid Washington a similar tribute: "I have ever consider'd that the United States are indebted for their Republican form of Government, solely to the firm & determine'd Republicanism of George Washington at this time."[33]

Afterword

NOT LONG AFTER George Washington put an end to the Newburgh Conspiracy, on April 29, 1783, John Armstrong wrote Horatio Gates. He saw that they had no chance of reviving the plot. "It is now ... too late," he wrote to Gates, who was in Virginia with his sick wife. "The soldiery are anxious to disperse, no ties, no promises will hold them longer, and with them will every loitering hope of ours break also." That was too bad because word from Colonel Ogden was that the army viewed "with horror and regret ... the mistaken step" of backing down on March 15; the officers felt "like contemptible penitents who have sinned beyond the prospect of salvation." They wanted "to have it to do over again," but peace had turned the soldiers' thoughts to home.

So who had caused the plot's collapse? Colonel Brooks! According to Ogden, he had been sent back from Philadelphia to the officers in the Hudson Highlands "to prepare their minds for some manly, vigorous Association with the other public Creditors." Rather than do that, though, "the timid Wretch" never revealed the plan to the officers. Instead he "betray'd it to the Commander in Chief, who ... was not to have been consulted 'till some later period."[1]

Were Ogden and Armstrong correct in naming Brooks as the person who caused the plot's collapse? Timothy Pickering certainly believed so. When he wrote Gates on May 28, he said he was inclined to think that what Ogden had said was true, that Brooks had betrayed the officers. Pickering had been the one to suggest that the Massachusetts colonel provide the officers in the Hudson Highlands with information not included in the letter McDougall and Ogden had written to Knox on the eighth of February. He did not say what that information was, but he almost certainly was referring to the plan to prepare the angry army for a union with other public creditors to force reluctant delegates and state legislatures to give Congress the taxation authority it needed to obtain revenue and redress their grievances. Brooks, though, did not provide the officers with that information. Instead he "with no little hesitation gave a recital of matters already mentioned in the letter with no addition of consequence."

The colonel had been "doubtless closetted by ____ _____ and ____ _____; and … too much influenced by their opinions, and made to believe that the public good required the concealment," Pickering opined. He was, after all, someone with "a high sense of honor."[2]

In addition to what Armstrong and Pickering wrote about Brooks's role in causing the plot to collapse, a memoir of the Massachusetts colonel that was written by one of his descendants portrays him as one of the key figures in helping Washington snuff out the conspiracy.[3] And the colonel was close to the Commander-in-chief,[4] so he certainly could have disclosed the plot to him.

Another possibility is that Brooks disclosed the plot to Knox, and the Massachusetts general then passed on the information to Washington. Rufus King, when describing a conversation he had with William Duer in October 1788, wrote, "Knox is said to have acquired some information on the subject [the plot] and to have communicated it to the Comr. in chief before the publication of the first address to the Army. … The manner in wh. he acquired information was such that the communication thereof to the Genl. gave universal dissatisfaction to the conspirators."[5] That last statement by King appears to indicate that Brooks was the person who disclosed the plot to Knox. Wouldn't the conspirators have been especially dissatisfied if someone considered one of their own, Brooks, had done so?

ABOUT ONE MONTH after Armstrong revealed to Gates what he had learned from Colonel Ogden about Brooks's role in the collapse of the plot, the major wrote another letter for the general. Still upset over how the events in the Hudson Highlands had played out, he called his fellow officers "fools and Rascals." McDougall, who had left Philadelphia in mid-May, would try to make them see that they had erred, that they had let an opportunity to achieve happiness and respectability slip away, but what they really needed, Armstrong felt, was a bold leader. If the men wanted to see their grievances get redressed, they needed someone like Anthony Wayne, not Washington, to lead them. Washington was just "the Illustrissimo of the age" and "of all his illustrious foibles … the affectation of Zeal in a cause he strove so anxiously to damn" was, in Armstrong's mind, "the most ridiculous; and like the lies of Falstaff, or Falstaff himself … gross and palpable."[6]

IN LATE JUNE 1783 Gates wrote Armstrong to relate what he had written to "an old friend and an honest man," Reverend William Gordon; Gordon had sent him a letter asking about "the secret history of the anonymous letters, etc." He believed "they were connected with some great financial arrangements." Claiming that he had "answered [Gordon's inquiry] frankly," Gates said, "Stewart was a kind of agent from our friends in congress and in the administration, with no object … beyond that of getting the army to co-operate with the civil creditors, as the way most likely for both to obtain justice." Their purpose was "to produce a strong remonstrance to Congress in favor of the object prayed for in a former one; and … the conjecture, that it was meant to offer the crown to Caesar, was without any foundation."[7]

MORE THAN FIVE years later, William Duer provided Rufus King with his views on the events in the Hudson Highlands. King subsequently summarized them in a written statement. Most of the officers, King wrote, did not look forward to the "arrival of peace and the approaching dissolution of the army." They thought the future offered them "a prospect of obscurity if not of actual misery. The American governments were not favorable to their claims. Their respectability wd. be lost by separation and their pretensions derided. They were without wealth or family influence and their military situation was more inviting and pleasant than any that they cd. expect or hope." Consequently, they sought "to perpetuate that situation or procure one more eligible for this purpose."[8]

BY LATE FEBRUARY 1797 Washington viewed the events of March 1783 with less alarm. Not wanting his strong denunciation of the Newburgh Addresses to hurt Armstrong's future prospects, he sent him a letter, in which he admitted that at the time he had written his speech he did not know the young major was the author of the addresses. Later he came to believe that "the object of the author was just, honorable and friendly to the country, though the means suggested by him were certainly liable to much misunderstanding and abuse."[9]

IN JANUARY 1820, almost four decades after the Newburgh Conspiracy had ended, Armstrong, using the pen name "John Montgars"—in part to ensure an "impartiality wholly uninfluenced by the name of the applicant"—wrote from New York to ask Pickering about it. He was working on a book and, he said, opinions on the events varied a great deal.[10]

Some believed that the army officers had a "deliberate and studied plan, to break down the civil authority and to erect on its ruins, a military despotism, and that it required the vast influence of Gen. Washington to prevent this dreadful catastrophe." Their view apparently was based on some things written in the addresses, the advice the officers gave in their resolutions after Washington's speech on the fifteenth, and "the acrimony with which the General speaks of the designs of the writer."

Another possibility was that "the clamor was altogether artificial and employed only to give a sort of political and moral finishing to the character of Washington and the army." Those who believed this was the case based their views on the fact that the writer was not punished for his actions, that he enjoyed "the continued friendship and confidence" of high-ranking officers while the army was intact and that later he was given a "succession of high political trusts." Montgars acknowledged that those were "striking ... facts," but not ones "sufficient to justify the conclusion, that a man of Washington's habitual dignity and uprightness, would connive at a pantomime of the kind alledged and much less that he would make himself the Punchinello of the shew."[11]

A third possibility was that "the letters were projected and written merely as auxiliaries to the fiscal measures of that day." This explanation was the most credible one, Montgars thought, since it was based on "some highly important and acknowledged facts Viz: the derangement in the public finances; —the fears and sufferings of public creditors, civil and military; the recommendation of a national impost by Congress as the only efficient means of complying with the public engagements; the adoption of this measure, by nine states out of the twelve and the very pertinacious and highly censurable rejection of it by Rhode Island." Besides those facts, there were ones "less known ... particularly the mission to the army of Col. W. Stewart ... and the representations made by him, of the prevailing sentiment of Congress and of the Dept. of finance, on the necessity of the army's *speaking* a more decisive language than had been hitherto held."[12]

Montgars then explained why "such importance" was attached to the officers' actions, which he considered "harmless" and well-intentioned: As the plan was "maturing," a letter was sent to Washington by a Virginia delegate, "advising him, that a conspiracy of the worst character, having for object the demolition of our free Constitution and the destruction of the General's authority, was in embryo and would shew itself in some overt act and that Robert and Gouverneur Morris and Alexander Hamilton were at the bottom of the plan."

The delegate, whom Montgars misidentified as "Mr. [Samuel] Hardy," meant well but had reasoned wrongly. His letter "led to suspicions, which ought never to have been excited." Since Washington held him in high regard, though, he could not ignore his warning. So, "as the first address appeared, it was identified with the schemes of the supposed conspirators and measures were immediately taken to stigmatise the author and defeat the advice he had given." Hence, when the officers met on the fifteenth, the general gave "a speech, strongly marked with suspicion of the designs of the writer or writers." He also read the delegate's letter, or some of it, including the part about the conspiracy. "Upon this, were founded the measures subsequently taken by the officers."[13]

Of course, Montgars was incorrect in his final assertion. Although Washington did read some of Joseph Jones's letter at the meeting of the officers, he certainly did not read what his friend had written about a conspiracy being hatched in Philadelphia.[14]

Soon after making that mistake, Montgars concluded his letter with an apology for its length.

He had gone on for so long only because he had to know what Pickering recalled about the events so he could "see truth prevail."[15]

How much the first explanation of the events bothered Armstrong became clear three years later, after Supreme Court Justice William Johnson wrote an account of Nathanael Greene's life, in which he charged that Gouverneur Morris had written the addresses as part of "the boldest and most portentous intrigue ... that ever threatened the liberties of this country," one designed to end in "the substitution of a *military despotism* for our present free institutions," one more extensive and dangerous than historians seemed to realize.[16]

This scandalous charge Armstrong could not let go unchallenged. Morris had about as much to do with writing the addresses "as he had in writing Solomon's Song, or the Psalms of David." Yes, he wanted Congress strengthened and he wished to use the army's influence. But that did not make him a conspirator! Morris was too smart to get involved in the type of conspiracy described. And although an eloquent writer, he was not capable of arousing the passions. He also was not the type "to mount a breach, or ... to suffer martyrdom for any system, religious or political."

And the army's influence was sought solely to ensure that the officers, soldiers, and public creditors were paid what they were owed, not to establish a sort of military despotism. What had really happened was very "far from being an attempt to close the war in usurpation and despotism." It was "an honest and manly, though perhaps indiscreet endeavor, to support public credit, and do justice to a long-suffering, patient, and gallant soldiery."

Upon his return to the Hudson Highlands, Walter Stewart was tasked with "drawing the attention of the army to the political crisis ... fast approaching, and to the course of proceeding under it, which would be most proper for them to adopt." While performing this task, "Stewart was frank, honest, assiduous; he saw all grades, and communicated freely with *all*, and whether justly or not, was under the most solemn conviction, that the creed of the army, *without a single exception*, was settled on three points: —1st. That they would look to the national government alone for compensation: 2d. That in prosecuting their claims, they would make common cause with the civil creditors of the Union: and 3d. That they would neither solicit nor accept furloughs, till the issue of the new appeal, to be made to the wisdom and justice of the States, should be distinctly known and officially promulgated."

Armstrong explained that the army had not publicly announced those sentiments because news of peace gave most of the men "some new reason for confiding in the promises of the public." Soon thereafter, though, as they watched and listened to "the partisans of State sovereignty," they understood that the arrival of peace actually made it less likely they were going to receive justice.

The officers had been summoned for a meeting to consider Ogden and McDougall's report, which supposedly indicated that the situation in Philadelphia boded ill for the officers' mission there, and to adopt some resolutions that could be forwarded to the general and to supportive delegates so they would have "a new and powerful lever" to use against the two states opposed to the impost. In order to ensure that their meeting was productive they needed "the interposition of a hand, which should touch with some ability the several chords of sympathy and feeling that belonged to the case." Without that the deliberations were certain to lack "tone and energy. ... They would be a dead letter." And so Major Armstrong was chosen to write the address.

In the last part of his review Armstrong focused on the conduct of Washington. As he had done when he wrote to Pickering under the name Montgars, he maintained that the general was greatly influenced by "a letter from a southern correspondent" warning of a most dangerous plot being hatched by the Financier, his assistant, and Hamilton. "Under its impulse, the general identified the *address* with the machinations of his enemies; ascribed it to the pen of one or more of the imaginary triumvirate, and denounced it as the first step in ... a deep and dangerous conspiracy." He then read the letter to the officers at the Temple of Virtue as "testimony ... that a conspiracy against the liberties of the country did exist."

But the charges made by the writer, who this time is identified in a footnote as (John) Harvie, were "entirely unsupported by any auxiliary testimony from the seat of government, and ... utterly unfounded in the facts it assumed," Armstrong insisted. Also, hadn't Washington later changed his mind about whether a dangerous plot was being hatched? Would he have become close friends with Robert Morris and made him a counselor if he had not? Would he have made Gouverneur Morris an ambassador to France and Alexander Hamilton a secretary of the treasury? Would he have written anything like the 1797 letter to Armstrong?[17]

Armstrong's claim that no conspiracy was afoot and that what he and his collaborators were doing posed no danger to the country may be viewed with a skeptical eye. Three years after Armstrong wrote his review of Johnson's book, Dr. James Thacher related to Timothy Pickering that Dr. Eustis, who "was in the secret," had told him of another letter written by the major. This one had been written after nothing positive had been achieved from his first two addresses and was "much worse" than those letters, but fortunately his friends were against publishing it and "finding himself already in trouble he deemed it most prudent to suppress it." Dr. Thacher believed that "had Armstrong met with much encouragement he would have been the means of effecting nearly the destruction of the Army and our country."[18]

However, a long letter from Brooks to Pickering, written eight months after Armstrong's review of Johnson's book appeared, can be seen as evidence that a military coup was not being plotted. "Judge Johnson's hypothesis, notwithstanding Mr. Gouverneur Morris's letters to General Green, is destitute of support. ... The thing was impossible, as the Judge ought to have seen." Morris was not with the officers in the Hudson Highlands when the two anonymous addresses were being written, copied and circulated; he was in Philadelphia.[19] That geographical separation, Brooks implied, precluded the possibility that nationalist politicians and officers were conspiring to replace the civilian leaders of the government with military rulers.

Ebenezer Huntington also thought no coup was being planned by anybody in Philadelphia but probably felt Armstrong's motives for writing the anonymous addresses were not innocent. Huntington had been away in Connecticut when they appeared and the meeting of the officers took place, but he learned all the details after he returned to West Point. He could not recall having "ever heard of any plot to overturn the republican institutions of our Country at that period … excepting so far as we may apply that term to the anonymous letters." He was sorry that the respected financier, his assistant, and Hamilton had been accused "without … proof."[20]

Even if no coup or mutiny was being planned before Washington's unexpected appearance at the Temple of Virtue, wouldn't one or the other have followed if the Commander-in-chief had not succeeded in soothing the officers? Brooks did not think so. He felt those behind the Newburgh Addresses "must have perceived how hazardous an enterprise it would be for the army to exact justice of Congress at the point of the bayonet." Making the same point Putnam had made in his answer to the addresses, Brooks emphasized that by threatening not to disband until it received justice the army "would find its situation desperate" and have to "either effect its object, or succumb & be punished as mutineers or rebels." And if it achieved its objective, "Ambition & cupidity would be generated, the justice first claimed lost sight of, & ultimately the destiny of an army, hitherto docile & virtuous, surrendered to the will of a popular Chief."

Though "the army's revolt, as recommended by the anonymous writer … was contemplated by some not only as feasible, but to be affected with the greatest facility," he believed "on that point an extreme degree of delusion existed." While some contended that "the interests of the individuals composing the army were the same, & that a sense of those common interests was so lively & strong as to form a bond of union that would continue indissoluble through all the vicissitudes of fortune until their demands were fully satisfied," Brooks said "nothing could have been more fallacious."

And what if Washington had decided to side with the conspirators? Brooks doubted that that would have been enough to tip the scales in favor of staging a coup. "Even among the officers, whose situations were similar," he wrote, "there could have been no union in the pursuit of an object of ever doubtful legitimacy: Washington himself could not have effected it." No matter how much the political situation in Philadelphia angered both officers and soldiers, they were more drawn towards their loved ones and "to whose society they were anxiously wishing to be restored" than to the cause of the Newburgh conspirators. Those officers willing to lead a mutiny or stage a coup needed the support of soldiers, but any call for them to rise up and seek justice at the ends of their bayonets "would have been but the watch word for them to abandon their veteran companions, & return to their friends & firesides."

The plotters could have looked to the southern army for help, but the men there were militia, "a species of force well adapted to the desultory mode of warfare pursued in the southern States, but composed of elements impossible to unite in the project recommended by the author of the Newburgh letters." Also, the "able, brave, ambitious & poor" commander of that army, General Greene, who was seen at the time of the conspiracy as someone who "possessed all the requisite qualities for great & daring enterprise," had no interest in becoming a part of the conspiracy; when he answered the feeler that Gouverneur Morris had sent in February 1783 to determine how receptive the general was to the nationalists' scheme, he displayed a "pulse indicative of greater sanity & firmness than might have been apprehended."[21]

It is hard to believe that the officers would have been anxious to unite with their troops to move against the government. The officers and soldiers generally came from different backgrounds, the former being better off financially and enjoying greater social status than the latter. In fact, one historian states that after 1776 the Continental Army's soldiery was made up mostly of the poor, vagrants, prisoners of war, indentured servants, slaves, and good-for-nothings. Their poverty and lack of status did not endear them to the officers. Many officers harshly disciplined their soldiers and regarded them as a "vulgar herd." They did not want to do anything to endanger their own positions in society, and if they had turned to their soldiers to force Congress and the state legislatures to redress their grievances, convulsions could have resulted and given those men a real understanding of the power they were able to exercise. Might they then have decided to use their bayonets against the officers who were part of the established social order?[22]

Even if the officers had been anxious to turn to their soldiers, they would not have found them willing to join forces to move against the government. In addition to the point made by Brooks, that both were anxious to return to their families, soldiers had not been promised a half-pay pension or commutation, and the idea of providing the officers with such generous postwar compensation was not something they liked.[23]

Writing to Pickering long after the war had ended, William Hull also made clear that he did not think a coup could have been effected: "An attempt to use the force of the remnant of the army in rebellion against the government of our country, would have been *absurd*, because success was too impracticable to be hoped for."[24]

But even if Brooks and Hull were right in saying that the idea of the officers using force to get what they wanted from the government was impracticable, General Washington could not afford to take any chances; he had to act decisively. The Newburgh conspirators' actions did pose a danger to the country. As Nathanael Greene noted when he made clear to Gouverneur Morris that he had no intention of becoming involved in the plot, the conspirators' plan could unleash some unforeseen chain of events and before they knew it cause the matter to spin violently out of control.[25] And, as Washington had observed to Hamilton after he ended the conspiracy, "The army is a dangerous instrument to play with."[26]

Acknowledgments

I recognize that many people helped make this book possible. I am particularly indebted to all the men and women who work behind the reference desk at the Henderson County Library in Hendersonville, North Carolina. When I had to use their interlibrary loan service to obtain individual books or multivolume sets of letters or papers from university and college libraries, they always eagerly forwarded my requests. Among the past and present workers there I especially want to thank Chris Kersten, Tony Cable, Simon T. Coultas, Debbie Huber, and Michele von Boeck. They helped me almost from the very beginning of this book project, not only forwarding my requests but also providing me with much assistance when I had computer problems.

I also want to thank the Massachusetts Historical Society, the New-York Historical Society, and the Gilder Lehrman Institute of American History. Through their courtesy I was allowed to use and quote from numerous collections of letters and other documents: the microfilm edition of the *Timothy Pickering Papers* and the Alexander Calvin and Ellen Morton Washburn Collection (the Massachusetts Historical Society); the *Alexander McDougall Papers*, MS 410, and the *Horatio Gates Papers*, MS 240 (the New-York Historical Society); and the *Henry Knox Papers* (the Gilder Lehrman Institute of American History). Ms. Anna Cook and Ms. Elaine M. Grublin helped me with my requests for permission to quote from the Massachusetts Historical Society's collections. Mr. Ted O'Reilly did the same for me when I approached the New-York Historical Society. And Mr. Tom Mullusky took care of that matter when I contacted the Gilder Lehrman Institute of American History.

In regard to the *Henry Knox Papers*, I want to note that I actually received photocopies of the letters I needed from Ms. Heather Merrill of the Massachusetts Historical Society, although the Gilder Lehrman Institute of American History was the place I had to contact to get permission to quote from them. The number of letters I used from that collection was significant and most of them were somewhat long, so Ms. Merrill had to spend much time photocopying them, and I appreciate her efforts to fill my requests.

Two more people whom I want to recognize are Tal Nadan of the New York Public Library and John Overholt of the Houghton Library at Harvard University. They provided with some information for citations that appear in the notes section in the back of the book.

Others deserving my gratitude are the many people who helped me when I visited the Hudson Highlands. Michael McGurty at the New Windsor Cantonment provided me with much information on the soldiers' huts and later, after I returned to North Carolina, answered several questions I had concerning the Temple of Virtue. Mel Johnson took time out from his schedule at George Washington's Headquarters at Newburgh to meet with me and answer questions I had about that site, the general, and the plot. Ms. Johanna Porr and Ms. Lynette Scherer gave me tours of the building and provided me with interesting tidbits concerning its various rooms and its occupants. Rita Forrester and Heather H. Georghiou of the Newburgh Free Library enthusiastically helped me when I needed to search through their material relating to the Revolutionary War.

Three more people who should be mentioned are Dr. Judith Miller and Jennifer Brathovde at the Library of Congress, and Karie Diethorn at Independence National Historic Park. They essentially steered me in right directions for some of my research.

Finally, I want to thank Larry Branscum, Mark Burdette, Amy Rogers, and Andrew Reed. Larry and Mark read the first draft of my manuscript and told me what its strengths and weaknesses were, thus giving me a good idea where revisions needed to be made. Amy and Andrew, critiquers for the North Carolina Writers' Network, then read my revised manuscripts and provided me with professional advice on what I needed to do to make it publishable. And I am indebted to Barbara Stone, who was most diligent in creating an index for this complex book.

Illustrations

We gratefully acknowlege the New York Public Library for its permission to use these images from the Print Collection and the Thomas Addis Emmet Collection of Illustrations Relating to the American Revolution and Early United States History.

P. 6	Gen. George Washington	Emmet Collection, Miriam and Ira D. Wallach Division of Art, Prints and Photographs, The New York Public Library, Astor, Lenox and Tilden Foundations.
P. 19	Robert Morris	Print Collection, Miriam and Ira D. Wallach Division of Art, Prints and Photographs, The New York Public Library, Astor, Lenox and Tilden Foundations.
P. 25	Gouverneur Morris	Print Collection, Miriam and Ira D. Wallach Division of Art, Prints and Photographs, The New York Public Library, Astor, Lenox and Tilden Foundations.
P. 58	Col. Walter Stewart	Emmet Collection, Miriam and Ira D. Wallach Division of Art, Prints and Photographs, The New York Public Library, Astor, Lenox and Tilden Foundations.
P. 86	Gen. Henry Knox	Emmet Collection, Miriam and Ira D. Wallach Division of Art, Prints and Photographs, The New York Public Library, Astor, Lenox and Tilden Foundations.
P. 110	Gen. Alexander MacDougall	Emmet Collection, Miriam and Ira D. Wallach Division of Art, Prints and Photographs, The New York Public Library, Astor, Lenox and Tilden Foundations.

| P. 166 | Alexander Hamilton | Print Collection, Miriam and Ira D. Wallach Division of Art, Prints and Photographs, The New York Public Library, Astor, Lenox and Tilden Foundations. |
| P. 194 | Gen. Horatio Gates | Emmet Collection, Miriam and Ira D. Wallach Division of Art, Prints and Photographs, The New York Public Library, Astor, Lenox and Tilden Foundations. |

The following images are used by permission of the Library of Congress Prints and Photographs Division, Washington, D.C. 20540.

P. x & back cover	*Washington's headquarters, Newburgh, N.Y.* Photographic print, ca. 1906. Courtesy Library of Congress, Prints & Photographs Division, Detroit Publishing Company Collection, Washington, D.C. 20540.
P. 232 & front cover	*George Washington, Esq'r. - Americanischer Generalissimus.* Etching, 1777-1778, unattributed artist. Courtesy Library of Congress Prints and Photographs Division, Washington, D.C. 20540.
P. 262	*View Near Hudson* of Newburgh, NY. Painted by William Guy Wall, engraved by John Hill, etcher, published by Henry I. Megarey, New York. Courtesy Library of Congress Prints and Photographs Division, Washington, D.C. 20540
Front cover	*The state-house in Philadelphia 1776.* Engraved by J. Serz. Published by Janentzky & Co., 1125 Chestnut Str., [1873], c1873. Courtesy Library of Congress Prints and Photographs Division, Washington, D.C. 20540.
P. 123	Colonel John Brooks. The original painting (artist unknown) is in The Huntington Library, Art Collections & Botanical Gardens in San Marino, CA. Used by permission.
P. 128	The drawing of the Temple of Virtue is ascribed to Massachusetts soldier William Tarbell, and was published in the October 1890 issue of the *Magazine of American History with Notes and Queries*.
Back cover	Photograph of the author by Paul Vincent, used by permission.

Chapter Notes

To save space I have not included subtitles with titles in these source notes. Also, if an author has written only one work, the title of that book is given only when I first cite it; in subsequent notes only his name and a page number appear. And some especially long titles of books and documents are abbreviated even when I first cite them.

I have frequently cited "Notes" and "Circular" as sources for material in this book. The former refers to the notes Madison took during the debates in Congress; the latter is used for any letter that was sent to all the state governors. I have also used abbreviations for the names of men who wrote letters and their addressees. The two keys given below should allow readers to discern who wrote and received the letters that I have cited as sources.

AH = Alexander Hamilton
AM = Alexander McDougall
AS = Arthur St. Clair
BH = (Governor) Benjamin Harrison
BL = Benjamin Lincoln
DC = David Cobb
EB = (President) Elias Boudinot
ER = Edmund Randolph
GC = (Governor) George Clinton
GM = Gouverneur Morris
GW = George Washington
HG = Horatio Gates
HK = Henry Knox
HL = (President) Henry Laurens
JA = John Armstrong

JB = John Brooks
JE = (Reverend) John Eliot
JH = (President) John Hanson
JJ = Joseph Jones
JM = James Madison
JW = James Wilson
MO = Matthias Ogden
NG = Nathanael Greene
PS = Philip Schuyler
RM = Robert Morris
SBW = Samuel B. Webb
SH = Samuel Hodgdon
SS = Samuel Shaw
TP = Timothy Pickering
WS = Walter Stewart

AMP = The Alexander McDougall Papers, MS 410

BLP = Allis, ed., The Benjamin Lincoln Papers

"Brooks's Memoir" = Brooks, "Memoir of John Brooks, Governor of Massachusetts," *New England Historical and Genealogical Register,* XIX, July 1865

Collection = *Collection of Papers, Relative to Half-Pay and Commutation of Half-Pay, Granted by Congress to the Officers of the Army*

Correspondence of the Revolution = Sparks, ed., *Correspondence of the American Revolution; Being Letters of Eminent Men to George Washington from the Time of His Taking Command of the Army to the End of His Presidency*

Diary of the Revolution = Moore, *Diary of the American Revolution from Newspapers and Original Documents*

General Orders = Boynton, ed., *General Orders of George Washington Issued at Newburgh on the Hudson, 1782–1783,* with an introduction by Alan C. Aimone

GLC = Gilder Lehrman Collection

Heath's Memoirs = Heath, *Memoirs of Major-General Heath, Containing Anecdotes, Details of Skirmishes, Battles, and Other Military Events, During the American War*

HGP = The Horatio Gates Papers, MS 240

HKP = The Henry Knox Papers, microfilm edition

Huntington's Letters = Blanchfield, *Letters Written by Ebenezer Huntington during the American Revolution*

JCC = Ford et al., eds., *Journals of the Continental Congress, 1774–1789*

Jones's Letters = Ford, ed., *Letters of Joseph Jones of Virginia, 1777–1787*

Knox's Correspondence = Drake, *Life and Correspondence of Henry Knox, Major-General in the American Revolutionary Army*

LDC = Smith et al., eds., *Letters of Delegates to Congress, 1774–1789*

LMCC = Burnett, ed., *Letters of Members of the Continental Congress*

LOC = Library of Congress

MHS = Massachusetts Historical Society

Morris's Diary and Letters = Morris, ed., *The Diary and Letters of Gouverneur Morris, Minister of the United States to France; Member of the Constitutional Convention*

Morris Selections = Sparks, *The Life of Gouverneur Morris, with Selections from his Correspondence and Miscellaneous Papers; Detailing Events in the American Revolution, the French Revolution, and in the Political History of the United States*

NYHS = New York Historical Society

PAH = Syrett, ed., *The Papers of Alexander Hamilton*

PGW = Abbot et al., eds., *The Papers of George Washington*

PJM = Hutchinson et al., eds., *The Papers of James Madison*

PNG = Conrad and Parks, eds., *The Papers of Nathanael Greene*

PRM = Catanzariti et al., eds., *The Papers of Robert Morris, 1781–1784*

Putnam's Memoirs = Buell, comp., *The Memoirs of Rufus Putnam and Certain Official Papers and Correspondence*

Recollections = Custis, *Recollections and Private Memoirs of Washington*

Shaw's Journals = Quincy, ed., *The Life and Journals of Major Samuel Shaw, the First American Consul at Canton: With a Life of the Author*

SP = Smith, ed., *The St. Clair Papers: The Life and Public Services of Arthur St. Clair, Soldier of the Revolutionary War, President of the Continental Congress, and Governor of the North-Western Territory, with His Correspondence and Other Papers*

Spirit = Commager and Morris, eds., *The Spirit of 'Seventy-Six: The Story of the American Revolution as Told by Participants*

TPP = Allis, ed., *The Timothy Pickering Papers*, microfilm edition

Webb's Correspondence = Ford, ed., *Correspondence and Journals of Samuel Blachley Webb*

WGW = Fitzpatrick, ed., *The Writings of George Washington from the Original Manuscript Sources, 1745–1799*

Although the Massachusetts Historical Society (MHS) provided all the photocopies of the letters from the Henry Knox Papers (*HKP*) cited below, the actual collection is owned by the Gilder Lehrman Institute of American History. In cases where those letters were quoted from, the Institute expressed a desire to be properly credited for allowing their usage. Consequently, the call numbers the Institute assigned to all those documents are given in brackets at the end of citations for those documents.

Introduction

1. Hudson's journal, quoted in Ruttenber, *History of the Town of Newburgh*, pp. 9–10; Eager, *Outline History of Orange County*, pp. 31, 203; Williams, *New York's Part in History*, p.103; Huey and Waite, *Washington's Headquarters, The Hasbrouck House*, p. 2; and Carmer, "Lordly Hudson," p. 6.
2. Ruttenber, pp. 19–20.
3. Eager, p. 43.
4. Ruttenber, pp. 20–21; and Eager, p. 44.
5. Ruttenber, p. 21.
6. Quoted ibid.
7. Ibid.; and quoted in Huey and Waite, pp. 3–4 (quote on p. 3).

8. Huey and Waite, p. 4.
9. Ruttenber, p. 128.
10. Anthony, *Washington's Headquarters, Newburgh, New York*, p. 9.
11. Ibid., pp. 9–10.
12. Ruttenber, pp. 24, 28, 30, 38–39, 128; and Huey and Waite, pp. 7, 10–11.
13. Huey and Waite, pp. 16–18, 35.
14. *Journal of Provincial Congress*, II, quoted in Dempsey, *Washington's Last Cantonment*, p. 10.
15. Ruttenber, p. 49.
16. Quoted ibid., pp. 50–52 (quote on p. 50).
17. Ruttenber, pp. 52–53; and quoted in Eager, p. 100.
18. Ruttenber, pp. 52–53; Eager, pp. 98–99.
19. Ruttenber, pp. 54–55.
20. Ibid., pp. 56–58; Corning, *Washington at Temple Hill*, pp. 2, 14; and Barratt, *Newburgh in the American Revolution*, p. 11.
21. Ruttenber, pp. 58–59; and Barratt, pp. 30–31.
22. Ruttenber, p. 58; and Huey and Waite, p. 2.
23. Barratt, p. 14.
24. Ruttenber, p. 58.
25. Barratt, pp. 7, 27.

Chapter One

1. SS to JE, Apr. 1783, Rhodehamel, ed., *American Revolution*, p. 787.
2. JA's Newburgh Address, ibid., pp. 774–77.
3. See chapter seventeen.
4. GW to AH, Mar. 12, 1783, *PAH*, III, pp. 286–88.
5. RM to JH, *PRM*, IV, p. 209.
6. Refer to the diary in *PRM*.
7. Higginbotham, *War of American Independence*, p. 289.
8. Sumner, *Financier and the Finances of the American Revolution*, I, p. 7; Jensen, *New Nation*, p. 38; Ferguson, *Power of the Purse*, pp. 35–40, 43 (table), 52n and 53; Higginbotham, p. 290; Bullock, "Finances of the United States from 1775 to 1789," p. 143 (chart); and "Continental Loan Office Certificates."
9. Ferguson, p. 40.
10. Sumner, I, pp. 101–02; "Continental Congress Lottery," pp. 1–4; and Mitchell, *Price of Independence*, p. 101.

11. Sumner, I, pp. 42–43, 84; Bullock, p. 130 (chart); and Ferguson, p. 30.
12. GW to BH, Dec. 18, 1778, Rhodehamel, ed., pp. 496–97.
13. GW to AM, Feb. 9, 1779, *WGW*, XIV, p. 83.
14. Miller, *Alexander Hamilton*, p. 45.
15. Oberholtzer, *Robert Morris*, p. 61.
16. Kaplan, "Pay, Pension, and Power," pp. 19–20.
17. Ferguson, pp. 57, 63–64, 67; "Continental Loan Office Certificates"; Rakove, *Beginnings of National Politics*, pp. 209–10; and quoted in Miller, *Alexander Hamilton*, p. 45.
18. Ferguson, p. 46.
19. Rakove, pp. 211–12; Mar. 18, 1780, *JCC*, XVI, p. 264 (quote); Ketcham, *James Madison*, p. 89; Brant, *Fourth President*, p. 50; Sumner, I, p. 85; Bullock, p. 137; Martin and Lender, *Respectable Army*, p. 151; Higginbotham, p. 293; and Ferguson, pp. 51–52.
20. JM to T. Jefferson, Mar. 27, 1780, *PJM*, II, p. 6.
21. Miller, *Alexander Hamilton*, p. 56.
22. Ferguson, pp. 65–66; and Henderson, *Party Politics in the Continental Congress*, p. 254.
23. Martin and Lender, p. 152.
24. Royster, *Revolutionary People at War*, p. 270.
25. Ibid.
26. Chidsey, *Loyalists*, p. 129.
27. Belcher, *First American Civil War*, II, pp. 34–35; and Bowman, *Morale of the American Revolutionary Army*, p. 24.
28. Sumner, I, p. 81.
29. Ibid.
30. Ibid., pp. 82, 95.
31. E. Huntington to A. Huntington, July 7, 1780, *Huntington's Letters*, pp. 86–88.
32. AH to J. Duane, Sept. 3, 1780, *PAH*, II, pp. 401–04.
33. GW to G. Mason, Oct. 22, 1780, *WGW*, XX, p. 242.
34. Article VIII, Articles of Confederation, in Bullock, pp. 118–19.
35. Sumner, I, p. 273.
36. Chernow, *Alexander Hamilton*, p. 170.
37. Ferguson, pp. 140–41.
38. RM to B. Franklin, quoted in Sumner, I, p. 274.
39. Rakove, p. 208; Bullock, p. 154; and Miller, *Triumph of Freedom*, p. 458 (example of a state that could not afford to send funds).
40. O. Wolcott, quoted in Miller, *Triumph of Freedom*, p. 659.

41. Van Doren, *Mutiny in January*, p. 34.
42. Ketcham, p. 116.
43. Alsop, *Yankees at the Court*, p. 187; and Flexner, *Washington*, p. 140.
44. GW to J. Laurens, Jan. 15, 1781, *WGW*, XXI, pp. 107–08.
45. Brant, p. 99; Brookhiser, *Alexander Hamilton*, p. 54; Higginbotham, p. 298; Morgan, *Birth of the Republic, 1763–89*, p. 107; Jan. 10 and Feb. 1, 3, 6-7, 1781, *JCC*, XIX, pp. 43, 105–06, 110–13, 123, 126; and Champagne, *Alexander McDougall and the American Revolution in New York*, p. 169.
46. Young, *Forgotten Patriot*, p. 123.
47. Higginbotham, p. 300.
48. Sumner, I, p. 1.
49. Ibid.

Chapter Two

1. My main sources for the biography of Robert Morris were Sumner, I; Wagner, *Robert Morris, Audacious Patriot*; Rappleye, *Robert Morris*; and Young. Ver Steeg, *Robert Morris*; and Oberholtzer provided little. My sources for quotations used in my biography of Morris are given separately in succeeding notes.
2. RM to J. Hancock, Dec. 23, 1776, *LDC*, V, p. 647.
3. GW to RM, Dec. 31, 1776, *PGW*, VII, p. 497.
4. RM to GW, Jan. 1, 1777, ibid., p. 508.
5. Young, p. 76.
6. Quoted in Wagner, p. 57.
7. Quoted in Tindall and Shi, *America*, p. 292.
8. Final essay in *Common Sense*, quoted in Hawke, *Paine*, p. 44.
9. Chernow, p. 170.
10. GW to J. Laurens, Apr. 9, 1781, *WGW*, XXI, pp. 438–39.
11. Sumner, I, p. 266.
12. Ketcham, p. 131.
13. AH to RM, Apr. 30, 1781, *PRM*, I, p. 32.
14. JW to RM, May 24, 1781, ibid., p. 78.
15. HG to RM, June 3, 1781, ibid., pp. 101–02.
16. RM to President Samuel Huntington, May 17, 1781, ibid., p. 66.
17. RM to B. Franklin, July 13, 1781, ibid., p. 283.
18. Circular, January 8, 1782, *PRM*, III, p. 508.

19. My description of the bank's management of finances and its capitalization comes from Plan for Establishing a National Bank, May 17, 1781, *PRM*, I, pp. 68–72; Wagner, p. 89; Young, pp. 118–19; Hammond, *Banks and Politics in America*, pp. 48–49, 51; Rakove, p. 302; Ferguson, p. 123; Sumner, II, pp. 24–26; and Higginbotham, p. 302. My sources for quotations used in this section are given separately in succeeding notes.
20. Plan for Establishing a National Bank, May 17, 1781, *PRM*, I, p. 71.
21. RM to J. Jay, July 13, 1781, ibid., p. 287.
22. *Rivington's Gazette*, May 12, 1781, quoted in *Diary of the Revolution*, II, pp. 425–426.
23. Young, p. 88; and Sumner, I, p. 95.
24. RM to the Governor of Cuba, July 17, 1781, *PRM*, I, pp. 311–14.
25. Circular, July 27, 1781, *PRM*, I, pp. 397–400.
26. I relied upon many sources for information on Morris's efforts to get cash for Yorktown: Smith, *New Age Now Begins*, II, p. 1668; Davis, *Campaign That Won America*, pp. 79–81; Adams, *Gouverneur Morris*, p. 134; Schultz, *Generous Strangers*, pp. 178–79; Bonsal, *When the French Were Here*, pp. 119, 127; Sumner, I, pp. 302–04, 308; Fleming, *Beat the Last Drum*, pp. 86–87, 92–93, 101; Mitchell, p. 110; Kline, *Gouverneur Morris and the New Nation*, pp. 203–04; Oberholtzer, pp. 86–87; Ketchum, ed., *American Heritage Book of the Revolution*, pp. 346, 355; and *Spirit*, p. 797. Sources for the quotations that appear in this section are given separately in succeeding notes.
27. GW to RM, Aug. 27, 1781, *WGW*, XXIII, pp. 50–52 (quotes on p. 52); and Fleming, *Beat the Last Drum*, p. 92.
28. GW to RM, Sept. 6, 1781, *WGW*, XXIII, p. 89.
29. RM, quoted in Davis, *Campaign That Won America*, p. 79.
30. Quoted in Schultz, p. 179.
31. Closen, quoted in Davis, *Campaign That Won America*, p. 82.
32. Major Popham, quoted ibid.
33. Smith, *New Age Now Begins*, II, p. 1669; Davis, *Campaign That Won America*, p. 82; Wallace, *Life of Henry Laurens*, p. 485; Hammond, pp. 49–50; and Young, pp. 120–21.
34. Circular, Oct. 19, 1781, *PRM*, III, p. 87.
35. My biography of Gouverneur Morris comes mostly from Adams and Kline. Other sources are *Morris Selections*, I; Mintz, *Gouverneur Morris and the American Revolution*; Swiggett, *Extraordinary Mr. Morris*; Crawford, *Unwise Passions*; Kirschke, *Gouverneur Morris*; Brookhiser, *Gentleman Revolutionary*; *Morris's Diary and Letters*; Ferling, *Leap in the Dark*; Wright, "'Nor Is Their Standing Army to Be Despised,'" in Hoffman and Albert, eds., *Arms and Independence*; Peters, *More Perfect Union*; and Van Doren, *Great Rehearsal*. Sources for quotations in my

biography of Gouverneur Morris and sources for the section describing the "Hickey Plot" are given separately in succeeding notes.

36. Will of L. Morris, Nov. 19, 1760, *Morris Selections*, I, p. 4n.
37. Quoted in Adams, p. 20.
38. GM to T. Penn, May 20, 1774, *Morris Selections*, I, p. 25.
39. Kline, p. 42.
40. GM to L. Morris, Feb. 25, 1775, quoted in Adams, p. 58.
41. Ellis, *Epic of New York City*, p. 160; Wheeler, *Voices of 1776*, p. 152; Alsop, p. 47; Jones, *History of New York during the Revolutionary War*, pp. 416–17; Fleming, *1776*, pp. 297–98; Smith, *New Age Begins*, I, pp. 718–22; Langguth, *Patriots*, pp. 373–74; McCullough, *1776*, pp. 132–33; Bobrick, *Angel in the Whirlwind*, p. 211; Schecter, *Battle for New York*, pp. 65, 95–96; Adams, p. 68; Kline, p. 60; and GW, quoted in Diamant, *Chaining the Hudson*, p. 43.
42. GM to J. Jay, Feb. 1, 1778, *LDC*, IX, p. 4.
43. GM to GC, Feb. 17, 1778, ibid., p. 117.
44. GM to GC, Mar. 16, 1778, ibid., p. 303.
45. Instructions to B. Franklin, Oct. 22–26, 1778, *JCC*, XII, p. 1041.
46. Observations on the Finances of America, October 1778, ibid., p. 1051.
47. Ibid., pp. 1050–51.
48. Quoted in *Morris's Diary and Letters*, I, p. 13.
49. Diary, Aug. 4, 1781, *PRM*, II, p. 14.
50. Boatner, *Encyclopedia of the American Revolution*, p. 275.
51. Brant, p. 52.
52. Chidsey, *Loyalists*, 129; and Miller, *Triumph of Freedom*, p. 659.
53. Ketcham, p. 141.
54. RM to B. Franklin, Nov. 27, 1781, quoted in Sumner, I, p. 97.

Chapter Three

1. Flexner, *George Washington in the American Revolution*, pp. 470–73; and Brady, *Martha Washington*, p. 141.
2. Nov. 2, 1781, *JCC*, XXI, pp. 1089–91.
3. Kline, pp. 207–08.
4. Ver Steeg, p. 83; Kirschke, pp. 128, 135; Rappleye, p. 285; Brookhiser, *Gentleman Revolutionary*, p. 70; Kline, p. 216; and diary, Dec. 3, 1781, *PRM*, III, p. 317 (quote). The sources don't agree on how often they met, but the diary shows that they originally planned to meet once a week.

5. RM to the Mass., R.I., and Md. governors, Jan. 3, 1782, *PRM*, III, p. 482.
6. Young, p. 122; Wagner, p. 89; Sumner, II, pp. 28–29, 34; Hammond, p. 49; and Brookhiser, *Gentleman Revolutionary*, p. 68.
7. Quoted in Wagner, p. 89.
8. GM to J. Jay, Jan. 20, 1782, *PRM*, IV, p. 82.
9. Kline, p. 254; and diary, Jan. 24, 26 and Feb. 7, 1782, *PRM*, IV, pp. 107–08, 115, 178 (1st quote on p. 108, 2nd and 3rd on p. 178).
10. Diary, Sept. 18, 1781, *PRM*, II, p. 290.
11. Agreement with R. R. Livingston and GW, *PRM*, IV, p. 201; and Sumner, I, pp. 234–35.
12. Quoted in Hawke, p. 123.
13. Sumner, I, p. 235.
14. RM to JH, Feb. 11, 1782, *PRM*, IV, pp. 205–13 (quotes on pp. 205 and 209); and Ver Steeg, p. 133.
15. Henderson, pp. 293–94.
16. GM to F. Rendon, Mar. 5, 1782, *PRM*, IV, pp. 352–58 (quotes on p. 358); and Kline, pp. 232–33.
17. Paine, "American Crisis," in Conway, ed., *Writings of Thomas Paine*, p. 343.
18. Quoted in Hawke, p. 125.
19. R. R. Livingston to RM, Mar. 18, 1782 and RM to R. R. Livingston, Apr. 2, 1782, *PRM*, IV, pp. 419, 499 (quotes in 2nd letter, p. 499).
20. Humphreys, *Life of David Humphreys*, I, p. 247 (first date only); and Freeman, *George Washington*, V, p. 411 (both dates). The first date is based on what General William Heath wrote, the second on a report in the April 10, 1782, *Pennsylvania Journal*.
21. GW to Chastellux, Aug. 10, 1782, *WGW*, XXIV, p. 495; Chadwick, *George Washington's War*, p. 436; and Fowler, "American Crisis," p. 3 (quote).
22. Lord North, Nov. 25, 1781, quoted in Fleming, *Beat the Last Drum*, p. 343.
23. Longford, ed., *Oxford Book of Royal Anecdotes*, p. 310 (fast-talking); and King George III, quoted in Hibbert, *George III*, p. 162.
24. King George III, quoted in Alsop, p. 230.
25. King's draft message, *Spirit*, pp. 1281–82.
26. History Channel, *Revolution*, part XI.
27. Brandt, *Man in the Mirror*, p. 198.
28. Details appear throughout Diamant. Also, see Monell, *Washington's Headquarters, Newburgh, N.Y. and Adjacent Localities*, p. 85; Thane, *Fighting Quaker*, p. 45; and Corning, pp. 8–12, 14.
29. P. Townsend letter, Mar. 10, 1845, in *General Orders*, pp. 106–07.
30. Ibid., p. 107.
31. Ibid.

32. T. Machin to AM, quoted in Diamant, p. 156 (1,700 feet).
33. P. Townsend letter, Mar. 10, 1845, in *General Orders*, p. 107. TP, in Diamant, p. 173, gives a different estimate: "upward of 60 tons." Mel Johnson, a longtime historic site assistant at George Washington's Headquarters at Newburgh, puts the number within the range offered by Townshend.
34. Many pages in Diamant. On p. 146 he says the chain had seven hundred-fifty links, but on p. 177 he says "800-odd" links. The difference is not explained. The length of links is from p. 173, where Timothy Pickering is quoted, and an average for salvaged ones is given on p. 183. The weight is an average for salvaged ones that appears on p. 183.
35. Loyalist spy's report, quoted in Diamant, p. 158.
36. Ibid., 133, p. 172.
37. Loyalist spy's report, ibid., p. 158.
38. Family record of A. Hasbrouck, quoted in Huey and Waite, p. 34.
39. Guided tour of George Washington's Headquarters at Newburgh. She received sixty-nine pounds for his stay in Newburgh.
40. Colonel H. Hughes, quoted in Fowler, "An American Crisis," p. 3.
41. Chastellux, quoted in Humphreys, I, p. 247.
42. J. Donnelly, quoted in Ruttenber, p. 104.
43. Chastellux, Dec. 5, 1782, quoted in Huey and Waite, p. 36.
44. My description of the first floor rooms is based on guided tours of George Washington's Headquarters at Newburgh.
45. Tour by Lynette Scherer and conversation with Mel Johnson at George Washington's Headquarters at Newburgh; Fowler, "An American Crisis," p. 4; Dempsey, pp. 28, 31; and Humphreys, I, p. 247.
46. Monell, pp. 52–54 (quotes on pp. 53 and 54).
47. Boller, *Presidential Wives*, p. 5.
48. Aimone's introduction in *General Orders*, p. iii; and Monell, p. 15.
49. Anthony, p. 49; Monell, p. 5; and quoted in Dempsey, p. 30.
50. Tours of George Washington's Headquarters at Newburgh; *General Orders*, p. 6; and Anthony, pp. 43, 49–51.
51. GW to T. Tilghman, Jan. 10, 1783, *WGW*, XXVI, p. 29.
52. Diary, Apr. 19, 1782, *PRM*, V, pp. 19, 20n3.
53. RM to JH, Apr. 24, 1782, ibid., p. 47.
54. RM to NG, Apr. 24, 1782, ibid., p. 50.
55. H. Swift to GW, May 6, 1782, *GW Papers, 1741–1799,* LOC (quotes); GW to H. Swift, May 6, 1782, *WGW*, XXIV, pp. 227–28; after orders, May 12, 1782, ibid., p. 249; and Fowler, *American Crisis*, p. 91.

56. NG to RM, Apr. 22, 1782, *PRM*, V, pp. 35–36, 38n4.
57. Circular, May 16, 1782, ibid., pp. 190–92.
58. RM to JH, May 17, 1782, ibid., p. 203.
59. RM to JH, May 17, 1782, and diary, May 20, 1782, ibid., pp. 204n3, 226 (quote on p. 226); Ferguson, p. 148; and Ver Steeg, p. 135.
60. RM to T. Tillotson, May 20, 1782, *PRM*, V, pp. 229–30 (quote on p. 230).

Chapter Four

1. L. Nicola to GW, May 22, 1782, *GW Papers, 1741–1799*, LOC; Basler, "History Lives at Cantonment"; "New Windsor Revolutionary History"; and tour of George Washington's Headquarters at Newburgh given by Ms. Johanna Porr. The last three sources cited here are for the troop estimate. Numbers vary depending upon what source is used. Aimone in *General Orders*, iv, says nine thousand, while Wensyel in "Newburgh Conspiracy" says seven to eight thousand.
2. GW to L. Nicola, May 22, 1782, *WGW*, XXIV, pp. 272–73.
3. Haggard, "Nicola Affair," p. 158.
4. L. Nicola to GW, May 23, 1782, *GW Papers, 1741–1799*, LOC.
5. L. Nicola to GW, May 24, 1782, ibid.
6. L. Nicola to GW, May 28, 1782, ibid.
7. Berkin, "George Washington and the Newburgh Conspiracy," in Hollinshead, ed., p. 39.

Chapter Five

1. Hatch, *Administration of the American Revolutionary Army*, pp. 77–78; GW to J. Hancock, and committee of second lieutenants to GW, Sept. 21, 1775, *PGW*, II, pp. 26, 32–33 (quote on p. 26); Kaplan, pp. 17, 23; June 14, 1775, *JCC*, II, p. 89; and Nov. 4, 1775, *JCC*, III, p. 322.
2. Petition from the townfolk of Harvard, Dec. 27, 1775, quoted in Hatch, p. 78.
3. Hatch, p. 78.
4. HK to J. Adams, Aug. 21, 1776, *HKP*, reel 3, MHS [GLC02437.00423].
5. Hatch, p. 79.
6. *Pensions Enacted by Congress for American Revolutionary War Veterans*; Johnson, "Army and Politics, 1783–1784," pp. 1–2; and Glasson, *Federal Military Pensions in the United States*, p. 20.
7. Eight Continental field officers to GW, Nov. 1777, *PGW*, XII, pp. 448, 451n1 (quote on p. 451).
8. Remarks on the proposed reform of the army, Nov. 1777, ibid., p. 453.
9. J. Warren's oration, Mar. 5, 1772, Williston, comp., *Eloquence of the United States*, V, p. 11.
10. Unsigned article in the *Boston Gazette*, Oct. 17, 1768, Cushing, ed., *Writings of Samuel Adams*, I, pp. 252–253.

11. Higginbotham, p. 207; Champagne, p. 157; and Ferguson, p. 156.
12. GW to HL, Dec. 23, 1777, *PGW*, XII, p. 686.
13. A. Waldo's Valley Forge diary, cited in Kaplan, p. 15.
14. E. Gerry to GW, Jan. 13, 1778, *LDC*, VIII, pp. 575–76 (quote on p. 576); Glasson, pp. 25–26; and Kaplan, p. 22.
15. Extract from a representation made by GW to a committee, Jan. 29, 1778, *Collection*, pp. 3–5.
16. GW to HL, Mar. 24, 1778, *WGW*, XI, p. 139.
17. Glasson, p. 27.
18. T. Burke to R. Caswell, Apr. 9, 1778, *LDC*, IX, pp. 394–95.
19. GW to HL, Apr. 10, 1778, *WGW*, XI, p. 237.
20. HL to W. Livingston, Apr. 19, 1778, *LDC*, IX, p. 444.
21. HL, quoted in Smith, *New Age Now Begins*, II, p. 1028; and *LDC*, VIII, p. xxv (untiring Laurens).
22. Ct. delegates to J. Trumbull, Sr., May 18, 1778, *LDC*, IX, p. 707.
23. Ibid.
24. J. Lovell to S. Adams, Jan. 13, 1778, ibid., VIII, p. 581.
25. U.S. House of Representatives, *Resolutions*, p. 9; and Glasson, p. 30.
26. HL, quoted in Smith, *New Age Now Begins*, II, p. 1029.
27. GW to GM, and GW to HL, May 18, 1778, *WGW*, II, pp. 413, 415; and Glasson, p. 30.
28. Glasson, p. 30.
29. GW to GM, May 8, 1779, *WGW*, XV, pp. 25–26.
30. GW to JA, May 18, 1779, ibid., p. 98.
31. Glasson, pp. 18, 32; diary, July 3, 1782, *PRM*, V, pp. 522n13; and Martin and Lender, p. 150.
32. Quoted in Haggard, p. 155.
33. For more on this subject refer to chapter eleven and its source notes.
34. Clarfield, *Timothy Pickering and the American Republic*, pp. 4 (father's occupation), 9 (appearance), 57; and TP, quoted in Miller, *Triumph of Freedom*, p. 469.
35. Quoted in Bowman, p. 56.
36. Dupuy and Hammerman, eds., *Peoples and Events of the American Revolution*, p. 198.
37. Flexner, *George Washington in the American Revolution*, p. 356.
38. Glatthaar and Martin, *Forgotten Allies*, p. 265; and Nelson, "Mutiny, Continental Army," in Fremont-Barnes et al., eds., *American Revolutionary War*, III, p. 1237.
39. GW to JJ, Aug. 13, 1780, *WGW*, XIX, p. 368.
40. GW to the President of Congress, Aug. 20, 1780, ibid., pp. 411–12 (quote on p. 412).
41. Resolutions of Aug. 12, 17, and 24, 1780, *AMP*, reel 3, NYHS.
42. Oct. 3, 1780, *JCC*, XVIII, pp. 893–97.

43. GW to the President, Oct. 11, 1780, *Collection*, p. 7.
44. Glasson, 34; and diary, July 3, 1782, *PRM*, V, p. 522n13.
45. Jensen, p. 32.
46. Hatch, p. 85.
47. Smith, *New Age Now Begins*, II, p. 1028.
48. Quoted ibid.
49. Quoted in Royster, p. 344.
50. Ibid.

Chapter Six

1. GW to RM, June 16, 1782, *PRM*, V, pp. 417–19.
2. Wagner, p. 91.
3. RM to G. Olney, June 23, 1782, *PRM*, V, p. 472.
4. RM to W. Greene, June 26, 1782, ibid., p. 485.
5. Diary, June 26, 1782, *PRM*, V, pp. 483–84 (quotes); Ver Steeg, p. 123; Kline, pp. 240–43; and Ferguson, pp. 149–50.
6. I used Thompson, "Info on General Walter Stewart, Ireland–PA, 1756–1796"; McGuire, *Philadelphia Campaign*, I, pp. 255–58, and II, p. 103; Lancaster, *From Lexington to Liberty*, p. 354; Morris, ed., p. 100; Smith, *Battle of Monmouth*, pp. 15–19; Stryker, *Battle of Monmouth*, pp. 149–85; Preston, *Short History of the American Revolution*, pp. 326–30; Hensley, "Walter Stewart," in Fremont-Barnes et al., eds., IV, p. 1791; Royster, p. 312 (April 1780 declaration/pledge); Boatner, p. 1059; Smith, *New Age Now Begins*, II, p. 1606; Palmer, *1794*, p. 14; and Van Doren, *Mutiny in January*, p. 51, for my biography of Walter Stewart. Sources for the quotes in this biography are given separately in the succeeding seven notes.
7. Quoted in Heitman, *Historical Register of Officers of the Continental Army*, pp. 520–21 (quotes on p. 521).
8. Hensley, op. cit., in Fremont-Barnes et al., eds., IV, p. 1791 ("Irish Beauty"); Lossing's explanation in *Recollections*, p. 355n (complexion quote); and WS, quoted in Tucker, *Mad Anthony Wayne and the New Nation*, pp. 133–34, 137 (quote on p. 134).
9. WS, quoted in Martin, *Private Yankee Doodle*, p. 187.
10. Van Doren, *Mutiny in January*, pp. 32–35, 55, 77–78 (A. Wayne to J. Reed, Dec. 16, 1780, quoted on p. 33); and Davis, *George Washington and the American Revolution*, pp. 353–54.
11. Denny's journal, Oct. 1781, Rhodehamel, ed., p. 724.
12. Lossing's explanation in *Recollections*, p. 355n.
13. Martin, p. 187.

14. RM to B. Franklin, Nov. 27, 1781, *PRM*, III, p. 269.
15. Ibid., p. 270.
16. Report to Congress on the Interest of Loan Office Certificates, June 27, 1782, *PRM*, V, p. 491.
17. Diary, June 28, 1782, ibid., p. 495; RM to JH, July 29, 1782, plan to erect a funding system, *PRM*, VI, p. 49n; Kline, p. 243; and Ver Steeg, p. 123.
18. Diary, June 28, 1782, *PRM*, V, p. 495.
19. Circular, July 29, 1782, *PRM*, VI, pp. 34–35 (including n5).
20. Remonstrance and petition to Congress from B. McClenachan, C. Petit, J. Ewing, and B. Rush, July 8, 1782, ibid., pp. 695–97.
21. Diary, July 9, 1782, *PRM*, V, pp. 548–49; Kline, pp. 243–44; and Ver Steeg, p. 123.
22. RM to G. Webb, July 9, 1782, *PRM*, V, p. 553.
23. NG to RM, July 10, 1782, ibid., p. 560.
24. AH to RM, July 22, 1782, *PRM*, VI, p. 8; and Ferguson, p. 148.
25. RM to JH, July 29, 1782, report on public credit, *PRM*, VI, pp. 56–72 (quotes on pp. 59–62); Rakove, pp. 311, 313; Kline, pp. 245–46; Ver Steeg, pp. 124–28; Mintz, p. 156; Ferguson, p. 151; and Wagner, p. 92.
26. RM to Governor Trumbull, July 31, 1782, *PRM*, VI, p. 112.
27. GW to W. Heath, June 22, 1782, *WGW*, XXIV, p. 371; and Kaplan, p. 29.
28. Officers of the Massachusetts Line to the Senate and House of Representatives of the Commonwealth of Massachusetts, in General Court Assembled, July 1782, *HKP*, reel 9, MHS [GLC02437.01514].
29. Diary, July 3, 1782, *PRM*, V, pp. 519–24n13 (J. Root, July 31, 1782, quoted on p. 524n13); and Fowler, *American Crisis*, pp. 140–44.

Chapter Seven

1. GM to M. Ridley, Aug. 6, 1782, *PRM*, VI, p. 148.
2. Davis, *George Washington and the American Revolution*, p. 448.
3. GW to the Secretary of Foreign Affairs, May 22, 1782, *WGW*, XXIV, p. 271.
4. GW to R. H. Harrison, Nov. 18, 1781, *WGW*, XXIII, p. 352.
5. Aug. 19, 1782, *General Orders*, p. 39.
6. Aug. 7, 1782, ibid., pp. 34–35.
7. Ibid., p. 35.
8. General orders, Aug. 7, 1782, *WGW*, XXIV, p. 488.
9. Mays, *Historical Dictionary of the American Revolution*, p. 16.
10. Quoted in Flexner, *George Washington in the American Revolution*, p. 482.

11. Ibid., pp. 482–83.
12. Ibid., p. 483.
13. See Bowman.
14. Randall, *George Washington*, p. 390; and Van Doren, *Mutiny in January*, pp. 232–33.
15. Flexner, *George Washington in the American Revolution*, p. 482.
16. Bowman, p. 33; and Cox, *Come All You Brave Soldiers*, p. 84. Baron de Kalb was the officer who guessed that the average profit was fifty percent.
17. GW to J. Reed, Dec. 12, 1778, *WGW*, XIII, p. 383.
18. The details of the army's relationship with Sands & Co. come from Ver Steeg, pp. 142–51; Hatch, p. 114; Sumner, II, pp. 61–62; Carp, *To Starve the Army at Pleasure*, pp. 215–16; Flexner, *George Washington in the American Revolution*, pp. 483–84; Mayer, *Belonging to the Army*, pp. 99–100; and Risch, *Supplying Washington's Army*, pp. 251–58. Sources for the quotes in the section on Sands & Co. are given separately in the succeeding seven notes.
19. Carp, p. 215.
20. J. Campbell to H. Hughes, Apr. 20, 1782, quoted ibid.
21. GW to RM, June 16, 1782, *WGW*, XXIV, p. 349.
22. GW to C. Sands, May 25, 1782, ibid., p. 285.
23. GW to RM, May 17–25, 1782, *PRM*, V, p. 209.
24. Ibid., p. 210.
25. GW to RM, Jan. 8, 1783, *WGW*, XXVI, p. 20.
26. Wensyel; General Harmar to AS, Sept. 29, 1782, *SP*, I, pp. 569–70; Clarfield, p. 62; Royster, p. 334; Flexner, *Washington*, pp. 170–71; Dempsey, p. 28; Oct. 30, 1782, *Heath's Memoirs*, p. 359; Skeen, *John Armstrong, Jr.*, p. 8; and Marshall, "Rise and Fall of the Newburgh Conspiracy."
27. Cutler, ed. *Dictionary of American History*, II, p. 514; and Mann, *Republic of Debtors*, p. 79.
28. Mann, p. 81.
29. Ibid., p. 79.
30. Ibid., pp. 85–91.
31. Tinkcom, "Revolutionary City," in Weigley, ed., *Philadelphia*, p. 150.
32. Mann, pp. 88–89.
33. RM to AH, Aug. 28, 1782, *PRM*, VI, pp. 270–71.
34. RM to JH, July 29, 1782, ibid., p. 51n; Ferguson, p. 151; and Johnson, p. 20.
35. GW to the President of Congress, Sept. 4, 1782, *WGW*, XXV, p. 121.
36. DC to R. T. Paine, Aug. 28, 1782, quoted in Dempsey, p. 33.
37. GW to the President of Congress, Sept. 4, 1782, *WGW*, XXV, p. 121.
38. NG to RM, Sept. 1, 1782, *PRM*, VI, p. 291.

39. Mitchell, p. 314; Sumner, II, p. 57; Wagner, p. 91; and Brant, p. 99.
40. Circular, May 9, 1782, *PRM*, V, p. 137.
41. RM to GW, Aug. 29, 1782, *PRM*, VI, p. 282.
42. AH to RM, Sept. 28, 1782, ibid., p. 460; Ferguson, pp. 151–52; Jensen, p. 66; and Morris, *Forging of the Union, 1781–1789*, p. 41.
43. RM to JH, July 29, 1782, *PRM*, VI, p. 51n; and Ferguson, pp. 151–52.
44. RM to JH, July 29, 1782, *PRM*, VI, p. 80n63.
45. Ver Steeg, p. 129; Kline, p. 248; Rakove, p. 313; Ferguson, p. 151; RM to JH, July 29, 1782, *PRM*, VI, pp. 51–52.
46. RM to Governor Greene, Oct. 24, 1782, *PRM*, VI, p. 656.
47. RM to Governor Greene, Sept. 3, 1782, ibid., p. 307.
48. Rakove, p. 313; and Bates, "Rhode Island and the Impost of 1781," p. 351.
49. Ibid., pp. 352–53.
50. Rappleye, p. 320.
51. *Providence Gazette*, Mar. 30, 1782, quoted in Bates, pp. 353, 357 (quotes on p. 353).
52. Bates, pp. 354, 358; and Miller, *Triumph of Freedom*, p. 668.
53. Palmer, p. 7; Flexner, *George Washington in the American Revolution*, p. 484; Dempsey, pp. 29, 34, 36; Bonsal, pp. 217, 228; Corning, p. 103; Humphreys, I, p. 255; and Sept. 14, 20–21, and Oct. 16, 1782, *Heath's Memoirs*, pp. 353, 357.
54. Dumas, quoted in Flexner, *George Washington in the American Revolution*, p. 484.
55. Steuben and GW, quoted in Davis, *Campaign That Won America*, p. 285; Fleming, *Perils of Peace*, pp. 13–14; and idem, *Beat the Last Drum*, pp. 335–36.
56. GW to BL, Oct. 2, 1782, Lengel, ed., *This Glorious Struggle*, pp. 251–52.
57. E. Cornell to RM, Oct. 5, 1782, *PRM*, VI, p. 501.
58. T. Tilghman to RM, Oct. 5, 1782, ibid., p. 509.
59. Kline, pp. 255–56.
60. Circular, Oct. 5, 1782, *PRM*, VI, pp. 496–97.
61. RM to NG and GW, Oct. 5, 1782, ibid., pp. 498–99.
62. RM to M. Ridley, Oct. 6, 1782, ibid., p. 512.
63. RM to the RI and Ga. governors, Oct. 17, 1782, ibid., p. 615n1; and Bates, p. 355.
64. Quoted in Bates, p. 355.
65. D. Howell to T. Foster, Oct. 9, 1782, *LDC*, XIX, pp. 244–45.
66. Ibid., pp. 244–45.
67. RI delegates to Governor Greene, Oct. 15, 1782, ibid., pp. 263–64.
68. RM to the RI and Ga. governors, Oct.17, 1782, *PRM*, VI, pp. 614–15.

69. GW to J. McHenry, Oct. 17, 1782, *WGW*, XXV, p. 269; and Flexner, *George Washington in the American Revolution*, p. 484.
70. Marshall.
71. GW to J. McHenry, Oct. 17, 1782, *WGW*, XXV, p. 269.
72. JM to ER, Oct. 22, 1782, *LMCC*, VI, p. 514 (quote); Mattern, *Benjamin Lincoln and the American Revolution*, pp. 138–39; and Champagne, pp. 184–85.
73. NC delegates to A. Martin, Oct. 22, 1782, *LDC*, XIX, p. 292; and RM to Governor Greene, Oct. 24, 1782, *PRM*, VI, p. 657.
74. RM to Governor Greene, Oct. 24, 1782, *PRM*, VI, pp. 657–58.
75. RM to AH, Oct. 16, 1782, *PAH*, III, p. 186.
76. Mattern, p. 138.
77. Report from the Continental Congress on a letter from the Speaker of the RI Assembly, Dec. 16, 1782, *PAH*, III, pp. 214–18 (quotes on pp. 215 and 218); Bates, p. 355; Rakove, p. 315; and Sumner, II, p. 66.
78. T. Paine to RM, Nov. 20, 1782, *PRM*, VII, p. 79n.
79. Bates, p. 358; Rakove, p. 315; Brookhiser, *Alexander Hamilton*, p. 54; and Miller, *Alexander Hamilton*, p. 90.

Chapter Eight

1. Johnson, pp. 6–7; Hatch, p. 144; Champagne, p. 184; and HK to Governor Hancock, Sep. 2, 1782, Massachusetts Archives, CCIV, #259.
2. JB to HK, Sept. 26, 1782, *HKP*, reel 10, MHS [GLC02437.01629]; Hatch, p. 145; Johnson, p. 7; and Champagne, p. 184.
3. HK to Governor Hancock, Sep. 2, 1782, Massachusetts Archives, CCIV, #259.
4. JB to HK, Sept. 26, 1782, *HKP*, reel 10, MHS (quotes) [GLC02437.01629]; Johnson, p. 7; and Jensen, p. 36.
5. Johnson, pp. 7–8; Hatch, p. 145; Jensen, p. 36; Champagne, p. 184; and JB to HK, Sept. 26, 1782, *HKP*, reel 10, MHS [GLC02437.01629].
6. HK to J. Lowell, Oct. 8, 1782, *HKP*, reel 10, MHS (quotes) [GLC02437.01650]; and Kaplan, pp. 30–31.
7. JB to HK, Oct.17, 1782, *HKP*, reel 10, MHS [GLC02437.01671].
8. S. Osgood to J. Lowell, Sep. 9, 1782, *LDC*, XIX, pp. 129–33 (all quotes); S. Osgood to HK, Dec. 4, 1782, *LMCC*, VI, p. 553.
9. JB to HK, Oct.17, 1782, *HKP*, reel 10, MHS [GLC02437.01671].
10. Ibid.

11. Quoted in Kaplan, p. 31.
12. Kaplan, pp. 31–32.
13. Kaplan, p. 128; SS to his father, Nov. 13, 1783, *Shaw's Journals,* p. 98 (1st quote); SS to JE, Apr. 1783, Rhodehamel, ed., p. 786 (2nd quote); and Hatch, p. 147.
14. Hatch, pp. 147–49.
15. Instructions for Colonel Webb, *Webb's Correspondence*, II, pp. 433–34.
16. SS to JE, Apr. 1783, Rhodehamel, ed., p. 786 (quotes); diary, Dec. 31, 1782, *PRM*, VII, p. 248n3; and Hatch, p. 147.
17. My main sources for this biography were "Henry Knox Brings Cannon to Boston, January 24, 1776"; and Callahan, "Henry Knox," in Billias, ed., *George Washington's Generals and Opponents.* sources for the quotes are given separately in the subsequent fifteen notes.
18. Quoted in "Henry Knox Brings Cannon to Boston."
19. Ibid.
20. Ibid.
21. Ibid.
22. Ibid.
23. Ibid.
24. Ibid.
25. Quoted in Smith, *New Age Now Begins*, I, p. 651.
26. Quoted in Schecter, p. 105.
27. Callahan, op. cit., in Billias, ed., p. 244.
28. HK to W. Knox, Sept. 23, 1776, *HKP*, reel 3, MHS [GLC02437.00449].
29. J. Adams, quoted in Martin and Lender, p. 106.
30. HK to L. Knox, n. d., and *Independent Chronicle*, Oct. 2, 1777, quoted in Callahan, op. cit., in Billias, ed., p. 250.
31. Quoted ibid., p. 253.
32. Unidentified enemy soldier, and SS to Lafayette, Apr. 15, 1792, quoted ibid., pp. 254–55.

Chapter Nine

1. HK to BL, Nov. 25, 1782, *HKP*, reel 10, MHS [GLC02437.10064].
2. Ellis, *Epic of New York City*, p. 141.
3. SS to JE, Apr. 1783, Rhodehamel, ed., pp. 786–87.
4. NG to RM, Dec. 3, 1782, *PRM*, VII, pp. 154–55.
5. BL to NG, Nov. 27, 1782, *PNG*, XII, p. 226.
6. BL to HK, Dec. 3, 1782, *HKP*, reel 10, MHS [GLC02437.01729].

7. SS to JE, Apr. 1783, Rhodehamel, ed., p. 787; HK to AM, Dec. 5, 1782, *HKP*, reel 10, MHS; diary, Dec. 31, 1782, *PRM*, p. 248fn2; Champagne, p. 5; MacDougall, *American Revolutionary*, p. 19; and Eager, p. 635. The last three sources listed here are for the description of Alexander McDougall.
8. Ramsay, *Life of George Washington*, p. 202; HK to Colonel Swift, Dec. 6, 1782, *Webb's Correspondence*, II, p. 436; Bancroft, *History of the Formation of the Constitution*, I, p. 93; Mitchell, p. 313; and Johnson, p. 13.
9. "To the Gentlemen the Committee of the Army appointed to Present their Address to the Honorable the Continental Congress," Dec. 7, 1782, *AMP*, reel 4, NYHS.
10. J. Paterson to HK, Dec. 9 (quotes) and Dec. 13, 1782, in Egleston, *Life of John Paterson*, pp. 282–83.
11. E. Huntington to A. Huntington, Dec. 9, 1782, *Huntington's Letters*, p. 102.
12. Officers' address and petition, *JCC*, XXIV, pp. 290–93.
13. Diary, Dec. 31, 1782, *PRM*, VII, p. 249n3.
14. JM, quoted in Brant, p. 100.
15. T. Paine to RM, Nov. 20, 1782, *PRM*, VII, p. 88.
16. Continental Congress to Governor Greene, Dec. 11, 1782, *PAH*, III, pp. 209–10.
17. Quoted in headnote to T. Paine to RM, Nov. 20, 1782, *PRM*, VII, p. 82.
18. Duncan, *Medical Men in the American Revolution*, p. 190.
19. Letter from AM, Dec. 12, 1782, quoted in MacDougall, p. 149.
20. AM to SBW, Dec. 15, 1782, *Webb's Correspondence*, II, p. 439.
21. HK to AM, Dec. 17, 1782, *AMP*, reel 4, NYHS; and diary, Dec. 31, 1782, *PRM*, VII, p. 249n3.
22. GW to JJ, Dec. 14, 1782, *WGW*, XXV, pp. 430–31.
23. My sources for the four paragraphs on the troubles with the New Jersey line officers are Martin, "'Most Undisciplined, Profligate Crew'" in Hoffman and Albert, eds., pp. 119–121; GW to W. Maxwell, May 7, 1779 and to the President, May 11, 1779, *WGW*, XV, pp. 13–15, 42–44; and Martin and Lender, p. 149. Sources for quotes that appear in those four paragraphs are given separately in the succeeding three notes.
24. GW to W. Maxwell, May 7, 1779, *WGW*, XV, pp. 13–15.
25. GW to the President, May 11, 1779, ibid., p. 43.
26. Quoted in Martin and Lender, p. 149.
27. Report by the Continental Congress on a letter from the Speaker of the R. I. Assembly, Dec. 16, 1782, *PAH*, III, pp. 213–22.
28. HK to AM, Dec. 17, 1782, *AMP*, reel 4, NYHS.
29. Ibid.; and Mattern, p. 139.

30. HK to BL, Dec. 20, 1782, *HKP*, reel 10, MHS [GLC02437.01754]; and the same letter in *Knox's Correspondence*, p. 77.
31. SS to JE, Dec. 22, 1782, *Shaw's Journals*, pp. 99–100.
32. SS to JE, Apr. 1783, Rhodehamel, ed., p. 787; diary, Dec. 31, 1782, *PRM*, VII, p. 248n3; and SS to JE, Dec. 22, 1782, *Shaw's Journals*, p. 99.
33. AM to SBW, Dec. 15, 1782, *Webb's Correspondence*, II, p. 439; and AM to HK, Dec. 14, 1782, *HKP*, reel 10, MHS.
34. Champagne, p. 185.
35. Diary, Nov. 15, 1782, and AS to RM, Nov. 18, 1782, *PRM*, VII, pp. 51, 60 (quotes on p. 60).
36. RM to AS, Nov. 18, 1782, ibid., pp. 61–62.
37. AS to RM, Nov. 19, 1782, ibid., pp. 65–66.
38. AS to AM, MO, and JB, Dec. 1782, *SP*, I, pp. 573–576 (quotes on pp. 575–76).

Chapter Ten

1. Diary, Dec. 21, 1782, *PRM*, VII, p. 226.
2. Diary, Dec. 31, 1782, ibid., p. 247n3.
3. Quoted in Ver Steeg, p. 130 (1st quote); Smith, *James Wilson*, pp. 178–79; Rappleye, p. 329; and S. Wharton to the Delaware Council, Jan. 6, 1783, *LMCC*, VII, p. 3 (2nd quote).
4. S. Osgood to J. Lowell, Jan. 6, 1783, *LDC*, XIX, p. 540 (1st quote); Brant, p. 101; notes, Dec. 24, 1782, *PJM*, V, p. 442 (2nd quote).
5. JM to ER, Dec. 24, 1782, *PJM*, V, p. 449 (quote); Smith, *New Age Now Begins*, II, p. 1763; and T. Paine to RM, Nov. 20, 1782, *PRM*, VII, pp. 84n–86.
6. S. Osgood to J. Lowell, Jan. 6, 1783, *LDC*, XIX, p. 540.
7. Hawke, pp. 134–35; Miller, *Alexander Hamilton*, p. 90; T. Paine to RM, Nov. 20, 1782, *PRM*, VII, pp. 84n–86; and Staples, *Rhode Island in the Continental Congress*, p. 428.
8. S. Osgood to J. Lowell, Jan. 6, 1783, *LDC*, XIX, p. 540.
9. Notes, Dec. 24, 1782, *PJM*, V, p. 442.
10. GM to NG, Dec. 24, 1782, quoted in Corbin, *Two Frontiers of Freedom*, p. 58.
11. JM to ER, Jan. 14, 1783, *LDC*, XIX, p. 583.
12. Smith, *James Wilson*, p. 179.
13. Ibid.
14. Chastellux, quoted in Corning, p. 24; and in Monell, p. 55.
15. Oct. 26–27, 1782, *Heath's Memoirs*, pp. 357–58 (quotes on p. 358).
16. Quoted in Dempsey, p. 40 (1st quote); Oct. 28, 1782, *Heath's Memoirs*, p. 358 (2nd quote); and Corning, 103.

17. Refer to the first source note for chapter four.
18. Conversation with Mike McGurty at the New Windsor Cantonment; and Aimone's introduction in *General Orders*, pp. iv, vi.
19. General orders, Oct. 28, 1782, *WGW*, XXV, p. 303.
20. HG to Steuben, Nov. 22, 1782, quoted in Dempsey, pp. 29, 41, 46–47 (quote on p. 41); Oct. 28, 1782, *Heath's Memoirs*, p. 358 (last quote).
21. HG to Steuben, Nov. 22, 1782, quoted in Dempsey, pp. 41 (quote), 46–48; conversation with Mike McGurty at the New Windsor Cantonment; Fowler, "An American Crisis," p. 9; and Monell, p. 40.
22. "New Windsor Cantonment."
23. Gates's orders, Jan. 5, 1783, *General Orders*, p. 63.
24. Aimone's introduction and Dec. 25, 1782, *General Orders*, pp. v, 62; and Corning, p. 108.
25. Wensyel.
26. Royster, p. 332.

Chapter Eleven

1. Flexner, *Young Hamilton*, p. 394; and Rappleye, p. 331.
2. AM to HK, Jan. 9, 1783, *HKP*, reel 11, MHS [GLC02437.01819].
3. Belcher, II, p. 40.
4. JM to ER, Dec. 30, 1782, *PJM*, V, p. 473.
5. *AMP*, MacDougall and Champagne were my main sources for the biography of Alexander McDougall. Smith, *New Age Now Begins*, I; Schecter; Aug. 28, 1782, *General Orders*; Shannon; "General Alexander McDougall, Citizen and Soldier, 1732–1786," and the quote sources also provided information. The sources for those quotes are given separately in the succeeding twenty-five notes.
6. AM, "To the Betrayed Inhabitants of the City and Colony of New York," in MacDougall, pp. 159–63.
7. AM, "To the Freeholders, and Freemen and Inhabitants of the Colony of New York; and to all the friends of liberty in North America," Feb. 9, 1770, *Holt's Journal*, quoted in MacDougall, p. 29.
8. Quoted in McDougall, p. 34.
9. Ibid.
10. Ibid.
11. AM's indictment for libel, Apr. 27, 1770, in Shannon, p. 243.
12. Ibid.
13. AM, "To the FREE and LOYAL INHABITANTS of the CITY and COLONY of NEW YORK" [Defense of non-importation agreements], May 16, 1770, NYHS [GLC02552].

14. Ibid.
15. Quoted in MacDougall, p. 97.
16. General orders for attacking Germantown, Oct. 3, 1777, *PGW*, XI, p. 375.
17. GW to the President, Oct. 7, 1777, *WGW*, IX, p. 322.
18. "The Memorial of the General Officers Serving in the Army of the United States," Nov. 18, 1779, in Shannon, pp. 269–73.
19. NG to AM, n. d., *AMP*, reel 3, NYHS.
20. AM to NG, May 29, 1780, ibid.
21. General officers' memorial, July 11, 1780, ibid.
22. NG's instructions to AM, July 11, 1780, ibid.
23. "Notes of the different Subjects contained in two memorials delivered to Congress in behalf of the American Army by Major General McDougall," Aug. 1780, *AMP*, reel 4, NYHS.
24. Resolution of Aug. 12, 1780, *AMP*, reel 3, NYHS. In addition to this source and the ones cited for the following two items, I used the August 24, 1780 resolution for this paragraph.
25. Resolution of Aug. 17, 1780, *AMP*, reel 3, NYHS.
26. "Notes of the different Subjects contained in two memorials delivered to Congress in behalf of the American Army by Major General McDougall," Aug. 1780, *AMP*, reel 4, NYHS.
27. AM to W. Malcolm, Apr. 21, 1781, Butler, ed., *Papers of the Continental Congress, 1774–1789*, reel 179, # 161.
28. AM to GC, Mar. 28, 1782, *AMP*, reel 4, NYHS.
29. Ibid.
30. AM to GW, Aug. 26, 1782, *AMP*, reel 4, NYHS.
31. Kail et al., eds., *Who Was Who in the American Revolution*; Johnson et al., eds, II; *Virtual American Biographies,* "John Brooks"; and "Brooks's Memoir" were my main sources for this biography. Duncan, pp. 7 and 77, is the source for the item about this country having only one medical college at that time and the apprenticeship info. Fleming, *Now We Are Enemies*; Champagne, pp. 117–18; McKenzie, *Barefooted, Bare Leg'd, Bare Breech'd*, pp. 60–61, 75; *Putnam's Memoirs*, pp. 89–94, 176; and the Hamilton biographies by Randall and Flexner were my other sources for the biography of Brooks. Sources for the quotations in this biographical section are given separately in the succeeding eight notes.
32. JB, quoted in McKenzie, p. 60.
33. R. W. Williams, quoted in "Brooks's Memoir," pp. 194–95.
34. Ibid.
35. Unidentified historian, quoted ibid., pp. 194–95.
36. JB, quoted in McKenzie, p. 75.

37. For this section describing Washington's desire for "uniformity ... army" and men of "character and abilities" for subinspector positions, Brooks's performance as an assistant to Steuben, and his participation at the Battle of Monmouth I used the following: GW to JB, Mar. 24, 1778, quoted in "Brooks's Memoir," p. 195; Hatch, p. 152; and Smith, *Battle of Monmouth*, pp. 9, 16.
38. June 5, 1782, *General Orders*, p. 27.
39. R.Putnam to GW, Dec. 17, 1782, in *Putnam's Memoirs*, p. 97.
40. My sources for the biography of Matthias Ogden were the following: Unger, "Matthias Ogden," in Fremont-Barnes et al., eds., III, p. 1362; *Virtual American Biographies*, "Robert Ogden"; Wheeler, comp., *Ogden Family in America*, pp. 133–34; Boatner, pp. 814–15; Billias, "Horatio Gates," in Billias, ed., pp. 85–87; Nelson, *Horatio Gates*, pp. 57–67; Lefkowitz, *George Washington's Indispensable Men*, p. 169; Morris, ed., p. 95. McGuire, *The Surprise of Germantown, or the Battle of Clivedon, October 4th, 1777*, p. 70; Eckert, *Wilderness War*, pp. 379–80, 384; Ketchum, ed., p. 307. Bobrick, pp. 392–93; Smith, *New Age Now Begins*, II, pp. 1514–16; Nagy, *Rebellion in the Ranks*, p. 42; Judd, ed., *Revolutionary War Memoir and Settled Correspondence of Philip Van Cortlandt*, I, p. 88n.44; Ziegler, *King William IV*, pp. 39–40; Irving, *Life of George Washington*, III, pp. 612–13; Hatch, p. 152; Randall, *Alexander Hamilton*, pp. 276–77; and Kline, p. 257. The sources for quotations in this section are given separately in the succeeding three notes.
41. Quoted in Boatner, p. 815.
42. J. P. Martin, quoted in Smith, *New Age Now Begins*, II, p. 1515.
43. J. P. Martin, quoted in Bobrick, p. 393.
44. Refer to my biography of Hamilton in chapter fourteen and the notes for that section.
45. JB to AH, July 4, 1779, *PAH*, II, p. 91 (quote); and JB to AH, Aug. 8, 1779, *PAH*, II, pp. 125–26.

Chapter Twelve

1. My main sources for the description of Philadelphia were Tinkcom, op. cit., in Weigley, ed.; and Schoepf, *Travels in the Confederation*. My other sources for unquoted material were Kirschke, pp. 113, 115, 317n2.; Boatner, p. 856; History Channel, *Washington's Generals: Lord Cornwallis*; Chernow, p. 173; Mintz, p. 107; Van Doren, *Benjamin Franklin*, p. 130; idem, *Great Rehearsal*, pp. 139, 247–48; Scharf and Westcott, *History of Philadelphia*, II, p. 966; Found and Hartnoll, eds., *Concise Oxford Companion to the Theatre*, p. 477; Ford, *Washington and the Theatre*, pp. 29–30; and Hendrickson, p. 375. The list of trades/professions is based on a description of Philadelphia in 1789–1790 in *Great Rehearsal* and on Schoepf's description of the city in the summer of 1783. My sources for quotations are given separately in the succeeding four notes.
2. RM, quoted in Tinkcom, op. cit., in Weigley, ed., p. 134.

3. NG, quoted in Bowman, p. 55.
4. Quoted in Tinkcom, op. cit., in Weigley, ed., p. 151.
5. Ibid., p. 144.
6. Miller, *Triumph of Freedom*, p. 434.
7. Morgan, p. 105; and Corbin, p. 35 (quote).
8. Henderson, pp. 2, 158.
9. Chernow, p. 173.
10. Corbin, p. 35.
11. Higginbotham, p. 214.
12. Hendrickson, p. 377.
13. Ibid., p. 375.
14. Corbin, p. 33.
15. Higginbotham, p. 214.
16. Ibid.; Ferling, *Leap in the Dark*, p. 255; Hendrickson, p. 375; Fleming, *Beat the Last Drum*, p. 103; and Miller, *Triumph of Freedom*, p. 434.
17. Miller, *Triumph of Freedom*, p. 659; and Hatch, p. 20.
18. RM to J. Duane, Sept. 8, 1778, *LDC*, X, p. 607.
19. GM to R. R. Livingston, [Jan. 1781] and Feb. 21, 1781, quoted in Rakove, pp. 233–34.
20. HL, quoted in Miller, *Triumph of Freedom*, p. 433.
21. Extract of the Articles of Confederation sent by Dr. Judie Miller at the LOC; Van Doren, *Great Rehearsal*, pp. xii, 5; Henderson, p. 157; Rakove, p. 355; and Ruttenber, p. 61.
22. Corbin, pp. 34, 36.
23. Mattern, pp. 139–40.
24. Diary, Dec. 31, 1782, *PRM*, VII, p. 247 (quotes); Siry and Newman, "Newburgh Conspiracy," in Krawczynski, ed., *History in Dispute*, XII, p. 228; Kline, p. 259; and Marshall.
25. Ver Steeg, p. 136.
26. Johnson, p. 21.
27. Ibid.
28. GM to J. Jay, Jan. 1, 1783, *PRM*, VII, pp. 256–57.
29. Kline, p. 58.
30. A. Clairy to AM, MO and JB, Jan. 5, 1783, quoted in Champagne, p. 187.
31. Fowler, "An American Crisis," p. 1; e-mail from Karie Diethorn, chief curator of Independence National Historic Park (room's description); notes, Jan. 6, 1783, *PJM*, VI, p. 15 (quote); SS to JE, Apr. 1783, Rhodehamel, ed., p. 787; and Glasson, p. 37.
32. Committee of the army's report to Knox, Feb. 8, 1783, *Collection*, pp. 14–15.

33. Champagne, pp. 189, 258n22.
34. Notes, Jan. 6, 1783, *PJM*, VI, p. 16.
35. Notes, Jan. 7, 1783, *PJM*, VI, pp. 18–19 (quotes); and RM to J. Pierce, Jan. 20, 1783, *PRM*, VII, p. 329n.
36. Va. delegates to BH, Jan. 7, 1783, *PJM*, VI, pp. 20–21.
37. JM to ER, Jan. 7, 1783, ibid., p. 22.
38. Gates's orders, Jan. 5, 1783, *General Orders*, p. 63; Dempsey, pp. 87–88, 92–96; and Corning, pp. 108–09.
39. Fowler, *American Crisis*, p. 165; Gates's orders, Jan. 5, 1783, *General Orders*, p. 63; HG, quoted in Dempsey, p. 92; Corning, pp. 108–09; Boatner, p. 1129 (biographical material); and Kail et al., eds., p. 156 (biographical material).
40. AM to HK, Jan. 9, 1783, *HKP*, reel 11, MHS [GLC02437.01819].
41. RM to EB, Jan. 9, 1783, *PRM*, VII, pp. 287–88n1; notes, Jan. 8–10, 1783, *PJM*, VI, p. 24 ; Ver Steeg, pp. 169–70; and Sumner, II, pp. 89–90.
42. RM to EB, Jan. 9, 1783, *PRM*, VII, pp. 287–88.
43. GW to JA, Jan. 10, 1783, *WGW*, XXVI, pp. 24–27 (quotes on pp. 25–27).
44. GW to T. Tilghman, Jan.10, 1783, ibid., pp. 27–30 (quotes on p. 27).
45. Freeman, V, p. 428; and Flexner, *George Washington in the American Revolution*, p. 499.
46. Fishman, "Presbyopia's Finest Hour," pp. 65–66.
47. Notes, Jan. 9–10, 1783, *PJM*, VI, p. 26 (quote); Champagne, p. 189; Johnson, p. 34; Hatch, p. 153; and Shannon, p. 197.
48. Gates's orders, Jan. 9, 1783, *General Orders*, p. 63.
49. Aimone's introduction and Gates's orders, Jan. 9, 1783, ibid., pp. v, 64 (quotes on p. 64).
50. Ibid., pp. vi, 64 (quotes on p. 64).
51. Document dated Jan. 10, 1783, cited in Dempsey, p. 96.
52. Diary, Jan. 11, 1783, and RM to Luzerne, Jan. 13, 1783, *PRM*, VII, pp. 292, 300 (quote on p. 292).
53. RM to B. Franklin, Jan. 11, 1783, ibid., p. 294 (quotes); and Sumner, II, p. 90.
54. AH to GC, Jan. 12, 1783, *LMCC*, VII, pp. 13–14.
55. Notes, Jan. 13, 1783, *PJM*, VI, pp. 31–33 (quotes); and Champagne, p. 5 (Alexander McDougall's speech impediment), p. 189.
56. Champagne, p. 190.
57. Notes, Jan. 13, 1783, *PJM*, VI, p. 33.
58. Kohn, *Eagle and Sword*, p. 22.
59. Johnson, p. 33.
60. Diary, Jan. 14, 1783, *PRM*, VII, p. 309n3.
61. JM to ER, Jan. 14, 1783, *PJM*, VI, p. 40.

62. Gates's orders, Jan. 14, 1783, *General Orders*, p. 64.
63. Dempsey, p. 101; and Corning, p. 109.
64. General orders, Jan. 8, 1783, *WGW*, XXVI, p. 23 (quote); and Dempsey, p. 96.
65. Gates's orders, Jan. 15, 1783, *General Orders*, p. 65.
66. Diary, Jan. 15, 1783, and RM to J. Pierce, Jan. 20, 1783, *PRM*, VII, pp. 310-11n7, 330n.
67. Ibid., pp. 310, 330 (quote on p. 310).
68. *The New York Packet, and the American Advertiser*, Jan. 16, 1783, quoted in Corning, p. 107.
69. *The New York Packet, and American Advertiser*, Jan. 16, 1783, quoted in Dempsey, p. 88. The dimensions given in the article may be incorrect. Refer to Dykman, "Historic Temple at New Windsor, 1783."
70. Gates's orders, Jan. 17, 1783, *General Orders*, p. 65.
71. RM to J. Adams, Jan. 16, 1783, *PRM*, VII, pp. 313-14n1 (quotes on p. 313).
72. Diary, Jan. 17, 1783, *PRM*, VII, p. 315.
73. JB to H. Jackson, Jan. 19, 1783, *Alexander Calvin and Ellen Morton Washburn Autograph Collection*, Manuscripts, reel 7, # 54B, MHS.
74. Translation of Luzerne to RM, Jan. 18, 1783, *PRM*, VII, pp. 319-21.
75. RM to J. Pierce, Jan. 20, 1783, ibid., p. 337.
76. RM to NG, Jan. 20, 1783, ibid., p. 326.
77. NG to Governor L. Hall, Jan. 20, 1783, *PNG*, XII, p. 380.

Chapter Thirteen

1. Diary, Jan. 21, 1783, *PRM*, VII, p. 345.
2. JM to ER, Jan. 22, 1783, *PJM*, VI, pp. 55-56.
3. GM to J. Rutledge, Feb. 3, 1783, *PRM*, VII, p. 393n; and Dempsey, pp. 109-10.
4. Notes, Jan. 24, 1783, *PJM*, VI, p. 127n25.
5. RM to the President, Jan. 24, 1783, *PRM*, VII, p. 368 (quotes); Dempsey, p. 110; and Champagne, p. 191.
6. Notes, Jan. 24, 1783, *PJM*, VI, p. 120.
7. I used the following for my description of the report prepared by the Grand Committee and the debates and resolutions of January 24: Dempsey, pp. 109-10; Glasson, pp. 37-38; Champagne, p. 191; Randall, *Alexander Hamilton*, p. 277; Flexner, *Young Hamilton*, p. 400; Johnson, pp. 39-42; Henderson, pp. 328-29; and notes, Jan. 24, 1783, *PJM*, VI, pp. 121-23. The sources for my quotations are given separately in the succeeding four notes.
8. Notes, Jan. 24, 1783, *PJM*, VI, p. 122.
9. Ibid., p. 121.

10. Ibid., pp. 121–22.
11. Ibid., p. 122.
12. Gates's orders, Jan. 21, 1783, *General Orders*, p. 65.
13. Resolutions by the United States Congress Assembled, Jan. 25, 1783, in *Collection*, pp. 12–13 (quote on p. 13); notes, Jan. 24–25, 1783, *PJM*, VI, pp. 122, 128fn36–30; Jan. 25, *JCC*, XXIV, p. 93; SS to JE, Apr. 1783, Rhodehamel, ed., p. 787; Glasson, p. 38; Johnson, pp. 39–42; Champagne, p. 191; Randall, *Alexander Hamilton*, p. 277; Siry, op. cit., in Krawczynski, ed., XII, p. 222; Ver Steeg, p. 171; and Kohn, "Inside History of the Newburgh Conspiracy," p. 195.
14. Quoted in Wagner, p. 56.
15. Notes, Jan. 27, 1783, *PJM*, VI, pp. 134–35 (quotes), 140n14.
16. Ibid., p. 135.
17. Ibid., pp. 135–36.
18. Ibid., p. 136.
19. Ibid., p. 137.
20. Ibid.
21. Ibid.
22. Ibid., pp. 137–38.
23. Gates's orders, Jan. 25–26, 1783, *General Orders*, p. 66.
24. Notes, Jan. 28, 1783, *PJM*, VI, p. 141.
25. Ibid., p. 142.
26. Ibid.
27. Ibid.
28. Ibid.
29. Ibid., pp. 142–43.
30. Quoted in Smith, *James Wilson*, p. 177.
31. Notes, Jan. 28, 1783, *PJM*, VI, p. 143.
32. Ibid.
33. Ibid.
34. Ibid., pp. 143–47.
35. Ibid., pp. 147–48.
36. Ibid. (quotes on p. 148).
37. Ibid., p. 148.
38. Ibid., pp. 148–49 (quote on p. 148).
39. Ibid., p. 149.
40. A. Lee to S. Adams, Jan. 29, 1783, *LMCC*, VII, p. 28.

41. Notes, Jan. 29, 1783, *PJM*, VI, pp. 159–60.
42. Ibid., p. 160.
43. Ibid., pp. 160–61 (quotes on p. 161).
44. Ibid., pp. 161–62.
45. Ibid., pp. 162–63.
46. Ibid., p. 163.
47. Ibid., pp. 163–64 (quotes on p. 164), 169n36, 37.
48. Ibid., p. 164.
49. Ibid., pp. 164–65.
50. Notes, Jan. 30, 1783, ibid., pp. 170–71. Besides Madison's notes and sources for quotations that are cited above, a number of other works helped me when I wrote the section about the debates that took place from January 28 to January 30: Smith, *James Wilson*, pp. 180–82; McDonald, *E. Pluribus Unum*, pp. 25–26; Randall, *Alexander Hamilton*, p. 278; Hendrickson, pp. 386–87; Brant, pp. 102–03; Henderson, pp. 329–31; Corbin, pp. 48, 50; and Chernow, p. 176.
51. Sumner, II, p. 68.
52. Ibid.
53. Mitchell, pp. 320–21; and Smith, *James Wilson*, pp. 182–83.
54. NG to BL, Feb. 2, 1783, *PNG*, XII, p. 402 (quote); and NG to RM, Feb. 2, 1783, ibid., p. 405.
55. Diary, Feb. 4, 1783, *PRM*, VII, p. 400.
56. RI delegates to W. Greene, Feb. 4, 1783, *LMCC*, VII, pp. 29–30.
57. Notes, Feb. 4, 1783, *PJM*, VI, pp. 187–88 (quotes come from these pages). Other sources used for the section detailing the debate on the report concerning the officers' request for commutation and the delegates' votes: Notes, Feb. 4, 1783, *PJM*, VI, p. 189n7; Henderson, p. 335; Glasson, p. 38; and Johnson, pp. 43–44. John Taylor Gilman again suggested referring the issue to the states on February 25. For more information on his proposal and the debate surrounding it see p. 350 and the corresponding end note.
58. Diary, Feb. 5, 1783, *PRM*, VII, p. 405; Johnson, p. 40n79; and Mintz, pp. 159–60.
59. Diary, Feb. 5, 1783, *PRM*, VII, p. 405.
60. Quoted in Dempsey, pp. 105–06 (quotes on p. 106); Gates's orders, Jan. 29, 1783, *General Orders*, p. 66; and Corning, p. 109.
61. Gates's orders, Feb. 4, 1783, *General Orders*, p. 67 (quotes); and Corning, p. 110.
62. *New York Packet and American Advertiser*, Feb. 13, 1783, quoted in Dempsey, pp. 116–17; and Aimone's introduction, *General Orders*, p. ix.
63. Feb. 6, 1783, *JCC*, XXIV, pp. 112–13.
64. Ibid., pp. 114–16 (quote on p. 115); and Henderson, p. 332.

Chapter Fourteen

1. GM to HK, Feb. 7, 1783, *PRM*, VII, p. 417.
2. AM and MO to HK, Feb. 8, 1783, *HKP*, reel 11, MHS [GLC02437.10515].
3. Champagne, pp. 193–94; Ferguson, p. 159; Fowler, "American Crisis," p. 12; Higginbotham, p. 408; Rappleye, pp. 341–42; RM to J. Pierce, Jan. 20, 1783, and GM to HK, Feb. 7, 1783, *PRM*, VII, pp. 332n, 419n11 and headnote; Siry and Newman, op. cit., in Krawczynski, ed., p. 223; and Kohn, *Eagle and Sword*, p. 24.
4. BH to the Va. delegates, Jan. 31, 1783, *PJM*, VI, p. 176.
5. Va. delegates to BH, Feb. 11, 1783, ibid., p. 219.
6. "Brutus" (AM) to HK, Feb. 12, 1783, *HKP*, reel 11, MHS [GLC02437.01912].
7. Notes, Feb. 12, 1783, *PJM*, VI, pp. 225–26 (quote on p. 225).
8. JM to ER, Feb. 18, 1783, ibid., p. 256.
9. Notes, Feb. 12, 1783, ibid., pp. 225–26 (quotes on p. 226).
10. M. Ridley to GM, Dec. 14, 1783, *PRM*, VII, p. 207n1. Historians differ on when the news arrived. The ship likely arrived on the 12th and Congress got the news the following day. See Morris's diary, Feb. 13, 1783, *PRM*, VII, p. 431.
11. Notes, Feb. 13, 1783, *LDC*, XIX, p. 692.
12. AH to PS, Feb. 18, 1781, *PAH*, II, pp. 563–64 (quotes on p. 564).
13. AH to J. McHenry, Feb. 18, 1781, ibid., p. 569.
14. Historians disagree on the date. I chose the one in *PAH*, III, p. 253.
15. AH to GW, Feb. 13, 1783, *PAH*, III, pp. 254–56.
16. Notes, Feb. 20, 1783, *PJM*, VI, p. 266.
17. R. Livingston to J. Adams, Feb. 13, 1783, quoted in Sumner, II, p. 75.
18. JM to ER, Feb. 13, 1783, *LDC*, XIX, p. 693.
19. Kohn, "Inside History of the Newburgh Conspiracy," p. 198 (arrival on Feb. 13); and JA to HG, Apr. 29, 1783, *LMCC*, VII, p. 155n3.
20. Smith, *James Wilson*, p. 183.
21. AH to GC, Feb. 14, 1783, *PAH*, III, p. 256.
22. My main sources for the biography of Alexander Hamilton were Randall, *Alexander Hamilton*, and Hendrickson. Other sources were Chernow; Miller, *Alexander Hamilton*; Brookhiser, *Alexander Hamilton*; Lefkowitz, pp. 109–10, 253; Kelly, *Best Little Stories from the American Revolution*, p. 160; MacDougall, pp. 55–57, 134–35; Langguth, p. 517; Ferling, *Leap in the Dark*, p. 245; AH to GC, Feb. 13 and Mar. 12, 1778, *PAH*, I, pp. 425–28, 439–42; AH to GC, Feb. 13, 1778, *PAH*, I, pp. 426–27; and GW to AH, Apr. 27, 1781, *WGW*, XXII, p. 3; Cornwallis's dispatch to Sir H. Clinton, Oct. 15, 1781, in Carrington, *Battles of the American Revolution*, p. 639; Davis,

Campaign That Won America, p. 225; and those cited in the succeeding notes for quotes and the content of Hamilton's "Continentalist" articles.

23. History Channel, *Duel: Hamilton vs. Burr.*
24. Quoted in Lefkowitz, p. 109.
25. Quoted in Randall, *Alexander Hamilton*, p. 75.
26. Ibid., p. 78.
27. Ibid.
28. Quoted in MacDougall, p. 55.
29. Quoted in Lefkowitz, p. 110.
30. Quoted in Randall, p. 136.
31. J. McHenry's journal, quoted ibid., p. 177.
32. AH to GC, Feb. 13, 1778, *PAH*, I, p. 425.
33. Ibid., p. 427.
34. Ibid.
35. GW to AH, Apr. 27, 1781, *WGW*, XXII, p. 3.
36. Continentalist I, July 12, 1781, *PAH*, II, pp. 650–51.
37. Continentalist III, Aug. 9, 1781, ibid., pp. 660–61.
38. The preceding two notes give my main sources for all the material on the articles by "the Continentalist." Other sources that I used for my description of those four articles are Continentalist II and IV, July 19, 1781, and Aug. 30, 1781, *PAH*, II, pp. 654–57, 669–70; and pp. 649, 652, and 662–65 in Continentalist I and Continentalist III, respectively.
39. Dr. Thacher's journal, *Spirit*, p. 1233.
40. Ibid.
41. Ibid.
42. Denny's journal, Oct. 11, 1781, Rhodehamel, ed., p. 723.
43. Denny's journal, Sept. 1–Nov. 1, 1781, ibid., p. 724.
44. Martin, *Private Yankee Doodle*, p. 235.
45. Ibid.
46. Ibid.
47. Quoted in Davis, *Campaign That Won America*, p. 227.
48. Quoted in Flexner, *Young Hamilton*, p. 364.
49. Quoted in Smith, *New Age Now Begins*, II, p. 1702.
50. Quoted in Randall, *Alexander Hamilton*, p. 244.
51. GM to NG, Feb. 11, 1783, *PRM*, VII, pp. 425–26n1.
52. RM to J. Pierce, Jan. 20, 1783, ibid., p. 333n.

53. Sketch by W. Tarbell of the 7th Massachusetts in Dykman.
54. Aimone's introduction and Feb. 15, 1783, *General Orders*, pp. vi, 68 (quotes on p. 68); and Dempsey, p. 123.
55. GW to D. Rittenhouse, Feb. 16, 1783, Lengel, ed., p. 262.
56. Notes, Feb. 18, 1783, *PJM*, VI, p. 249.
57. Ibid.
58. Ibid., pp. 249–50.
59. Ibid., p. 250.
60. Ibid.
61. Ibid., p. 251.
62. Ibid.
63. Ibid.
64. GW to WS, Jan. 18, 1783, and GW to Steuben, Feb. 18, 1783, *WGW*, XXVI, pp. 46–47, 143 (quotes on pp. 47 and 143).

Chapter Fifteen

1. Notes, Feb. 19, 1783, *PJM*, VI, pp. 258–59.
2. Ibid., p. 259.
3. Ibid.
4. Notes, Feb. 19, 1783, *PJM*, VI, p. 259; Miller, *Alexander Hamilton*, pp. 88–89; Rakove, p. 315; and Sumner, II, p. 68.
5. Notes, Feb. 19, 1783, *PJM*, VI, pp. 259, 262n6.
6. Ibid., pp. 259–60.
7. Ibid., p. 260.
8. Ibid.
9. Ibid., pp. 260, 263n18.
10. Ibid., pp. 260–61.
11. Ibid., p. 261.
12. Ibid.
13. "Brutus" (AM) to HK, Feb. 19, 1783, *HKP*, reel 11, MHS [GLC02437.01933].
14. Notes, Feb. 20, 1783, *PJM*, VI, pp. 264–65.
15. Ibid., p. 265.
16. Ibid., p. 266.
17. HG to R. Peters, Feb. 20, 1783, Sol Feinstone Collection, reel 1.
18. "On the Prospect of Peace," ibid.

19. NG to RM, Feb. 20, 1783, *PRM*, VII, p. 445.
20. Mattern, p. 141.
21. HK to AM, Feb. 21, 1783, *HKP*, reel 11, MHS [GLC02437.10097].
22. HK to GM, Feb. 21, 1783, *PRM*, VII, pp. 448–49.
23. Notes, Feb. 21, 1783, *PJM*, VI, pp. 270–72.
24. Ibid., pp. 272–73.
25. Ibid., p. 273.
26. Ibid.
27. Ibid.
28. Ibid.
29. Ibid., pp. 273, 277n27 and 28.
30. Diary, Feb. 22, 1783, *PRM*, VII, p. 450.
31. SS to JE, Feb. 23, 1783, *Shaw's Journals*, p. 100.
32. Quoted in Bates, p. 357; and Ferguson, pp. 147, 152–54.
33. Notes, Feb. 25, 1783, *PJM*, VI, pp. 282–84n2 and 4 (quotes); Feb. 25, 1783, *JCC*, XXIV, p. 147; and Glasson, p. 39.
34. JM to ER, Feb. 25, 1783, *PJM*, VI, pp. 285–87 (quotes on pp. 286–87).
35. Steuben to HK, Feb. 25, 1783, *HKP*, reel 11, MHS [GLC02437.01952].
36. Feb. 26, 1783, *JCC*, XXIV, pp. 149–51.
37. Ibid., p. 151; and RM to EB, Feb. 26, 1783, *PRM*, VII, p. 470.
38. RM to GW, Feb. 27, 1783, *PRM*, VII, p. 475.
39. GW to JJ, Dec. 14, 1782, *WGW*, XXV, p. 431n.
40. JJ to GW, Feb. 27, 1783, *Jones's Letters*, pp. 97–100, 102 (quotes on pp. 98–100).
41. Notes, Feb. 27, 1783, *PJM*, VI, pp. 297–98 (quotes); Hatch, p. 158; and Jensen, p. 73.
42. Notes, Feb. 27, 1783, *PJM*, VI, p. 298 (quotes); and Hatch, p. 158.
43. Notes, Feb. 27, 1783, *PJM*, VI, pp. 298–99.
44. Ibid., p. 299.
45. "Brutus" (AM) to HK, Feb. 27, 1783, *HKP*, reel 11, MHS [GLC02437.01959].
46. Notes, Feb. 28, 1783, *PJM*, VI, pp. 300–01 (quote on p. 300); Feb. 28, 1783, *JCC*, XXIV, pp. 154–56; and Glasson, p. 39.
47. Quoted in RM to J. Pierce, Jan. 20, 1783, *PRM*, VII, p. 334n.
48. HK to AM, Mar. 3, 1783, *AMP*, reel 4, NYHS. In a draft of this letter in *HKP*, reel 11, MHS, HK crossed out "rutus."
49. HK to AM, Mar. 3, 1783, *AMP*, reel 4, NYHS. In addition to the Feb. 28 letter, there was one dated Feb. 24. Neither MHS nor NYHS has the letters.

50. HK to BL, Mar. 3, 1783, *HKP*, reel 11, MHS [GLC02437.01974 and GLC02437.01976].
51. Ibid., # 179, MHS.

Chapter Sixteen

1. GW to AH, Mar. 4, 1783, *PAH*, III, pp. 277–79.
2. Nelson, *Horatio Gates*; and Billias were my main sources for the biography of Gates. Ketchum was useful. *American Revolutionary War*, II and IV (Schuyler and the northern department); *Dictionary of American Biography*, IV; Morris's encyclopedia; Williams; Brandt, Wallace's "Benedict Arnold" and Higginbothm's "Daniel Morgan" in Billias's book; the History Channel's *Revolution* (Part V); Raddall's *Paths of Destiny*; and Lengel's biography of George Washington were used for events up to but not including the Conway Cabal. GW to HG, Oct. 30, 1777, *WGW*, IX; GW to T. Conway, Nov.16, 1777, *PGW*, XII; Chadwick, p. 262; GW to HG, Feb. 9, 1778, *PGW*, XIII; Peckham, "Marquis de Lafayette" in Billias, ed.; Buckman, *Lafayette*; Unger, *Lafayette*; Higginbotham; Boatner; Randall, *Alexander Hamilton*; Langguth; Freeman, *IV*; Lefkowitz; Schultz; Champagne; Bobrick; Chadwick; and Hatch were used for the Conway Cabal and its aftermath. For the period from Gates's taking command of the southern army until his return after a forced retirement over Camden I used Chidsey, *War in the South*; Buchanan, *Road to Guilford Courthouse*; History Channel, *Washington's Generals: Lord Cornwallis*; Carrington; Oct. 5, 1782, *Heath's Memoirs*; Aug. 29, 1782, *General Orders*; Flexner, *Young Hamilton*; Russell, *American Revolution in the Southern Colonies*, p. 165 (hair powder); and Landers, *Battle of Camden, South Carolina* (hair powder). Patterson; Davis, *George Washington and the American Revolution*; Smith, *New Age Now Begins*, II; History Channel, *Washington's Generals: Horatio Gates*; Flexner, *Washington*; *Diary*, II; Leach, *Arms for Empire*, pp. 363-66; Van Every, *Forth to the Wilderness*, pp. 88-90; and Thane also provided bits of material. Sources for quotations and some paraphrased parts of letters are given separately in succeeding notes.
3. Ketchum, p. 52.
4. Quoted in Nelson, *Horatio Gates*, p. 6.
5. Quoted ibid., p. 24.
6. J.Trumbull to HG, July 12, 1776, quoted ibid., p. 61.
7. Ibid., p. 63.
8. S. Chase and C. Carroll to J. Hancock, May 27, 1776, *LDC*, IV, p. 82.
9. MO to A. Burr, July 26, 1776, quoted in Nelson, *Horatio Gates*, pp. 65–66.
10. U. Hay to GC, Aug. 13, 1777, quoted in Billias, op. cit., in Billias, ed., p. 90.
11. HG to J. Burgoyne, Sept. 2, 1777, *Spirit*, p. 560.
12. Captain Warren, quoted in Brandt, p. 133.
13. HG to Governor Clinton, Oct. 4, 1777, quoted in Billias, op. cit., in Billias, ed., p. 95.

14. Quoted in Nelson, *Horatio Gates*, p. 137.
15. GW to R. H. Lee, Oct.16, 1777, *PGW*, XI, p. 529.
16. Ibid.
17. GW to T. Conway, Nov. 5, 1777, *PGW*, XII, p. 129.
18. T. Conway to GW, Nov. 5, 1777, ibid., p. 130.
19. T. Conway to GW, Nov. 16, 1777, ibid., p. 277.
20. T. Mifflin to HG, Nov. 28, 1777, *HGP*, reel 6, NYHS.
21. HG to T. Conway, Dec. 3, 1777, *HGP*, reel 6, NYHS [actual letter is in MS Sparks 22 at Harvard's Houghton Library].
22. HG to GW, Dec. 8, 1777, *HGP*, reel 6, NYHS [actual letter is held by the LOC].
23. GW to HL, Jan. 2, 1778, *PGW*, XIII, p. 119.
24. GW to HG, Jan. 4, 1778, ibid., pp. 138–39.
25. T. Conway to GW, Jan. 10, 1778, ibid., pp. 195–96 (quotes on p. 195).
26. HG to GW, Jan. 23, 1778, *HGP*, reel 6, NYHS.
27. Lafayette, quoted in Thane, p. 123.
28. Lafayette to GW, Feb. 23, 1778, *PGW*, XIII, p. 649.
29. HG to GW, Feb. 19, 1778, *HGP*, reel 6, NYHS.
30. B. Stoddert to HG, Feb. 25, 1778, ibid.
31. GW to P. Henry, Mar. 28, 1778, *PGW*, XIV, p. 336.
32. GW to L. Carter, May 30, 1778, *WGW*, XI, p. 494.
33. GW to J. Jay, Apr. 14, 1779, *WGW*, XIV, p. 385.
34. RM, quoted in Young, p. 102.
35. HG to BL, July 4, 1780, *HGP*, reel 11, NYHS [actual letter is credited to the following: *HGP*. Manuscripts and Archives Division. The New York Public Library. Astor, Lenox, and Tilden Foundations].
36. HG to President Huntington, July 20, 1780, ibid.
37. O. Williams, quoted in Smith, *New Age Now Begins*, II, p. 1408.
38. Quoted in Carrington, p. 516.
39. Quoted in Landers, p. 47.
40. AH to J. Duane, Sept. 6, 1782, *PAH*, II, pp. 420–21 (quote on p. 421).
41. AH to J. Duane, Sept. 6, 1783, *PAH*, II, p. 420 (quote); Nelson, *Horatio Gates*, pp. 270–71; Higginbotham, p. 411; and Nelson, "Horatio Gates at Newburgh, 1783," pp. 144, 146.

Chapter Seventeen

1. GW to BH, Mar. 4, 1783, *WGW*, XXVI, pp. 183–85.
2. Ferguson, p. 160; Wagner, p. 99; "Lucius" to RM, Mar. 5, 1783, *PRM*, VII, p. 501n; and JM to ER,

Apr. 8, 1783, *PJM*, VI, p. 439.

3. A. Lee to S. Adams, Mar. 5, 1783, *LMCC*, VII, p. 68.
4. Rappleye, pp. 351n, 569; and "Lucius" to RM, Mar. 5, 1783, *PRM*, VII, pp. 504–05 (quotes).
5. R. Peters to HG, Mar. 5, 1783, *HGP*, reel 13, NYHS.
6. Nelson, *Horatio Gates*, p. 268.
7. Sumner, II, p. 96.
8. The sources for my description of the funding plan recommendations and the relationships between larger states with western lands and smaller landless ones are the following: Report on Restoring Public Credit, Mar. 6, 1783, *PJM*, VI, pp. 311–14 incl. n8 (quotes on p. 313); Smith, *James Wilson*, p. 185; Ketcham, p. 118; Brant, pp. 103–04; Miller, *Alexander Hamilton*, p. 96; Rakove, pp. 322, 337; Jensen, pp. 74–75; Miller, *Triumph of Freedom*, pp. 653–54 ("boundless empire" quote on p. 653); Van Every, p. 315; and Morgan, p. 109.
9. After orders, Mar. 6, 1783, *General Orders*, pp. 68–69 (quote on p. 69).
10. H. Wetmore to J. Pierce, Mar. 7, 1783, quoted in headnote to RM to J. Pierce, Jan. 20, 1783, *PRM*, VII, p. 335.
11. RM to EB, Mar. 8, 1783, ibid., pp. 525–28.
12. NG to RM, Feb. 2, 1783, ibid., pp. 391–92n1 (quotes on p. 391).
13. GW to RM, Mar. 8, 1783, ibid., pp. 538–39.
14. NG to Governor Guerard, Mar. 8, 1783, *PNG*, XII, pp. 494–96.
15. The sources for my description of the actions of Stewart and the plotters on March 8 – 9, the former's large holdings in securities, his feelings towards prominent Philadelphia creditors, and his earlier meetings with disenchanted officers and members of the creditors' committee are Kline, pp. 268–69; Higginbotham, p. 410; Ferguson, p. 159; Flexner, *George Washington and the American Revolution*, p. 502; Johnson, pp. 78–79; McDonald, p. 27; statement by R. King on his conversation with W. Duer, Oct. 12, 1788, King, ed., *Life and Correspondence of Rufus King*, I, p. 622 ("should meet ... Commander in Chief" quote); Palmer, p. 14; Skeen, *John Armstrong, Jr.*, pp. 9–11 (K. Armstong quoted—"setting ... unison"—on p. 10) ; idem, "Newburgh Conspiracy Reconsidered," pp. 275–76; Clarfield, p. 78; Boatner, p. 780; Nelson, *Horatio Gates*, p. 272; Wensyel; and HG to JA, June 22, 1783, Bancroft, I, p. 318 ("a kind of agent ... administration" quote).
16. GW to AH, Mar. 12, 1783, *PAH*, III, pp. 286–88; and Wensyel.
17. Anonymous notification of an officers' meeting, Mar. 10, 1783, *Collection*, 16.
18. Wensyel.
19. Kohn, *Eagle and Sword*, pp. 18, 29; Boatner, p. 781; Fowler, "An American Crisis," p. 15; Belcher, II, pp. 42–43; Nelson, *Horatio Gates*, p. 273; Gordon, *History of the Rise, Progress, and Establishment of the Independence of the United States*, IV, p. 355; and *Morris Selections*, I, p. 253.

20. My sources for the biography of John Armstrong are Skeen, *John Armstrong, Jr.*, pp. x, 3, 6–8; Patterson, pp. 20, 168, 280, 367; Whitney, *Colonial Spirit of '76*, p. 105; and Landers, p. 16. The sources for quotes in this biography are given separately in the succeeding two notes.
21. JA to HG, Jan. 14, 1781, quoted in Skeen, *John Armstrong, Jr.*, p. 7.
22. JA to his father, 1781, quoted ibid., pp. 7–8.
23. JA's Newburgh Address, Rhodehamel, ed., pp. 774–77.
24. Armstrong, "Review of Judge Johnson's Life of General Greene," p. 41.
25. TP to SH, Mar. 16, 1783, quoted in Kohn's rebuttal to Skeen, "Newburgh Conspiracy Reconsidered," p. 292.
26. Memoir section, Judd, ed., p. 68.
27. Mar. 22, 1783, *Heath's Memoirs*, p. 367.
28. GW to BH, Mar. 19, 1783, *WGW*, XXVI, p. 240.
29. TP to SH, Mar. 16, 1783, *TPP*, reel 34, MHS; and Corbin, p. 63.
30. W. P. Smith to EB, Apr. 22, 1783, Gerlach, ed., *New Jersey in the American Revolution*, p. 320.
31. Quoted in Kohn's rebuttal to Skeen, "Newburgh Conspiracy Reconsidered," p. 295.

Chapter Eighteen

1. Champagne, pp. 196, 259n39; Johnson, p. 97; Glasson, pp. 39–40; and AM to HK, Mar. 15, 1783, *HKP*, reel 12, MHS [GLC02437.02005].
2. GW to AH, Mar. 12, 1783, *PAH*, III, pp. 286–88.
3. Palmer, p. 3.
4. Eyewitness, quoted in "Brooks's Memoir," p. 195.
5. BL to NG, Mar. 10–12, 1783, *PNG*, XII, p. 505.
6. SS to JE, Apr. 1783, Rhodehamel, ed., p. 787.
7. Ibid.
8. Skeen, *John Armstrong, Jr.*, p. 12; Lefkowitz, p.15; Preston, p. 483; Corbin, p. 63; and DC to TP, Nov. 9, 1825, *TPP*, reel 32, MHS.
9. Eyewitness, quoted in "Brooks's Memoir," p.195; and Patterson, p. 342. The latter cites MHS's Brooks Papers, but MHS has no such collection. Also, the eyewitness quoted is unnamed; there is no date for the quote; and there are no source notes in Patterson's book. However, it seems somewhat likely that Washington went to Brooks to ensure that the officers not leave their quarters. Brooks, as the cantonment's chief medical officer, was nearby; Washington knew him well; and the conspirators later identified Brooks as the person who had betrayed them.
10. Mar. 11, 1783, *General Orders*, pp. 69–70.
11. Randall, *George Washington*, p. 222.

12. Flexner, *Washington*, p. 158.
13. HK to GW, Mar. 11, 1783, GLC, NYHS.
14. JM to ER, Mar. 11, 1783, *PJM*, VI, pp. 326–27.
15. Notes and JM to ER, Mar. 11, 1783, ibid., pp. 322–23, 327n5.
16. Notes, Mar. 11, 1783, ibid., p. 323.
17. Dr. Thacher, quoted in Wheeler, p. 289.
18. Memoir section, Judd, ed., p. 68.
19. Pickering's notebooks, *TPP*, reel 46, p. 329, MHS.
20. Gordon, IV, p. 356.
21. Wensyel.
22. In addition to the sources cited in the preceding four notes, I used Corning, p. 118; Preston, p. 484; Humphreys, I, p. 266; Royster, p. 336; Dempsey, p. 134; and Ramsay, p. 206 for this paragraph and the two paragraphs that precede it.
23. GW to Luzerne, Mar. 19, 1783, *WGW*, XXVI, p. 236.
24. Diary, Mar. 12, 1783, *PRM*, VII, pp. 557–58.
25. "Lucius" to RM, Mar. 12, 1783, ibid., pp. 559–61.
26. GW to HK, Mar. 12, 1783, GLC, NYHS; Ramsay, p. 202; and Fowler, "An American Crisis," p. 18. The last two sources listed here were used only for the very brief description of Huntington (friend … signatory …).
27. GW to JJ, Mar. 12, 1783, Rhodehamel, ed., pp. 778–80.
28. GW to AH, Mar. 12, 1783, *PAH*, III, pp. 286–88.
29. Second anonymous address, *JCC*, XXIV, pp. 298–99.
30. GW's report to EB, ibid., p. 294; and *Collection*, p. 16.
31. GW's report to EB, *JCC*, XXIV, p. 294.
32. Chadwick, p. 442.
33. HK to AM, Mar. 12, 1783, *HKP*, reel 12, MHS [GLC02437.01999].
34. HK to BL, Mar. 12, 1783, ibid., [GLC02437.02000].
35. W. Floyd to GC, Mar. 12, 1783, *LMCC*, VII, p. 72.
36. General orders, Mar. 13, 1783, *WGW*, XXVI, pp. 221–22.
37. RM to NG, Mar. 14, 1783, *PRM*, VII, pp. 574–75 (quotes on p. 575).
38. DeGregorio, *Complete Book of Presidents*, p. 1; Smith, *New Age Now Begins*, II, p. 1769; and T. Jefferson, quoted in Brookhiser, *George Washington on Leadership*, pp. 200, 202–03 (quote on p. 203).
39. Freeman, V, p. 433n.
40. Fowler, "An American Crisis," p. 17.

41. Wensyel.
42. Washington, Forms of Writing, and the Rules of Civility and Decent Behavior In Company and Conversation, ante 1747, *GW Papers, 1741–1799*, LOC.
43. TP to R. W. Pickering, Mar. 11, 1783, *TPP*, reel 1, MHS.
44. TP to R. W. Pickering, Mar. 14, 1783, ibid.

Chapter Nineteen

1. AM to HK, Mar. 15, 1783, *HKP*, reel 12, MHS [GLC02437.02005].
2. Preston, p. 484.
3. Draft reply to the anonymous addresses, Mar. 15, 1783, in Hatch, pp. 205–08.
4. Sketch by W. Tarbell of the 7th Massachusetts in Dykman, 1783.
5. Oct. 28, 1782, *Heath's Memoirs*, p. 358.
6. Ibid.
7. Ibid.
8. Many sources were used for my description of the officers' arrival and my identification of who attended the meeting: Ferling, *Leap in the Dark*, p. 251; Belcher, II, p. 45fn1; Fowler, "An American Crisis," pp. 10, 16; Chadwick, pp. 443, 445; Anthony, p. 38; Robertson and McDonald, "Newburgh Conspiracy"; Flexner, *George Washington in the American Revolution*, p. 505; Dempsey, p. 88; TP to R.W. Pickering, Jan. 28, 1783, *TPP*, reel 1, MHS; and Preston, p. 484. Also refer to the sources cited in the succeeding four notes.
9. Pickering's notebooks, *TPP*, reel 46, p. 330, MHS.
10. Rappleye, p. 348.
11. Boatner, p. 994.
12. Eager, p. 136.
13. Wensyel; Monell, p. 33; and Mitchell, p. 326. Mitchell has George Washington meeting with both Henry Knox and Nathanael Greene, which could not have been possible; Greene was in the South.
14. SS to JE, Apr. 1783, Rhodehamel, ed., p. 787.
15. Wensyel.
16. SS to JE, Apr. 1783, Rhodehamel, ed., p. 787.
17. History Channel, *Washington the Warrior*.
18. Lafayette, quoted in Schultz, p. 46.
19. Lafayette, quoted in *Recollections*, 484.
20. DeGregorio, p. 1.
21. Count Fersen, quoted in Fleming, *Beat the Last Drum*, p. 76.

22. Randall, *George Washington*, pp. 4, 403.
23. Patterson, p. 342; Berkin, op. cit., in Hollinshead, ed., p. 45; Martin and Lender, p. 192; Ferling, *Leap in the Dark*, p. 251; Ellis, *His Excellency*, p. 144; Freeman, V, p. 434.
24. SS to JE, Apr. 1783, *Shaw's Journals*, p. 103.
25. Ellis, *His Excellency*, p. 79; and Aimone's introduction in *General Orders*, p. iii.
26. Washington, Forms of Writing, and the Rules of Civility and Decent Behavior In Company and Conversation, ante 1747, *GW Papers, 1741–1799*, LOC.
27. SS to JE, Apr. 1783, Rhodehamel, ed., p. 787.
28. Ibid., pp. 787–88; Wensyel; Freeman, V, p. 434; and Fowler, "An American Crisis," p. 17.
29. Wensyel; Preston, p. 484; Chadwick, p. 443; Flexner, *George Washington in the American Revolution*, p. 505; and J. A. Wright to J. Webb, Mar. 16, 1783, quoted in *WGW*, XXVI, p. 229fn40.
30. Fowler, "An American Crisis," p. 17.
31. GW's speech, Rhodehamel, ed., pp. 781–82.
32. Flexner, *Washington*, p. 177.
33. GW's speech, Rhodehamel, ed., pp. 782–83.
34. Flexner, *Washington*, p. 177.
35. GW's speech, Rhodehamel, ed., pp. 783–85.
36. TP to SH, Mar. 16, 1783, *TPP*, reel 34, MHS (quote); Ferling, *Leap in the Dark*, p. 252; and idem, *Almost a Miracle*, p. 556.
37. Wensyel.
38. DC, cited by Lefkowitz, p. 259.
39. Hatch, pp. 172–73 (including notes).
40. SS to JE, Apr. 1783, *Shaw's Journals*, p. 103.
41. TP to SH, Mar. 16, 1783, *TPP*, reel 34, MHS.
42. Flexner, *Washington*, p. 177.
43. Freeman, V, p. 435.
44. TP, quoted in Fowler, "An American Crisis," p. 17.
45. SS to JE, Apr. 1783, Rhodehamel, ed., p. 788.
46. DC to TP, Nov. 9, 1825, *TPP*, reel 32, MHS; Ferling, *Almost a Miracle*, p. 556; Hendrickson, p. 391; and Freeman, V, p. 435.
47. SS to JE, Apr. 1783, *Shaw's Journals*, p. 104.
48. J. Trumbull, quoted in DC to TP, Nov. 9, 1825, *TPP*, reel 32, MHS.
49. GW, quoted in Ramsay, pp. 206–07.
50. GW, quoted in Ruttenber, p. 68; and quoted in Headley, "Last Days of Washington's Army at Newburgh." Headley has him putting on the glasses before his prepared statements.

51. GW, quoted in Corning, p. 120.
52. GW, quoted in Preston, p. 485.
53. GW, quoted in Humphreys, I, p. 267.
54. Ferling, *First of Men*, p. 311.
55. J.Trumbull, cited in DC to TP, Nov. 9, 1825, *TPP*, reel 32, MHS.
56. Chadwick, p. 446.
57. SS to JE, Apr. 1783, *Shaw's Journals*, p. 104; J. Trumbull, cited in DC to TP, Nov. 9, 1825, *TPP*, reel 32, MHS; PS, cited by Belcher, II, p. 45; and Nelson, *Horatio Gates*, p. 275.
58. Wensyel.
59. Humphreys, I, p. 268; and Davis, *George Washington and the American Revolution*, p. 452.
60. Nelson, *Horatio Gates*, p. 275; and Flexner, *George Washington in the American Revolution*, p. 507.
61. Besides sources cited below for quotes and other items, I used MacDougall, pp. 151–52, Chadwick, p. 445; Ellis, *His Excellency*, p. 144; Patterson, pp. 342–43; and Robertson and McDonald for actions from his reading Jones's letter to his departure.
62. SS to JE, Apr. 1783, *Shaw's Journals*, p. 104.
63. GW, quoted in Marx, *Health of the Presidents*, pp. 18–24 (quote on p. 18); Fowler, *American Crisis*, p. 163; and Ferling, *First of Men*, p. 259.
64. Smith, *Patriarch*, p. 19.
65. Burns and Dunn, *George Washington*, pp. 52–53 (quotes on p. 52).
66. Brookhiser, *George Washington on Leadership*, p. 74.
67. McDonald, forward to Addison, *Cato*, p. viii; Corbin, pp. 72–73; Chernow, p. 106; Brady, p. 123; Burian, *George Washington's Legacy of Leadership*, p. 337; and resolution passed in 1774, W. Bradford to his sister Rachel, March 14, 1778, and resolutions of Oct. 12 and 16, 1778, quoted in Ford, *Washington and the Theatre*, pp. 24 (1st quote), 26–27 (2nd and 3rd quotes on p. 27).
68. McDonald's forward to Addison, pp vii–viii.
69. Corbin, p. 72; and Henderson, p. 91.
70. Brady, p. 123.
71. McDonald, forward and introduction to Addison, pp. ix, xvii–xx; and act I, scene I, fn.5.
72. Addison, act II, scene I, lines 23–24, 43–44 (quote), 52–53, and 80.
73. Brookhiser, *George Washington on Leadership*, p. 224.
74. Ferling, *First of Men*, p. 249.
75. Addison, act II, scene VI, lines 39–40 (1st quote); and idem, act III, scene V, line 20(2nd quote)–22.
76. Examples of fear for Roman liberty can be found in ibid., act I, scene II, lines 9–10, and in act II, scene II, lines 28–29.
77. Ibid., act II, scene II, line 41.

78. Wood, *Creation of the American Republic*, p. 68.
79. Addison, act I, scene I, lines 13–14.
80. Ibid., act IV, scene II, lines 29–30.
81. Ibid., act V, scene IV, line 108.
82. Ibid., act II, scene V, lines 64–65.

Chapter Twenty

1. Report of the Convention of Officers, Mar. 15, 1783, in *Collection*, p. 28.
2. Ibid., p. 29.
3. Ibid.
4. Ibid.
5. Ibid.
6. Ibid.
7. Ibid.
8. Ibid., pp. 29–30.
9. Ibid., p. 29.
10. TP to SH, Mar. 16, 1783, *TPP*, reel 34, MHS.
11. Ibid.
12. E. Hand to General Irvine, Apr.19, 1783, Bancroft, I, p. 307.
13. Pickering's notebooks, *TPP*, reel 46, p. 331, MHS.
14. Statement of R. King on his conversation with W. Duer, Oct. 12, 1788, King, ed., I, p. 622.
15. PS to S. Van Rensselaer, Mar. 17, 1783, Lossing, *Life and Times of Philip Schuyler*, II, p. 427n.
16. In addition to the sources cited in the first fifteen notes for this chapter, I used many other works for the section that describes events from the time of George Washington's departure until the minutes are forwarded by him to Congress: Proceedings of the meeting, *General Orders*, p. 118; TP to SH, Mar. 16, 1783, *TPP*, reel 34, MHS; Siry, op. cit., in Krawczynski, ed., p. 224; Nelson, *Horatio Gates*, p. 276; Ruttenber, pp. 70–71; Corning, p. 120; Boatner, p. 781; Freeman, V, p. 435; Wensyel; Humphreys, I, p. 268; Monell, p. 33; Johnson, p. 90; Dempsey, p. 148; Fowler, "An American Crisis," p. 18; Royster, p. 337; Chadwick, p. 446; Belcher, II, p. 45; and Mitchell, p. 328.
17. SS to JE, May 3, 1783, *Shaw's Journals*, pp. 106–07.
18. JA to TP, Oct. 6, 1825 (quote), and DC to TP, Nov. 9, 1825, *TPP*, reel 32, MHS; and SS to JE, May 3, 1783, *Shaw's Journals*, pp. 106–07.
19. PS to S. Van Rensselaer, Mar. 17, 1783, Lossing, II, p. 427n.
20. HK to BL, Mar. 16, 1783, *HKP*, reel 12, MHS [GLC02437.02009].

21. D. Humphreys to BL, Mar. 19, 1783, quoted in Dempsey, p. 134; Van Doren, *Mutiny in January*, p. 63; and Lefkowitz, p. 202. The last two works are for biographical information.
22. J. A. Wright to SBW, Mar. 16, 1783, *Webb's Correspondence*, III, pp. 5–6.
23. SS to JE, Apr. 1783, Rhodehamel, ed., pp. 788–89.
24. W. P. Smith to EB, Apr. 22, 1783, Gerlach, ed., pp. 320–21.
25. G. Benet to his mother, Apr. 15, 1783, quoted in Corning, p. 93.
26. Letters from Philadelphia, Feb. 18, 1783, in Sir G. Carleton's dispatch of Mar. 15, 1783, in Bancroft, I, pp. 296–97 (quotes); and Dempsey, p. 133.
27. Letters from Philadelphia, Feb. 20, 1783, in Sir G. Carleton's dispatch of Mar. 15, 1783, in Bancroft, I, p. 297.
28. Extract of a letter from a person in Philadelphia to his friend in New England, in Sir G. Carleton's No. 60 of Mar. 15, 1783, ibid., pp. 298–300.
29. Letter from Philadelphia, Mar. 7, 1783, ibid., p. 300.

Chapter Twenty-One

1. GW to the President, Mar. 16, 1783, *Collection*, p. 22.
2. Notes, Mar. 17, 1783, *PJM*, VI, p. 348.
3. EB to GW, Mar. 17, 1783, *LMCC*, VII, p. 84.
4. AH to GW, Mar. 17, 1783, *PAH*, III, pp. 291–93.
5. Mar. 18, 1783, *General Orders*, p. 72.
6. GW to EB, Mar. 18, 1783, Lengel, ed., pp. 271–73 (quotes); Corbin, p. 68; and notes, Mar. 22, 1783, *PJM*, VI, p. 375.
7. GW to JJ, Mar. 18, 1783, *WGW*, XXVI, pp. 232–34.
8. GW to L. Washington, Mar. 19, 1783, ibid., pp. 245–46.
9. Leibiger, *Founding Friendship*, p. 28.
10. Notes, Mar. 18, 1783, *PJM*, VI, p. 350.
11. Many sources were used for the description of actions taken in Congress from March 20 to March 22: March 20 and 22, 1783, *JCC*, XXIV, pp. 204fn1, 207–08; Jensen, pp. 76–77; Champagne, p. 197; Dempsey, p. 157; Kohn, *Eagle and Sword*, p. 33; Fowler, "An American Crisis," pp. 18–19; Ruttenber, p. 72; Kohn, "Inside History of the Newburgh Conspiracy," p. 212; E. Dyer to J. Trumbull, Sr., Apr. 12, 1783, *LDC*, XX, p. 173 ("would quiet … Army" quote); notes, Mar. 20, 1783, *PJM*, VI, p. 370 ("extorted … our affairs" quote); Continental Congress Report on Half Pay to the Army, Mar. 21, 1783; BL to HK, Mar. 22, 1783, *BLP*, reel 6, MHS; and *PAH*, III, p. 302fn. The last source listed here explains that the endorsement on the report indicates it was read on the 21st, although the journal entry is dated the 22nd.

12. Fowler, "An American Crisis," p. 19; Ferguson, p. 164; and resolution of Mar. 22, 1783, U.S. House of Representatives, *Resolutions*, pp. 14–15.

Chapter Twenty-Two

1. Notes, Mar. 22, 1783, *PJM*, VI, p. 375.
2. EB to GW, Mar. 23, 1783, in general orders for Mar. 29, 1783, *General Orders*, p. 74 (quotes); Abbott, *New York in the American Revolution*, p. 267; Ruttenber, p. 72; Humphreys, I, p. 270; Davis, *George Washington and the American Revolution*, p. 452; Dempsey, p. 152; and Morris, ed., p. 109.
3. AH to GW, Mar. 24, 1783, *PAH*, III, p. 304.
4. AH to GW, Mar. 25, 1783, *Correspondence of the Revolution*, IV, pp. 10–12.
5. Ibid., pp. 12–14 (quotes on pp. 13–14).
6. Mar. 28, 1783, *General Orders*, p. 73 ("certainty" quote is from an extract of a letter from the French minister to GW, Mar. 24, 1783, within the order).
7. Quoted in Dempsey, pp. 157–58; and EB to GW, Mar. 23, 1783, in general orders, Mar. 29, 1783, *General Orders*, p. 74.
8. GW to AH, Mar. 31, 1783, *PAH*, III, pp. 309–10.
9. NG to GM, Apr. 3, 1783, in *Morris Selections*, I, pp. 251–52.
10. GW to T. Bland, Apr. 4, 1783, *WGW*, XXVI, pp. 285–90.
11. GW to AH, Apr. 4, 1783, *PAH*, III, pp. 315–16.

Chapter Twenty-Three

1. Abbott, pp. 267–68.
2. AH to GW, Apr. 8, 1783, *LDC*, XX, pp. 148–51n1 (quotes on pp. 148–50).
3. Abbott, pp. 267–68; Burrows and Wallace, *Gotham*, p. 256 (quote); and Bosak, "History of New York City Police Department."
4. Diary, Apr. 9, 1783, *PRM*, VII, pp. 682–83.
5. EB to GW, Apr. 12, 1783, *LMCC*, VII, p. 135.
6. GW's circular, Apr. 14, 1783, *WGW*, XXVI, pp. 318–19.
7. RM to AH, T. Bland, T. Fitzsimmons, S. Osgood, and R. Peters, Apr. 14, 1783, *PRM*, VII, pp. 701–02.
8. GW to AH, Apr. 16, 1783, *PAH*, III, pp. 329–30.
9. Notes, Apr. 4, 1783, *PJM*, VI, pp. 432, 434n8; Rakove, pp. 322, 337; Ferguson, p. 161; Flexner, *Young Hamilton*, p. 414; Miller, *Alexander Hamilton*, p. 97; quoted in Brant, pp. 103–05 ("no bait for Virginia" quote on p. 105); Sumner, II, p. 69; Jensen, pp. 75–76; Mitchell, p. 329; Henderson, p. 338.

10. Quoted in Ruttenber, pp. 73–74; Corning, p. 115; Dempsey, pp. 162, 173–74; Aimone's introduction and general orders, Apr. 18, 1783, *General Orders*, pp. x, 78–80; Apr. 19, 1783, *Heath's Memoirs*, p. 371; Fish, p. 23; Humphreys, I, p. 271; Wensyel; and Fowler, "An American Crisis," p. 19.
11. GW to AH, Apr. 22, 1783, *PAH*, III, pp. 334–36.
12. GW to T. Tilghman, Apr. 24, 1783, in Bancroft, I, pp. 308–09.
13. Address to the States, Apr. 26, 1783, *PJM*, VI, pp. 488–94.
14. Johnson, pp. 161–62; and Leibiger, p. 29.

Chapter Twenty-Four

1. Diary, May 3, 1783, *PRM*, VII, p. 789.
2. RM to J. Pierce, Jan. 20, 1783, ibid., p. 335n.
3. GW to J. Huntington and GW to HK, May 14, 1783, *WGW*, XXVI, pp. 429 (incl. note)–430 (quotes); and Jensen, p. 80 (reason for petition).
4. Diary, May 15, 1783, and RM to N. Gorham, AH, and R. Peters, May 15, 1783, *PRM*, VIII, pp. 44–45, 49–59 (quotes on pp. 50–51).
5. GM to NG, May 18, 1783, ibid., p. 92.
6. HG to TP, May 19, 1783, *TPP*, reel 18, MHS.
7. TP to HG, May 28, 1783, *TPP*, reel 5, MHS.
8. WS to HG, May 28, 1783, *HGP*, reel 13, NYHS [actual letter is credited to the following: *HGP*. Manuscripts and Archives Division. The New York Public Library. Astor, Lenox, and Tilden Foundations].
9. Continental Congress Motion that Furloughs be Granted to NCOs and Soldiers, May 26, 1783, *PAH*, III, p. 364.
10. General orders, June 2, 1783, *WGW*, XXVI, p. 464.
11. JA to HG, May 30, 1783, *HGP*, reel 13, NYHS.
12. June 2, 1783, *General Orders*, p. 83.
13. June 5, 1783, *Heath's Memoirs,* pp. 374–76.
14. GW's response to Heath's petition, June 6, 1783, *Collection*, pp. 34–35; and June 6, 1783, *Heath's Memoirs*, pp. 377–79. The letter from Morris that is mentioned in this section is dated May 29, 1783. It can be found in *PRM*, VIII, pp. 130–31.
15. GW to the President, June 7, 1783, *Collection*, p. 36; and June 7, 1783, *Heath's Memoirs*, p. 380.
16. McDonald, p. 30; and Royster, p. 342.
17. Dempsey, pp. 209–10, 219–20; and June 6–9, 1783, *Heath's Memoirs*, pp. 382–83.
18. GW to Lafayette, June 15, 1783, *WGW*, XXVII, p. 12.
19. Circular, June 8, 1783, *WGW*, XXVI, pp. 483–96.

Chapter Twenty-Five

1. WS to HG, June 20, 1783, *HGP*, reel 13, NYHS.
2. Flexner, *George Washington in the American Revolution*, p. 514.
3. WS to HG, June 20, 1783, *HGP*, reel 13, NYHS.
4. Dempsey, p. 233.
5. Ibid., p. 231; Corning, p. 122; June 20 and 23, 1783, *Heath's Memoirs*, pp. 384–85; and June 20, 1783, *General Orders*, pp. 88–89.
6. Johnson, pp. 191–92; AM to Col. Wyllys, July 27, 1783, *Webb's Correspondence*, III, p. 24; AM to HK, July 25, 1783, *HKP*, reel 13, MHS; and AM to AS, Aug. 6, 1783, Miscellaneous Manuscripts Collection, LOC.
7. AM to AS, Aug. 6, 1783, Miscellaneous Manuscripts Collection, LOC.
8. AM to Colonel Wyllys, July 27, 1783, *Webb's Correspondence*, III, p. 24.
9. Johnson, pp. 193–98.
10. Dempsey, pp. 242–244; and Corning, pp. 121–22.
11. Monell, p. 6.
12. GW's farewell orders, Nov. 2, 1783, *General Orders*, pp. 120–24 (quote on p. 122).
13. Knox, "Letter from Henry Knox, 1783" (quotes). The source cited here is a transcript produced by the Claremont Institute from the actual letter, which is owned by the Gilder Lehrman Institute. The actual letter's call number is GLC02437.10199.
14. Hatch, pp. 192–93.
15. The sources for quotes that I cited in the succeeding eleven notes also provided me with much of the paraphrased material in this and the other twelve paragraphs that describe New England's opposition to commutation. In addition to those sources, though, I did have to use some other sources: Johnson, pp. 185, 201, 207–10, 216–17, 234, 236–37, 240–41; Royster, pp. 345, 347–48; Glasson, pp. 47–48; Rakove, pp. 323, 338; J. Adams to RM, July 10–11, 1783, and RM to Gov. Hancock, Sept. 20, 1783, *PRM*, VIII, pp. 268, 275, 533–34n1; S. Adams to _____, of Ct., from draft, Sept. 25, 1783, in Bancroft, I, pp. 329–30; and Fiske, *Critical Period in American History*, pp. 112–13.
16. Quoted in Johnson, p. 186.
17. Quoted in Glasson, pp. 43–44.
18. Quoted in Johnson, p. 238.
19. "Constant Customer" of *Connecticut Courant and Weekly Intelligencer*, May 13, 1783, quoted in Glasson, p. 44.
20. *Salem Gazette*, Aug. 21, 1783, quoted in Johnson, p. 179.
21. Ibid., p. 180.
22. Ibid., p. 182n46.

23. JM to ER, Sept. 8, 1783, *LMCC*, VII, p. 291.
24. Colonel J. Chester to Lieutenant Colonel Huntington, Sept. 22, 1783, quoted in Johnson, p. 202.
25. "Honorius," *Salem Gazette,* Sept. 18, 1783, quoted ibid., pp. 204–05.
26. Governor Trumbull, *Salem Gazette,* Dec. 4, 1783, quoted ibid., p. 211.
27. Mitchell, p. 330.
28. Rakove, pp 338–40.
29. Glasson, pp. 49–50.
30. House documents, 2nd session, 19th Congress, 1826–1827, quoted ibid., pp. 50–51 (quotes on p. 51); "Pensions Enacted by Congress for Revolutionary War Veterans"; U.S. House of Representatives, *Resolutions*, p. 17; Martin and Lender, p. 197; Higginbotham, p. 412; Fowler, "An American Crisis," p. 19.
31. GW to EB, Mar. 18, 1783, Lengel, ed., pp. 272–73.
32. Thomas, *Reminiscences of the Last Sixty-five Years, Commencing with the Battle of Lexington*, I, p. 125.
33. DC to TP, Nov. 9, 1825, *TPP*, reel 32, MHS.

Afterword

1. JA to HG, Apr. 29, 1783, *LMCC*, VII, p. 155n3 (quotes); Dempsey, p. 178; and Apr. 16, 1783, *General Orders*, p. 77. The last two works cited are for Horatio Gates's being with his sick wife in Va.
2. TP to HG, May 28, 1783, *TPP*, reel 5, MHS.
3. "Brooks's Memoir," p. 195.
4. Fowler, "An American Crisis," p. 16.
5. Statement of R. King on his conversation with W. Duer, Oct. 12, 1788, in King, ed., I, p. 622.
6. JA to HG, May 30, 1783, *HGP*, reel 13, NYHS (quotes); Champagne, p. 199 (time of departure).
7. HG to JA, June 22, 1783, in Bancroft, I, p. 318.
8. Statement of R. King on his conversation with W. Duer, Oct. 12, 1788, King, ed., I, pp. 621–22.
9. GW to JA, Feb. 23, 1797, *WGW*, XXXV, p. 397.
10. "John Montgars" to TP, Jan. 20, 1820, *TPP*, reel 31, MHS; and JA to TP, Oct. 6, 1825 (quote), *TPP*, reel 32, MHS.
11. "John Montgars" to TP, Jan. 20, 1820, *TPP*, reel 31, MHS.
12. Ibid. Armstrong's emphasis on the word *"speaking"* almost certainly was meant to let Pickering know that no violent *action* was planned.
13. Ibid.
14. JB to TP, Sept. 6, 1823, and Dr. Thacher to TP, Jan. 5, 1826, *TPP*, reel 32, MHS; and Pickering's notebooks, *TPP*, reel 46, pp. 177, 329–332, MHS.

15. "John Montgars" to TP, Jan. 20, 1820, *TPP*, reel 31, MHS.
16. W. Johnson, quoted and cited in Armstrong, "Review of Judge Johnson's Life of General Greene," pp. 25–26.
17. Ibid., pp. 26–43 (quotes on pp. 34, 37, 40–43).
18. Dr. Thacher to TP, Jan. 5, 1826, *TPP*, reel 32, MHS (quotes); and Hatch, p. 161.
19. JB to TP, Sept. 6, 1823, *TPP*, reel 32, MHS.
20. E. Huntington to TP, Dec. 28, 1825, ibid.
21. JB to TP, Sept. 6, 1823, ibid.
22. Martin, op. cit., in Hoffman and Albert, eds., pp. 124, 138–39 (quote on p.138).
23. Bancroft, I, p. 81.
24. Extract of W. Hull to TP, n. d., Pickering and Upham, *Life of Timothy Pickering*, I, p. 436.
25. NG to GM, Apr. 3, 1783, in *Morris Selections*, I, pp. 251–52.
26. GW to AH, Apr. 4, 1783, *PAH*, III, pp. 315–16.

Bibliography

Abbot, W. W., et al., eds. *The Papers of George Washington*. Revolutionary War Series. 18 volumes to date. Charlottesville: University Press of Virginia, 1985–.

Abbott, Wilbur C. *New York in the American Revolution*. New York: Charles Scribner's Sons, 1929.

Adams, William Howard. *Gouverneur Morris: An Independent Life*. New Haven: Yale University Press, 2003.

Addison, Joseph. *Cato: A Tragedy and Selected Essays*. Edited by Christine Dunn Henderson and Mark E. Yellin, and with a foreword by Forrest McDonald. Indianapolis: Liberty Fund, 2004.

Alexander Calvin and Ellen Morton Washburn Autograph Collection. Manuscripts. Reel 7. Massachusetts Historical Society.

The Alexander McDougall Papers, 1757-1795. 4 reels. New York: New York Historical Society, 1942.

Allis, Frederick S., Jr., ed. *The Benjamin Lincoln Papers*. Reel VI. Boston: Massachusetts Historical Society, 1967.

_____. *Timothy Pickering Papers*. 69 reels. Boston: Massachusetts Historical Society, 1966.

Alsop, Susan Mary. *Yankees at the Court: The First Americans in Paris*. Garden City: Doubleday & Co., 1982.

Ambrose, Stephen. *Duty, Honor, Country: A History of West Point*. Baltimore: Johns Hopkins Press, 1966.

Anthony, Walter C. *Washington's Headquarters, Newburgh, New York: A History of its Construction and its Various Occupants*. Newburgh: Historical Society of Newburgh Bay and the Highlands, 1928.

Armstrong, John. "Review of Judge Johnson's Life of General Greene." *United States Magazine and Literary and Political Repository*. Vol. I, No. I (January 1823).

Bancroft, George. *History of the Formation of the Constitution of the United States of America*. Vol. I. New York: D. Appleton and Company, 1882. Reprint, Littleton: Fred B. Rothman & Co., 1983.

Barratt, Albert Gedney. *Newburgh in the American Revolution*. [mid-1920s?]

Basler, George. "History Lives at Cantonment." n.p., n.d. Photocopy from unidentified newspaper in the Newburgh Free Library's folder titled *New Windsor Cantonment*.

Bates, Frank Greene. "Rhode Island and the Impost of 1781." *Annual Report of the American Philosophical Association for the Year 1894*. Washington, D.C.: Government Printing Office, 1895.

Belcher, Henry. *The First American Civil War: First Period, 1775–1778*. Vol. II. London: MacMillan & Co., 1911.

Berg, Fred Anderson. *Encyclopedia of Continental Army Units: Battalions, Regiments and Independent Corps*. Harrisburg: Stackpole Books, 1972.

Billias, George Athan, ed. *George Washington's Generals and Opponents: Their Exploits and Leadership*. New York: De Capo Press, 1994.

Blanchfield, G. W. F., ed. *Letters Written by Ebenezer Huntington during the American Revolution*. New York: C. F. Heartman, 1914.

Boatner III, Mark M. *Encyclopedia of the American Revolution*. New York: David McKay Co., 1974.

Bobrick, Benson. *Angel in the Whirlwind: The Triumph of the American Revolution*. New York: Simon and Schuster, 1997.

Boller, Paul F. *Presidential Wives*. New York: Oxford University Press, 1988.

Bonsal, Stephen. *When the French Were Here: A Narrative of the Sojourn of the French Forces in America, and their Contribution to the Yorktown Campaign*. Garden City: Doubleday, Doran and Company, 1945.

Bosak, Michael E. J. "History of New York City Police Department: George, George and More George or The Genesis of American Law Enforcement in New York City." *New York City Police Memorial*. 1999. Accessed Sept. 30, 2013. http://nypd.police-memorial.com/history-of-nypd/

Bowman, Allen. *The Morale of the American Revolutionary Army*. Port Washington: Kennikat Press, 1943.

Boynton, Major Edward C., ed. & comp. *General Orders of George Washington Issued at Newburgh on the Hudson, 1782–1783*. With an introduction by Alan C. Aimone. Harrison: Harbor Hill Books, 1973.

Brady, Patricia. *Martha Washington: An American Life*. New York: Penguin Books, 2005.

Brandt, Clare. *The Man in the Mirror: A Life of Benedict Arnold*. New York: Random House, 1994.

Brant, Irving. *The Fourth President: A Life of James Madison*. Indianapolis: Bobbs-Merrill Co., 1970

Brookhiser, Richard. *Alexander Hamilton: American*. New York: Free Press, 1999.

_____. *Gentleman Revolutionary: Gouverneur Morris–The Rake Who Wrote the Constitution*. New York: Free Press (a division of Simon and Schuster), 2003.

_____. *George Washington on Leadership*. New York: Basic Books, 2008.

Brooks, Charles. "Memoir of John Brooks, Governor of Massachusetts." *New England Historical and Genealogical Register*. Vol. XIX, No. 3 (July 1865).

Buchanan, John. *The Road to Guilford Courthouse: The American Revolution in the Carolinas*. New York: John Wiley & Sons, 1997.

Buckman, Peter. *Lafayette: A Biography*. New York: Paddington Press, 1977.

Buell, Rowena, comp. *The Memoirs of Rufus Putnam and Certain Official Papers and Correspondence*. Boston and New York: Houghton, Mifflin and Company, 1903.

Bullock, Charles J. "The Finances of the United States from 1775 to 1789, with Especial Reference to the Budget." *Bulletin of the University of Wisconsin*. Economics, Political Science, and History Series. Vol. I (1894–1896), No. 2. Madison: University of Wisconsin, 1897.

Burian, A. Ward. *George Washington's Legacy of Leadership*. New York: Morgan James Publishing, 2007.

Burnett, Edmund C., ed. *Letters of Members of the Continental Congress*. 8 vols. Washington, D.C.: Carnegie Institution of Washington, 1921–1936.

Burns, James MacGregor, and Susan Dunn. *George Washington*. New York: Times Books, Henry Holt & Co., 2004.

Burrows, Edwin G., and Mike Wallace. *Gotham: A History of New York City to 1898*. New York: Oxford University Press, 1999.

Butler, John P., ed. *Papers of the Continental Congress, 1774–1789*. Roll 179. Washington, D. C.: National Archives Microfilm Publications, 1959.

Carmer, Carl. "The Lordly Hudson." *American Heritage*. Vol. X, No. 1 (December 1958).

Carp, E. Wayne. *To Starve the Army at Pleasure: Continental Army Administration and American Political Culture, 1775–1783*. Chapel Hill: University of North Carolina Press, 1984.

Carrington, Henry B. *Battles of the American Revolution, 1775–1781*. New York: Promontory Press, [1974?]

Catanzariti, John, et al., eds. *The Papers of Robert Morris, 1781–1784*. 9 vols. Pittsburgh: University of Pittsburgh Press, 1973–1999.

Chadwick, Bruce. *George Washington's War: The Forging of a Revolutionary Leader and the American Presidency*. Naperville: Sourcebooks Inc., 2004.

Champagne, Roger J. *Alexander McDougall and the American Revolution in New York*. Schenectady: The New York State American Revolution Bicentennial Commission in conjunction with Union College Press, 1975.

Chernow, Ron. *Alexander Hamilton*. New York: Penguin Press, 2004.

Chidsey, Donald Barr. *The Loyalists: The Story of Those Americans Who Fought Against Independence*. New York: Crown Publishers, 1973.

_____. *The War in the South*. New York: Crown Publishers, 1969.

Clarfield, Gerard H. *Timothy Pickering and the American Republic*. Pittsburgh: University of Pittsburgh Press, 1980.

Collection of Papers, Relative to Half-Pay and Commutation of Half-Pay, Granted by Congress to the Officers of the Army. Fishkill: Samuel Loudon, 1783.

Commager, Henry Steele, and Richard B. Morris, eds. *The Spirit of 'Seventy-Six: The Story of the American Revolution as Told by Participants*. New York: Harper & Row, 1975.

Conrad, Dennis M., and Roger N. Parks, eds. *The Papers of Nathanael Greene*. Vol. XII. Chapel Hill: University of North Carolina Press, 2002.

Conway, Moncure Daniel. *The Writings of Thomas Paine*. New York: Knickerbocker Press, 1906.

Corbin, John. *Two Frontiers of Freedom*. New York: Charles Scribner's Sons, 1940.

Corning, A. Elwood. *Washington at Temple Hill*. Newburgh: Lanmere Publishing Co., 1932.

Cox, Caroline. *A Proper Sense of Honor: Service and Sacrifice in George Washington's Army*. Chapel Hill: University of North Carolina Press, 2004.

Cox, Clinton. *Come All You Brave Soldiers: Blacks in the Revolutionary War*. New York: Scholastic Inc., 2002.

Crawford, Alan Pell. *Unwise Passions: The True Story of a Remarkable Woman and the First Great Scandal of Eighteenth Century America*. New York: Simon & Schuster, 2000.

Cushing, Harry Alonzo, ed. *The Writings of Samuel Adams*. Vol. I. New York: G. P. Putnam's Sons, 1904.

Custis, George Washington Parke. *Recollections and Private Memoirs of Washington*. With a memoir of the author by his daughter and illustrative and explanatory notes by Benson J. Lossing. Philadelphia: J. W. Bradley, 1861.

Cutler, Stanley I., ed. *Dictionary of American History*. Vol. II. New York: Charles Scribner's Sons, 2003.

Davis, Burke. *The Campaign That Won America: The Story of Yorktown*. New York: Dial Press, 1970.

———. *George Washington and the American Revolution*. New York: Random House, 1975.

DeGregorio, William A. *The Complete Book of Presidents*. New York: Dembner Books, 1989.

Dempsey, Janet. *Washington's Last Cantonment: "High Time For a Peace."* Monroe: Library Research Associates, 1987.

Diamant, Lincoln. *Chaining the Hudson: The Fight for the River in the American Revolution*. New York: Carol Publishing Group, 1989.

Drake, Francis S. *Life and Correspondence of Henry Knox, Major-General in the American Revolutionary Army*. Boston: Samuel G. Drake, 1873.

Duel: Hamilton vs. Burr. History Channel.

Duncan, Louis C. *Medical Men in the American Revolution, 1775–1783*. Carlisle Barracks: Medical Field Service School, 1931. Reprint, New York: Augustus M. Kelley, 1970.

Dupuy, R. Ernest, and Trevor N. *An Outline History of the American Revolution*. New York: Harper & Row, 1975.

Dupuy, Trevor N., and Gay M. Hammerman, eds. *People and Events of the American Revolution*. Dunn Loring: T. N. Dupuy Associates, 1974.

Dykman, J. O. "The Historic Temple at New Windsor, 1783." *Magazine of American History* 24, no. 4. (October 1890). Accessed Sept. 30, 2013. http://democraticthinker.wordpress.com/2010/01/03/temple-of-virtue/.

Eager, Sam'l W., Esq. *An Outline History of Orange County with an Enumeration of the Names of Its Towns, Villages, Rivers, Creeks, Lakes, Ponds, Mountains, Hills, and Other Known Localities and Their Etymologies or Historical Reasons Therefore; Together with Local Traditions and Short Biographical Sketches of Early Settlers, Etc.* Newburgh: S. T. Callahan, 1846–1847.

Eckert, Allan W. *The Wilderness War: A Narrative.* Boston: Little, Brown and Company, 1978.

Egleston, Thomas. *The Life of John Paterson: Major-General in the Revolutionary Army.* New York: G. P. Putnam's Sons, 1898.

Ellis, David M., et al. *A Short History of New York State.* Ithaca: Cornell University Press, 1957.

Ellis, Edward Robb. *The Epic of New York City.* New York: Old Town Books, 1966.

Ellis, Joseph J. *His Excellency: George Washington.* New York: Alfred A. Knopf, 2004.

Ferguson, E. James. *The Power of the Purse: A History of American Public Finance, 1776–1790.* Chapel Hill: The University of North Carolina Press, 1961.

Ferling, John. *A Leap in the Dark: The Struggle to Create the American Republic.* New York: Oxford University Press, 2003.

_____. *Almost a Miracle: The American Victory in the War of Independence.* New York: Oxford University Press, 2007.

_____. *The First of Men: A Life of George Washington.* Knoxville: University of Tennessee Press, 1988.

Fischer, David Hackett. *Washington's Crossing.* New York: Oxford University Press, 2004.

Fish, Hamilton. *George Washington in the Highlands, or Some Unwritten History.* Newburgh: Newburgh News, 1932.

Fishman, Ronald S. "Presbyopia's Finest Hour." *Archives of Ophthalmology.* Vol. CXX, No. 1 (January 2002).

Fiske, John. *The Critical Period of American History, 1783–1789.* Boston: Houghton Mifflin Company, 1888.

Fitzpatrick, John C., ed. *The Writings of George Washington from the Original Manuscript Sources, 1745–1799.* 39 vols. Washington, D.C.: United States Government Printing Office, 1931–1944.

Fleming, Thomas. *1776: Year of Illusions.* New York: W. W. Norton & Co., 1975.

_____. *Beat the Last Drum.* New York: St. Martin's Press, 1963.

_____. *Liberty: The American Revolution.* New York: Viking, 1997.

_____. *Now We Are Enemies: The Story of Bunker Hill.* New York: St. Martin's Press, 1960.

_____. *The Perils of Peace: America's Struggle for Survival after Yorktown.* New York: Harper Collins, 2007.

Flexner, James Thomas. *George Washington in the American Revolution (1775–1783).* Boston: Little, Brown and Company, 1968.

_____. *The Young Hamilton.* Boston: Little, Brown and Company, 1978.

_____. *Washington: The Indispensable Man*. New York: New American Library, 1984.

Ford, Paul Leicester. *Washington and the Theatre*. New York: Dunlap Society, 1899. Reissue, New York: Benjamin Blom, 1967.

Ford, Worthington C., ed. *Correspondence and Journals of Samuel Blachley Webb*. 3 vols. Lancaster: Wickersham Press, 1893–1894. Reprint, New York: New York Times & Arno Press, 1969.

_____. *Letters of Joseph Jones of Virginia, 1777–1787*. Washington, D. C.: State Department, 1889. Reprint, New York: New York Times & Arno Press, 1971.

Ford, Worthington C., et al., eds. *Journals of the Continental Congress, 1774–1789*. 34 vols. Washington, D.C.: U. S. Government Printing Office, 1904–1937.

Found, Peter, and Phyllis Hartnoll, eds. *The Concise Oxford Companion to the Theatre*. Oxford: Oxford University Press, 1992.

Fowler, William M., Jr. "An American Crisis: The Newburgh Address." Speech given at Mount Vernon, July 20, 2006. Accessed Sept. 30, 2013. www.lehrmaninstitute.org/lehrman/newburgh.pdf.

_____. *American Crisis: George Washington and the Dangerous Two Years After Yorktown, 1781–1783*. New York: Walker & Co., 2011.

Freeman, Douglas Southall, and John Alexander Carroll and Mary Wells Ashworth. *George Washington: A Biography*. 7 vols. New York: Charles Scribner's Sons, 1948–1957.

Fremont-Barnes, Gregory, et al., eds. *American Revolutionary War: A Student Encyclopedia*. 5 vols. Santa Barbara: ABC-CLIO, 2007.

The George Washington Papers, 1741–1799. Library of Congress.

Gerlach, Larry R., ed. *New Jersey in the American Revolution, 1763–1783: A Documentary History*, Trenton: New Jersey Historical Commission, 1975

Gilder Lehrman Collection. New York Historical Society.

Glasson, William H. *Federal Military Pensions in the United States*. Edited by David Kinley. New York: Oxford University Press, 1918.

Glatthaar, Joseph T., and James Kirby Martin. *Forgotten Allies: The Oneida Indians and the American Revolution*. New York: Hill and Wang, 2006.

Gordon, William. *The History of the Rise, Progress, and Establishment, of the Independence of the United States; Including an Account of the Late War; and of the Thirteen Colonies, from Their Origin to That Period*. Vol. IV. Freeport: Books for Libraries Press, 1969.

"The Great Chain." *A Revolutionary Day along Historic US Route 9W*. Accessed Sept. 30, 2013. www.revolutionaryday.com/usroute9/garrison/default.htm

Gross, Daniel, and the editors of *Forbes* magazine. "Robert Morris: America's First Financier." *Forbes Greatest Business Stories of All Time*. New York: John Wiley & Sons, Inc., 1996.

Haggard, Robert F. "The Nicola Affair: Lewis Nicola, George Washington, and American Military Discontent during the Revolutionary War." *Proceedings of the American Philosophical Society*. Vol. CXLII, No. 2 (June 2002).

Hammond, Bray. *Banks and Politics in America from the Revolution to the Civil War*. Princeton: Princeton University Press, 1957.

Hatch, Louis Clinton. *The Administration of the American Revolutionary Army*. London: Longmans, Green, and Co., 1904.

Hawke, David Freeman. *Paine*. New York: Harper & Row, 1974.

Headley, Joel Tyler. "Last Days of Washington's Army at Newburgh." *Harper's New Monthly Magazine*. Vol. LXVII, No. 401 (October 1883).

Heath, William. *Memoirs of Major-General Heath, Containing Anecdotes, Details of Skirmishes, Battles, and Other Military Events, During the American War*. Boston: I. Thomas and E. T. Andrews, 1798.

Heitman, Francis B. *Historical Register of Officers of the Continental Army During the War of the Revolution, April, 1775 to December, 1783*. Washington, D.C.: Rare Book Shop Publishing Company, 1914.

Henderson, H. James. *Party Politics in the Continental Congress*. New York: McGraw-Hill Book Company, 1974.

Hendrickson, Robert. *Hamilton I (1757-1789)*. New York: Mason/Charter, 1976.

"Henry Knox Brings Cannon to Boston, January 24, 1776." *Mass Moments*. 2013. Accessed Sept. 30, 2013. www.massmoments.org/moment.cfm?mid=29

The Henry Knox Papers. 55 reels. Boston: Massachusetts Historical Society, 1960.

Hibbert, Christopher. *George III: A Personal History*. New York: Basic Books, 1998.

Higginbotham, Don. *The War of American Independence: Military Attitudes, Policies, and Practice, 1763-1789*. New York: The Macmillan Company, 1971.

Hoffman, Ronald, and Peter J. Albert, eds. *Arms and Independence: The Military Character of the American Revolution*. Charlottesville: University Press of Virginia, 1984.

Hollinshead, Byron, ed. *I Wish I'd Been There*. New York: Doubleday, 2006.

The Horatio Gates Papers, 1726-1828. 20 reels. Sanford: Microfilming Corporation of America, 1978.

Huey, Paul R., and John G. Waite. *Washington's Headquarters, the Hasbrouck House: An Historic Structure Report*. New York: New York State Historic Trust, Parks and Recreation, 1971.

Humphreys, Frank Landon. *The Life of David Humphreys, 1751-1818*. Vol. I. New York: Knickerbocker Press, 1917.

Hutchinson, William T., et al., eds. *The Papers of James Madison*. 17 vols. Chicago: University of Chicago Press, 1962-1991.

Irving, Washington. *Life of George Washington*. Vol. III. New York: P. F. Collier & Son, 1901.

Jensen, Merrill. *The New Nation: A History of the United States During the Confederation, 1781-1789*. New York: Alfred A. Knopf, 1967.

Johnson, Allen, et al., eds. *Dictionary of American Biography*. 22 volumes to date. New York: Charles Scribner's Sons, 1927-.

Johnson, Carl Ferdinand. "The Army and Politics, 1783–1784." Master's thesis, University of Wisconsin, 1949.

Jones, Thomas. *History of New York during the Revolutionary War*. New York: Arno Press, 1968.

Jordan, Louis. "Continental Congress Lottery." *Colonial Currency*. Accessed Sept. 30, 2013. www.coins.nd.edu/ColCurrency/CurrencyText/CC-78descrip.html.

———. "Continental Loan Office Certificates." *Colonial Currency*. Accessed Sept. 30, 2013. www.coins.nd.edu/ColCurrency/CurrencyText/FiscalDocsUS.html.

Judd, Jacob, ed. *The Revolutionary War Memoir and Selected Correspondence of Philip Van Cortlandt*. Tarrytown: Sleepy Hollow Restorations, 1976.

Kail, Jerry, and the editors of *Who's Who in America*. *Who Was Who in the American Revolution*. Indianapolis and New York: Bobbs-Merrill Company, 1976.

Kaplan, Sidney. "Pay, Pension, and Power: Economic Grievances of the Massachusetts Officers of the Revolution." *The Boston Public Library Quarterly*. Vol. III (1951).

Karsten, Peter, ed. *The Military in America: From the Colonial Era to the Present*. New York: Free Press, 1980.

Kelly, C. Brian. *Best Little Stories from the American Revolution*. Nashville: Cumberland House, 1999.

Ketcham, Ralph. *James Madison: A Biography*. New York: Macmillan Company, 1971.

Ketchum, Richard M., ed. *The American Heritage Book of the Revolution*. New York: American Heritage Publishing Co., 1958.

———. *Saratoga: Turning Point of America's Revolutionary War*. New York: Henry Holt & Co., 1997.

King, Charles, R., ed. *The Life and Correspondence of Rufus King*. Vol. I (1755–1794). New York: G. P. Putnam's Sons, 1894.

Kirschke, James J. *Gouverneur Morris*. New York: St. Martin's Press, 2005.

Kline, Mary-Jo. *Gouverneur Morris and the New Nation, 1775–1788*. New York: Arno Press, 1978.

Knox, Henry. "Letter from Henry Knox, 1783." *Rediscovering George Washington*. 2002. Accessed Sept. 30, 2013. www.pbs.org/georgewashington/collection/pre-pres_1783.html

Kohn, Richard H. *Eagle and Sword: The Federalists and the Creation of the Military Establishment in America, 1783–1802*. New York: Free Press, 1975.

———. "The Inside History of the Newburgh Conspiracy: America and the Coup d'Etat." *The William & Mary Quarterly*. 3rd series. Vol. XXVII, No. 2 (April 1970).

Krawczynski, Keith, ed. *History in Dispute*. Vol. XII. Detroit: St. James Press, 2003.

Lancaster, Bruce. *From Lexington to Liberty: The Story of the American Revolution*. Garden City: Doubleday & Company, 1955.

Landers, H. L. *The Battle of Camden, South Carolina, August 16, 1780*. Washington, D.C.: United States Government Printing Office, 1929.

Langguth, A. J. *Patriots: The Men Who Started the American Revolution*. New York: Simon & Schuster, 1988.

Leach, Douglas Edward. *Arms for Empire: A Military History of the British Colonies in North America, 1607–1763*. New York: Macmillan Co., 1973.

Leckie, Robert. *George Washington's War: The Saga of the American Revolution*. New York: Harper Collins, 1992.

Lefkowitz, Arthur S. *George Washington's Indispensable Men: The 32 Aides-de-Camp Who Helped Win American Independence*. Mechanicsburg: Stackpole Books, 2003.

Leibiger, Stuart. *Founding Friendship: George Washington, James Madison, and the Creation of the American Republic*. Charlottesville: University Press of Virginia, 1999.

Lengel, Edward G. *General George Washington: A Military Life*. New York: Random House, 2005.

_____, ed. *This Glorious Struggle: George Washington's Revolutionary War Letters*. New York: Harper Collins, 2007.

Longford, Elizabeth, ed. *The Oxford Book of Royal Anecdotes*. New York: Oxford University Press, 1989.

Lossing, Benson J. *The Life and Times of Philip Schuyler*. Vol. II. New York: Sheldon & Company, 1873.

MacDougall, William L. *American Revolutionary: A Biography of General Alexander McDougall*. Westport: Greenwood Press, 1977.

Mann, Bruce H. *Republic of Debtors: Bankruptcy in the Age of American Independence*. Cambridge: Harvard University Press, 2002.

Marshall, George L., Jr. "The Rise and Fall of the Newburgh Conspiracy: How George Washington and his Spectacles Saved the Republic." *Archiving Eearly America*. Fall 1997. Accessed Sept. 30, 2013. www.earlyamerica.com/review/fall97/wshngton.html/.

Martin, James Kirby, and Mark Edward Lender. *A Respectable Army: The Military Origins of the Republic, 1763–1789*. Arlington Heights: Harlan Davidson, 1982.

Martin, Joseph Plumb. *Private Yankee Doodle: Being a Narrative of Some of the Adventures, Dangers and Sufferings of a Revolutionary Soldier*. Edited by George F. Scheer. Boston: Little, Brown and Company, 1962.

Marx, Rudolph. *The Health of the Presidents*. New York: G. P. Putnam's Sons, 1960.

Massachusetts Archives. Volume CCIV. State House, Boston.

Mattern, David B. *Benjamin Lincoln and the American Revolution*. Columbia: University of South Carolina Press, 1995.

Mayer, Holly A. *Belonging to the Army*. Columbia: University of South Carolina Press, 1996.

Mays, Terry M. *Historical Dictionary of the American Revolution*. Lanham: Scarecrow Press, 1999.

McCullough, David. *1776*. New York: Simon & Schuster, 2005.

McDonald, Forrest, *E. Pluribus Unum: The Formation of the American Republic, 1776–1790*. Boston: Houghton Mifflin Company, 1965.

McGuire, Thomas J. *The Philadelphia Campaign*. 2 vols. Mechanicsburg: Stackpole Books, 2006–2007.

_____. *The Surprise of Germantown, or, the Battle of Cliveden, October 4th, 1777*. Cliveden and Gettysburg: Cliveden of the National Trust for Historic Preservation and Thomas Publications, 1994.

McKenzie, Matthew G. *Barefooted, Bare Leg'd, Bare Breech'd: The Revolutionary War Service of the Massachusetts Continental Line*. Boston: The Massachusetts Society of the Cincinnati, 1995.

Middlekauff, Robert. *The Glorious Cause: The American Revolution, 1763–1789*. New York: Oxford University Press, 1982.

Miller, John C. *Alexander Hamilton: Portrait in Paradox*. New York: Harper & Row, 1959.

_____. *Triumph of Freedom, 1775–1783*. Boston: Little, Brown and Company, 1948.

Mintz, Max M. *Gouverneur Morris and the American Revolution*. Norman: University of Oklahoma Press, 1970.

Miscellaneous Manuscripts Collection. Library of Congress.

Mitchell, Broadus. *The Price of Independence: A Realistic View of the American Revolution*. New York: Oxford University Press, 1974.

Monell, J. J. *Washington's Headquarters, Newburgh, N.Y. and Adjacent Localities*. Newburgh: E. M. Ruttenber & Son, 1872.

Moore, Frank. *Diary of the American Revolution from Newspapers and Original Documents*. Vol. II. New York: New York Times & Arno Press, 1969.

Moran, Donald Norman. "The Last Crisis of the American Revolution." American Revolution.org. Accessed Sept. 30, 2013. www.americanrevolution.org/wnewburg.html /.

Morgan, Edmund S. *The Birth of the Republic, 1763–89*. Chicago: University of Chicago Press, 1956.

Morris, Anne Cary, ed. *The Diary and Letters of Gouverneur Morris, Minister of the United States to France; Member of the Constitutional Convention*. Vol. I. New York: Charles Scribner's Sons, 1888.

Morris, Richard B., ed. *Encyclopedia of American History*. New York: Harper & Brothers, 1953.

_____. *The Forging of the Union, 1781–1789*. New York: Harper and Row Publishers, 1987.

Nagy, John A. *Rebellion in the Ranks: Mutinies of the American Revolution*. Yardley: Westholme, 2008

Nelson, Paul David. *Horatio Gates: A Biography*. Baton Rouge: Louisiana State University Press, 1976.

_____. "Horatio Gates at Newburgh, 1783: A Misunderstood Role." With a rebuttal by Richard H. Kohn. *The William & Mary Quarterly*. 3rd Series. Vol. XXIX, No. 1 (January 1972).

"New Windsor Cantonment." *A Revolutionary Day along Historic US Route 9W*. Accessed Sept. 30, 2013. www.revolutionaryday.com/usroute9w/windsor/.

"New Windsor Revolutionary History." *Town of New Windsor, Orange County, New York.* 2013. Accessed Sept. 30, 2013. http://town.new-windsor.ny.us/About/TownHistorian/RevolutionaryHistory.aspx

Oberholtzer, Ellis Paxson. *Robert Morris: Patriot and Financier.* New York: Macmillan Company, 1903.

Palmer, Dave R. *1794: America, Its Army, and the Birth of the Nation.* Novato: Presidio Press, 1994.

Patterson, Samuel W. *Horatio Gates: Defender of American Liberties.* New York: Columbia University Press, 1941.

"Pensions Enacted by Congress for Revolutionary War Veterans." Accessed Sept. 30, 2013. http://vagensearch.com/AmericanRevolution/Pensions.html.

Perkins, James Breck. "The Sinews of War." *France in the Revolution.* AmericanRevolution.org. Accessed Sept. 30, 2013. www.americanrevolution.org/frconfiles/fr17.html

Peters, William. *A More Perfect Union.* New York: Crown, 1987.

Pickering, Octavius, and Charles Wentworth Upham. *The Life of Timothy Pickering.* Vol. I. Boston: Little, Brown, and Company, 1867.

Preston, John Hyde. *A Short History of the American Revolution.* New York: Pocket Books, 1933.

Quincy, Josiah, ed. *The Life and Journals of Major Samuel Shaw, the First American Consul at Canton: With a Life of the Author.* Boston: W. Crosby and H. P. Nichols, 1847.

Raddall, Thomas H. *The Path of Destiny.* Edited by Thomas B. Costain. New York: Popular Library, 1957.

Rakove, Jack N. *The Beginnings of National Politics: An Interpretive History of the Continental Congress.* New York: Alfred A. Knopf, 1979.

Ramsay, David. *The Life of George Washington: Commander in Chief of the Armies of the United States in the War Which Established Their Independence; and First President of the United States.* London: Luke Hanfard & Sons, 1807.

Randall, Willard Sterne. *Alexander Hamilton: A Life.* New York: Harper Collins Publishers, 2003.

———. *George Washington.* New York: Henry Holt and Company, 1997.

Rappleye, Charles. *Robert Morris: Financier of the American Revolution.* New York: Simon & Schuster, 2010.

Resch, John. "Continental Army Veterans: From Outcasts to Icons." *VFW Magazine.* June–July 2002.

The Revolution. History Channel.

Rhodehamel, John, ed. *The American Revolution: Writings from the War of Independence.* New York: Library of America, 2001.

Risch, Erna. *Supplying Washington's Army.* Special studies series. Washington, D.C.: Center of Military History, United States Army, 1981.

Robertson, John R., and Bob McDonald. "The Newburgh Conspiracy." *A Brief Profile of the Continental Army.* Last updated January 17, 2007. Accessed Sept. 30, 2013. www.revwar75.com/ob/newburgh.htm.

Royster, Charles. *A Revolutionary People at War: The Continental Army and American Character, 1775–1783*. Chapel Hill: The University of North Carolina Press, 1979.

Russell, David Lee. *The American Revolution in the Southern Colonies*. Jefferson: McFarland & Co., 2000.

Ruttenber, E. M. *History of the Town of Newburgh*. Newburgh: E. M. Ruttenber and Co., 1859.

Scharf, John Thomas, and Thompson Westcott. *History of Philadelphia, 1609–1884*. Vol. II. Philadelphia: L. H. Everts & Co., 1884.

Schecter, Barnet. *The Battle for New York: The City at the Heart of the American Revolution*. New York: Walker & Co., 2002.

Schoepf, Johann David. *Travels in the Confederation [1783–1784]*. Translated and edited by Alfred J. Morrison. Philadelphia: William J. Campbell, 1911.

Schultz, Pearle Henriksen. *Generous Strangers: Six Heroes of the American Revolution*. New York: Vanguard Press, 1975.

Shannon, Sister Anna Madeleine. "General Alexander McDougall, Citizen and Soldier, 1732–1786." Dissertation, Fordham University, 1957.

Skeen, C. Edward. *John Armstrong, Jr., 1758–1843*. Syracuse: Syracuse University Press, 1981.

_____. "The Newburgh Conspiracy Reconsidered." With a rebuttal by Richard H. Kohn *The William & Mary Quarterly*. 3rd Series. Vol. XXXI, No. 2 (April 1974).

Smelser, Marshall. *The Winning of Independence*. Chicago: Quadrangle Books, 1972.

Smith, Page. *A New Age Now Begins: A People's History of the American Revolution*. 2 vols. New York: McGraw-Hill Book Co., 1976.

_____. *James Wilson: Founding Father, 1742–1798*. Chapel Hill: University of North Carolina Press, 1956.

Smith, Paul H., et al., eds. *Letters of Delegates to Congress, 1774–1789*. 26 vols. Washington, D. C.: Library of Congress, 1976–2000.

Smith, Richard Norton. *Patriarch*. New York: Houghton Mifflin Company, 1993.

Smith, Samuel Stelle. *The Battle of Monmouth*. Monmouth Beach: Philip Freneau Press, 1964.

Smith, William Henry, ed. *The St. Clair Papers: The Life and Public Services of Arthur St. Clair, Soldier of the Revolutionary War, President of the Continental Congress, and Governor of the North-Western Territory, with His Correspondence and Other Papers*. Vol. I. New York: Da Capo Press, 1971.

The Sol Feinstone Collection of the American Revolution. Compiled by Delores Howland. Reel 1. Philadelphia: Rhistoric Publications, 1969.

Sparks, Jared, ed. *Correspondence of the American Revolution; Being Letters of Eminent Men to George Washington, from the Time of His Taking Command of the Army to the End of His Presidency*. Vol. IV. New York: Books for Libraries Press, 1970.

———. *The Life of Gouverneur Morris, with Selections from his Correspondence and Miscellaneous Papers; Detailing Events in the American Revolution, the French Revolution, and in the Political History of the United States.* Vol. I. Boston: Gray & Bowen, 1832.

Staples, William Read. *Rhode Island in the Continental Congress, with the Journal of the Convention that Adopted the Constitution, 1765–1790.* Edited by Reuben Albridge Guild. Providence: Providence Press, 1870.

Stryker, William S. *The Battle of Monmouth.* Port Washington: Kennikat Press, 1970.

Sumner, William Graham. *The Financier and the Finances of the American Revolution.* 2 vols. New York: Dodd, Mead and Company, 1891. Reprint, New York: Augustus M. Kelley, 1968.

Swiggett, Howard. *The Extraordinary Mr. Morris.* Garden City: Doubleday & Company, 1952.

Syrett, Harold C., and Jacob E. Cooke, eds. *The Papers of Alexander Hamilton.* 27 vols. New York: Columbia University Press, 1961–1987.

Thane, Elswyth. *The Fighting Quaker: Nathanael Greene.* New York: Hawthorn Books, 1972.

Thomas, E. S. *Reminiscences of the Last Sixty-five Years, Commencing with the Battle of Lexington. Also, Sketches of His Own Life and Times.* Volume I. Hartford: Case, Tiffany and Burnham, 1840.

Thompson, Maggie Pulgar. "Info on General Walter Stewart, Ireland–PA, 1756–1796." *The Generations Network.* December 16, 2008. Accessed Sept. 30, 2013. http://genforum.genealogy.com/stewart/messages/14845.html

Tindall, George Brown, and David E. Shi. *America: A Narrative History.* New York: W. W. Norton and Company, 1999.

Tucker, Glenn. *Mad Anthony Wayne and the New Nation: The Story of Washington's Front-line General.* Harrisburg: Stackpole Books, 1973.

Unger, Harlow Giles. *Lafayette.* Hoboken: John Wiley & Sons, 2002.

U.S. House of Representatives. *Resolutions, Laws, and Ordinances, Relating to the Pay, Half Pay, Commutation of Half Pay, Bounty Lands, and Other Promises Made by Congress to the Officers and Soldiers of the Revolution; to the Settlement of the Accounts between the United States and the Several States; and to Funding the Revolutionary Debt.* Washington, D.C.: Genealogical Publishing Co., 1998.

Van Doren, Carl. *Benjamin Franklin.* New York: Viking Press, 1938.

———. *Mutiny in January.* New York: Viking Press, 1943.

———. *The Great Rehearsal.* New York: Vikiing Press, 1948.

Van Every, Dale. *Forth to the Wilderness: The First American Frontier, 1754–1774.* New York: New American Library, 1961.

Ver Steeg, Clarence L. *Robert Morris: Revolutionary Financier.* New York: Octagon Books, 1972.

Virtual American Biographies. "John Brooks." 2001. Accessed Sept. 30, 2013. http://famousamericans.net/johnbrooks.

———. "Robert Ogden." 2001. Accessed Sept. 30, 2013. http://famousamericans.net/robertogden.

Wagner, Frederick. *Robert Morris, Audacious Patriot*. New York: Dodd, Mead & Company, 1976.

Wallace, David Duncan. *The Life of Henry Laurens, with a Sketch of the Life of Lieutenant-Colonel John Laurens*. New York: Knickerbocker Press, 1915.

Washington's Generals. History Channel.

Weigley, Russell F., ed. *Philadelphia: A 300-Year History*. New York: W. W. Norton & Co., 1982.

Wensyel, James W. "The Newburgh Conspiracy." *American Heritage*. April/May 1981.

Westermann, Edward B., "Contemporary Civil-Military Relations: Is the Republic in Danger." *Airpower Journal*. Summer 1995.

Wheeler, Richard. *Voices of 1776: The Story of the American Revolution in the Words of Those Who Were There*. Greenwich: Fawcett Publications, 1972.

Wheeler, William Ogden, comp. *The Ogden Family in America, Elizabethtown Branch, and Their English Ancestry; John Ogden, the Pilgrim, and His Descendants, 1640–1905, Their History, Biography & Genealogy*. Edited by Lawrence Van Alstyne and Reverend Charles Burr Ogden. Philadelphia: J. B. Lippincott Co., 1907.

Whitney, David C. *Colonial Spirit of '76: The People of the Revolution*. Chicago: Encyclopedia Britannica Educational Corporation, 1974.

Williams, Sherman. *New York's Part in History*. New York: D. Appleton and Company, 1915.

Williston, E. B., comp. *Eloquence of the United States*. Vol. V. Middletown: E. & H. Clark, 1827.

Wood, Gordon S. *The Creation of the American Republic, 1770–1787*. Chapel Hill: University of North Carolina Press, 1969.

Wright, Esmond, ed. *History of the World: The Last Five Hundred Years*. New York: Bonanza Books, 1984.

Young, Eleanor. *Forgotten Patriot: Robert Morris*. New York: Macmillan Company, 1950.

Ziegler, Philip. *King William IV*. New York: Harper & Row, 1973.

Index

"A Farmer" (pen name of David Howell), 75

Academy of Philadelphia, 24

Adams, John Quincy, 283

Adams, John, 48, 80-81, 90, 131, 165, 236, 280

Adams, Samuel, 49, 50, 55, 154, 207, 281

Addison's *Cato: A Tragedy*, Joseph, 242-44

addresses of conspirators. See Newburgh addresses

Albany, NY, 34, 74, 87, 196, 201, 228

Algonquin Indians, 2

Allen, Ethan, 86

American minister to France. See Franklin, Benjamin

American Philosophical Society, 130

anonymous addresses. See Newburgh addresses

anonymous author, Newburgh addresses. See Armstrong, John, Jr.

anonymous call for March 11, 1783, meeting, 212-13, 219, 220, 221, 222, 223, 225, 226, 238, 246, 251, 289

Armstrong, Horatio Robert, 214

Armstrong, John, Jr., 7, 212, 218, 219, 221, 224, 225, 236, 238, 239, 243, 244, 246-47, 251, 257, 268, 271-72, 285, 286, 291, 292; biography of, 213-17; George Washington admits to not having known that Armstrong had written address, 287; Johnson's biography of Nathanael Greene reviewed by, 289-90; under pen name "John Montgars" (1820), recollections of conspiracy requested by, 287-89, 290

Armstrong, John, Sr., 118, 137, 213

Armstrong's addresses. See Newburgh addresses

army pay arrears, 7, 8, 10, 13, 32, 34, 38-42, 43-47, 54, 60, 61, 62, 65-66, 67, 68, 69, 72, 76, 77-78, 85, 94-95, 96, 103, 119-20, 122, 124, 133, 137, 139-40, 142, 143, 146, 147, 153, 155-57, 159, 174-75, 181, 185, 187, 191-92, 212, 234, 236, 237, 249, 251, 253, 258, 272, 274, 280, 289; one month's pay for army, 23, 141, 142, 143-44, 146, 147, 159, 174, 191, 210, 219, 258, 270; Rhode Island votes to give state battalion three months' pay, 57; three months' pay for army, 77, 258, 264, 265, 270, 273; two months' pay for officers in Hudson Highlands, 77; two months' pay approved in response to generals' petition, 121; two months' pay for southern army, 143

Arnold, Benedict, 124, 197; treason of, 28, 54, 214, 218

Arnold, Jonathan, 80-81, 98, 134, 147, 159

Articles of Confederation, 8, 15, 26, 68, 75, 106, 132, 147, 149, 151, 157, 159, 163, 173, 182, 183, 185, 186, 210, 284

Assistant Secretary of War. See Jackson, William

Assunpink Bridge, 89

Assunpink Creek, 90

Audibert, Philip, 23

Austria, 1

Badge of Military Merit, 69-70

Baltimore, MD, 76

Bank of North America, 21-22, 24, 31-32, 130, 265

Bank of Pennsylvania, 19, 21

Barber, Francis, 126

Barber, William, 175-76, 213

Belvoir (Fairfax plantation, Virginia), 242

Bemis Heights, 123, 196

Benet, George, 249.

Berkeley County, VA, 195

Berkshire Hills, MA, 87

Bills of credit, 9-11, 25; devaluation of, 11-12, 54

Bland, Theodorick, 147, 148, 149, 152, 155, 156, 157, 163, 177, 188, 191, 257, 258, 264

Blue Ridge Mountains, 209

Board of War, 134, 199, 200, 201, 202

Boston Massacre, 86, 88, 113

Boston Port Act, 115, 168

Boston Tea Party, 115

Boston, 24, 70, 76, 82, 83, 86, 88, 91, 95, 113, 124, 129, 167, 278, 280-81; British evacuation of, 88

Boudinot, Elias, 225, 251, 252-53, 255, 256, 264

bounties: eighty-dollar completion-of-service, 97, 272; enlistment, to be paid by states objecting to reductions of line regiments, 72; enlistment, from Massachusetts towns, 124; promised but not given caused discontent, 69; for signing up early, 85; ten-dollar, to extend enlistment, 18-19, 125, 195; of three gold Portuguese half-johannes for new Pennsylvania recruits, 61; for withdrawal of petition by New Jersey Line, 100

boycott of British goods, 115

Braddock, Edward, 194-95

Brandywine, Battle of, 58-59, 91, 125, 169, 198, 199, 203

Breymann, Heinrich von, redoubt of, 123, 197, 214

Briar Hill, 59

Bridge's Massachusetts Regiment, Ebenezer, 122

Bronx River, 116, 117

Brookhiser, Richard, 242

Brooklyn Heights, 116

Brooks, John, 82-85, 95, 96, 99, 102, 103, 109, 126, 129, 132-33, 134, 135, 138-40, 142-44, 145, 146, 158, 161, 162, 166, 173, 174, 181, 192, 213, 219, 245-46, 249; biography of, 122-24; charged with causing plot's collapse, 285-86; friendship with Alexander Hamilton, 126; plan and feasibility of military coup disavowed by, 290-92. See also delegation of army to Congress

"Brutus" (pen name of Alexander McDougall), 113, 163, 179, 191

Bunker Hill, Battle of, 86, 122, 124

Burgoyne, John, 122-23, 194, 196-97, 214

Burke, Thomas, 15, 51-52

Burlington, VT, 228

Burnet, Robert R., 236

Burns, James MacGregor, 242

Burr, Aaron, 196

Butler, Richard, 61

Butter Hill, 1, 3, 36, 106, 277

Cambridge, MA, 48, 85, 86, 87, 124

Camden, Battle of, 28, 54, 204-5, 214

Canaan, CT, 281

Canada, 45, 110, 116, 195, 196; Canadians, 214; expedition to, 201-2; Quebec, 124-25

Carleton, Guy, 68, 249, 264

Carlisle, PA, 213, 214

Carroll, Daniel, 106, 134, 160, 179

Cato: A Tragedy (play by Joseph Addison), 242-44

certificates: of the army's commissary and quartermaster departments, 10-11, 12; commutation, 254, 280-81, 283; Continental loan office, 8-9, 175, 184, 208, 222; Henry Knox and Rufus Putnam propose that Massachusetts Line be paid with, 66; Lewis Nicola and, 45; New York legislature's view for non-payment of soldiers with, 122; in official report on March 15, 1783, officers' meeting George Washington advocates for the army the issue of, 253; part of debt to Baron Von Steuben paid with, 76; yielding six percent recommended by Grand Committee, 146. See also notes payable; securities

cessation of hostilities, royal proclamation of, 263, 264, 269

chain barriers across Hudson River, 35-36, 118

Charleston, SC: British evacuation of 99, 141; British victory at, 28, 54

Charlotte, NC, 205

Chatterton Hill, 116, 168

Chesapeake Bay, 22

Chester, PA, 23, 59

Chew, artillery barrage against home of Benjamin, 91, 118

Church of England, 2

City Tavern, 131

civil war, fear of, 140, 186, 252

Clairy, Arthur, 134

Clark, Abraham, 33, 99

Clermont, SC, 204

Clinton, George, 27, 34, 121-22, 138-39, 166, 169-70, 226-27, 282

Clinton, Henry, 59

Clymer, George, 41

Cobb, David, 240, 284

Colden, Cadwallader, 111, 113

College of New Jersey (now Princeton), 12, 124, 167, 213

College, Academy, and Charitable School of Philadelphia, The. See University of the State of Pennsylvania

Committee at Camp (committee sent to Valley Forge by Congress), 27, 50, 51, 169

Committee of Fifty, 115

Committee of Fifty-One, 115, 126

Committee of One Hundred, 115

Committee of Sixty, 115

Committee of the army. See delegation of army to Congress

Common Sense, 32

commutation, 84, 93, 96, 97, 104, 140, 145, 147, 147-48, 158-59, 162, 166, 181, 185, 188, 190-91, 208, 218, 227, 233, 235, 251, 264, 271, 272, 275, 278, 282, 283, 292; approved by Congress, 254, 255, 256; congressional votes against, 147-48, 158-59, 218; opposition in Massachusetts and Connecticut to Commutation Act, 279-82

Concord, Battle of, 115, 122

Condict, Silas, 134

Congress: address to the states, April 26, 1783, 268; approves recommendation that Robert Morris give men at least one month's pay, 147; Constitution ratified by, 284; declaration of cease-fire by, 267; denunciation of theatre performances by, 242; description of, 131-32; final peace treaty ratified by, 279; financing the war, 8, 9, 13-14, 21, 25, 27, 28, 31, 32, 33, 40-41, 148, 150, 155, 156, 209; furloughs authorized by, 271-73; general funding for, 13, 27, 28, 31, 32, 33, 40, 41, 103, 135, 145, 146-58, 160, 161, 162, 163, 165, 173, 174-75, 176, 177-78, 179, 180, 181, 182, 183-84, 186-87, 188-89, 190, 207, 208, 209-10, 211, 220, 254, 256, 257, 258, 259, 263, 265-66, 268, 269, 275, 278; preliminary peace treaty ratified by, 265, 267; requisitions to states for funds for, 14-15, 27, 30, 32, 33, 40, 41, 44, 54, 57, 62, 63-64, 75, 145, 149, 150, 153, 156, 157, 160, 163, 183, 184, 186, 210, 264, 275; taxation authority for, 8, 13, 14, 20, 22, 27, 28, 32, 33, 41-42, 44, 57, 65, 66, 68, 80, 121, 126, 133, 134, 139, 145, 146, 147, 148, 149, 151, 152, 153, 154, 156, 160, 164, 171, 175, 176, 183, 187, 209, 210, 212, 263, 271, 275, 282, 286. See also duties on imports

committees of: on assessing state land values, 106, 160; on commutation, 148, 158, 162, 188; to consider Morris's circular to the states, 41; on debt to France, 136-37; to develop funding program, 184, 190, 209, 220; to lobby Rhode Island General Assembly, 105-6; to produce an address to the states, 268; in response to Robert Morris's resignation, 209; to review Morris's tax proposal, 33; to study Rhode Island's unfavorable vote on Impost, 99; of the whole, 155, 163, 179, 184. See also Committee at Camp; Grand Committee

Connecticut: Alexander McDougall's stop in, 118; commercial relationship with Rhode Island and impact of Impost, 75, 177-78; congressional delegates from, 52, 67, 148, 149, 151, 156, 190, 191, 218, 227 (See Dyer, Eliphalet; Ellsworth, Oliver; Root, Jesse; Wolcott, Oliver); creditors from, 74; desertion by troops from, 54; governor appeals to state legislature to do right by the army, 282; officers and reduction of forces, 66, 132; opposition to pensions for army officers, 254; residents' criticism of the Commutation Act, 281-82; Robert Morris dismisses complaints about taxes to governor of, 65; sergeants petition for half-pay pensions, 267, 270; signatories to Hudson Highlands officers' petition to Congress, 95, 222; state legislature (General Assembly) and commutation, 271, 281-82; troops' mutinies, 28, 39, 60, 69

Connecticut Courant and Weekly Intelligencer, "Constant Customer" of, 281

conspirators' plot. See nationalists' plot

Continental loan offices. See certificates: Continental loan office

Constitution Island, 106

Constitution, ratification of, 284

Continental Regiment of Artillery, 86

"Continentalist, the" (pen name of Alexander Hamilton), 170, 173

convention of the states, call for national, 154, 173, 182

Conway Cabal, the, 118, 197-203, 205

Conway, Thomas, 197-203

Cornell, Ezekiel, 77, 78

Cornwallis, 61, 89-90, 204

Corps of Invalids, 43

Coxe's Mill, NC, 203

Crane, John, 85

creditors, 8, 61-64, 101, 142, 145, 149, 150, 152, 155-57, 165, 174-79, 181, 182, 184

domestic, 25, 74, 173, 175, 205, 211-12; New York, 74; Pennsylvania, 62, 63, 73, 74, 150, 152, 154, 157, 176, 177, 178, 184, 205, 212; Virginia, 178, 184

foreign: Cuba (Havana), Spanish court at, 22, 32, 135, 142; Europe, 28, 98, 137, 157, 165, 208; France, 8, 15, 20-21, 23-24, 31, 40, 61-62, 74, 136-37, 138, 140, 143, 159, 264; Holland, 8, 80-81, 159, 193; Spain, 8

Crompond, NY, 76

"Crown Letter," 43-46, 47, 53, 57; Washington's response to, 45-46. See also Nicola, Lewis

Cuba: Havana, 18; governor of, 22. See also creditors, foreign

Cummins, Michael, 112, 114

Custis, George Washington Parke, 61, 237

Custis, John "Jack" Parke, 30

Dans Kammer, 36

Deane, Silas, 90

debtors' prisons, 72, 253

Dedham, MA, 280

DeGrasse, Admiral, 23

DeLancey family, 111

Delaware: conditional approval of Impost, 282; congressional delegates from, 218

Delaware River, 118, 169; Washington crossing, Christmas 1776, 89

delegation of army to Congress, December 1783, 94, 95-96, 99, 102, 105, 109, 124, 126, 129, 132-33, 134, 137, 138-39, 142-44, 145-46, 158, 161-62, 173, 179, 181, 191-92, 246, 249, 289; advice from General St. Clair for, 103-4; arrival in Philadelphia, 109, 132, 138, 161, 163; departure for Philadelphia, 102-3; initial report from McDougall, 136; meeting with Grand Committee, 139-40, 141, 161; official presentation of petition by, 134, 161; selection of, 95. See also McDougall and Ogden report from Philadelphia; petition of Hudson Highlands officers

Department of Finance, 21, 288; establishment of, 16

Department of Foreign Affairs, establishment of, 16

Department of Marine, 30, 168; establishment of, 16

Department of War, establishment of, 16

depreciation: of commutation certificates, 283; of currency, 10-12, 15, 18, 21, 28, 29, 33, 43, 45, 46, 53, 69, 122, 171, 208

desertions, 27, 40, 51, 54, 55, 69, 115, 125, 195; British, 197

Deviser's Ferry, 169

Dickinson, Philemon, 134

Digby, Robert, 126

Dilworth Village, PA, 59

disbandment of army, 40-41, 103, 144, 164, 173, 192, 212, 215, 223, 235, 236, 239, 249, 253, 264, 265, 269, 270, 274, 277, 279, 287; threat of early, 211; threat of refusal to disband, 7, 43, 46, 67, 138, 163, 164, 178, 179, 182, 186, 187, 189, 190, 216, 217, 233-34, 238, 256, 257, 268, 271, 291

Donnelly, James, 37

Dorchester Heights, 88

du Coudray, Phillipe, 90

Duane, James, 13

Duer, William, 286, 287

Duke of Leed's head housekeeper, 194

Dunn, Susan, 242

duties on imports, 27-28, 173, 190, 209, 210, 220, 254, 266, 268; Impost of 1781, 15-16, 20, 22, 24, 31, 32-33, 41, 47, 61, 62, 65, 75-76, 78-79, 80-81, 82, 94, 95, 98, 99, 100-1, 105-6, 109, 121, 143, 145, 149, 151, 153-57, 158, 163, 174-75, 177-78, 179, 181, 182, 185, 187, 189-90, 207, 209, 210, 211, 221, 247, 263, 266, 268, 278, 279-80, 282, 288, 290

Dyer, Eliphalet, 149, 191, 203, 218, 227, 233, 254

Earl of Egremont, 195

East India Company, 114-15, 167

East River, 115, 116

Easton, PA, 100

8th Massachusetts Regiment, 122

Eliot, John, 102, 184-85, 240, 247

Elizabethtown Academy, 167

Elizabethtown, NJ, 125

Ellison, house of John. See Gates's headquarters

Ellsworth, Oliver, 151, 156, 268

Eltham, Virginia, estate of Washington's brother-in-law, 30

England, 2, 110, 111, 113, 114, 148, 195, 216, 242, 255; Bristol, 17; Falmouth, 263; House of Commons, 35; House of Lords, 249; London, 195, 216, 242; Parliament, 25, 35, 93, 111, 113, 151, 163, 167, 216, 220; prime minister, 34, 35; Royal Council, 2

Englishtown, NJ, 59

Esopus, NY, 4, 213

Europe, 170. See also creditors, foreign

Eustis, William, 85, 95, 102, 212, 247, 290

Evans, Israel, 107, 108, 136, 160, 277

Ewing, John, 62, 212

Fairfax, family of, 242

Farmer, 19

Farmington, CT, 281

Fearnaught, 205

Ferling, John, 241

Fersen, Axel, 237

Fields, the (New York City), 111, 112, 115, 126, 167

Financier, the. See Morris, Robert

financing the war. See Congress

1st New York Regiment, 115; desertion from, 54

1st Regiment, New Jersey Line, 125

Fish, Nicholas, 212

Fishkill, NY, 39, 43, 71, 106, 117

Fitzsimmons, Thomas, 99, 148, 150, 152, 154, 158, 160, 162, 178, 184, 188, 190, 209, 220, 264, 265; army discontent discussed at home of, 179-80; 186

Floyd, William, 226-27

Flucker, Lucy, 86

Fort Montgomery, 3, 4, 35, 36

Fort Bunker Hill, 168

Fort Clinton, 3, 35

Fort Constitution, 4, 117

Fort Crown Point, 125, 195, 196

Fort Duquesne, 194

Fort George, Grand Battery beneath, 168

Fort Putnam, 266, 267

Fort Schuyler, 54

Fort Ticonderoga, 86, 87, 125, 195, 196, 205

45th Regiment, Nova Scotia, 195

Framingham, MA, 87

France, 1, 2, 19, 28, 90, 110, 199, 201, 222, 255, 290; American minister to, 28, 138; French army and navy, 19; French troops, 73, 76-77; intendant of French army, 23; joins war effort, 122; Paris, 20, 93, 133, 255. See also creditors, foreign

Franklin, Benjamin, 14, 18, 28, 29, 30, 138

Fraunces' Tavern, 111, 279

Frederick the Great, 198

Fredericksburg, VA, 30

Freehold, NJ, 59

Freeman, Douglas Southall, 228

Freeman's Farm, battle at, 196-97

Freeman's Journal, 208, 222, 248

French and Indian War, 17, 110, 136, 213, 220; Braddock's expedition to Fort Duquesne, 194-95

French minister. See Luzerne

funding for Congress. See Congress, general funding for

furloughs granted to army, 270, 272, 273, 274

Gates, Elizabeth, 208-9, 285

Gates, Horatio, 7, 28, 37, 54, 58, 118, 119, 212, 213, 271, 277, 285, 286-87; apology to George Washington, 202; appointment of Robert Morris praised by, 21; at Battle of Camden, 54, 204-5; at Battles of Saratoga, 123, 196-97; before settling in America, 194-95; biography of, 194-205; challenged to duel, 202, 214; and construction of huts at New Windsor Cantonment, 107; and construction of Temple of Virtue, 108, 138, 141, 142, 147, 150, 159-60, 174; and the Conway Cabal, 197-203; death of only child, 214; declines expedition against the Indians in Mohawk Valley, 203; at Fort Ticonderoga, 125, 196-96; letter to R. Peters and poem by, 180-81, 208; made commander of New Windsor Cantonment, 205; president, Board of War, 200; reasons for joining plot, 205; suspected by Washington of involvement in conspiracy, 193-94; at Temple of Virtue, March 15, 1783, 236, 237, 245, 247; urged to become part of independent army in Hudson Highlands, 196; wife's sickness, 208-9, 285

Gates, Robert (father of Horatio), 194

Gates, Robert (son of Horatio), 213, 214

Gates's headquarters (Ellison's house), 212, 213

General Barrington, 110

general funding for Congress. See Congress, general funding for

general revenue. See Congress, general funding for

General Washington, 222

"General Washington's Watch Chain," 36

George III, 34-35, 113, 242; speech to Parliament, December 1782, 93, 163, 179, 220

Georgia: absence of congressional representation, 134; governor of, 79, 144; and taxes, including Impost, 75, 78, 105, 144, 153, 158, 181, 210, 282

Germain, Lord, 34

German soldiers, 123, 197

Germantown, Battle of, 59, 91, 117-18, 125, 203

Gerry, Elbridge, 50

Gervais, John Lewis, 148, 158, 162

Gilman, John Taylor, 159, 185-86

Glover, John, 89, 116

Gordon, William, 217, 221, 286-87

Gorham, Nathaniel, 149, 155, 175, 179, 184, 186, 188, 190, 191, 209, 220, 264, 265, 270

Grand Committee, the, 74, 134, 136, 137, 162; meets with delegation of army, 139-40, 141, 161; report to Congress by, 146-47

subcommittee to report on army's grievances, 140-41, 145, 146, 162

Grand Convention, 281-82

Green Mountain Boys, 86

Green Spring, VA, 61

Greene, Nathanael, 30, 39-40, 43, 50, 64, 73-74, 78, 90, 94, 106, 118, 119, 129, 141, 143, 144, 145, 158, 181, 210, 211, 227, 257, 271, 289, 290; encouraged to join conspiracy, 173, 257; command of southern army turned over to, 205; nationalists' plot rejected by, 257, 292-93

Greene, William, 31, 57, 79, 80, 98

Greenway, Robert, 17

Gregory, Isaac, 205

Guerard, Benjamin, 211

Half Moon, 1

half-pay pensions, 7, 8, 27, 34, 43, 44, 47, 49, 50, 51, 52, 53, 54, 55, 56, 66, 72, 82, 83, 84, 85, 93, 94, 95, 96, 97, 103, 104, 119, 120, 132, 133, 139, 140, 147, 148, 150, 158-59, 161, 162, 170, 172, 181, 185, 186, 189, 190, 191, 208, 212, 218, 227, 236, 237, 251, 252, 254, 264, 267, 275, 278, 281, 283, 292

Hamilton, Alexander, 13, 20, 64, 73, 74, 98, 99, 100, 101, 126, 132, 133, 140, 141, 145-52, 157, 158, 160, 162, 175, 177, 178, 179, 180, 184, 188, 190, 193-94, 201, 205, 206, 209, 220, 221, 224, 235, 251, 254, 255-56, 26-57, 263-64, 265, 266, 267, 268, 270; appointed New York's receiver of Continental taxes, 172-73; appointment of congressional tax collectors pushed by, 151-52; appointment of Robert Morris praised by, 21; army involvement in conspiracy intimated to Governor Clinton by, 138-39; articles under pen name "the Continentalist" written by, 170-71, 173; biography of, 166-73; breach with Commander-in-chief, 164; charged with involvement in conspiracy, 288, 290-91; in the Continental Army, 13, 26, 165, 168-72; friendship with Alexander McDougall, 126, 134, 167, 168; friendship with John Brooks, 126; on inactive army list, 172; possible involvement in conspiracy dismissed by Armstrong, 290; urges Washington to take charge of army's efforts for redress, 164-65, 173, 173-74, 180; reprimanded by Washington for considering the idea of redress by force, 258-59, 293

Hamilton, James, Jr., 166

Hamilton, James, Sr., 166

Hancock, John, 31, 82, 280

Hand, Edward, 245, 247

Hanson, John, 38, 41

Hardy, Samuel, 288

Harlem River, 24

Harrison, Benjamin, 10, 162, 207

Harrison, NY, 214

Hartford, CT, 15, 26, 39, 281

Harvard, MA, 48

Harvie, John, 290

Hasbrouck House. See Washington's headquarters, Newburgh

Hasbrouck, Catherine "Tryntje", 36-37

Hasbrouck, Jonathan, 2, 36-37

Havana, Cuba, 18. See also creditors, foreign

Hawkins, Francis, 228

Head of Elk, MD, 23

Heath, William, 10, 65, 71, 216, 272

Henry IV's Edict of Nantes, 1

Henry, Patrick, 203

Hessians, 89, 116, 117, 168, 169, 171-72

Hickey Plot, 26, 115, 126

Hickey, Thomas, execution of, 26

Hillsboro, NC, 203, 205

Hingham, MA, 132

Holland, 1, 44, 68, 114. See also creditors, foreign

Holten, Samuel, 184, 190

Horsmanden, Daniel, 112

House of Employment, 130

Howard, Captain, 245-46

Howe, William, 88, 116, 117, 129, 196, 281

Howell, David, 75-76, 78-79, 80-81, 98, 185; articles under pen name "A Farmer" published by, 75

Hudson Highlands, 7, 30, 34, 35, 39, 44, 65, 67, 73, 77, 80, 85, 93, 96, 98, 108, 117, 118, 124, 138, 142, 143, 150, 158, 161, 162, 166, 174, 176, 181, 190, 191, 192, 196, 205, 209, 210, 211, 218, 219, 222, 224, 226, 233, 235, 244, 253, 269, 274, 277, 279, 285, 286, 287, 289, 290

Hudson River, 1, 2, 3, 35, 36, 37, 73, 87, 88, 106, 107, 118, 125, 220, 222, 266, 274

Hudson Valley, 122

Hudson, Henry, 1

Hughes, James Miles, 212

Hull, William, 82, 83, 85, 292

Humane Society, 130

Humphreys, David, 46, 248

Humpton, Richard, 38

Huntington, Ebenezer, 13, 96, 291

Huntington, Jedediah, 85, 136, 222, 270

Hutchinson, Israel, 116

Impost of 1781. See duties on imports

Independent Gazetteer, 207

Indian Queen Inn, 137

Indians, 2, 45, 115, 180; expedition against, in Mohawk Valley, 203; "Mohawks" threaten anyone who assists in landing or storing tea in New York, 114; served under Burgoyne, 196, 214. See also French and Indian War

inflation, 69; examples of, 10, 12, 29

Ireland, 58

"Irish Beauty, the" (nickname for Walter Stewart), 60

Islay, Scotland, island of, 109

Jackson, William, 141

Jamaica, 17

Jay, John, 32, 133, 168

Jefferson, Thomas, 11, 12, 184, 228

Jockey Club, 131

Johnson, William, 289, 290

Jones, Joseph, 99, 105, 188-89, 223, 253, 254; informs George Washington of plot (letter of February 27, 1783), 188-89, 224, 228, 240-41, 284, 288

Judd, William, 66, 184

"Junius," 216

Kalb, Johann, 201

King, Rufus, 286, 287

King's College, 24, 167

Klinkersberg. See Butter Hill

Knox, Henry, 37, 48-49, 65-66, 82, 84, 85, 93, 94, 95, 124, 132, 136, 161-64, 166, 179, 181-82, 185, 187-88, 190-92, 219, 220, 222-23, 233, 236, 248, 270, 278, 279, 285; advocates the establishment of military academies, 89; approval of Philadelphia mission given to McDougall, 102; biography of, 86-92; McDougall and Lincoln notified of officers' meeting and Armstrong's address by, 226; moving of artillery from Fort Ticonderoga to Cambridge, 86-88; nationalists' plot rejected by, 181-82; at March 15, 1783, meeting of the Hudson Highlands officers, 236, 245-46, 247; petition written by, 96-98; preparations for Congress to receive petition made by, 102; rout of the Hessians, 89; suspected of disclosing plot to Washington, 286; warns John Lowell of "the extreme uneasiness of the Massachusetts Line," 83

Knox, William, 89

La Triomphe, 255

Lafayette, 23, 59, 61, 91, 169, 171, 201-2, 236-37

Lake Champlain, 195

Lake George, 86, 88

Lancaster, PA, 277

land grants to veterans, 45, 47, 49, 61, 72, 119, 121; formation of new western state, 45, 47

Landais, Pierre, 38

Laurens, Henry, 50-53, 132, 203

Laurens, John, 15, 20, 23, 31

Lee, Arthur, 33, 151, 152, 154-57, 177-78, 183-84, 186, 207-8

Lee, Charles, 59, 124

Lee, Richard Henry, 198, 200

Lee, Billy, 38, 237

Leicester, MA, 87

Levine, Johann, 166

Lexington, Battle of, 3, 86, 115, 168, 266, 267

Library Company of Philadelphia, 130

Lincoln, Benjamin, 30, 34, 66, 77, 93, 132, 158, 197, 219, 226, 248, 270, 284; report to Knox on army distress, 94-95, 102, 192; visit to New Windsor Cantonment, 78, 79, 80, 94, 192

"Little Lion, the" (nickname for Alexander Hamilton), 169

Livingston, Henry Beekman, 117

Livingston, Robert, 30, 32, 34, 166, 169, 270; army unrest reported to John Adams by, 165

Livingston, William, 168

London, 115, 167

London Book Store, 86

London, England, 195, 216, 242

Long Island, 122, 281; Battle of, 88, 116

Louis XIV, 1

Louvois, French Minister of War, 1-2

Lovell, James, 203

Lowell, John, 41, 83, 84

Loyalists, 25, 26, 86, 118, 167, 196, 204, 264; "nest of Tories," 2

"Lucius," 208, 222

Luken's Mill, 59

Luzerne, French minister, 23, 138, 140, 143, 256

Machin, Thomas, 36

Madison, James, 12, 29, 41, 98, 99, 106, 109, 134, 135, 136-37, 140, 141, 145, 146, 150, 152-54, 159, 160, 162, 163, 166, 175, 178, 179, 183-84, 186-87, 190-91, 207, 209, 220, 254, 266, 268-69; informed of Virginia's repeal of Impost, 105; learns of plot and Washington's popularity decline, 179-80; writes Edmund Randolph in cipher of growing army unrest, 165-66, 186; writes Thomas Jefferson of devaluation plan, 11-12

Mahakeneghtuc (Mohegan). See Hudson River

March 15, 1783, meeting of the Hudson Highlands officers. See Temple of Virtue

Marlborough, MA, 87

Marshall, Christopher, 10

Martin, Joseph Plumb, 61

Martinque, invasion of, 195

Martyr's Reach, 35

Maryland: Battalion, 274; congressional delegates from, 28, 79; and fear of being bankrupted by Virginia, 209-10; governor of, 31; and half pay for duration officers, 53; and Impost, 32, 105; Robert Morris, Sr.'s work in, 17; troops' huts, 107; troops in battle at Chatterton Hill, 116-17; troops' march south after Yorktown, 30

Mason, George, 13

Massachusetts: colonels from five regiments petition General Heath over pay arrears, 10; congressional delegates from, 33, 83, 84, 132, 149, 158, 184, 203, 280 (See Gorham, Nathaniel; Holten, Samuel; Lovell, James; Osgood, Samuel); exodus of regiments from New Windsor Cantonment, 274; governor of, 31, 82, 280; movement of artillery from Fort Ticonderoga through, 87-88; officers' petition and appeals to state legislature (1781 and 1782), 65-67, 82-84, 93, 124; opposition to Commutation Act and Impost, 280; 282; regimental officers begin movement for redress of Hudson Highlands army's grievances, 85; reduction of regiments from, 132; regiments from, 116, 122, 124, 141, 144; regiments leave for West Point, 277; Samuel Adams gets state to accept Commutation Act, 281; signatories to Hudson Highlands officers' petition to Congress, 95; soldiers believe enlistments are up and leave West Point, 54, 69; state legislature (General Court), 32, 82, 83, 84-85, 124, 280, 281; troops' huts, 107

Matthews, David, 26

McClenachan, Blair, 58, 62, 63, 211

McCrea, Jane, 196

McDougall, Alexander, 26, 55, 95-96, 99, 102-3, 124, 126, 129, 132-33, 134, 135, 136, 137, 138-40, 142-43, 145-46, 158, 159, 161-62, 166, 167-68, 173, 179, 181, 184, 188, 190-92, 201, 202, 218, 219, 226, 245, 246, 249, 254, 278, 279, 285, 286; arrest and imprisonment of, 112-13, 114, 167; asks for Knox's opinion on plan to unite army and creditors, 136; biography of, 109-22; as "Brutus", informs Knox of growing threat that army won't disband, 163; campaign to educate public on commutation, 278; financial sacrifices and appeals to Congress and New York legislature for back pay, 121-22; friendship with Alexander Hamilton, 126, 134, 167-68; on "Hickey Plot" committee, 26, 126; informs Knox of vote against commutation, 233. See also delegation of army to Congress

McDougall, Elizabeth, 109

McDougall, Ranald, 109, 111

McDougall, Ranald Stephen, 132

McHenry, James, 79

McWilliams, William, 198, 202

Medford, MA, 122

Mercer, Hugh, 213

Mercer, John Francis, 163, 174, 175, 178, 184, 186, 189-90

Merchants' Coffee House (New York City), 114

Middletown, CT, 281, 282

Mifflin, Thomas, 105-6, 199, 200, 202

Mohawk Valley Indians, expedition against, 203

Mohegan Indians, 1

Monmouth Courthouse, 59, 91

Monmouth, Battle of, 59-60, 124, 125, 169

Monongahela River, 194

Montgars, John (pen name of John Armstrong, Jr.), 287-89, 290

Moore, Harry, 111

Moore, Major, 212

Morgan, Daniel, 197

Morris, Gouverneur, 30, 32, 106, 126, 131-32, 132, 152, 161, 162, 166, 169, 181, 182, 206, 257, 271, 289, 290, 291, 292-93; accident and peg leg, 28, 29; biography of, 24-29; as congressional delegate from New York, 26-28, 131-32; displayed guile in treatment of militia battalion, 133-34; explains financial problems to Spain's representative, 33; on "Hickey Plot" committee, 26, 126; makes motion to Congress for lifelong pension, 53; observes that continued war would necessitate a strong government, 68; poses specter of a military coup, 133; proposes army and creditors unite to pressure legislatures, 161; publishing as "an American," advocates greater authority for

Congress, 28; sends feeler on nationalists' scheme to Nathanael Greene, 173, 257, 292; suspected of involvement in plot, 219, 266, 288, 289, 290, 291; visits Valley Forge as Committee at Camp member, 27, 51, 169

Morris, Lewis, 24

Morris, Robert, 14, 29, 30, 31, 32, 33, 34, 38-40, 40-41, 57-58, 61-63 64, 65, 66, 71, 72, 73-75, 77-78, 80, 94, 98, 103, 105, 106, 129, 132, 133, 134-35, 136-37, 138, 140, 141-43, 143-44, 145, 147, 152, 154, 158, 159, 169, 172, 173, 181, 184, 185, 203, 205, 206, 210, 222, 234, 254, 264, 265, 266, 270-71, 273, 280, 282, 290; appointment as Superintendent of Finance and reactions to, 16, 19, 21; and the Bank of North America, 21-22, 24, 31-32, 130; biography of, 17-24; claimed as fellow plotter, 180, 212; as congressional delegate from Pennsylvania, 18, 131; critical response to resignation, 207-8, 209, 222, 250; developed reputation as schemer, 19; and efforts to secure funds from Cuba, 22, 135, 142; resignation of, 146, 188, 210-11, 220, 227-28, 247, 265; urges union of creditors to influence legislatures, 62; and the Yorktown campaign, 22-24; suspected of leading Newburgh Conspiracy, 259, 288, 291

Morris, Robert, Sr., 17

Morris, Sarah, 24

Morrisania (childhood home of Gouverneur Morris), 24, 29

Morristown, NJ, 34, 38, 54, 90, 125, 213

Mount Vernon, 30, 38

Moylan, Stephen, 132

Muhlenberg, Peter, 118

mutinies: of Connecticut troops, 28, 39, 60, 69; fear of, 34, 99, 138, 139, 154; of Massachusetts troops, 54, 69; of New Jersey troops, 124; of New York troops, 54, 69; of Pennsylvania troops, 40, 44, 61, 69, 70, 124, 277

Nancy, 167

Nash, Abner, 105-6, 134

Nassau Hall, Princeton, 169

national debt. See public debt

national lotteries, 9

nationalists, 19-20, 41, 66, 67, 101, 109, 151, 157, 160, 164, 175, 180, 181, 186, 206, 208, 252, 254, 258

nationalists' plot to influence congressional funding, 193, 221, 247, 255; after-event analysis of, 285-93; attempt to recruit George Washington for, 164-65, 173, 180 [see also 193]; attempt to recruit Nathanael Greene for, 173, 292; George Washington suspects Horatio Gates is leader of, 193; nationalists' wariness of involving Gates in, 206; reasons for involvement of Gates in, 205; threat of army mutiny, coup, or refusal to disband, 7, 43, 46, 67, 133, 138-39, 154-55, 163, 164, 166, 178, 179, 182, 186, 187-88, 189, 190, 193-94, 216, 217, 223, 233-34, 238, 243, 246, 256, 257, 258-59, 263, 265, 268, 271, 291; union of creditors and army, 57-58, 103, 106, 134, 136, 161, 162, 173, 176, 181-82, 205, 212, 223, 251-52, 263

Nevis, island of, 166

New Building, New Windsor Cantonment. See Temple of Virtue

New England: congressional delegates from, 148, 158; New Englanders, fear of emergence of privileged caste of officers among, 49, 190; popularity of Gates with politicians from, 203; town meetings in, 279

New Hampshire: Brigade, 160, 274; congressional delegates from, 159, 218 (See Gilman, John Taylor; White, Phillips); exodus of brigade from New Windsor Cantonment, 274; printers in campaign to educate public on commutation, 278; signatory to Hudson Highlands officers' petition to Congress, 95; troops' huts, 107

New Jersey: congressional delegates from, 33, 99, 148, 158, 218 (See Condict, Silas); creditors from, 74; Line officers' threat to resign en masse and legislature's reaction, 100; mutiny of troops from, 54; printers in campaign to educate public on commutation, 278; signatory to Hudson Highlands officers' petition to Congress, 95; state legislature provided funds for Congress, 40; state legislature's opposition to pensions for army officers, 52; troops' exodus from New Windsor Cantonment, 274; troops' huts, 107; regiment from, 125

New London, CT, 281

New Rochelle, NY, 24

New Windsor Cantonment, 37, 79, 94, 106-8, 124, 135-36, 138, 141-42, 147, 160, 174, 180, 192, 205, 221, 223, 224, 235, 249, 265, 266, 267, 269, 274, 277; auction of huts and Temple of Virtue, 279; building of huts, 107, 141-42; closing of camp, 277; tension in camp, 221. See also Temple of Virtue

New Windsor, NY, 4, 36, 37, 71, 106, 141, 164

New York: arrival of Palatines in, 1, 2; broadsides for inhabitants of, 111-12, 113, 167; Committee of Safety urges Horatio Gates to become part of independent army in Hudson Highlands, 196; congressional delegates from, 13, 26-28, 101, 131-32; 160, 167, 170, 205, 226-27, 251, 256, 265, 266 (See Duane, James; Floyd, William; Hamilton, Alexander); Council, 113; creditors from, 74; exodus of regiments from New Windsor Cantonment, 274; first constitution of, 26; governor of, 26, 27, 34, 111, 121-22, 138, 166, 169-70, 226-27, 282; receiver of Continental taxes (tax collector), 64, 172-73, 282; regiments from, 115, 170; signatory to Hudson Highlands officers' petition to Congress, 95; troops in battle at Chatterton Hill, 116-17; troops' huts, 107; troops' mutinies, 54, 69; state legislature (General Assembly, New York Provincial Congress, and New York Provincial Convention) of: 3, 25, 26, 111, 113, 114, 115, 121, 122, 134, 166, 167, 168, 266; proposes national convention of states to strengthen Congress, 64, 73, 173; rejected Commutation Act, 279; support for Impost turned down by Congress, 282; votes to use requisitioned funds to pay line troops, 34

New York City, 2, 26, 35, 36, 88, 107, 109-16, 126, 129, 167, 168, 249, 263, 264; British evacuation of, 279; British occupation of, 116; broadsides for inhabitants of, 111-12, 113, 167; the Fields, 111, 112, 115, 126, 167; George Washington calls anonymous addresser "Emissary ... from New York," 239; Harlem Heights, 88; mayor of, 26; merchants vs. McDougall, 113-15; New Gaol, 72, 113; "tea party," 115, 167

New York Packet, The, and the American Advertiser (*New-York Packet*), 141, 170, 173, 278

Newburgh addresses, 7, 46, 212, 213, 214-17, 218, 219, 220, 221, 224, 225, 226, 236, 237, 238, 243, 244, 245, 246, 247, 251, 257, 268, 269, 286-87, 288, 289, 290-91, 292; circulated in camp, 213, 219, 223, 224, 237; Rufus Putnam's response to, 233-35, 291; second address, 224-25

Newburgh headquarters. See Washington's headquarters

Newburgh, NY, 1, 2, 3-4, 24, 34, 36-38, 57, 106, 235, 241, 267, 274, 279

Newport, RI, 76, 113

Nicola, Lewis, 43-47, 48, 53, 57. See also "Crown Letter"

19th Continental Infantry, 122

North Briton, 113

North Carolina: arrival of John Armstrong in, 214; congressional delegates from, 15, 51, 105, 152 (See Burke, Thomas; Nash, Abner; Williamson, Hugh); state legislature, 203; troops' flight from Camden, 204-5

North, Prime Minister Lord, 34, 35

Northborough, MA, 87

Norton's Tavern, 95, 98

notes payable, 142, 273

officer resignations, 10, 50, 51, 52, 53, 54, 55, 56, 79, 90; offer to resign by Thomas Conway, 199, 202

Ogden, Matthias, 95, 96, 99, 102-3, 109, 129, 132-33, 134-35, 138-40, 142-44, 145, 146, 158, 159, 161-62, 166, 173, 181, 192, 219, 246, 249; biography of, 124-26; charges Brooks with causing plot's collapse, 285-86; Horatio Gates praised by, 196. See also delegation of army to Congress; McDougall and Ogden report from Philadelphia

Ogden and McDougall report from Philadelphia, 161-62, 166, 181, 213, 219, 234, 245, 285, 289

"old leven, the" (Horatio Gates), 193

"Old Man" and "Patsy", 38

"old Square Toes." See Willing, Thomas

Olney, George, 57

Olney, Jeremiah, 57

Olney's battalion, 57

"On the Prospect of Peace" (poem by Gates), 180

Oneida Indians, 54

Osgood, Samuel, 33, 83-84, 93, 105-6, 132, 134, 136-37, 148, 158, 162, 188, 264, 265

Pacific Ocean, 209

Paine, Tom, 20, 24, 29, 32, 33, 98, 105

Palatinate (German), 1

Palatines, 1, 2; petition to Lords Commissioners of Trade and Plantations, 2

Paris, France, 93, 133, 255

Parker, James, 112

Parliament, 35, 93, 111, 113, 151, 163, 167, 216, 220

Paterson, John, 96

pay of civilian officials, 79, 100, 139, 267

paymaster general. See Pierce, John

peace treaty: final, 255, 256, 279; preliminary, 93, 163, 222, 265, 267

Peale, Charles Wilson, 130

Peekskill, NY, 4, 73, 117, 202

Pendleton, Mr., 105

Pennsylvania: ban on theatrical performances in, 130; Bank of, 21; Committee of Safety, 18; congressional delegates from, 18, 21, 99, 131, 148, 155, 165, 177, 208 (See Fitzsimmons, Thomas; Morris, Robert; Peters, Richard; Smith, Jonathan Bayard; Wilson, James); and half pay for duration officers, 53, 55, 103; Line desires general funding for Congress, 103; state legislature (General Assembly), 33, 60, 73, 74, 131, 150, 152, 154, 178, 282; regiments from, 58, 59, 60; Supreme Executive Council, 61, 277; troops' advice for delegation of the army, 103-4; troops' march south after Yorktown, 30; troops' mutinies, 40, 44, 60-61, 69, 70, 124, 277. See also creditors, domestic

Pennsylvania Hospital, 130

Pennsylvania Journal, 33

Pennsylvania Packet, 28, 207

Pennsylvania State House, 131, 134, 277

pensions: acts by Congress from 1818 to 1832 pertaining to, 283; for disabled, 49, 97, 283. See also half-pay pensions

permanent revenue. See Congress: general funding for

Peters, Richard, 134, 140, 165, 179, 188, 208, 264, 270

Petit, Charles, 62, 211-12

petitions: of Connecticut sergeants for half-pay pensions, 267, 270; decades after war, of old officers for overdue pensions, 283; fear that delegates' tables will be covered with, 39; of generals against promotion of Thomas Conway, 201; of Hudson Highlands officers, 85, 93-99, 102-4, 105, 109, 124, 133, 134, 135, 136, 137, 142-43, 146, 153, 154, 161, 162, 181, 191, 215, 222, 245, 246, 249, 253, 269, 289; of junior officers for pay raise, 48; of Massachusetts colonels concerning pay, 10; of Massachusetts officers to state legislature, 65-66, 67, 82-84, 93; of neglected generals and delegates' response to, 54, 55, 119-20, 121; of New Jersey officers to state legislature, 100; of officers to states concerning pay, 32; of unpaid officers fearing early furloughs and discharges, 272, 273; of public creditors, 62-63, 74, 154. See also delegation of army to Congress

Philadelphia, 7, 10, 11, 15, 17, 18, 22, 23, 24, 28, 30, 33, 34, 40, 44, 53, 55, 58, 60, 61, 66, 67, 72, 73, 78, 79, 80, 83, 84, 93, 94, 95, 96, 99, 102-3, 105, 109, 115, 119, 120, 121, 122, 124, 125, 126, 132, 133, 134, 136, 137, 141, 142, 143, 150 160, 161, 162, 163, 169, 173, 174, 176, 177, 179, 180, 181, 183, 191, 192, 196, 205, 212, 213, 214, 218, 219, 220, 222, 223, 226, 228, 245, 246, 249, 254, 258, 277, 278, 283, 285, 288, 291; British occupation of, 9, 27, 125, 129, 202, 203; British evacuation of, 91, 129; description of, 129-31; public creditors of, 62, 63, 73, 74, 175, 176, 205, 211-12

Phoenix, 88

Pickering, Timothy, 36, 54, 216, 221, 228-29, 271, 279, 287, 289, 290, 292; belief that John Brooks caused plot's collapse, 285-86; and construction of huts and Temple of Virtue, 107, 136, 141; at March 15, 1783, officers' meeting, 236, 240, 245-47

Pierce, John, 38, 143-44, 162, 210, 265, 273, 283

Plater, George, 28

plotters' scheme. See nationalists' plot

Poughkeepsie, NY, 121

President of Congress, 38, 50, 55, 100, 146, 199, 203, 210, 225, 246, 251, 252-53, 255, 256, 264, 273. See also Boudinot, Elias; Hanson, John; Laurens, Henry

Prince William Henry, 263

Princeton, 61, 168; Battle of, 169, 213

Providence Gazette, 75

Providence, RI, 98

Public Building, New Windsor Cantonment. See Temple of Virtue

public debt, 8, 22, 27, 31, 33, 38-39, 62, 64, 74, 79, 80, 142, 146, 148, 151, 152, 174, 186-87, 190, 191, 208, 210, 222, 235, 275

Purple Heart, 69

Putnam, Rufus, 65-66, 82, 83, 85, 124, 245, 280; responds to Newburgh addresses, 233-35, 291

Quartering Act, 111, 112

Quassaick (Algonquin), 2

Quebec, Canada, 124

Rall, Johann, 89

Ramapo, NY, 4

Ramsey, David, 149-50, 156

Randolph, Edmund, 109, 145, 165, 186, 220

Rappleye, Charles, 24

Raritan River, 168

Reading Company of Minutemen, 122

Reading, MA, 122

redoubt number three, West Point, 236

reduction of forces: January 1, 1781, 55-56, 66, 184; January 1, 1783, 72, 132-33

Reed, Joseph, 61

Rendon, Francisco, 33

requisitions for state funds. See Congress, requisitions to states for funds for

Rhode Island: approval by Congress for delegation to be sent to, 98, 105; approval of Impost by state legislature, 282; Arthur Lee predicts state's approval of Impost if duration is limited, 156; congressional delegates from, 75, 80-81, 148, 159, 218 (See Arnold, Jonathan; Howell, David); George Washington criticizes state for crying about loss of sovereignty, 274; governor of, 31, 57, 79, 80, 98; mock burial of currency by residents of, 22; Newport begins trading with British, 113; opposition to pensions or commutation for army officers, 52, 148, 218; opposition to and vote against Impost, 32, 62, 75-76, 78-79, 80-81, 82, 94, 98, 100-1, 105-6, 153, 177-78, 182, 185, 207, 288; Robert Morris criticizes state legislature for endangering "national Safety," 80; state legislature (General Assembly) praises its delegates to Congress, 185; support for Impost from James Varnum of, 75; vote by state legislature to give Jeremiah Olney's battalion three months' pay, 57;

Richmond, Christopher, 213

Richmond, VA, 163, 214

Ridley, Matthew, 68

Ringwood Furnace, 36

Rittenhouse, David, 137, 174, 228, 240

Ritzema, Rudolphus, 116

Roberts, John, 112

Rochambeau, General, 15, 23

Rochefontaine, Stephen, 136

Rock Redoubt, 171, 172

Rockingham, Prime Minister Lord, 35

Rocky Hill, NJ, 279

Root, Jesse, 41, 67

Rose, 88

Royal American Regiment, 195

Royal Gazette, 22

Rugeley's Mill, 204

"Rules of Civility & Decent Behaviour In Company and Conversation," 228, 237

Rush, Benjamin, 62, 203, 211

Rutledge, John, 41, 134, 136-37, 140, 141, 145, 146, 150, 154, 155-57, 162, 174, 175, 177-79, 184, 190, 209, 220

Saint Esprit, 110

Salem, MA, 54

Sanders Creek, 204

Sands and Company, 71-72

Sands, Comfort, 71

Sandy Hook, NJ, 167

Saratoga, 228; Battles of, 35, 122, 123, 197, 214

Schenectady, NY, 228

Schuykill River, 90, 131

Schuyler, Philip, 74, 195, 196, 205, 235, 247, 248

Scotland, 249; Islay, island of, 109

Scott, Charles, 118

2nd Massachusetts, 141

2nd Pennsylvania, 60

Secretary of Foreign Affairs. See Livingston, Robert

Secretary of the Treasury, 290

Secretary of War. See Lincoln, Benjamin

securities, 96, 234, 254, 258

Sergeant, Jonathan Dickinson, 62

7th Massachusetts Regiment, 124

Shaw, Samuel, 91, 102, 184-85, 219, 236, 240, 241, 247, 248

Shee, John, 62

Shrewsbury, MA, 87

Simsbury, CT, 281

Six Nations, campaign against, 100, 125

Smallwood, William, 116

Smith, Jonathan Bayard, 50, 203

Smith, Richard Norton, 242

Smith, William Peartree, 216, 248-49

Smith, William, 25

Snake Hill, 107

Sons of Liberty, 111, 112, 113, 114, 115, 126, 167

South Carolina: congressional delegates from, 149-50, 156, 175 (See Laurens, Henry; Ramsey, David; Rutledge, John); Gates and the Battle of Camden, 203-5; governor of, 211; Nathanael Greene's concern over state legislature and Impost, 158, 181, 210, 211; opposition to lifetime pension for army officers, 52; after Yorktown, march of Virginia, Maryland, and Pennsylvania men to, 30

Southborough, MA, 87

Southington, CT, 281

Southwark Theatre, 130-31

Spain, 32, 255. See also creditors, foreign

Spencer, MA, 87

Springfield, MA, 87

St. Clair, Arthur, 213, 278; advises delegation of army, recommending union of army and creditors, 103-4

St. Croix, island of, 110, 167

St. Leger, Barry, 196

Stamp Act, 18, 75, 111

Stephen, Adam, 118

Sterling Iron Works, 4, 36

Steuben, Baron von, 76, 123, 187-88

Stevens's Virginia militia, Edward, 204

Stewart, Major T., 212

Stewart, Walter, 7, 62, 175-76, 211-12, 271, 277; biography of, 58-61; meeting of conspirators at Gates's headquarters, 212; role in conspiracy of, 176, 211-12, 219, 223, 224, 287, 288, 289

Stirling, Lord, 198, 200

Stoddert, Benjamin, 202

Storm King Mountain. See Butter Hill

Suffolk County, MA, 280

Sullivan, John, 90, 100, 118, 125

Superintendent of Finance. See Morris, Robert

Swift, Herman, 39

Tarbell, William, 235

tax collectors, 100, 101, 149, 150, 151, 152, 153, 154, 155, 156, 157, 163, 179, 209, 221, 266; for New York, 64, 172-73, 282; for Virginia, 63

taxation authority of Congress. See Congress, taxation authority for

taxes, 12, 13, 33, 58, 62, 63, 74, 75, 76, 80, 106, 111, 113, 144, 148, 154, 155, 168, 175, 210. See also duties on imports

Tea Act, 114

tea party, Manhattan, 115, 167; threat by "Mohawks," 114

Temple of Virtue: anniversary celebration of alliance with France at, 159-60; anonymous (unauthorized) call for Hudson Highlands officers to meet at, 212-13, 219, 220, 221, 222, 223, 225, 226, 238, 246, 251, 289; cessation of hostilities marked at, 267; construction of, 107-8, 135-36, 138, 141, 141-42, 147, 150, 159-60, 174, 205, 210; description of, 235; George Washington's rescheduling of (unauthorized) meeting, 219, 222, 223, 225, 226, 229, 251; as initial stage of troops' homeward march, 274; Israel Evans names building, 108; last sermon at, 277; March 15, 1783, meeting of the Hudson Highlands officers at, 7, 67, 227, 228-29, 235, 237-49, 251, 252, 255, 257, 268, 269, 284, 285, 286, 287, 288, 290, 291; resolutions of officers' committee at March 15, 1783, meeting, 245-47, 252, 287; sale of, 279; surprise as element of Washington's appearance at March 15, 1783, meeting, 219-20, 236, 284, 291

Thacher, James, 221, 290

3rd Pennsylvania Battalion, 58

13th Pennsylvania Regiment, 59, 60

Thomson, Charles, 30

Tilghman, Tench, 38, 77-78, 105, 137, 164, 268

"To the Betrayed Inhabitants of the City and Colony of New York," 111-12, 167

"To the Citizens of America, who are the Creditors of the United States," 74

"To the Free and Loyal Inhabitants of the City and Colony of New York," 113

Tories, 180-81; "nest of Tories," 2

Townshend, Peter, 36

Townshend, Thomas, 249

"Traveller's Rest" (Gates's plantation), 195

Trenton, 89; Battle of, 89, 169, 213; Hessian outpost at, 169

Troup, Robert, 201, 202

Trumbull, Jonathan, 65, 282

Trumbull, Jonathan, Jr., 46, 228

Tryon, William, 26

Tufts, Simon, 122

Tupper, Benjamin, 136, 138, 141, 159

Turtle Creek, 194

Tyger, 110

union of creditors and angry army. See nationalists' plot

University of the State of Pennsylvania, 130

Valley Forge, 3, 50, 59, 91, 123, 200, 201, 221, 242; Brooks and Hamilton at, 126; Committee at Camp's visit, 27, 51, 169

Van Cortlandt, Philip, 85, 96, 221

Varnum, James, 75

Vermont, 228, 282

Verplanck's Point, 73, 106

Virginia: Arthur Lee predicts state's approval of Impost if duration is limited, 156; congressional delegates from, 33, 99, 135, 140-41, 145-46, 147, 151, 152, 162, 163, 166, 175, 177, 186, 188-89, 198, 220, 223-24, 288 (See Bland, Theodorick; Jones, Joseph; Lee, Arthur; Lee, Richard Henry; Madison, James; Mercer, John Francis); creditors from, 178, 184; diversion of funds needed for defense by, 144; French arrival from, 73; funding plan offered "no bait for ...," 266; George Washington hoped to return to, 38; governor of, 10, 135, 162, 203, 207; and half pay for duration officers, 53; Horatio Gates asked by sick wife to return to, 208; Horatio Gates with sick wife in, 285; Maryland's fear of being bankrupted by, 209-10; officer resignations, 10, 51; ratification of Impost, 32-33; receiver of Continental taxes, 63; repeal of Impost, 105, 106, 132, 145, 149, 151, 153-54, 177, 178, 182, 185, 207; reluctance to provide requisitioned funds, 63-64, 145, 148-49; state legislature (General Assembly), 154; Stevens's militia, 204; troops march south after Yorktown, 30

Wall Street (New York City), 114

Walnut Street Prison, 130

Waltham, MA, 87

Warren, Joseph, 49

wartime profiteering, 70-72, 184; speculation in loan office certificates, 175, 222

Washington at Temple Hill, 241

Washington, George: alerts Congress on arrival of officers' petition, 99; alerts Robert Morris to officers' growing impatience, 57; apprises Secretary of War of army's unrest, 77; assessed as public speaker by Thomas Jefferson, 228; "... blind in the service of my country," 240; breach in relations with Horatio Gates, 197-203; chides Hamilton for suggesting redress by force, 258-59, 265; complains to the Financier about Comfort Sands, 71; early (1777-80) advocacy of half-pay, 50-52, 53, 55, 252; element of surprise in appearance at March 15, 1783, officers' meeting, 219-20, 236, 284, 291; emphasizes army's desperate state to John Laurens, 20-21; expresses faith in Congress at March 15, 1783, officers' meeting, 239; farewell dinner at Fraunces' Tavern for, 279; final orders, 279; financial sacrifices during war, 237; health of, 137, 228, 240-42, 284; meets with brigade commanders to stop conspiracy, 221; official report on March 15, 1783, officers' meeting and plea for justice, 252-53, 255, 269; physical presence of, 236-37; praise for speech at officers' meeting and actions ending conspiracy, 248-49, 284; reaction to Morris's resignation, 210-11; realizes address author is army officer, 224; rebukes Lewis Nicola for "Crown Letter," 45-46; receives anonymous notice of March 11, 1783, officers' meeting, 212; receives copy of Armstrong's address, 218; receives funds for soldiers' bounties, 19; report to Congress of unauthorized officers' meeting and anonymous address, 225, 251; reported decline in popularity of, 165, 180, 189; requests one-month's pay for troops prior to Yorktown, 22-23; rescheduling of unauthorized officers' meeting, 219, 222, 223, 225, 226, 229, 251; resigns as Commander-in-chief, 279; rumored guilt in conspiracy, 226; spectacles (reading glasses), 137, 174, 228, 240-42, 284; speech and actions of March 15, 1783, 7-8, 235, 236, 237-44, 248, 249, 252, 269, 288; summons Knox to his headquarters, 220, 222; suspects Gates is behind plot, 193-94; and the theatre, 130, 242; urges government to compensate army before disbandment, 253-54, 257-58, 264; urges states to give up "local prejudices," 274-76, 278; warns Congress of negative results from troop reduction, 55; warns Jones and Hamilton of possible horrors if Congress fails to act, 223-24; warns McHenry that army's patience is near an end, 79; writes to Armstrong (February 1797) about events of March 1783, 287, 290

Washington, Lund, 253-54

Washington, Martha, 30, 34, 37, 38

Washington's headquarters, Newburgh, NY, 36-38, 70, 124, 220, 267, 279; arrival at, 4, 34; visit of Walter Stewart, 212

Washington's Life Guard, 38

Watertown, MA, 87

Wayland, MA, 87

Wayne, Anthony, 59-60, 61, 118, 286

Webb, Samuel Blachley, 85, 99, 248

Webster, Pelatiah, 66, 184

West Indies, 76, 110

West Point, 35, 36, 54, 71, 76, 95, 106, 121, 122, 136, 220, 226, 236, 266, 277, 291; committee to draft Hudson Highlands officers' petition chosen at, 85, 93

western lands, ceding of, 27, 74, 76, 81, 209, 210, 266

Weston, MA, 87

Wethersfield, CT, 281

Wetmore, Hezekiah, 174, 191, 210

Wharton and Bowes Book Store, 86

Whigs, 79, 180, 181

White Plains, NY, 116, 118, 122; Battle of, 168

White, Phillips, 134

Wilkes, John, 113, 216

Wilkinson, James, 198, 201; challenges Gates to duel, 202, 214

William IV, 126

Williams, Otho H., 214

Williamson, Hugh, 152, 156, 158, 178-79

Willing & Morris, 18

Willing, Charles, 17

Willing, Thomas, 17, 18

Wilson, James, 106, 148, 149, 150, 151, 154, 155, 157, 158, 159, 160, 162, 174, 175, 178-79, 188, 221; appointment of Robert Morris praised by, 21

Winsted, CT, 281

Witherspoon, John, 12, 50, 167

Wolcott, Oliver, 134, 149, 156, 191

Worcester, MA, 24, 87

Wright, Joseph Allen, 248

Yale, 13, 248

"Yankee Pumpkin Vine," 36

Yates, Abraham, Jr., 282

York, PA, 27, 202

Yorktown, Battle of, 24, 30, 34, 61, 69, 91, 171

Youth Behaviour, 228

Pisgah Press

Also available from Pisgah Press

Letting Go: Collected Poems 1983-2003 $14.95	Donna Lisle Burton
Unbelievable: Faith, Reason, & the Search for Truth $16.00	Joseph R. Haun w. A. D. Reed
MacTiernan's Bottle $14.95	Michael Hopping
rhythms on a flaming drum $16.95	Michael Hopping
I Like It Here! Adventures in the Wild & Wonderful World of Theatre $30.00	C. Robert Jones
Fragments $16.00	Martin A. Keeley
Oscar & the Royal Avenue Cats $15.00	Martin A. Keeley
A Green One for Woody $15.95	Patrick O'Sullivan
Reed's Homophones: a comprehensive book of sound-alike words $10.00	A.D. Reed
Trang Sen $19.50	Sarah-Ann Smith
Killer Weed $14.95	RF Wilson

To order:

Pisgah Press, LLC
PO Box 1427, Candler, NC 28715
www.pisgahpress.com

www.ingramcontent.com/pod-product-compliance
Lightning Source LLC
Chambersburg PA
CBHW051207290426
44109CB00021B/2367